Experiences

Experiences

FLORENCE H. MORGAN   **FRED MORGAN**

Harcourt Brace Jovanovich, Inc.

New York   Chicago   San Francisco   Atlanta

Cover photo: Manfred Kage from Peter Arnold

© 1975 by Harcourt Brace Jovanovich, Inc.

All rights reserved. No part of this publication may be reproduced or transmitted in any form or by any means, electronic or mechanical, including photocopy, recording, or any information storage and retrieval system, without permission in writing from the publisher.

ISBN: 0-15-525813-3

Library of Congress Catalog Card Number: 74-29433

Printed in the United States of America

Copyrights and Acknowledgments

For permission to use the selections reprinted in this book, the authors are grateful to the following publishers and copyright holders:

ATHENEUM PUBLISHERS, INC. for "London Road." From *As I Walked Out One Midsummer Morning* by Laurie Lee. Copyright © 1969 by Laurie Lee. Reprinted by permission of Atheneum Publishers.

HEYWOOD HALE BROUN AND THE ESTATE OF CONSTANCE BROUN for "Holding a Baby," by Heywood Broun; copyright 1921, 1949. Reprinted by permission of Heywood Hale Broun and the Estate of Constance Broun.

CAMBRIDGE UNIVERSITY PRESS for "A Fight." Adapted from *Theocritus*, edited by A. S. F. Gow, published by Cambridge University Press. Copyright 1952 by Cambridge University Press. Reprinted by permission of the publisher.

DODD, MEAD & COMPANY for "The Great Lover" and "Heaven" by Rupert Brooke. Reprinted by permission of Dodd, Mead & Company, Inc. from *The Collected Poems of Rupert Brooke*. Copyright 1915 by Dodd, Mead & Company. Copyright renewed 1943 by Edward Marsh. For "Madness." Reprinted by permission of Dodd, Mead & Company, Inc. from *Orthodoxy* by G. K. Chesterton. Copyright 1908 by Dodd, Mead & Company. Copyright renewed.

DOUBLEDAY & COMPANY, INC. for "Auda" and "Arab Feasting" from *Seven Pillars of Wisdom* by T. E. Lawrence. Copyright 1926, 1935 by Doubleday & Co., Inc. For "The Pattern-Makers" from *Swallowing the Anchor* by William McFee. Copyright 1923 by William McFee. Reprinted by permission of Doubleday & Co., Inc.

HARCOURT BRACE JOVANOVICH, INC. for "Marrakech." From *Such, Such Were the the Joys* by George Orwell, copyright, 1945, 1952, 1953, by Sonia Brownell Orwell. *Thunderstorm* from "Limestone" by Adalbert Stifter is reprinted from his volume *Limestone and Other Stories*, translated and copyright © 1968 by David Luke. Reprinted by permission of Harcourt Brace Jovanovich, Inc.

WILLIAM HEINEMANN LTD. for "The Tactless Man" and "The Flatterer" by Theophrastus. Adapted from *The Characters of Theophrastus* translated by John Maxwell Edmonds. Copyright 1929 by William Heinemann Ltd. Reprinted by permission of William Heinemann Ltd.

THE HOKUSEIDO PRESS for "What is Zen?" by R. H. Blyth and "The Thief and the Moon" by Ryokan. From *Zen in English Literature and Oriental Classics* by R. H. Blyth. Copyright 1947, 1960 by The Hokuseido Press. Reprinted by permission of The Hokuseido Press.

HOLT, RINEHART AND WINSTON, INC. for "Justice." From *The Fire on the Mountain and Other Ethiopian Stories* by Harold Courlander and Wolf Leslau. Copyright 1950 by Holt, Rinehart and Winston, Inc. Reprinted by permission of Holt, Rinehart and Winston, Inc.

Acknowledgments

HOUGHTON MIFFLIN COMPANY for "Old Man Facing Death." From *Raw Material* by Oliver La Farge. Copyright 1942, 1943, 1944 and 1945 by Oliver La Farge. Copyright 1972 by Consuelo Le Farge. Originally published in *The New Yorker*. Reprinted by permission of the publisher Houghton Mifflin Company.

DAVID McKAY COMPANY, INC. for "The Governor of Los Teques." From *Young Man of Caracas* by T. R. Ybarra, published by Ives Washburn. Copyright 1941 by David McKay Company, Inc., reprinted with permission.

MACMILLAN PUBLISHING CO., INC. for "The Grasshopper and the Ant." Reprinted with permission of Macmillan Publishing Co., Inc. from *A Son of the Middle Border* by Hamlin Garland. Copyright 1917 by Hamlin Garland, renewed 1945 by Mary I. Lord and Constance G. Williams.

JOHN MURRAY (PUBLISHERS) LTD. for "Evolution of the Horse." Reprinted from *Earth's Company* by Leslie Reid. Copyright by John Murray (Publishers) Ltd. Reprinted by permission of John Murray (Publishers) Ltd.

THE NEW YORKER for "Red" by Niccolo Tucci. The original story was long and had a different ending than the present version, but there was insufficient time to print the version the author preferred. Reprinted by permission; © 1972 The New Yorker Magazine, Inc.

W. W. NORTON & COMPANY, INC. for "Old Houses," "The Hospital," and "The Hand." Reprinted from *The Notebooks of Malte Laurids Brigge* by Rainer Maria Rilke. By permission of W. W. Norton & Company, Inc. Copyright 1949 by W. W. Norton & Co., Inc.

HAROLD OBER ASSOCIATES INCORPORATED for "Discovery of a Father" by Sherwood Anderson. Published in *The Reader's Digest*, November, 1939. Copyright 1939 by Eleanor Copenhaver Anderson. Renewed. Reprinted by permission of Harold Ober Associates, Incorporated.

LAWRENCE POLLINGER LTD for "Lie Thee Down, Oddity" by T. F. Powys. Copyright 1934 by the estate of T. F. Powys. Reprinted by permission of Lawrence Pollinger, Ltd.

OXFORD UNIVERSITY PRESS for "The Peloponnesian War: Final Defeat of the Athenian Forces." From *Thucydides: The History of the Peloponnesian War* edited in translation by Sir R. W. Livingstone and published by Oxford University Press. For "In What Way Princes Must Keep Faith." From *The Prince* by Niccolò Machiavelli, translated by Luigi Ricci, revised by E. R. P. Vincent, published 1935 by Oxford University Press. For "A Working Class Mother" and "Old Men in Libraries." From *The Uses of Literacy* by Richard Hoggart, published 1970 by Oxford University Press. Reprinted by permission of the publisher.

ROBERT PAYNE for "Chariots Go Forth to War" by Tu Fu. From *The White Pony*, edited by Robert Payne and published by The John Day Co., Inc. Copyright 1947 by Robert Payne. Reprinted by permission of Robert Payne.

PRINCETON UNIVERSITY PRESS for "Fools Are Happy." From *The Praise of Folly* by Desiderius Erasmus, translated by Hoyt Hopwell Hudson (copyright 1941 © 1969 by Princeton University Press; Princeton Paperback, 1970), pp. 47–58. Reprinted by permission of Princeton University Press.

G. P. PUTNAM'S SONS for "Conversation." Reprinted by permission of G. P. Putnam's Sons from *Solomon in All His Glory* by Robert Lynd. Copyright 1923 by Robert Lynd.

RANDOM HOUSE, INC. for "Three Dreams." From *Markings*, by Dag Hammerskjold, translated by Leif Sjoberg and W. H. Auden. Copyright © 1964 by Alfred A. Knopf, Inc. and Faber and Faber Limited. Reprinted by permission of Alfred A. Knopf, Inc. For excerpt from "The Judgment of the Birds." Reprinted from *The Immense Journey*, by Loren Eiseley, by permission of Random House, Inc. Copyright © 1956 by Loren Eiseley. For "An Autumn Night in the Hills." Reprinted from *The Complete Works of John M. Synge*, by courtesy of Random House, Inc.

THE SOCIETY OF AUTHORS for "Hall-Bedrooms." From *The Verdict of Bridlegoose* by Llewellyn Powys, published by Jonathan Cape Ltd. Copyright 1927 by the Estate of Llewellyn Powys. For "A House of Correction." From *Earth Memories* by Llewellyn Powys, published by W. W. Norton & Company, Inc. Copyright 1938 by the Estate of Llewellyn Powys. Reprinted by permission of The Society of Authors.

Acknowledgments

HELEN THURBER for "The Moth and the Star," "The Courtship of Arthur and Al," "The Unicorn in the Garden," and "The Rabbits Who Caused All the Trouble." Copyright © 1940 by James Thurber. Copyright © 1968 by Helen Thurber. From *Fables for Our Time*, published by Harper and Row. Originally printed in *The New Yorker*. Reprinted by permission of Helen Thurber.

THE VIKING PRESS for "Base Details." From *Collected Poems* by Siegfried Sassoon. Copyright 1918 by E. P. Dutton & Co. Copyright renewed 1946 by Siegfried Sassoon. All rights reserved. Reprinted by permission of The Viking Press, Inc.

Preface

Experiences seeks to involve students in life. It suggests that they begin at the beginning, with their own senses, and then develop their abilities to generalize for themselves on the basis of what their senses tell them. It also tries to show that writers are remembered for their original observations rather than for taking sides in the forgotten quarrels of their times. *Experiences* attempts to achieve relevance to living itself, not to the over-debated issues of the day.

As the title indicates, students are encouraged to approach writing through their own experiences. Writing, we believe, is not primarily a matter of grammar, sentence structure, and paragraph organization. Learning to write by studying the mechanics of composition is like learning to drive by taking a car apart: it may be a good idea to know how the car functions in case it stops running well, but this knowledge does not make a good driver. One becomes a good driver through observation, experience, and practice, and that is also how one becomes a good writer.

Like driving, writing may be improved by following good examples. One purpose of *Experiences* is to show students how others do the job. This purpose has determined the choice of selections; relevance to student writing, as well as literary quality, have been the controlling factors.

The selections have been dated only to remind students that some good ideas were expressed before our own day. Except for a few allusions that have been glossed where we felt it would be helpful, ideas stand independent of their specific historical contexts. The book has been organized to make these ideas progressively accessible to the student of writing. Its four parts develop the student's skills from direct observation to abstract generalization. We have emphasized in our introductions, discussion questions, and

Preface

notes the writing skills exemplified by our selections rather than their literary or historical importance. *Experiences* is dedicated to writing, not to literary history.

Writing is a product of experiences transmuted through individuals who, in turn, are products of their accumulated experiences. We believe that too much attention is often paid to analysis of the self, as though it were some sort of tangible entity rather than an aggregate of experiences that should be augmented and enriched by being related to one another. In our view, writing students should sharpen their perception and try to make sense of the world outside themselves. Inadequacies of "self" are really flaws in perception, and when students can observe well and generalize soundly, they will both know and express themselves better.

We hope students will discover that writing is a means of discovering reality, not escaping from it. We also hope they will be able to use *Experiences* actively, as a means for organizing their perceptions. Most of the selections were written with enthusiasm; we hope this enthusiasm will prove contagious, and that students will learn to use writing as one of their tools for the mastery of life.

Florence H. Morgan
Fred Morgan

Contents

Preface　vii

Part I
Observing　1

Chapter 1　Observing Things　3

The Great Lover, Rupert Brooke　3
　A Note on Emotional Language　4
A Storm, Mark Twain　5
The Thunderstorm, Adalbert Stifter　7
The Wind, Roger Ascham　9
The Whirlwind, Benjamin Franklin　10
Shanties at Walden Pond, Nathaniel Hawthorne　12
The House Beautiful, Mark Twain　13
Hall-Bedrooms, Llewellyn Powys　16
Old Houses, Rainer Maria Rilke　19
Writing Suggestions　21

Plate 1　*Six Persimmons*, Mu Ch'i　23
Plate 2　"Palm Tree, Nassau," Winslow Homer　26

ix

Contents

Chapter 2 Observing Individuals   27

Miss Birdseye, Henry James   27
A Working Class Mother, Richard Hoggart   28
Auda, T. E. Lawrence   30
The Old Apple Dealer, Nathaniel Hawthorne   32
Old Man Facing Death, Oliver LaFarge   35
Red, Niccolo Tucci   40
Writing Suggestions   47

Plate 3 *Erasmus,* Hans Holbein   48
Plate 4 *Dr. Johnson,* Sir Joshua Reynolds   50

Chapter 3 Observing a Scene   52

A Fight, Theocritus   52
A Slave Galley, John Evelyn   54
Description of a City Shower, Jonathan Swift   56
Arab Feasting, T. E. Lawrence   58
The Inside of an Omnibus, Leigh Hunt   62
Conversation, Robert Lynd   66
Old Men in Libraries, Richard Hoggart   70
An Autumn Night in the Hills, J. M. Synge   72
Writing Suggestions   77
   A Note about Writing in General   78

Plate 5 *The Feast of St. Nicholas,* Jan Steen   81
Plate 6 *Stag at Sharkey's,* George Wesley Bellows   83

Part II
Observing & Generalizing   85

Chapter 4 Beginning with Direct Observation: Informal Generalizing   87

The Social Instinct among Animals, Gilbert White   87
The Judgment of the Birds, Loren Eiseley   88
The Finger-Nail and the Note, Samuel Butler   90
Beer and My Cat, Samuel Butler   91
Small Economies, Elizabeth Cleghorn Gaskell   92
On the Use of Language, Oliver Goldsmith   94
Marrakech, George Orwell   98
A House of Correction, Llewellyn Powys   104
   A Note on Irony   107
Writing Suggestions   108

Plate 7 *Maxime Dethomas,* Henri de Toulouse-Lautrec   110

Contents

Chapter 5   Beginning with Direct Observation: Explaining   112

The Line, Herman Melville   113
The Pattern-Makers, William McFee   115
Writing Suggestions   126

Plate 8   "Snowy Egret," John James Audubon   128

Chapter 6   Beginning with Generalized Observations   130

The Tactless Man, Theophrastus   131
The Flatterer, Theophrastus   131
The Hunter, Samuel Butler   132
The Languid Lady, Edward Young   133
Song, John Donne   134
On Quick and Slow Wits of Pupils, Roger Ascham   135
Madness, G. K. Chesterton   137
Dying, Jeremy Taylor   139
Darwin among the Machines, Samuel Butler   140
Idols of the Mind, Francis Bacon   144
   A Note on Organization   157
Writing Suggestions   159

Plate 9   "Venus" of Willendorf and *Venus de Milo*   160
Plate 10   *The Spirit of the Dead Watching*, Paul Gauguin   162

Chapter 7   Beginning with the Observations of Others   164

The Governor of Los Teques, T. R. Ybarra   164
The Peloponnesian War: Final Defeat of the
   Athenian Forces, Thucydides   167
The Evolution of the Horse, Leslie Reid   176
What Is Zen?, R. H. Blyth   178
Writing Suggestions   193

Plate 11   "The Vision of St. John," Albrecht Dürer   195
Plate 12   *Persephone*, Thomas Hart Benton   198

Part III
The Direct Experience   199

Chapter 8   The Outward Experience   201

Mauled by a Lion, David Livingstone   201
Getting Up on Cold Mornings, Leigh Hunt   203
The Country Visit, Soame Jenyns   205
The Grasshopper and the Ant, Hamlin Garland   207

xi

Contents

London Road, Laurie Lee   213
Writing Suggestions   223

Plate 13   "The Great Wave off Kanagawa," Hokusai   224
Plate 14   *Joseph the Carpenter*, Georges de la Tour   226

Chapter 9   Inner Experience   228

The Good-Morrow, John Donne   229
Three Dreams, Dag Hammerskjöld   230
Discovery of a Father, Sherwood Anderson   231
Tribulations of a Cheerful Giver, William Dean Howells   235
Visions in a Fever, George Gissing   243
The Hospital, Rainer Maria Rilke   245
The Hand, Rainer Maria Rilke   249
The Pains of Opium, Thomas De Quincey   251
Writing Suggestions   259

Plate 15   *Puberty*, Edvard Munch   261
Plate 16   Etching from *Imaginary Prisons*, Giovanni Battista Piranesi   263

Part IV
Experiencing & Generalizing   265

Chapter 10   Informal Generalizing   267

A Moose Hunt, Henry David Thoreau   267
Walking Tours, Robert Louis Stevenson   277
Holding a Baby, Heywood Broun   283
Writing Suggestions   286

Plate 17   *Stag Hunt*, Gnosis   288
Plate 18   *The Bath*, Mary Cassatt   290

Chapter 11   Expressing a View of Life   293

An Apology for Idlers, Robert Louis Stevenson   293
Success in Life, Walter Pater   301
The Essential Things, John Ruskin   303
Chariots Go Forth to War, Tu Fu   306
The Thief and the Moon, Ryokan   307
Writing Suggestions   308

Plate 19   *Crucifixion*, Mathias Grünewald   309
Plate 20   *The Trinity*, Allessandro Allori   312
Plate 21   "Old Friends," Winslow Homer   313
Plate 22   *Listening to the Wind in the Pines*, Ma Lin   316

Chapter 12 Giving Advice   317

To a Young Lady on Her Marriage, Jonathan Swift   317
Letter to His Son, Philip Stanhope, Lord Chesterfield   322
Advice to Youth, Mark Twain   325
In What Way Princes Must Keep Faith, Niccolò Machiavelli   328
Writing Suggestions   330

Chapter 13 Satire and Fable   332

Base Details, Siegfried Sassoon   332
The Latest Decalogue, Arthur Hugh Clough   333
Letter to Lord Chesterfield, Samuel Johnson   334
Fools Are Happy, Erasmus of Rotterdam   335
A Modest Proposal, Jonathan Swift   342
The Penitent, Robert Louis Stevenson   349
Four Fables for Our Time, James Thurber   349
Justice, an Ethiopian folk tale   352
Lie Thee Down, Oddity, T. F. Powys   354
Writing Suggestions   361
   A Note on Parody   362
Heaven, Rupert Brooke   362

Plate 23 "Couple," George Grosz   364
Plate 24 *Secretary*, Richard Stankiewicz   366

Index of Authors and Titles   368

Index of Plates and Artists   370

I
Observing

The primary purpose of writing is to communicate what you have observed or experienced through your senses. Its secondary purpose is to communicate what you think and feel about your observations and experiences. Although writing also has many more complex functions, these are the basic ones. Knowledge and imagination begin in the senses; good writing begins in sharp observation. Our first concern, then, will be with firsthand observations and with putting these observations into the words that best communicate them.

Observing is not a simple matter. There are countless ways of seeing the same object. (When we use the word "seeing" we mean observing with all the senses, not sight alone.) Each individual sees differently from others because of different backgrounds, different prior experiences, and different interests: a landscape painter and a farmer will not see quite the same farm. Even the same individual will see differently at different times because of changing attitudes and increasing knowledge: if you were to go back to a farm you visited as a child, you would not see it the same way.

In Part I you will encounter a number of writers, each with his own way of seeing and each with his own techniques for persuading you to see as he does. You will answer questions designed to bring out these differences in perception and technique and, at the end of Part I, you will find some sugges-

Observing

tions for your own writing based on direct observation. If you have never done this kind of writing, we believe you will enjoy it. By the time you have reached Part II, you will have sharpened your powers of observation and will be ready to begin generalizing on a sounder basis.

1

Observing Things

In our first selection, Rupert Brooke does not give us a generalization such as "I am in love with life," a statement that might make us yawn or reply, "So what?" Instead he offers a list of particular things he loves. But it is not just a list: each item is presented either in emotionally charged language or in words that evoke a strong sensual image. The effect is to waken us to the delights of using our senses on the ordinary things around us.

Rupert Brooke

The Great Lover

(1911)

These I have loved:
              White plates and cups, clean-gleaming,
Ringed with blue lines; and feathery, faery dust;
Wet roofs, beneath the lamp-light; the strong crust
Of friendly bread; and many-tasting food;
Rainbows; and the blue bitter smoke of wood;
And radiant raindrops couching in cool flowers;
And flowers themselves, that sway through sunny hours,
Dreaming of moths that drink them under the moon;
Then, the cool kindliness of sheets, that soon
Smooth away trouble; and the rough male kiss

Observing

>Of blankets; grainy wood; live hair that is
>Shining and free; blue-massing clouds; the keen
>Unpassioned beauty of a great machine;
>The benison of hot water; furs to touch;
>The good smell of old clothes; and other such—
>The comfortable smell of friendly fingers,
>Hair's fragrance, and the musty reek that lingers
>About dead leaves and last year's ferns....
>   Dear names,
>And thousand other throng to me! Royal flames;
>Sweet water's dimpling laugh from tap or spring;
>Holes in the ground; and voices that do sing;
>Voices in laughter, too; and body's pain,
>Soon turned to peace; and the deep-panting train;
>Firm sands; the little dulling edge of foam
>That browns and dwindles as the wave goes home;
>And washen stones, gay for an hour; the cold
>Graveness of iron; moist black earthen mould;
>Sleep; and high places; footprints in the dew;
>And oaks; and brown horse-chestnuts, glossy-new;
>And new-peeled sticks; and shining pools on grass;—
>All these have been my loves.

A NOTE ON EMOTIONAL LANGUAGE

Each word we use has a denotation and a connotation. The denotation is the thing the word represents: if you are asked for the denotation of "lemonade," you hold up a glass of lemonade. The connotation is made up of the emotional associations stimulated by the word. For you the connotation of "lemonade" might be picnics, summer days on the front porch, memories of your family, and so on. When Rupert Brooke uses "the blue bitter smoke of wood," he is deliberately recalling to our minds such experiences as sitting in front of a fireplace in winter or camping in the forest, experiences that usually have pleasant associations. He does not use words primarily for their denotations, as a tax-collector might, but for their connotations. Writing that is done primarily for the reader's pleasure is likely to be highly connotative.

Often two or more words with the same denotation—that is, referring to the same object—will have quite different connotations. For example, you can refer to your senator as a statesman or as a politician; the senator hasn't changed, but you have expressed two different emotional attitudes toward him. An odor might be a perfume or a stink, depending on whether you like it or dislike it. When you write you will often find similar choices of words before you, and you will want to choose the word with the connotation that fits the feeling you wish to communicate.

Words with strong associations are called "emotionally charged" words. Emotionally charged language is often used in attempts to distort the reader's

benison: blessing.

perception of fact or to persuade the reader to share the writer's view. Thus you should be aware of it when you encounter it, and you should examine its purpose. In the case of Rupert Brooke's poem, you recognize that, while the emotional charge is strong, the purpose is entirely benevolent: he wants us to enjoy life more. But in cases where a writer or speaker is asking you to act in some way that affects your welfare or that of others—to vote, to buy something, to give money, to join a revolution—then you will want to analyze both his language and his motives.

Most of the writers in *Experiences* use emotionally charged language to some degree. You should be aware of both the degree and the purpose of its emotionalism. More important, you should know when you are using emotional language in your own writing and be able to employ it consciously, not naively. At the end of this chapter and elsewhere in the book you will find some writing suggestions that offer a chance to practice deliberate use of emotional language.

As we have seen, Rupert Brooke uses emotionally charged words to evoke in our minds the things he loves in such a way that we are invited to feel strongly about them. Mark Twain is less insistent that we feel as he does but, in the following description, lets us know how he feels about a thunderstorm.

Mark Twain

A Storm

(1883)

By and by, when the fog began to clear off, I noticed that the reflection of a tree in the smooth water of an overflowed bank, six hundred yards away, was stronger and blacker than the ghostly tree itself. The faint, spectral trees, dimly glimpsed through the shredding fog, were very pretty things to see.

We had a heavy thunder-storm at Natchez, another at Vicksburg, and still another about fifty miles below Memphis. They had an old-fashioned energy which had long been unfamiliar to me. This third storm was accompanied by a raging wind. We tied up to the bank when we saw the tempest coming, and everybody left the pilot-house but me. The wind bent the young trees down, exposing the pale underside of the leaves; and gust after gust followed, in quick succession, thrashing the branches violently up and down, and to this side and that, and creating swift waves of alternating green and white, according to the side of the leaf that was exposed, and these waves raced after each other as do their kind over a wind-tossed

pilot-house: a forward deckhouse containing the steering wheel and navigating equipment; Twain was a river pilot aboard a Mississippi steamboat.

Observing

field of oats. No color that was visible anywhere was quite natural—all tints were charged with a leaden tinge from the solid cloud-bank overhead. The river was leaden, all distances the same; and even the far-reaching ranks of combining whitecaps were dully shaded by the dark, rich atmosphere through which their swarming legions marched. The thunder-peals were constant and deafening; explosion followed explosion with but inconsequential intervals between, and the reports grew steadily sharper and higher-keyed, and more trying to the ear; the lightning was as diligent as the thunder, and produced effects which enchanted the eye and set electric ecstasies of mixed delight and apprehension shivering along every nerve in the body in unintermittent procession. The rain poured down in amazing volume; the ear-splitting thunder-peals broke nearer and nearer; the wind increased in fury and began to wrench off boughs and tree-tops and send them sailing away through space; the pilot-house fell to rocking and straining and cracking and surging, and I went down in the hold to see what time it was.

DISCUSSION

1. Comparing Brooke's poem with Twain's description, which do you feel communicates emotion more effectively? Try to pin down the reasons for your choice in terms of the writers' use of words.
2. We have said that Brooke *evokes* the things he loves: that is, he does not merely list them, but presents them in terms that appeal to our senses and make them real to us. What are some of the evocative words he uses? What sense or senses does each appeal to?
3. Everyone sees in his own way, and it would be hard to find two people less alike in their perceptions than Rupert Brooke and Mark Twain. What evidences of differing personalities do you notice? How might Twain react to some of the things in Brooke's poem, and how might Brooke feel about the storm Twain describes?
4. Point out some words and phrases in Twain's piece that are purely descriptive of the storm itself and others that indicate his feelings about the storm. Into which class do words like "natural," "rich," "deafening," and "diligent" fall?

Even more restrained is the following account of a thunderstorm by a German writer who was a master of direct, simple prose. At first reading he seems to be giving us a straightforward, almost scientifically detached observation of a natural event; yet when we have finished we are left with a feeling about the storm that is quite different from the feeling Mark Twain gives us.

Adalbert Stifter

The Thunderstorm

(1848)

Suddenly there was a brief glimmer all around us, reddening the rocks. It was the first flash of lightning, but it had been silent, and no thunder followed it.

We walked on. Presently there was more lightning, and as the evening had already darkened appreciably, and the light was diffused by the opaque cloud layer, the limestone turned rose-red before our eyes at every flash.

When we reached the point at which our ways parted, the priest stopped and looked at me. I conceded that the storm was breaking, and said that I would go home with him.

So we took the road leading to the Kar, and walked down the gentle rocky slope into the meadow.

On reaching the presbytery, we sat down for a little on the wooden bench in front of the house. The storm was now in full development and was standing from end to end of the sky like a dark rampart. Presently, against this unbroken darkness, across the foot of the storm wall, we saw long puffed-up streaks of drifting white vapor. So over there the storm had perhaps already begun, although where we were there was still not a leaf or a blade of grass stirring. Those drifting swollen clouds are often bad omens in stormy weather; they always presage violent gales and often hail and flooding. And the flashes of lightning were now being followed by clearly audible thunder.

Finally we went into the house.

The priest said that when there was a storm at night, it was his habit to place a lighted candle on his table and to sit quietly in front of it until the storm was over. During the day, he said, he sat at the table without a candle. He asked me if I had any objection to his observing this custom on the present occasion too. I reminded him of his promise not to put himself out in the slightest degree on my account. So he accompanied me through the entrance hall into the familiar little room, and invited me to take off my things.

I usually carried with me on a leather strap over my shoulder a case containing drawing materials, and also some surveying instruments. Fastened next to the case was a satchel where I kept my cold food, my wine, my drinking glass, and my wine cooler. I took these things off and hung them over the back of a chair in a corner of the room. I stood my long measuring rod against one of the yellow cupboards.

Meanwhile the priest had left the room, and he now entered carrying a candle. It was a tallow candle in a brass candlestick. He placed the candlestick on the table and laid a pair of brass snuffers beside it. Then we both sat down at the table and remained seated, waiting for the storm.

It now seemed imminent. When the priest had brought the candle, the small remnant of daylight that was still coming through the windows had

Observing

vanished. The windows stood like black panels, and night had fallen completely. The lightning was more vivid, and in spite of the candle each flash lit up every corner of the room. The thunder became more solemn and menacing. Thus things continued for some time. Then at last came the first blast of the storm wind. The tree in front of the house trembled softly for a moment, as if stricken by a fleeting breeze, then it was still again. A little while later there was another tremor, more prolonged and profound. Shortly afterwards came a violent blast, all the leaves rustled, the branches seemed to be shuddering, to judge by the noise we heard from indoors; and now the roar continued unabated. The tree by the house, the hedges surrounding it, and all the bushes and trees of the neighborhood were caught up in one great rushing howl that merely waxed and waned by turns. Through it came the peals of thunder. They grew more and more frequent and penetrating. But the storm had still not reached us. There was still an interval between lightning and thunder, and the lightning, brilliant though it was, came in sheets and not in forked flashes.

At last the first raindrops struck the windows. They hammered singly against the glass but soon there were more of them, and before long, the rain was streaming down in torrents. It increased rapidly, with a hissing, rushing sound, until in the end it was as if whole continuous massive volumes of water were pouring down onto the house, as if the house were throbbing under the weight of it and one could feel the throbbing and groaning from inside. Even the rolling thunder was scarcely audible through the roar of the water; the roaring water became a second thunder. Finally the storm was immediately overhead. The lightning fell like lanyards of fire, the flashes were followed instantly by the hoarse thunderclaps which now triumphed over all the rest of the uproar, and the windowpanes shuddered and rattled under their deep reverberating echoes.

I was glad now that I had followed the priest's advice. I had seldom experienced such a storm. The priest was sitting quietly and simply by the table in his little room, with the light of the tallow candle shining on him.

At last there came a crash of thunder that seemed to try to lift the whole house up out of its foundations and hurl it down, and a second crash followed at once. Then there was a short pause, as often happens in the course of such phenomena; the rain broke off for a moment as if in alarm; even the wind stopped. But soon everything was as before; and yet the main onslaught had been broken, and everything continued more steadily. Little by little the storm abated. The gale fell to no more than a steady wind, the rain weakened, the lightning paled, and the thunder became a dull mutter that seemed to be retreating across-country.

At last, when the rain had died down to a mere continuous drizzle and the lightning to a flicker, the priest stood up and said: "It is over."

DISCUSSION

1. What emotionally charged words can you find in "The Thunderstorm"? Comparing them with the words used by Mark Twain, do you find them more, or less emotional? Are such words more, or less frequently used?

2. Most of Stifter's description is devoted to the phenomena of the storm itself. But there are several short passages about other things. What are these things? Do they have any one quality in common? What is their function in heightening the impression of threat and violence in the storm?
3. How is Stifter's way of seeing a storm different from Mark Twain's?

So far our writers have been concerned with communicating their feelings, as opposed to their thoughts, about what they have observed. The following two selections offer examples of different ways we can think about what we observe. We can look for knowledge for a particular purpose we have in mind, as Roger Ascham does in "The Wind"; or we can observe simply to learn of the nature of the thing itself, as Benjamin Franklin does in "The Whirlwind." "The Wind" is taken from a manual of archery called *Toxophilus* ("The Bow-and-Arrow Lover"). Ascham's way of seeing is conditioned by his interest in the way the action of the wind will affect the flight of an arrow.

Roger Ascham

The Wind

(1545)

The wind is sometime plain up and down, which is commonly most certain, and requireth least knowledge, wherein a mean shooter, with mean gear, if he can shoot home, may make best shift. A side wind trieth an archer and good gear very much. Sometime it bloweth aloft, sometime hard by the ground; sometime it bloweth by blasts, and sometime it continueth all in one; sometime full side wind, sometime quarter with him, and more; and likewise against him, as a man with casting up light grass, or else if he take good heed, shall sensibly learn by experience. To see the wind with a man his eyes it is unpossible, the nature of it is so fine and subtile; yet this experience of the wind had I once myself, and that was in the great snow that fell four years ago. I rode in the high way betwixt Topcliff-upon-Swale and Boroughbridge, the way being somewhat trodden before, by way-faring men; the fields on both sides were plain, and lay almost yard-deep with snow; the night afore had been a little frost, so that the snow was hard and crusted above; that morning the sun shone bright and clear, the wind was whistling aloft, and sharp, according to the time of the year; the snow in the high way lay loose and trodden with horses' feet; so as the wind blew, it took the loose snow with it, and made it so slide upon the snow in the field, which was hard and crusted by reason of the frost over night, that thereby I might see very well the

mean: poor.

Observing

whole nature of the wind as it blew that day. And I had a great delight and pleasure to mark it, which maketh me now far better to remember it. Sometime the wind would be not past two yards broad, and so it would carry the snow as far as I could see. Another time the snow would blow over half the field at once. Sometime the snow would tumble softly; by and by it would fly wonderful fast. And this I perceived also, that the wind goeth by streams, and not whole together. For I should see one stream within a score on me; then the space of two score, no snow would stir; but, after so much quantity of ground, another stream of snow, at the same very time, should be carried likewise, but not equally, for the one would stand still, when the other flew apace and so continue sometime swiftlier, sometime slowlier, sometime broader, sometime narrower, as far as I could see. Nor it flew not straight, but sometime it crooked this way, sometime that way, and sometime it ran round about in a compass. And sometime the snow would be lift clean from the ground up to the air, and by and by it would be all clapt to the ground, as though there had been no wind at all, straightway it would rise and fly again. And that which was the most marvel of all, at one time two drifts of snow flew, the one out of the west into the east, the other out of north into the east. And I saw two winds, by reason of the snow, the one cross over the other, as it had been two high ways. And, again, I should hear the wind blow in the air, when nothing was stirred at the ground. And when all was still where I rode, not very far from me the snow should be lifted wonderfully. This experience made me more marvel at the nature of the wind, than it made me cunning in the knowledge of the wind; but yet thereby I learned perfectly that it is no marvel at all though men in wind lose their length in shooting, seeing so many ways the wind is so variable in blowing.

While Ascham begins his observations with a practical purpose in mind, he cannot resist commenting on the fascination of the subject itself. Benjamin Franklin, a lively observer of everything around him, is freely interested in the whirlwind for its own sake. Perhaps in the long run Franklin's attitude is the more practical of the two, for we know from his other writings that he stored all sorts of information, which he later used to develop theories and inventions. This passage is taken from a letter to a friend.

Benjamin Franklin

The Whirlwind

(1755)

Being in *Maryland*, riding with Colonel *Tasker*, and some other gentlemen to his country-seat, where I and my son were entertained by that amiable and worthy man with great hospitality and kindness, we saw in

compass: circle.

Observing Things

the vale below us, a small whirlwind beginning in the road, and showing itself by the dust it raised and contained. It appeared in the form of a sugar-loaf, spinning on its point, moving up the hill towards us, and enlarging as it came forward. When it passed by us, its smaller part near the ground, appeared no bigger than a common barrel, but widening upwards, it seemed, at 40 or 50 feet high, to be 20 or 30 feet in diameter. The rest of the company stood looking after it, but my curiosity being stronger, I followed it, riding close by its side, and observed its licking up, in its progress, all the dust that was under its smaller part. As it is a common opinion that a shot, fired through a water-spout, will break it, I tried to break this little whirlwind, by striking my whip frequently through it, but without any effect. Soon after, it quitted the road and took into the woods, growing every moment larger and stronger, raising, instead of dust, the old dry leaves with which the ground was thick covered, and making a great noise with them and the branches of the trees, bending some tall trees round in a circle swiftly and very surprizingly, though the progressive motion of the whirl was not so swift but that a man on foot might have kept pace with it; but the circular motion was amazingly rapid. By the leaves it was now filled with, I could plainly perceive that the current of air they were driven by, moved upwards in a spiral line; and when I saw the trunks and bodies of large trees inveloped in the passing whirl, which continued entire after it had left them I no longer wondered that my whip had no effect on it in its smaller state. I accompanied it about three quarters of a mile, till some limbs of dead trees, broken off by the whirl, flying about and falling near me, made me more apprehensive of danger; and then I stopped, looking at the top of it as it went on, which was visible, by means of the leaves contained in it, for a very great height above the trees. Many of the leaves, as they got loose from the upper and widest part, were scattered in the wind; but so great was their height in the air, that they appeared no bigger than flies. My son, who was by this time come up with me, followed the whirlwind till it left the woods, and crossed an old tobacco-field, where, finding neither dust nor leaves to take up, it gradually became invisible below as it went away over that field. The course of the general wind then blowing was along with us as we travelled, and the progressive motion of the whirlwind was in a direction nearly opposite, though it did not keep a strait line, nor was its progressive motion uniform, it making little sallies on either hand as it went, proceeding sometimes faster and sometimes slower, and seeming sometimes for a few seconds almost stationary, then starting forward pretty fast again. When we rejoined the company, they were admiring the vast height of the leaves now brought by the common wind, over our heads. These leaves accompanied us as we travelled, some falling now and then round about us, and some not reaching the ground till we had gone near three miles from the place where we first saw the whirlwind begin. Upon my asking Colonel *Tasker* if such whirlwinds were common in *Maryland*, he answered pleasantly, "No, not at all common; but we got this on purpose to treat Mr. Franklin." And a very high treat it was, too.

sugar-loaf: old-fashioned sugar-loaves were conical.

Observing

DISCUSSION

1. Which writer, Ascham or Franklin, would you judge to be the better observer? Support your choice with examples. What qualities make one better than the other?
2. Does either writer make use of any senses other than sight? Where?
3. Could such observations as Franklin's be of any practical use? What possible use? Aside from practical use, is there any other reason for making such observations? What values are involved?

If Benjamin Franklin came to any conclusions from his observation of the whirlwind, they would be conclusions about the nature of air movements and the uses they could be put to. His thinking would be confined to the thing observed and its possible practical applications. In the next selection, Nathaniel Hawthorne demonstrates another way of looking at things, a way that, like Franklin's, has definite limitations.

Nathaniel Hawthorne

Shanties at Walden Pond

(1843)

In a small and secluded dell that opens upon the most beautiful cove of the whole lake, there is a little hamlet of huts or shanties inhabited by the Irish people who are at work upon the railroad. There are three or four of these habitations, the very rudest, I should imagine, that civilized men ever made for themselves—constructed of rough boards, with the protruding ends. Against some of them the earth is heaped up to the roof, or nearly so; and when the grass has had time to sprout upon them, they will look like small natural hillocks, or a species of anthills—something in which Nature has a larger share than man. These huts are placed beneath the trees, oaks, walnuts, and white-pines, wherever the trunks give them space to stand; and by thus adapting themselves to natural interstices, instead of making new ones, they do not break or disturb the solitude and seclusion of the place. Voices are heard, and the shouts and laughter of children, who play about like the sunbeams that come down through the branches. Women are washing in open spaces, and long lines of whitened clothes are extended from tree to tree, fluttering and gambolling in the breeze. A pig, in a sty even more extemporary than the shanties, is grunting and poking his snout through the clefts of his habitation. The household pots and kettles are seen at the doors; and a glance within shows the rough benches that serve for chairs, and the bed upon the floor. The visitor's nose takes note of the fragrance of a pipe. And yet, with all these homely items, the repose and sanctity of the old wood do not seem to be destroyed or profaned; she overshadows these poor people, and assimilates them somehow or other to the character of her natural inhabitants. Their presence did not shock me any more than if I had merely discovered a squirrel's nest in a tree. To be sure, it is a torment to see the great, high, ugly embankment of the railroad, which is here thrusting itself into the lake, or along its margin, in close vicinity to this picturesque little hamlet. I have seldom seen anything more beautiful than the cove on the border of which the huts are situated; and the more I looked, the lovelier it grew. The trees overshadowed it deeply; but on one side there was some brilliant shrubbery which seemed to light up the whole picture with the effect of a sweet and melancholy smile. I felt as if spirits were there—or as if these shrubs had a spiritual life. In short, the impression was indefinable; and, after gazing and musing a good while, I retraced my steps through the Irish hamlet, and plodded on along a wood-path.

DISCUSSION

1. In a brief statement sum up Hawthorne's reason for liking the settlement of the railroad workers.
2. Why does he find the embankment ugly?
3. In light of what he says here, how do you think Hawthorne would react to a modern city? What are some reasons he might give to support his reaction?
4. Which of the senses does Hawthorne employ? Point out phrases in which each sense figures.
5. Do you think Hawthorne is entirely honest with himself? That is, would he have been content to live as the workers lived or is he looking at the phenomenon entirely from the outside? Is there another way of looking at these shanties different from his?
6. Assuming that Hawthorne himself enjoyed the comforts of a good house, which he did, is there any possible compromise between his admiration of the way the shanties fit into the natural scene without spoiling it and his own love of comfort?

In the following chapter from *Life on the Mississippi*, Mark Twain also makes an esthetic judgment, but a negative one, as he looks at the inside of a typical upper-middle-class house of the southern Mississippi region.

Mark Twain

The House Beautiful

(1883)

Every town and village along that vast stretch of double river-frontage had a best dwelling, finest dwelling, mansion—the home of its wealthiest and most conspicuous citizen. It is easy to describe it: large grassy yard, with paling fence painted white—in fair repair; brick walk from gate to door; big, square, two-story "frame" house, painted white and porticoed like a Grecian temple—with this difference, that the imposing fluted columns and Corinthian capitals were a pathetic sham, being made of white pine, and painted; iron knocker; brass door-knob—discolored, for lack of polishing. Within, an uncarpeted hall, of planed boards; opening out of it, a parlor, fifteen feet by fifteen—in some instances five or ten feet larger; ingrain carpet; mahogany center-table; lamp on it, with green-paper shade —standing on a gridiron, so to speak, made of high-colored yarns, by the young ladies of the house, and called a lamp-mat; several books, piled and disposed, with cast-iron exactness, according to an inherited and unchangeable plan; among them, Tupper, much penciled; also, *Friendship's Offering*, and *Affection's Wreath*, with their sappy inanities illustrated in die-away mezzotints; also, Ossian; *Alonzo and Melissa*, maybe *Ivanhoe*; also "Album," full of original "poetry" of the Thou-hast-wounded-the-spirit-that-loved-thee breed; two or three goody-goody works—*Shepherd of Salisbury Plain*, etc.; current number of the chaste and innocuous *Godey's Lady's Book*, with painted fashion-plate of wax-figure women with mouths all alike—lips and eyelids the same size—each five-foot woman with a two-inch wedge sticking from under her dress and letting on to be half of her foot. Polished air-tight stove (new and deadly invention), with pipe passing through a board which closes up the discarded good old fireplace. On each end of the wooden mantel, over the fireplace, a large basket of peaches and other fruits, natural size, all done in plaster, rudely, or in wax, and painted to resemble the originals—which they don't. Over middle of mantel, engraving—"Washington Crossing the Delaware"; on the wall by the door, copy of it done in thunder-and-lightning crewels by one of the young ladies—work of art which would have made Washington hesitate about crossing, if he could have foreseen what advantage was going to be taken of it. Piano—kettle in disguise—with music, bound and unbound, piled on it, and on a stand near by: "Battle of Prague"; "Bird Waltz"; "Arkansas Traveler"; "Rosin the Bow"; "Marseillaise Hymn"; "On a Lone Barren Isle" (St. Helena); "The Last Link Is Broken"; "She Wore a Wreath of Roses the Night When Last We Met"; "Go, Forget Me, Why Should Sorrow o'er That Brow a Shadow Fling"; "Hours That Were to Memory Dearer"; "Long, Long Ago"; "Days of Absence"; "A Life on the Ocean Wave, a Home on the Rolling Deep"; "Bird at Sea"; and spread open on the rack where the plaintive singer has left it, "*Ro*-holl on, silver *moo*-hoon, guide the *trav*-el-err on his *way*," etc. Tilted pensively against the piano, a guitar—guitar capable of playing the Spanish fandango by itself, if you give it a start. Frantic work of art on the wall—pious motto, done on the premises, sometimes in colored yarns, sometimes in faded grasses: progenitor of the "God Bless Our Home" of modern commerce. Framed

ingrain: made of fiber dyed before weaving.
Tupper, Friendships Offering, and so on: the books Mark Twain refers to are for the most part popular sentimental and moral works of the time with little or no permanent value.

in black moldings on the wall, other works of art, conceived and committed on the premises, by the young ladies; being grim black-and-white crayons; landscapes, mostly: lake, solitary sailboat, petrified clouds, pre-geological trees on shore, anthracite precipice; name of criminal conspicuous in the corner. Lithograph, "Napoleon Crossing the Alps." Lithograph, "The Grave at St. Helena." Steel plates, Trumbull's "Battle of Bunker Hill," and the "Sally from Gibraltar." Copper plates, "Moses Smiting the Rock," and "Return of the Prodigal Son." In big gilt frame, slander of the family in oil: papa holding a book ("Constitution of the United States"); guitar leaning against mamma, blue ribbons fluttering from its neck; the young ladies, as children, in slippers and scalloped pantalettes, one embracing toy horse, the other beguiling kitten with ball of yarn, and both simpering up at mamma, who simpers back. These persons all fresh, raw, and red—apparently skinned. Opposite, in gilt frame, grandpa and grandma, at thirty and twenty-two, stiff, old-fashioned, high-collared, puff-sleeved, glaring pallidly out from a background of solid Egyptian night. Under a glass French clock dome, large bouquet of stiff flowers done in corpsy-white wax. Pyramidal what-not in the corner, the shelves occupied chiefly with bric-à-brac of the period, disposed with an eye to best effect: shell, with the Lord's Prayer carved on it; another shell—of the long-oval sort, narrow, straight orifice, three inches long, running from end to end—portrait of Washington carved on it; not well done; the shell had Washington's mouth, originally—artist should have built to that. These two are memorials of the long-ago bridal trip to New Orleans and the French Market. Other bric-à-brac: Californian "specimens"—quartz, with gold wart adhering; old Guinea-gold locket, with circlet of ancestral hair in it; Indian arrow-heads, of flint; pair of bead moccasins, from uncle who crossed the Plains; three "alum" baskets of various colors—being skeleton-frame of wire, clothed on with cubes of crystallized alum in the rock-candy style—works of art which were achieved by the young ladies; their doubles and duplicates to be found upon all what-nots in the land; convention of desiccated bugs and butterflies pinned to a card; painted toy dog, seated upon bellows attachment—drops its under-jaw and squeaks when pressed upon; sugar-candy rabbit—limbs and features merged together, not strongly defined; pewter presidential-campaign medal; miniature cardboard wood-sawyer, to be attached to the stovepipe and operated by the heat; small Napoleon, done in wax; spread-open daguerreo-types of dim children, parents, cousins, aunts, and friends, in all attitudes but customary ones; no templed portico at back, and manufactured landscape stretching away in the distance—that came in later, with the photograph; all these vague figures lavishly chained and ringed—metal indicated and secured from doubt by stripes and splashes of vivid gold bronze; all of them too much combed, too much fixed up; and all of them uncomfortable in inflexible Sunday clothes of a pattern which the spectator cannot realize could ever have been in fashion; husband and wife generally grouped together—husband sitting, wife standing, with hand on his shoulder—and both preserving, all these fading years, some traceable effect of the daguerreotypist's brisk "Now smile, if you please!" Bracketed over what-not—place of special sacredness—an outrage in watercolor, done by the

Observing

young niece that came on a visit long ago, and died. Pity, too; for she might have repented of this in time. Horsehair chairs, horsehair sofa which keeps sliding from under you. Window-shades, of oil stuff, with milkmaids and ruined castles stenciled on them in fierce colors. Lambrequins dependent from gaudy boxings of beaten tin, gilded. Bedrooms with rag carpets; bedsteads of the "corded" sort, with a sag in the middle, the cords needing tightening; snuffy feather-bed—not aired often enough; cane-seat chairs, splint-bottomed rocker; looking-glass on wall, school-slate size, veneered frame; inherited bureau; wash-bowl and pitcher, possibly—but not certainly; brass candlestick, tallow candle, snuffers. Nothing else in the room. Not a bathroom in the house; and no visitor likely to come along who has ever seen one.

That was the residence of the principal citizen, all the way from the suburbs of New Orleans to the edge of St. Louis.

DISCUSSION

1. Mark Twain's description is mostly a "catalogue"—a list of the objects he observes. How effective do you find this method? To what extent does its effectiveness depend on the subject? Can you think of other subjects that could be handled this way and some that could not? What quality of a subject enables it to be "catalogued" effectively?
2. What generalizations can you make about the "principal citizen" who lives in the house Twain describes? What items mentioned by Twain support each generalization?
3. Mark Twain's way of seeing many of the objects in the house is different from the way the owner would see them. Taking a few specific examples, how might the owner see these things? What factors might condition the owner's way of seeing?

Unlike Hawthorne, who remains outside his subject, and Mark Twain, who regards his with amused detachment, Llewellyn Powys, poor and with little choice as to where he lives, is uncomfortably involved with some rooming houses, a flophouse, and a cheap restaurant in New York City. He describes these interiors and their inhabitants with the intense revulsion of one forced into close association with them.

Llewellyn Powys

Hall-Bedrooms

(1927)

In the early part of December my brother once more left for the West, and it became clear to me that if I was to support myself by my pen I

Lambrequins: short, fancy cloths usually used to drape over shelves.

would have to find a cheaper room than the spacious fortified barrack in which we had been living. If I could hire a hall-bedroom for ten or twelve dollars a month, I would be able, I thought, to get on all right. For several mornings I searched in the poorer streets toward the river. It was a peculiarly depressing occupation. Dressed in my old African red shirt and a pair of khaki trousers, I mounted scores of stone steps, steps worn and chipped, to pull at scores of broken bell-handles, in order to interview scores of bedraggled landladies. I had had no conception that such people were still living. It was amazing. One after another they stood before me, decrepit human alley-cats, with knots of grey unbrushed hair falling upon their soiled blouses, like the elf-locks one sees in the manes of aged mares that are past work, and yet retain a sufficient fund of energy to display certain vicious characteristics developed by them through long years of ill-usage. Quite apart from the degrading effect of penury, I think that the profession of renting rooms has a most evil influence on human beings. To make one's living out of providing so simple a necessity as a rain-proof roof must bring into play a kind of atavistic meanness, the meanness of a taloned female who has secured a good cleft in the rock or a good forked branch. How sordid and squalid were the rooms into which I was conducted, rooms that smelt of gas, rooms that gave out the faint, chill aroma of damp, fly-blown wallpaper, rooms that affected one's spirits with the lugubrious, concentrated weight of all the forgotten rainy afternoons that had ever fallen upon New York City. Some of these old women would eye me with a kind of salacious avarice, others with an unmoved, bloodshot glare, as if they were already making exact calculations as to the number of soiled dollar-notes that my depravity and despair were likely to bring to their tattered purses, before I fell to even lower levels of life. With nervous tread I would tiptoe over the frayed oilcloth carpets, to look out of the window, carpets that had, perhaps, been lying in the same place through the bitter Januaries and the humid Augusts of sixty New York seasons, carpets worn bare to the boards below by the muddy, uneven boot-heels of numberless single-room bachelors. And to look out of these small back windows, with one of these hostile women at my side, women whose indrawn personalities were as powerful as the clinging, adhesive tentacles of a defiled fish, on to the backs of houses, with washtubs suspended from the nails by each window, on to desolate roofs and walls stained with filth and grime, was to receive a revelation as to the pernicious power that a foul human environment might have upon the mind. With a feeling of infinite nostalgia I remembered how once I had ridden over wide African plains, where the hoofs of my stallion had clicked against the bones of lions; where there had been places so removed from mankind and the traps they lay for one another, that a sow rhinoceros could suckle her young, completely ignorant that there existed in the world an erect anthropoid as unprecedented in its cunning and ferocity as *homo sapiens*.

   I had often noticed a hotel on Sixth Avenue which advertised rooms at twenty-five cents a night, and it seemed to me that I might perhaps persuade the landlord of it to rent me one of these on a more permanent basis. After all, I thought, if I could have a small room where my clothes

Observing

would be safe, and where I could do my typewriting, I would be happy enough. I turned into the place and climbed up a long flight of stairs, which led into a large waiting-room, where some twenty men were engaged in reading newspapers. The landlord approached me and I told him what I wanted. He was a competent fellow, with the disposition of a master of a workhouse, at once stern and kindly, but I was unable to interest him in my affairs. "This place would not do for you," he kept repeating. Eventually I persuaded him to show me the twenty-five cent rooms. They were cubicles opening on to a narrow central passage, which was dark as night. My guide urged me in a whisper to walk as quietly as possible along this grim catacomb, lest I should wake the sleepers on each side of me. I left the house, descending once more the wide staircase, each step of which was tipped with iron, never to enter it again. I used to look at it often enough, though, as I waited for the downtown elevated train at Eighth Street, craning my neck like a speckled starling on a roof-top, to get a better view of the waiting-room, which remained always full of men reading crumpled newspapers, with apparently no gaps in their ranks. And, as I looked at that melancholy, dispirited interior, I would think of those others, further within, who like rats in their darkened, dolorous holes were enjoying for "25 cents" a blessed respite from the heartless, ferret-like ferocity prevailing on the other side of the swinging-door encased in triple brass, of this retreat "for bachelors only."

As a matter of fact, all my trouble had been wasted; for when I announced to my landlady that I intended to leave, she suggested that I occupy a small room on the same landing as the staircase which led to the roof, a bedroom which I found in every way suitable, and where I was to live for the next few months. Charles Divine, the poet and short story writer, inhabited the floor below me, and I would often consult him as to the secrets of the trade we followed, and envy him his mastery of a technique which still seemed to me extremely intricate and extremely difficult. For in spite of all my efforts I remained very poor. I would spend hour upon hour studying a little paper called "How to Write!" With envy in my heart I would read the autobiographical accounts of how this or that author became successful, became the master of so many thousand of dollars a year, in no time at all. I would study this remarkable publication in a cheap restaurant frequented by draymen, a restaurant which presented a plate-glass front to two separate streets. There we would sit like queer fish in an illuminated aquarium, for all men's eyes to see. Now and again we would get up and leave our places and go to the counter to have our cups of thick white china filled with coffee at five cents a cup. And it would be so cold often outside, with the snow fluttering down on the pavement, that one could not fail to be grateful for the warmth of the place, for the warm atmosphere that enveloped one as soon as one pushed the door open, an atmosphere smelling of dirty sawdust, tobacco, and stale human sweat. Sometimes I would have my lunch as well as my breakfast in this establishment, but I never did so without regretting it afterwards. The food was more fit for the debased appetite of famished hyenas than for human beings; and one could not help wondering how long ago it must have been since the day when the grass-eaters, at whose greasy bones we gnawed, had been driven in from their pastures for the last time. There I would sit, with my elbows resting on the table of sham marble, reading my absurd magazine and filling my coffee with more and more sugar, dipped out of a bowl with a spoon coated over with grains of sweetness congealed by the coffee of earlier guests; and as I sipped the brown syrup I would look at a heap of unripe grapefruit, whose pale lemon-coloured skins, more than anything else, seemed to suggest the bitter meagreness of the provender upon which at this period of my life it had pleased the good God that I should live.

DISCUSSION

1. What is the proportion of description to comment in this selection? Is the description factual or is it presented in emotional terms? Point out examples.
2. Isolate a dozen or so descriptive details. Are these well chosen to convey the impression Powys wants to make? What do they have in common? What are some details he may have left out because they do not contribute to this impression?
3. Taking into account what Powys is aiming at (impressing the reader with the sordidness of being poor in the city) would he have done better to offer more detail and less comment? Why, or why not?
4. Powys regards these sordid places and people with sad seriousness, because he is necessarily involved with them. What are some ways a more detached observer might see them? Point out particular examples from the piece that could be seen in another light.

Llewellyn Powys observes the squalidness of poverty at first hand, but tries to keep it outside of himself. Rilke goes a step further in the thoughts and feelings that grow out of his observation. In the person of the fictional student Malte Laurids Brigge, who is on the verge of a nervous breakdown and whose senses are therefore abnormally keen, he is not only vividly aware of the ugliness of human life but recognizes with terror that this ugliness is a part of him, that it has entered his soul, that the decaying wall whose history he reads is a reflection of himself.

Rainer Maria Rilke

Old Houses

(1910)

Will anyone believe that there are such houses? No, they will say I am misrepresenting. This time it is the truth, nothing omitted, and naturally nothing added. Where should I get it from? Everyone knows I am poor.

Observing

Everyone knows it. Houses? But, to be precise, they were houses that were no longer there. Houses that had been pulled down from top to bottom. What *was* there was the other houses, those that had stood alongside of them, tall neighboring houses. Apparently these were in danger of falling down, since everything alongside had been taken away; for a whole scaffolding of long, tarred timbers had been rammed slantwise between the rubbish-strewn ground and the bared wall. I don't know whether I have already said that it is this wall I mean. But it was, so to speak, not the first wall of the existing houses (as one would have supposed), but the last of those that had been there. One saw its inner side. One saw at the different storeys the walls of rooms to which the paper still clung, and here and there the join of floor or ceiling. Beside these room-walls there still remained, along the whole length of the wall, a dirty-white area, and through this crept in unspeakably disgusting motions, worm-soft and as if digesting, the open, rust-spotted channel of the water-closet pipe. Grey, dusty traces of the paths the lighting-gas had taken remained at the ceiling edges, and here and there, quite unexpectedly, they bent sharp around and came running into the colored wall and into a hole that had been torn out black and ruthless. But most unforgettable of all were the walls themselves. The stubborn life of these rooms had not let itself be trampled out. It was still there; it clung to the nails that had been left, it stood on the remaining handsbreadth of flooring, it crouched under the corner joints where there was still a little bit of interior. One could see that it was in the paint, which, year by year, it had slowly altered: blue into moldy green, green into grey, and yellow into an old, stale rotting white. But it was also in the spots that had kept fresher, behind mirrors, pictures, and wardrobes; for it had drawn and redrawn their contours, and had been with spiders and dust even in these hidden places that now lay bared. It was in every flayed strip, it was in the damp blisters at the lower edges of the wallpapers; it wavered in the torn-off shreds, and sweated out of the foul patches that had come into being long ago. And from these walls once blue and green and yellow, which were framed by the fracture-tracks of the demolished partitions, the breath of these lives stood out—the clammy, sluggish, musty breath, which no wind had yet scattered. There stood the middays and the sicknesses and the exhaled breath and the smoke of years, and the sweat that breaks out under armpits and makes clothes heavy, and the stale breath of mouths, and the fusel odor of sweltering feet. There stood the tang of urine and the burn of soot and the grey reek of potatoes, and the heavy, smooth stench of ageing grease. The sweet, lingering smell of neglected infants was there, and the fear-smell of children who go to school, and the sultriness out of the beds of nubile youths. To these was added much that had come from below, from the abyss of the street, which reeked, and more that had oozed down from above with the rain, which over cities is not clean. And much the feeble, tamed domestic winds, that always stay in the same street, had brought along; and much more was there, the source of which one did not know. I said, did I not, that all the walls had been demolished except the last—? It is of this wall I have been speaking all along. One would think I had stood a long time before it; but I'm willing to swear that I began to run as soon as I had recognized that wall. For that is the terrible thing, that I did recognize it. I recognize everything here, and that is why it goes right into me: it is at home in me.

DISCUSSION

1. This paragraph is worth studying closely. It is compact, conveying a wealth of precise images in a few words. It is clear: we always know exactly what we are looking at. And at the same time it strongly communicates disgust and fear with a minimum of emotional words that express these emotions directly. What words can you find that tell you directly what the writer's emotions are? What words imply what he feels? What images convey emotions to the reader purely through the things described, without the writer's having to comment? It might be useful to make a rough count of examples of these three ways of communicating emotion to see what the proportions are. Strong writing *shows* the reader the things that give rise to the emotion rather than telling what the emotion is. To say, for example, "The dog cringed and whined as the man struck it again and again with his cane" is far more effective than to say "I hate people who abuse animals." Note how Rilke employs this principle. Instead of saying "Old houses fill me with disgust and fear," he *shows* us the old houses exactly as they appear to him.
2. Of all our senses the sense of smell has the most immediate suggestive associations: a smell brings back an old memory instantly or evokes a pleasant or unpleasant association. How does Rilke use this sense? Does he actually smell all the things he mentions in the last third of the paragraph? What is the effect of converting his impressions into odors rather than telling us about these things factually?
3. What is the main difference between the way Llewellyn Powys sees his sordid surroundings and the way Rilke sees the old houses? Which writer describes more vividly? Which carries his thoughts further?

WRITING SUGGESTIONS

1. In the manner of Rupert Brooke in "The Great Lover," though not necessarily in rhyme, list some objects and experiences you like. List them as experiences, even though they may be things. Rather than saying "summer rain," for example, indicate the experience you enjoy in connection with that summer rain: "the smell of rain soaking fallen leaves," "the tiny cold shocks of raindrops against my skin," "the sound of rain drumming on the roof while I am snug indoors," and so on. Try to indicate in this way a dozen or more experiences you enjoy.
2. Visualize a heavy rain falling in a location that is very familiar to you, such as your back yard or street. Describe in as much detail as you can what the *water* is doing, both before and after it reaches the ground. Stay entirely

Observing

with the water itself, bringing in other things such as wind, objects, or mud only as they affect, or are affected by, the water. Squeeze your visual memory for detail; note also what you hear, smell, and feel. You should be able to write several substantial and evocative paragraphs.

3. Taking a cue from Mu Ch'i's painting *Six Persimmons* on page 23, but using words, describe the contrast between, say, a green banana and an overripe one. You can do this best with the bananas actually before you, for then you will observe new things that are not in your memory. Do not confine yourself to the sense of sight, as Mu Ch'i had to; use also your senses of smell, taste, touch, and even, perhaps, hearing. Other subjects for such a contrast might be a new wallet and a worn one, a new piece of lumber and an old, weathered one, or clean, dry clothing and rain-soaked clothing. You can probably think of other likely subjects that are rich in sense data.

4. Write two descriptions of the same familiar room at home, school, or elsewhere, one of them objective, simply giving a clear and complete word-picture of it and the other emotionally colored by a definite attitude toward it. Your attitude need not be genuine for the purposes of this exercise. You might assume, for example, that this room is your favorite place to relax or that it disgusts you in every way, or that it makes you think of a prison. Be one-sided: write of nothing but its comfortable qualities or of its disgusting qualities, or of its resemblances to a prison.

5. Recall an interesting house you have been in, preferably an old one, or even an abandoned one. Describe it in such a way as to communicate the *feelings* it gives you. Keep in mind that these feelings are probably created not only by the things you see but by the things you feel (warmth or chill, textures) and by the things you smell and hear as well.

6. Choose a city block, a group of farm buildings, a row of old warehouses, or even a section of a suburban street. Find a place to sit and take notes and work up a description of the place in considerable detail. Slant your description to bring out your opinion of the scene, but without in any way stating that opinion. Don't use words like "beautiful," "ugly," "interesting," "dull," and so on, but convey your feeling through the details you select and those you omit, and by the way you present them. For example, the same brick wall could be described as "richly textured" or as "dirty and crumbling," thus giving two entirely different impressions of it.

7. Try a catalogue approach similar to Mark Twain's in "The House Beautiful." Choose a house you know pretty well, whose contents clearly reflect the character of the people who live in it, and describe these objects, selecting the ones that tell us the most about their owners.

Plate 1
Mu Ch'i (mid-13th Century): *Six Persimmons*

   Like many Chinese paintings, this one is deceptively simple. The writers of the Japanese poems called "Haiku" (see "The Thief and the Moon," p. 307) limit themselves to seventeen syllables and try to make those syllables communicate as much as possible. Similarly Mu Ch'i sets himself the task of saying a great deal with a single brush and color, using as few strokes as he can: his brush has touched the surface about twenty to twenty-five times. Aside from the sophisticated rhythm and balance he has achieved, he has communicated a good deal about his persimmons.

1. There is a relationship between the shade of each persimmon and its shape. What shape are the lighter ones? The darker? What does this relationship tell us?
2. What would happen to the persimmon on the left if you dropped it on the floor? What would happen to the large one in the center? How do you know this?
3. Through the medium of vision, what other senses has Mu Ch'i called into play? How has he done it in each case?
4. Why has he placed his persimmons in the bottom half of his picture space instead of in the center? What is the effect of this low placement?
5. Imagine yourself planning a picture called "Six Bananas." What positions would you choose to show the bananas in? Why? How would you communicate the same qualities of the bananas that Mu Ch'i brings out in his persimmons? Could you do it effectively in black and white? How?

PLATE 1   Mu Ch'i, **Six Persimmons,** c. 1269. *Daitoku-ji, Kyoto.*

PLATE 2   Winslow Homer (1836–1910), **Palm Tree, Nassau.** *The Metropolitan Museum of Art, Lazarus Fund, 1910.*

Plate 2
Winslow Homer (1836–1910): "Palm Tree, Nassau"

When Roger Ascham and Benjamin Franklin wanted to tell us what the wind was doing, they found they had to do so in terms of the snow and leaves being moved by the wind. In the same way Winslow Homer painted not only a palm tree, but the wind as well, through its effects on the things before him.

1. Besides the palms, what things tell us a wind is blowing? What do they tell us about its strength? Is it a steady or fitful wind? What else can you say about its quality? How does the artist communicate this quality?
2. What senses other than sight are called into play by the painting? Exactly what things in the picture stimulate these senses?
3. Imagine that you want to paint a city street scene in such a way as to communicate that it is raining, but without depicting water in any form. What devices would you use to imply the presence of rain?
4. Comparing Winslow Homer's painting with Mu Ch'i's (Plate 1), what devices do you find they have in common? If Mu Ch'i had painted the palm tree, in what ways would you expect his picture to be different from Homer's?

2

Observing Individuals

Our ways of seeing differ more when we are observing other individuals than at any other time. We cannot help assuming some sort of attitude as soon as we see another person, and that attitude has a great deal to do with the qualities in him that we become aware of. In the following brief description from *The Bostonians*, Henry James regards Miss Birdseye critically; another observer might accept her at her own evaluation, as an altogether admirable woman.

Henry James

Miss Birdseye

(1886)

She was a little old lady, with an enormous head; that was the first thing Ransom noticed—the vast, fair, protuberant, candid, ungarnished brow, surmounting a pair of weak, kind, tired-looking eyes, and ineffectually balanced in the rear by a cap which had the air of falling backward, and which Miss Birdseye suddenly felt for while she talked, with unsuccessful irrelevant movements. She had a soft, pale face, which (and it was the effect of her whole head) looked as if it had been soaked, blurred, and made vague by exposure to some slow dissolvent. The long practice of philanthropy had not given accent to her features; it had rubbed out their transitions, their meanings. The waves of sympathy, of enthusiasm, had wrought upon them in the same way in which the waves of time finally modify the surface of old marble busts, gradually washing away their sharpness, their details. In her large countenance her dim little smile scarcely showed. It was a mere sketch of a smile, a kind of installment, or payment on account; it seemed to say that she would smile more if she had time, but that you could see, without this, that she was gentle and easy to beguile.

DISCUSSION

1. James' language, while not strong or obvious, is nevertheless emotional and subjective. Try to separate the factual elements of his description word by word from the interpretive elements. How many pieces of factual description—that is, description everyone would agree to regardless of his feeling toward Miss Birdseye—can you find?
2. Try to make up a description of Miss Birdseye, in two or three sentences, that would not contradict any facts James gives us, but that would give an entirely different impression of her.

James describes Miss Birdseye in such a way that we must either disagree with him or take a definite, one-sided attitude toward her. He gives us the material that contributes to this attitude and withholds the rest. In the following extraordinary sketch, Richard Hoggart does something both more difficult and more honest: he records the unpleasant, even grotesque facts about his subject in uncompromising language and then persuades us that these facts form an integral part of an admirable character.

Richard Hoggart

A Working Class Mother

(1957)

... Her clothes looked as though they had been picked up individually from second-hand-clothing shops, and she wasn't very clean. Over a torn, old and grubby blouse and skirt she had for the street an ex-army gascape; from that there stuck what might have been the head of one of the witches in *Macbeth*. She must have been in her middle forties, so that her face could not be called young; but it was not yet old or 'past everything'. It was well-lined but not haggard; it was scored with hard work, insufficient attention and the lines which 'making shift', doggedness, fighting for your own and an overriding bravado bring. Her left eye had a violent cast and her lower lip a drop to the right, so that on the whole the bravado won. But it was a *farouche* bravado, even when she was in the easiest of spirits. Her hair was a dirty mouse colour, hanging in straggly locks from either side of an old felt hat which she wore rammed hard and unshapenly to the head, held in place by a large pin with a piccaninny's head carved on the blunt end—a relic of a day at the sea, I suppose. Her shoes were split, sloppy and entirely uncleaned; her lisle stockings hung in circles from the knees. Her voice was raucous and had been developed over the years by area and backyard 'callings' (the 'a' is pronounced as in 'shall') and 'bawlings-out'. She was not, as those who knew her only slightly thought, a widow: her husband had been in a mental home for about a dozen years, during which time she had looked after the family single-handed. Her effective married life had begun with three days' holiday at home, and had ended five or six years later, when 'They took 'im away'. So there she was at forty-odd with five of them to look after, or more accurately four, since the eldest son of eighteen was in the army. Then there was a fourteen-year-old girl who was 'bright' and had won a scholarship to the local grammar-school, a boy of ten who looked like resembling her, a girl of seven who had inherited several kinds of ill-health, and a girl of four, already pasty and with a continual cold.

They were all solidly ranged behind the mother and very cheerful, as she was. She had the spirits, and I say this with no intention of disparaging her, of a mongrel bitch. She fought hard and constantly for her children, but it never 'got 'er down', though she often exploded with temper among them. She was without subservience or deference, or a desire to win pity; she was careless of many things affecting her children and refused to worry or to take life earnestly. She asked those she worked for 'not to mention it to the Guardians', but did not cadge or respond to a gift in a way which might have suggested that further gifts would be gratefully received. If someone gave her a dress or an item of food she took it with a short word of thanks, and that was all. No doubt she often felt she could have done with some of the surplus money her employers seemed to have, but she obviously had no envy of their manner of life. The young middle-class housewives for whom she did the heavy work in a vigorous if careless-at-the-edges and knockabout fashion soon learned that any social pretensions or attempts at patronage would have been out of place. The truth was that she had a fuller life than some of those for whom she worked. Thus, if she had a day off, she thought nothing of moving with all available members of the family to the nearest seaside resort, which wasn't far, for a noisily enjoyable day, ending with fish-and-chips for all.

DISCUSSION

1. Again, separate fact from judgment in this description. What proportion is strictly factual? How does this proportion compare with the amount of factual content in "Miss Birdseye"?

2. Would it be possible to take the same facts and use them to give an impression of bad character? What are some interpretive words that could be used for this effect?

3. Our background has a great deal to do with the way we see things. From

Observing

Hoggart's insight into the mother he describes, could you guess anything about the author's background? Is it likely, for example, that he was born in a wealthy and snobbish family? How was his background probably different from that of James?

Both James and Hoggart are concerned to persuade us, James that the famous philanthropist is really a pathetic dupe, Hoggart that the vulgar and unkempt creature he describes is an independent and courageous fighter for her family. Both writers tell us pretty directly what they feel about their subjects. But it is the facts that persuade us of the virtues of the working-class mother, not the author's opinions. Often the facts alone are enough to tell the story, as in the following account of T. E. Lawrence's first meeting with an Arab warrior. (In the war against Turkey, an ally of Germany, Colonel Lawrence is looking for a potential Arab leader to help him capture the port of Akaba.)

T. E. Lawrence

Auda

(1926)

... The tribal propaganda was marching forward: all was for the best, and I was about to take my leave when Suleiman, the guestmaster, hurried in and whispered to Feisal, who turned to me with shining eyes, trying to be calm, and said, 'Auda is here'. I shouted, 'Auda abu Tayi', and at that moment the tent-flap was drawn back, before a deep voice which boomed salutations to Our Lord, the Commander of the Faithful. There entered a tall, strong figure, with a haggard face, passionate and tragic. This was Auda, and after him followed Mohammed, his son, a child in looks, and only eleven years old in truth.

Feisal had sprung to his feet. Auda caught his hand and kissed it, and they drew aside a pace or two and looked at each other—a splendidly unlike pair, typical of much that was best in Arabia, Feisal the prophet, and Auda the warrior, each filling his part to perfection, and immediately understanding and liking the other. They sat down. Feisal introduced us one by one, and Auda with a measured word seemed to register each person.

We had heard much of Auda, and were banking to open Akaba with his help; and after a moment I knew, from the force and directness of the man, that we would attain our end. He had come down to us like a knight-errant, chafing at our delay in Wejh, anxious only to be acquiring merit for Arab freedom in his own lands. If his performance was one-half his desire, we should be prosperous and fortunate. The weight was off all minds before we went to supper.

We were a cheerful party; Nasib, Faiz, Mohammed el Dheilan Auda's politic cousin, Zaal his nephew, and Sherif Nasir, resting in Wejh for a few days between expeditions. I told Feisal odd stories of Abdulla's camp, and the joy of breaking railways. Suddenly Auda scrambled to his feet with a loud 'God forbid', and flung from the tent. We stared at one another, and there came a noise of hammering outside. I went after to learn what it meant, and there was Auda bent over a rock pounding his false teeth to fragments with a stone. 'I had forgotten,' he explained, 'Jemal Pasha gave me these. I was eating my Lord's bread with Turkish teeth!' Unfortunately he had few teeth of his own, so that henceforward eating the meat he loved was difficulty and after-pain, and he went about half-nourished till we had taken Akaba, and Sir Reginald Wingate sent him a dentist from Egypt to make an Allied set.

Auda was very simply dressed, northern fashion, in white cotton with a red Mosul head-cloth. He might be over fifty, and his black hair was streaked with white; but he was still strong and straight, loosely built, spare, and as active as a much younger man. His face was magnificent in its lines and hollows. On it was written how truly the death in battle of Annad, his favourite son, cast sorrow over all his life when it ended his dream of handing on to future generations the greatness of the name of Abu Tayi. He had large eloquent eyes, like black velvet in richness. His forehead was low and broad, his nose very high and sharp, powerfully hooked: his mouth rather large and mobile: his beard and moustaches had been trimmed to a point in Howeitat style, with the lower jaw shaven underneath.

Centuries ago the Howeitat came from Hejaz, and their nomad clans prided themselves on being true Bedu. Auda was their master type. His hospitality was sweeping; except to very hungry souls, inconvenient. His generosity kept him always poor, despite the profits of a hundred raids. He had married twenty-eight times, had been wounded thirteen times; whilst the battles he provoked had seen all his tribesmen hurt and most of his relations killed. He himself had slain seventy-five men, Arabs, with his own hand in battle: and never a man except in battle. Of the number of dead Turks he could give no account: they did not enter the register. His Toweiha under him had become the first fighters of the desert, with a tradition of desperate courage, a sense of superiority which never left them while there was life and work to do: but which had reduced them from twelve hundred men to less than five hundred, in thirty years, as the standard of nomadic fighting rose.

Auda raided as often as he had opportunity, and as widely as he could. He had seen Aleppo, Basra, Wejh, and Wadi Dawasir on his expeditions: and was careful to be at enmity with nearly all tribes in the desert, that he might have proper scope for raids. After his robber-fashion, he was as hard-headed as he was hot-headed, and in his maddest exploits there would be a cold factor of possibility to lead him through. His patience in action was extreme: and he received and ignored advice, criticism, or abuse, with a smile as constant as it was very charming. If he got angry his face worked uncontrollably, and he burst into a fit of shaking passion, only to be assuaged after he had killed: at such times he was a wild beast, and

Observing

men escaped his presence. Nothing on earth would make him change his mind or obey an order to do the least thing he disapproved; and he took no heed of men's feelings when his face was set.

He saw life as a saga. All the events in it were significant: all personages in contact with him heroic. His mind was stored with poems of old raids and epic tales of fights, and he overflowed with them on the nearest listener. If he lacked listeners he would very likely sing them to himself in his tremendous voice, deep and resonant and loud. He had no control over his lips, and was therefore terrible to his own interests and hurt his friends continually. He spoke of himself in the third person, and was so sure of his fame that he loved to shout out stories against himself. At times he seemed taken by a demon of mischief, and in public assembly would invent and utter on oath appalling tales of the private life of his hosts or guests: and yet with all this he was modest, as simple as a child, direct, honest, kind-hearted, and warmly loved even by those to whom he was most embarrassing—his friends.

DISCUSSION

1. Once more, separate comment from fact. What are some expressions of Lawrence's emotion or opinion? What are the facts? Do the facts speak for themselves, making Lawrence's opinion superfluous?
2. A single incident can reveal much about a person. What are several things we learn about Auda when he breaks his false teeth?
3. To what extent does Lawrence's being an Englishman color his way of seeing Auda? What kind of person might see him quite differently? For example, how might a dogmatic pacifist see him? A person who valued refined manners and personal hygiene? A member of his own tribe? What details might each of these persons emphasize?

Few of us have the luck to meet a character as spectacular as Auda, but all of us can observe people that would otherwise pass unnoticed in a crowd. In the following sketch, Nathaniel Hawthorne takes a close look at such a person and finds much that is interesting about him. Hawthorne's description is a model of careful observation.

Nathaniel Hawthorne

The Old Apple Dealer

(1846)

... I remember an old man who carries on a little trade of gingerbread and apples at the depot of one of our railroads....

He is a small man, with gray hair and gray stubble beard, and is invariably clad in a shabby surtout of snuff color, closely buttoned, and half concealing a pair of gray pantaloons; the whole dress, though clean and entire, being evidently flimsy with much wear. His face, thin, withered, furrowed, and with features which even age has failed to render impressive, has a frost-bitten aspect. It is a moral frost which no physical warmth or comfortableness could counteract. The summer sunshine may fling its white heat upon him, or the good fire of the depot room may make him the focus of its blaze on a winter's day; but all in vain; for still the old man looks as if he were in a frosty atmosphere, with scarcely warmth enough to keep life in the region about his heart. It is a patient, long-suffering, quiet, hopeless, shivering aspect. He is not desperate,—that, though its etymology implies no more, would be too positive an expression,—but merely devoid of hope. As all his past life, probably, offers no spots of brightness to his memory, so he takes his present poverty and discomfort as entirely a matter of course: he thinks it the definition of existence, so far as himself is concerned, to be poor, cold, and uncomfortable. It may be added, that time has not thrown dignity as a mantle over the old man's figure: there is nothing venerable about him: you pity him without a scruple.

He sits on a bench in the depot room; and before him, on the floor, are deposited two baskets of a capacity to contain his whole stock in trade. Across from one basket to the other extends a board, on which is displayed a plate of cakes and gingerbread, some russet and red-cheeked apples, and a box containing variegated sticks of candy, together with that delectable condiment known by children as Gibraltar rock, neatly done up in white paper. There is likewise a half-peck measure of cracked walnuts and two or three tin half pints or gills filled with the nut kernels, ready for purchasers. Such are the small commodities with which our old friend comes daily before the world, ministering to its petty needs and little freaks of appetite, and seeking thence the solid subsistence—so far as he may subsist—of his life.

A slight observer would speak of the old man's quietude; but, on closer scrutiny, you discover that there is a continual unrest within him, which somewhat resembles the fluttering action of the nerves in a corpse from which life has recently departed. Though he never exhibits any violent action, and, indeed, might appear to be sitting quite still, yet you perceive, when his minuter peculiarities begin to be detected, that he is always making some little movement or other. He looks anxiously at his plate of cakes or pyramid of apples and slightly alters their arrangement, with an evident idea that a great deal depends on their being disposed exactly thus and so. Then for a moment he gazes out of the window; then he shivers quietly and folds his arms across his breast, as if to draw himself closer within himself, and thus keep a flicker of warmth in his lonesome heart. Now he turns again to his merchandise of cakes, apples, and candy, and discovers that this cake or that apple, or yonder stick of red and white candy, has somehow got out of its proper position. And is

surtout: overcoat.

Observing

there not a walnut kernel too many or too few in one of those small tin measures? Again the whole arrangement appears to be settled to his mind; but, in the course of a minute or two, there will assuredly be something to set right. At times, by an indescribable shadow upon his features, too quiet, however, to be noticed until you are familiar with his ordinary aspect, the expression of frost-bitten, patient despondency becomes very touching. It seems as if just at that instant the suspicion occurred to him that, in his chill decline of life, earning scanty bread by selling cakes, apples, and candy, he is a very miserable old fellow.

But, if he thinks so, it is a mistake. He can never suffer the extreme of misery, because the tone of his whole being is too much subdued for him to feel anything acutely.

Occasionally one of the passengers, to while away a tedious interval, approaches the old man, inspects the articles upon his board, and even peeps curiously into the two baskets. Another, striding to and fro along the room, throws a look at the apples and gingerbread at every turn. A third, it may be of a more sensitive and delicate texture of being, glances shyly thitherward, cautious not to excite expectations of a purchaser while yet undetermined whether to buy. But there appears to be no need of such a scrupulous regard to our old friend's feelings. True, he is conscious of the remote possibility to sell a cake or an apple; but innumerable disappointments have rendered him so far a philosopher, that, even if the purchased article should be returned, he will consider it altogether in the ordinary train of events. He speaks to none, and makes no sign of offering his wares to the public: not that he is deterred by pride, but by the certain conviction that such demonstrations would not increase his custom. Besides, this activity in business would require an energy that never could have been a characteristic of his almost passive disposition even in youth. Whenever an actual customer appears the old man looks up with a patient eye: if the price and the article are approved, he is ready to make change; otherwise his eyelids droop again sadly enough, but with no heavier despondency than before. He shivers, perhaps folds his lean arms around his lean body, and resumes the lifelong, frozen patience in which consists his strength. Once in a while a school-boy comes hastily up, places a cent or two upon the board, and takes up a cake, or stick of candy, or a measure of walnuts, or an apple as red cheeked as himself. There are no words as to price, that being as well known to the buyer as to the seller. The old apple dealer never speaks an unnecessary word: not that he is sullen and morose; but there is none of the cheeriness and briskness in him that stirs up people to talk.

Not seldom he is greeted by some old neighbor, a man well to do in the world, who makes a civil, patronizing observation about the weather; and then, by way of performing a charitable deed, begins to chaffer for an apple. Our friend presumes not on any past acquaintance; he makes the briefest possible response to all general remarks, and shrinks quietly into himself again. After every diminution of his stock he takes care to produce from the basket another cake, another stick of candy, another apple, or

chaffer: bargain.

another measure of walnuts, to supply the place of the article sold. Two or three attempts—or, perchance, half a dozen—are requisite before the board can be rearranged to his satisfaction. If he have received a silver coin, he waits till the purchaser is out of sight, then he examines it closely, and tries to bend it with his finger and thumb: finally he puts it into his waistcoat pocket with seemingly a gentle sigh. This sigh, so faint as to be hardly perceptible, and not expressive of any definite emotion, is the accompaniment and conclusion of all his actions. It is the symbol of the chillness and torpid melancholy of his old age, which only make themselves felt sensibly when his repose is slightly disturbed.

DISCUSSION

1. Henry James, Richard Hoggart, and T. E. Lawrence all seem to approach their subjects with opinions already formed, and we are given an impression of their subjects that might not be the same as our own would be if we were the observers. Is this true of Hawthorne? Do you find him more objective than the others or less so? What is your evidence?

2. Hawthorne makes a good many comments as he goes along, mostly about the old man's seeming inability to feel extremes of emotion. Are these comments justified by the evidence Hawthorne shows us? If so, could he lead us more effectively to the same conclusion while refraining entirely from comment? How? (It is a truism of both writing and speaking that if you state an opinion, you get an argument; but if you get the other person to form the opinion himself as though it were his own, you get an agreement.)

It is one thing to observe a stranger; it is another to look closely at someone you have known all your life. Here Oliver LaFarge tells us about his own father and what his father's last days were like.

Oliver LaFarge

Old Man Facing Death

(1945)

The relationship and common interests of two artists came late with my father and me. For us three brothers the early one, the constant running through our lives, was the outdoors, first the boats and the horses, then fishing, hunting, and on according as our various experiences matched his one way or another.

For me it begins with candlelight and a whisper. Long before dawn there would be the step on the stairs and the yellow clarity of the candle reach-

Observing

ing through the doorway, spreading along the wall, growing stronger. Then his voice, conspiratorial, eager:

'Four o'clock, Inky. Get up.'

He would leave the candle and slip downstairs, very quiet, a man to whom it came natural to tread lightly. I dressed in a hurry and followed him. A lamp and two alcohol flames burned in the dining room. In one copper kettle eggs were boiling, in another, coffee, which otherwise I did not yet drink. There might be only me, or a brother or so as well. The eggs would be served soft-boiled. We hated soft-boiled eggs, but it never occurred to us to say a word. It was part of the ritual, along with the smell of the flames and hot copper and coffee, and my father constantly glancing out the window lest a gleam of white in the east proclaim us laggards.

All in whispers and soft movements. Guns ready. Rubber boots. The marsh and gun-oil smell of shooting jackets. Quietly down to the shore, the definite quality of escape, the canoe grating slightly on the beach, then the lap of water and the long paddle to the marshes.

You had the sense of being taken into a man's world; as Kipling said, of crossing to the men's side. A boy might be very much a pupil under instruction but at the same time my father let him feel that he was an equal partner in the joint enterprise of hunting. There was a thrilling promotion to equality in a private world. All hunting was illuminated by his artist's response to beauty and his trained perception, which he knew very well how to convey. When the duck came, when a trout rose to the fly, when there was a hen grouse with her chicks in the springtime or a butterfly hovering in sunlight, he could pull you alert and into perception with his quiet voice. There was an eternally fresh excitement in his speech and his eyes.

The voice was always quiet. He used the wild country as Indians do, in co-operation and communion with it, finding any form of noise a baneful disharmony. The impossible union of liquor and gunning which some men attempt, the loud talk sounding over waters, closing hearts and ears and eyes to the essence of hunting, were abomination to him. He called such sportsmen yahoos and taught us to hate the donkey-laugh in the woods as much as we do the mere killers. The Indians know a way of belonging to the manless country. Their ritual expresses the communion of love between a hunter and the game he seeks to kill. There is a way of being which fills with pleasure even the entirely luckless days when no game is seen or killed. These my father had.

Learning from him, we were always conscious of his reserves of experience. Canadian Indians accepted him as an equal canoeman. He was utterly at home in Arizona. He had sailed with our own Rhode Island fishermen long before a power-driven smack was dreamed of. The wild goose, the mountain goat, elk, salmon, moose and caribou, snowshoes, packhorses, tump-line and fishing smack were his familiars. We became men and in one point or another achieved some single experience which we could match in talk with some part of his, but the older we grew and the more we learned, the deeper grew our respect.

tump-line: a strap across the forehead used to support a back-pack.

This old man was practically indestructible. When he was seventy he decided I should have a real taste of Canadian-style duck-hunting in a canoe. He put me in the bow and took me up-river. With age he had shrunken very slightly, a light, slender man with no great appearance of strength about him. I knew he was good, but I did not expect the force of his final twist of the paddle at each stroke, the feel of the canoe leaping and turning under his hand, all in nearly perfect silence. The loudest sound, I think, was the fall of drops off his paddle as he reached forward. Coming back downriver I took bow paddle. He was nice about it, but the plain fact was that I was nowhere near man enough to make an adequate mate for his stern paddle.

It was about that time that the depression liquidated his architectural practice. It took some persuading to talk him out of starting over again from scratch. He had no intention of becoming idle and quickly found new uses for his skill and reputation.

It would not be quite true to say that he laughed off his first heart attack, but it did not stop him from travelling through Europe on a fellowship. The second one laid him low. He had fished that spring, killed his duck in the fall, then suddenly he was imprisoned in a small room with a good view over the bay. After months he would be allowed to walk about that floor, after yet longer he might be free to go downstairs, carefully.

For more than a year we visited with him in the room. Each of us received the same impression. Neither self-deceived nor a coward, he was visibly making himself ready for death. He let go, one by one, of minor interests and particularly of those, such as improvements in the place, which could be considered only in terms of years from now. He kept up those which were rewarding in themselves and out of them made himself a lively life. He entertained himself with us.

I still do not know if there is a smell of death. There was something in that room which had the emotional effect of a smell, one felt the presence of the old skull and bones. To him it must have been perched on the foot of the bed. It might come in ten minutes and it might not come for a year or more, there was no way of knowing. It could come quietly, instantly, or it could strike as a searing, unbearable pain in the full fury of a heart attack. None of this could be foreseen. It simply was always there, waiting. And he knew it.

In its presence he sat up radiating his great personal charm and his warmth at its most perfect. With me he talked intimately about my writing, following my ideas and endeavors with great interest, and endlessly we shared the tribes we knew in common or matched this odd thing about Guatemala with that of Canada. He was a very easy man to talk to. He offered the wisdom of his many years and at the same time he made himself contemporary.

When we came in from the river or the marshes we went to his room and gave him a blow-by-blow account. I started fishing at the big bend and put on a Queen of the Waters and a Whirling Dun. That big bastard was feeding under the log at the back of the bend, he rose to the Queen a

Queen of the Waters, Whirling Dun: types of artificial flies used for fishing.

Observing

couple of times but wouldn't touch it. The marsh marigolds were beautiful and there were some lady-slippers out. At the log below the reach there was a good one feeding. He took the Dun almost as soon as it hit the water, here he is. . . .

My father would listen, smiling, alert. At a lost fish or a missed shot he would exclaim with the same disgust as he had in the field, a success would give him the same pleasure. When he detected a flaw in technique he would advise as he always did.

Never, at any time, did he protest at being cooped up in that room. None of us, nor my mother, heard him pity himself for that, not even when we were on the marsh with a fine sou'wester blowing. He would damn the cook for a flavourless soup, row with my mother for ordering food he didn't care for, in ten minutes he could cure visitors he didn't like of coming to sit with him, when his vitality was up he could raise particular hell over small things. But he never complained about the big one, and whatever fear sat on him, he never referred to it.

The fear was there along with the courage to handle it. Death was in the room. You could not be there long and not know that. Coming down for the week-end and entering the room you were aware of it, it was oppressive and it filled you with wonder at this man. Then he made you forget it, and to the degree that you forgot it you recognized it again after you had gone. The memory of that time is made up of his warmth, wide-ranging talk, laughter, his quick response, and that eternal presence. The two elements were in balance with each other, one could not separate them.

He had a shelf outside his window on which he put feed for the birds. Some of them were becoming very tame. There was a rat which came up the grapevine onto the porch roof at sundown and raided the feed. He had also killed a bird. My father wanted to get him. How about laying for him with the twenty-eight?

I took the little shotgun down from the shelf by the door. There were shells in his bureau. I mounted the gun and loaded it. Now we were back in our private world. It was dusk and the rat would come soon.

'Quiet, Inky. Sit here on the bed. He's smart, if you move he'll spot you.'

The old voice, a whisper which you felt rather than heard and yet had the hunting timbre in it. The half smile and the lively eyes. We were hunting, sitting there in the growing darkness, he in the bed, I on it, waiting for a rat to show up. Hunting—my mind was divided, feeling his pleasure and thinking of the geese and duck coming in a howling snow-storm, of the big-horn and the moose and the mountain lion and the feats of skill and endurance. Hunting.

'Here he comes.'

You didn't need to understand the words, you knew the all-but-inaudible, thrilling tone since you first crouched in a blind with him and the V of duck showed in the sky. Raising the gun and the click of the safety was too much, the rat fled back down the vine.

'Shah!' It was what he always said, and he made an adequate curse out of it. 'They're so quick.'

'We'll try again tomorrow evening.'

I put the gun away and we went on with normal talk, but I was glad when I was called for supper. I needed time to cope with my sense of the pathetic.

His funeral was on the day before the season opened. That evening we spoke to my mother, and we all agreed that he would be most upset if we missed the opening day on his account. So the three of us went out and hunted for him. We felt tired, lax, and curiously peaceful. There was a great closeness to him in doing this, and none of us referred to him while we were out. We worked unusually carefully, and we had good luck. When my mother saw our bag, as many black duck as we had use for, she said:

'Oh, boys, your father would be so pleased.'

In a sense I have hunted with him ever since and discussed the problems that arose with him. Often I talk to him in Spanish, a language he loved and which was one of our common interests. Then he is the man of the first thirty-five years of my life, the woodsman who could always walk me groggy. At other times it occasionally happens that I think about my own death, and pray that it will be sudden. And if it comes slowly I wonder and doubt if I could turn the old skeleton into a mere visitor sitting to one side while I entertained myself by fascinating my friends.

DISCUSSION

1. From the information in this essay, what objective statements can you make about LaFarge's father? Are these statements very important ones? Where is the importance of the essay to be found?
2. Sometimes a portrait of an individual can be used to express a philosophy of life, to make a statement concerning values. What are some of the qualities and values that LaFarge seems to consider important?
3. What kind of person might see the old man quite differently? What sort of values might cause a person to dislike him?

Modern writers are often careful to preserve an appearance of neutrality toward their material, seeming to let the facts speak for themselves. On the surface, the following account seems to be a straightforward chronicle of events. Nevertheless, as we read it, we find that certain feelings are aroused in us about Red, about the author, and about our society. That the author has chosen to write about Red shows that he believes his subject to be significant; he is trying to tell us something, or at least to let reality tell us something.

Observing

Niccolo Tucci

Red

(1972)

A few years ago, a bum killed himself by jumping from one of the masts of the lightship Scotland, which was docked at the foot of Fulton Street. I knew him. He was called Red. No one knew his real name. Among acquaintances, he had a reputation for making long speeches and for having theories that no one understood but that sometimes made people laugh. When he wasn't making speeches, he might remain silent for weeks. On the street, he had for years introduced himself to strangers by saying, "Dime for a cup of coffee?" More recently, he had been saying, "Quarter for a cup of coffee?" He had gradually given up another activity, which he had called "collecting"; in fact, he had given up the whole city, with its immense wealth in newspapers and in objects of all sorts and sizes—umbrellas, electric wires, bulbs, bottles. This had advantages. A bum can travel light. He needn't have a heavy shopping bag weighing him down and cutting his fingers, and he doesn't have to decide whether to discard the newspapers he has carried for months in order to make room for new ones. I first met Red on a beautiful June morning, shortly after sunrise, at the Battery. It was a Saturday. On Saturdays and Sundays, I often walk all the way downtown from Sixty-seventh Street and Madison Avenue, where I live. I enjoy wandering alone through the financial district, which in its abandoned state becomes a place for meditation—like a dead city. The atmosphere lasts well into the afternoon, when tourists walk about aimlessly, as if they were in Pompeii. The fruit store beyond the five-cent turnstiles of the Staten Island Ferry is open on Sundays, and I usually buy myself bananas and pretzels, saving some money in spite of the wasted five cents, because they are cheaper than elsewhere. At any rate, on this particular Saturday, I encountered a bum in Battery Park whose gray hair was glued to the side of his face that he had been sleeping on (obviously in the dirt) and whose clothes were torn at the back, one sleeve hanging loose and showing a brownish-red arm with many scars, the other sleeve tied up with rather clean strings, like a salami. He was clutching a brand-new shoe under his left arm. On his feet were the last remnants of an old pair of shoes, tied together by a similar system of strings. He was whistling a twenties tune called "When My Baby Smiles at Me."

"How do you come to remember that tune?" I asked.

"I was a rich man once," he said cheerfully. "I went to night clubs, and I danced with rich girls to that tune." Then, as if there were a connection between the two things, he showed me the new shoe and said he had found it the day before. He insisted that I appreciate the quality of the leather, the perfection of the finish, the thickness of the double sole. Everything about that shoe pleased him.

"Wonderful," I said. "But where's the other shoe?"

He scouted the horizon—the harbor, with its ships—then looked at the seagulls above us, at the blue shadows of leaves on the asphalt pavement, at the rags on his feet, and said, "Man always strives for the impossible. But hope is one-legged. All it needs is two wings." He started to walk away, and I realized I had made a bad mistake. I ran after him and gave him a dollar, and that was my second mistake, because it was actually ten dollars—all I had in my pocket for the weekend. He took the money without thanking me, and left me.

Later that morning, I found myself in the midst of noises, smoke, and smells; the Brooklyn Bridge, to the north, stood high above me, thundering horribly with trucks and cars, which sent the bitter taste of exhaust over the rusty roofs of sheds adjoining the Fulton Fish Market, where empty strainers with bits of rotting fish clinging to them were glittering in the pink sunshine, garbage was burning in the streets, and oil was leaking from a parked truck that was puffing poison in my face. Across the river from me, smokestacks filled the sky with black clouds from which descended invisible cancer for smokers and nonsmokers alike. It wasn't one of those days when the sea manages to pierce the curtain of industrial development and salt it, iodize it, disinfect it.

Oscillating like metronomes, above a white hull, were the masts of the Coast Guard ship Eagle. Suddenly the bum with the shoe under his arm was at my side, saying, "Wouldn't you like to climb up there and feel the sea under your feet? I've never had the sea under my feet. Only the earth."

"That's all we have," I said.

"Don't forget the moon," he said. "Next year, we'll set foot on the moon."

"Not you or I," I said. "A couple of trained mechanics. And the price of their ticket, far exceeding the yearly budget of a large city, will be paid by us in taxes."

"I don't pay taxes," he said. "And I wouldn't if they asked me."

"You pay more for beer, or whatever it is you drink, and for whatever else you buy," I said. "You're being taxed."

"I don't care," he said. "I despise money anyway."

"You are luckier than I am," I said. "I respect money very much. But it seems to despise me."

"Then listen to me," he said. "Don't give it to bums. They are immoral. Especially those who sleep on the benches in Madison Square Park. I wouldn't be seen dead in that place. But also the bums on the Bowery. Don't trust them. They are stupid. They don't think. They have no conversation."

"Thanks for warning me," I said. "I'll make a mental note of that."

"Don't you be so goddam wise," he said.

I looked at him closely. His face was flushed. He seemed to be in a state of extreme anger.

"Do you think the bums can go on picking up after you?" he continued. "I used to collect empty bottles, old newspapers, and everything else. I ruined myself to save the city, but now I've given up."

I looked about me for help. We were alone. At a great distance from us, another bum was sitting in front of a pile of burning garbage.

Observing

"Looking for help?" the bum with the shoe said. "Do you need the police? Why don't you use your brain? No, that all goes into making money. So when you meet a man who knows how to talk to you, your money does all the talking and you run away from him."

I said nothing, and turned to go my way.

"Where do you think you are going?" he said. "How about showing me what you are worth. Not in hard cash—I don't give a damn about your cash—but with your head. Why did you talk to me this morning? I was happy, and you ruined my happiness. So I need another shoe, eh? Want to see what I do with your damn shoes that come in pairs? This." And he threw the shoe into the filth of the river. Obviously, the loss was painful to him, for he followed the shoe's course intently. I even thought I saw tears in his eyes. I dared not move. "How about that broken glass everywhere in the city?" he said, finally. "You have good shoes. You don't care. God mends my feet for free. All you can think of is to throw another bottle in my path. From rooftops. From windows. You missed my head by an inch last week. And then you cut my back and my arm. See? God mends my arm, but you don't mend my sleeve for free."

"But that's exactly what I was saying," I said. "You pay taxes—more so than anyone else."

"Who throws those bottles from the rooftops?" he said. "Who breaks them in my path?"

"I never threw a bottle in my life," I said. "Besides, I live uptown."

"So it's the Negroes and the Puerto Ricans—is that it?" he said.

"No, the kids," I said. "All kids, of all races and backgrounds. It's their idea of fun. A barbarous idea—new to me. When we were young, these things were unknown."

"Kids don't throw away what they can sell for cash," he said. "But, with prices going up every day, bottles worth two cents apiece only a few years ago drop down to zero. They're good enough to be thrown in my path. What's wrong with glass? The one thing that doesn't rot. I have seen bottles in museums, with my own eyes—unbroken through many civilizations. So why don't you pay fifteen cents apiece and keep the kids working and the city clean?" This was before "the environment" and "recycling" had entered everyone's vocabulary.

That was only the beginning of a long conversation that took place over a number of days and covered many subjects, but Red always steered away from any inquiries relating to his origins and to his name. He told me simply to call him Red. I made it a point to walk all the way down to the Battery even on weekdays, because his case fascinated me, even though it irritated me at the same time. I never told him I would be there again the next morning. In fact, I made it clear to him that I was a bit tired of his absurdities, but the next morning I was sure to find him there, and he never seemed surprised to see me come back. I must add that I did give him some money every day. Not as much as the first day—indeed, never more than fifty cents, but fifty cents at five in the morning is a very good beginning for a bum. So one day I decided to tell him that I couldn't go on helping him, because I had to go to Europe and also because I was not the rich man he had imagined. To my great surprise, he not only understood

Observing Individuals

but he offered to help me financially, to the extent of a few hundred dollars. This, I felt, authorized me to look into his personal finances. If he had all that money, he obviously possessed more than I did, so why didn't he spend it to make himself more presentable? I told him I didn't think people had a right to go around filthy and in rags, and pretend that it was a private matter. The moment I had finished, he said, "But then you agree with me. I cannot ride an image of myself out of this life. And *who am I? What* am I? I haven't opened a book in years." I secretly registered this as an important fact. He *had* cared for books.

"Why don't you tell me your real name?" I said. "That will help you understand who you are."

By then, we were walking uptown from the Battery. It seemed to me that he was turning morose, and I feared a new outbreak of the anger that had frightened me the first day. To keep him from brooding, I began to elaborate on the reasons an intellectual like him might have for becoming so secretive about his personal identity. "You tend to identify yourself with your intellectual achievement, and, having given this up, you have denied yourself even the use of your own name," I said. "Is that it?"

He said nothing, but he seemed interested. This gave me courage to go on.

"If you knew how little most intellectuals read, and how little they absorb of what they read, even after they have earned the respect of the world, you would realize that they don't deserve it," I said. "Have *I* opened a book in many years? No, and I close my eyes on all the good books I read, because I read them in bed after a strenuous day of lecturing, teaching, correcting papers, listening to the nonsense of others. But that's all irrelevant to our discussion. What is your name?"

He stared at me as if he hadn't heard me.

"Did you hear my question?" I asked.

"Yes, yes, of course," he said. "That's interesting. Go on. So they don't deserve it, you were saying. See? I was listening."

I decided to go on. "Now, dressing up like the others is one sure way to keep your identity hidden, while going around in rags reveals too much of your inner conflicts to people who have no right to pry into your background. Get it?"

He smiled and nodded, staring at the pavement in front of the Chase Manhattan Bank Building. He was obviously thinking.

"Even if you have reasons for keeping your name a secret forever," I said, "it is harder for you to do so in your present condition than it would be as a normal-looking person with a name you had adopted to cover up your past once and for all."

He was now listening with great intensity, and he did look like a hunted criminal trying to flatten himself against a wall so as not to be seen by the police and at the same time fearing every noise from behind the wall.

I thought it best not to show apprehension, but just then my apprehension became greater, because the "wall" at that moment was one of the windows of the Marine Midland Bank, and the night watchmen were right inside. What if they came out and Red had one of his temper tantrums? They had a right to ask what we were doing there, and would I want to

Observing

take his side? But there was more to worry me. If I feared a summons that would delay my trip to Europe, I was equally afraid of hurting Red's feelings. I knew what to expect from him when he spoke to an audience of one—and a friendly one, at that. Let a watchman threaten him with a nightstick, and God knew what would happen. "Red, please, let's go," I said. "What are you doing there?" He seemed to be listening to the building. His ear was pressed against a metal partition between two windows.

"This building is completely dead," he said.

"What do you mean?" I said. "Can't you see the night watchmen inside? Let's go, Red. It's dangerous."

"Dangerous?" he said. "I don't see why. The building has no voice. I've always known that. Look over there across the street. That was a building with a voice. They are tearing it down. The voice is gone. It's the first thing to go."

I headed for the building across the street, and Red followed me. We just made it, for one of the night watchmen came out.

"Interesting architecture," I said, very loudly. "It's really a shame they are tearing it down."

"The seamen's hotel down there was even better," he said. "They are tearing that down, too. And look at this sign. They put this sign up everywhere."

The sign was the usual warning to trespassers, with promise of a reward to anyone turning in trespassers or leading to their capture. "How do you like that?" he asked me. "We are trespassers, but they are aliens—the ones who are tearing it down. That building that lost its voice—you know what it was called? It was called the Singer Building, and it used to sing every morning with the voices of thousands of birds. And find me a window ledge or a roof where birds can nest along the walls of these new buildings!"

We were now standing under some scaffolding across the street from the Chase Manhattan Bank Building. Another building was coming down. A row of beautifully carved closet doors and shutters had been erected all around the wrecking site, but through fissures here and there we could see what resistance the wreckers were encountering from the ancient masonry. An acrid smell of rotting wood emanated from the half-demolished building. Red sniffed the air. "Smell the breath of the dead?" he asked me. Then he shouted, "Rape and murder, in there!" He went on, in his ordinary voice, "Did you see the crater down this way? That will be the World Trade Center. There were many birds in that area, but they left when the steel cage was built. You can catch buildings in cages but not birds. Tell me, are they doing the same thing to the mansions on Fifth Avenue? Putting them in a cage and killing them?"

"Yes," I said. "But how long has it been since you were in that area?"

"Years, I guess," he said. "Ever since they tore down that beautiful club at the corner of Fifth and Fifty-first, to replace it with Best & Co. Let's go listen to the birds at the U. S. Court House. That's become the last gathering place since the Singer Building began to come down."

We walked up past City Hall, and there, in the grayish morning mist, while the first drops of rain were falling on us, we heard the most wonderful concert of birds, coming from dark corners between windows and stone garlands all along the facade and the side of the Court House. Red stood there in the middle of Foley Square, his legs apart, listening.

After five minutes or so, Red said, "Let's go to the jail."

"To the jail?" I asked.

"Yes, to the jail," he said. "Three blocks from here, on Centre Street."

We walked up Centre Street until we came to the new Tombs. He pointed out to me that hands were moving at almost every window. A group of black women and children soon joined us on the sidewalk. Hands were raised in the rain, answering hands at the windows. A child next to us couldn't identify the window from which his father was calling. His mother tried to direct his eyes toward it but couldn't get him to stay quiet. "It's Saturday morning," Red whispered to me. "They come early for the visit."

We continued uptown on Centre Street. It was really raining now—a cold rain. Red's feet looked purple through his torn shoes.

"You know, here is another stupid thing they do," Red said. "All the streets of New York are full of steam heat, but the pedestrian gets none of it. If I were rich, I would have all the streets heated."

"Wouldn't it be easier to buy yourself a pair of shoes?" I asked.

"It's always easier to think only of yourself, first and last, and neglect the rest of suffering mankind," he answered, with anger. "I am thinking of others. And my plan would cost nothing."

"Really?"

"Much less than a day's fighting in Vietnam," he said. "Do you know how much heat is generated by one single bomb? Do you know how much iron is thrown away every hour in Vietnam? And these streets could be paved with iron bars, like those we have just seen. The subways would have light, and we would have heat; then I would have the subway closed down at midnight and the tracks cleaned by people. Just by people—you know? Even by me. I wouldn't mind."

We were walking up Lafayette Street now, and I had decided that I would take a bus at Astor Place, because that is where the Madison Avenue line begins, but Red insisted that we go and walk on the Bowery, which, from the jail, would be quite a detour for me, with all that rain coming down from the sky and up from the earth through my shoes. I was colder than I had almost ever been, even in the winter, because the weather forecast had spoken of an unusually warm day, precipitation probability near zero, wind at a few inches per hour; so here I was in my lightest summer suit, with no raincoat and no umbrella, and with sudden gusts of the nastiest possible wind bringing whiffs of dejection and garbage into my face.

"Why the Bowery, Red? Haven't you had enough of it? I have. Especially this morning."

But he was way ahead of me, walking at an exceptionally energetic pace for him, so I ran after him, in order not to hurt his feelings—all the way from there to Cooper Union, where he suddenly seemed to lose all his strength, just when I was beginning to recapture mine. The bus was there,

Observing

ready to leave. It meant all the difference between sitting in warm, dry air and standing in the rain, and I boarded it. Once comforted by the heat and transportation, I decided I must do something for Red, even if it seemed impossible. I simply must.

A week or so later, I decided to go downtown and look for Red. I found him listening to buildings, as usual. It was difficult for me to tell whether the shoes and rags he wore were those I had last seen him in or were new ones. He appeared glad to see me—as if he sought friendship. Or, at least, he liked to be seen to have friends by those who were incapable of friendship; namely, the bums on the Bowery. He evidently liked to impress bums and policemen alike by showing them the sight of him, a filthy bum, talking authoritatively to a man from "the other world."

I decided to treat Red as a friend, and told him candidly that I didn't like his suicidal way of living.

"Suicidal?" he shouted, in a fit of anger. "Su-i-ci-dal, *he* says." And he harangued the trees, the seagulls, and the whole Port of New York out to the Statue of Liberty. "I don't believe in suicide," he said. "I don't like those bums who try to be run over by cars in the Bowery. They are stupid. But if you want to kill yourself you'd better not talk about it, or you'll wind up in Bellevue. Just do it before they can get to you. And do it quietly."

As we were about to part company in front of the Court House, Red remembered that I was supposed to be in Europe that summer, and seemed very much disappointed when I said I didn't know whether I could go after all. "Oh, that's too bad," he said. "I like to think that I know somebody who is feeling the sea under his feet."

I felt I owed him a promise that I would go soon, and I promised him I would. Perhaps I really would.

I continued my early walks, but I intentionally avoided meeting Red. I saw him a couple of times but managed to change my route before he saw me. The last time I saw him was the very day he died. He was standing under the highway at the foot of Fulton Street, where we had met for the second time in one morning only a couple of months before, and he was staring at the masts of the Scotland, which had just been repainted.

The next day, I saw Red's picture—actually, one of a series of four pictures—in the *Times*, against the background of the Brooklyn Bridge, as he jumped from the mast. He looked like a long flying fish, crossing that beautiful network of wires against the sky. Someone had sold Red's suicide. And this exceptional picture must surely have won a photography contest somewhere.

DISCUSSION

1. Rather than speaking for him, as LaFarge does for his father, Tucci lets Red speak for himself in words and actions. But this is one of the most difficult things for a writer to do; he must listen and watch carefully, never dismissing as unimportant anything the other person says or does. What are some details of speech and action that an observer with less

respect for Red might have overlooked or judged too trivial to record?

2. Probably few people have observed and listened to a "bum" as carefully as Tucci does. Does he, or the reader, gain anything from this careful attention? Does Red in his surroundings suggest any insights into our way of life?

3. Henry James and Richard Hoggart approach their subjects with a pretty definite attitude already in mind; T. E. Lawrence is already prepared to admire Auda, having heard much about him before he meets him; Oliver LaFarge's way of seeing his father is conditioned by a lifetime of familiarity and affection. What conditions Tucci's approach to Red? What are some clues to his attitude? Does he seem open-minded, or does he see what he expects to see?

4. What motivations do you think cause Tucci to observe Red as carefully as he does? (Obviously, he cannot know beforehand that there is going to be a picture of Red's suicide in the paper.)

5. Tucci does not seem to be entirely candid with us concerning his own role. We find it hard to believe that the man who writes about Red is also the rather timid and unperceptive person who is afraid of him and asks him naive questions. Tucci, for the purpose of writing, has assumed a *persona* or mask. What does the author gain by representing himself as less intelligent than he really is? Besides the situation represented here, what are some other situations where it might be to a writer's advantage to adopt such a pose?

WRITING SUGGESTIONS

1. Choose a position in a bus station, on a bus, in a park, in a doctor's waiting room, or in some similar place where you can observe a stranger for some time without attracting attention to yourself. Take notes. Describe the stranger in considerable detail, but with complete objectivity: do not state any conclusions or suppositions at all. Do not even guess his age, but describe the physical evidences of age in such a way that your reader can guess it. Try to describe the stranger so completely that a painter could do a full-length portrait.

2. Try a subjective portrait like that of LaFarge's father. Describe a time in the life of a person very close to you, in terms of what that person meant to you, of the activities you shared with him, of the things you learned from him. You need not necessarily write about a person you are fond of; sometimes we are very close to a person with whom we have uncomfortable conflicts, and an irritating relationship is as interesting to explore as an affectionate one. Or, as often happens, such a relationship may be a combination of affection and friction. Tell it the way it looks to you.

3. Spend some time with a person you know, but who is not too close to you, while he is going about his normal activities and perhaps talking with you casually. Using Tucci's "Red" as a model, show us this person through his characteristic actions and opinions, with little or no comment of your own. Keep your writing objective. You may, as Tucci does, regard your own reactions and answers, but leave your reader to form his own conclusions.

Plate 3
Hans Holbein (1497–1543): *Erasmus*

When it comes to describing a person, the painter is far more limited by his medium than the writer. He cannot tell us how Auda broke his teeth and why; he cannot tell us a person's past history as Oliver LaFarge does in "Old Man Facing Death." He must rely entirely on what he can reveal by depicting facial and other physical features in a state of immobility. Considering this great limitation, it is surprising how much a fine portrait artist can communicate about his subject.

1. Erasmus (see "Fools Are Happy," p. 335) was the most famous scholar and satirist of his time. But if we knew nothing about him aside from what Holbein tells us through this portrait, what would we know? What personal characteristics can you infer from the picture, and what is your evidence?
2. In addition to obvious kinds of evidence such as the objects and clothing in the picture, what more subtle kinds of evidence point to the nature of the man? What seems to be implied by the positions of the mouth, the eyes, and the left hand, for example?

PLATE 3   Hans Holbein (1497–1543), **Erasmus.** *The Louvre, Paris, from Lauros-Giraudon.*

Plate 4
Sir Joshua Reynolds (1723–92): *Dr. Johnson*

Like Erasmus, Samuel Johnson (see "Letter to Lord Chesterfield," p. 334) was a famous scholar and satirist.

1. All of the writers in Chapter 2 show us their subjects in characteristic activities and situations—in their natural habitat, so to speak. The painters in this unit do the same. Holbein shows us Erasmus at his usual work, writing, presumably in a library or study. Here Reynolds portrays Dr. Johnson without any background, but in a characteristic pose. What does this pose imply as to Dr. Johnson's best-known activity? Why is no background necessary?
2. What sort of person would you expect Dr. Johnson to be as, say, a dinner companion? What evidence in the portrait leads you to this conclusion?
3. Examine Reynolds' use of color. How is it different from Holbein's? What impression does it create of Dr. Johnson's character and habitat?
4. Erasmus was a small man, Dr. Johnson a large one. Which painter most effectively communicates an impression of the size of his subject? Exactly how does he do this?
5. Judging from the portraits, which man would you prefer to spend a social evening with, Erasmus or Dr. Johnson? Why? How has each painter communicated the impressions that cause you to make this choice?

PLATE 4   Sir Joshua Reynolds (1723–92), **Dr. Johnson.** *The Tate Gallery, London. Photo by Vince Finnegan & Associates.*

3

Observing a Scene

One challenge to be faced when you set out to describe a complex scene is that of keeping things straight and making the various relationships clear to the reader. Here is an ancient Greek description of a fight, complete with cheering onlookers. The fight, between two legendary figures, is imaginary, but the action is obviously based on observations of real fights. The several ways in which the participants and their bands are named may confuse you at first, but once you get the names straight, you will find Theocritus' account of the actions masterfully clear.

Theocritus

A Fight

(270 B.C.)

When the two had strengthened their hands with straps of oxhide and wound the long thongs around their arms, they stepped together into the middle of the circle breathing slaughter against each other. Each tried hard to get the light of the sun behind him, but Polydeuces outwitted

Polydeuces: better known as Pollux, his Roman name. Castor and Pollux were legendary twin demigods credited with many heroic exploits.

the giant and the rays fell full on Amycus' face. He came on, heart full of anger, making play with his fists, but as he attacked the son of Tyndareus caught him a blow on the point of the jaw and angered him still more, so that he became confused and, head down, waded in with all his force. The Bebryces cheered, and on the other side the heroes shouted encouragement to the mighty Polydeuces, fearing that in the narrow space that Tityus-like creature would smother and defeat him. But the son of Zeus, stepping in on this side and that and cutting the skin first with one fist and then the other, kept Poseidon's son on the defensive from the beginning, in spite of all his confidence. Drunk with blows, he came to a standstill and spat crimson blood, while all the heroes shouted to see the grievous wounds about his mouth and jaws; his face swelled until his eyes were narrowed to slits. Then the prince confounded him with feints on every side, and when he saw him confused, drove his fist down on his brow above the nose and skinned his forehead to the bone, and stretched him on his back on the flowery grass.

Then, when he rose again, the fight became grim as with blows of the tough thongs they sought each other's death. But the chief of the Bebryces struck with his fists the chest and neck of his opponent, while the invincible Polydeuces pounded the other's face with disfiguring blows. And as he sweated the flesh of Amycus shrank, and from a giant in a little while he became small; but as the work waxed hotter the other's limbs grew ever stronger and of better color.

How, then, did the son of Zeus lay that glutton low? . . . Truly Amycus, eager for a great coup, leaned forward from his guard, grabbed with his left hand the left hand of Polydeuces, stepped in on his right foot and swung his mighty fist upward from the right flank. Had he landed the blow he would have done great harm to the king of Amyclae, but Polydeuces rolled his head aside and with his stout fist struck below the left temple, putting his shoulder into the punch, and from the gaping temple flowed dark blood. Then with his left he landed on the mouth so that the tight-set teeth rattled, and with an even faster rain of blows he battered the face until the cheeks were crushed and Amycus, reeling, stretched his length upon the ground and held up both his hands, declining further fight, for he was nearly dead. Then, O boxer Polydeuces, for all thy victory, thou didst him no further hurt; but he swore a mighty oath to thee, calling upon his father Poseidon in the sea, that he would nevermore molest a stranger.

A knock-down-drag-out fight is about the same in any place or time in history, but the galley slave is a phenomenon that fortunately can be seen

Amycus: on his voyage with Jason's Argonauts to recover the Golden Fleece, Polydeuces encountered Amycus, king of the Bebryces, who challenged all who passed his way to a boxing match. Since he was a champion, he always killed them in the match if they accepted; if they declined, he simply threw them into the sea.
son of Tyndareus: Polydeuces.
Poseidon's son: Amycus.
king of Amyclae: Polydeuces.

Observing

today only in the movies. In his diary Evelyn tells us something about the lives of galley slaves in 1644.

John Evelyn

A Slave Galley

(1644)

7th October. We had a most delicious journey to Marseilles, through a country sweetly declining to the south and Mediterranean coasts, full of vineyards and olive-yards, orange trees, myrtles, pomegranates, and the like sweet plantations, to which belong pleasantly-situated villas to the number of above 1500, built all of freestone, and in prospect showing as if they were so many heaps of snow dropped out of the clouds amongst those perennial greens. It was almost at the shutting of the gates that we arrived. Marseilles is on the sea-coast, on a pleasant rising ground, well-walled, with an excellent port for ships and galleys, secured by a huge chain of iron drawn across the harbour at pleasure; and there is a well-fortified tower with three other forts, especially that built on a rock; but the castle commanding the city is that of Notre Dame de la Garde. In the chapel hung up divers crocodiles' skins.

We went then to visit the galleys, being about twenty-five in number; the Capitaine of the Galley Royal gave us most courteous entertainment in his cabin, the slaves in the interim playing both loud and soft music very rarely. Then he showed us how he commanded their motions with a nod, and his whistle making them row out. The spectacle was to me new and strange, to see so many hundreds of miserably naked persons, their heads being shaven close, and having only high red bonnets, a pair of coarse canvas drawers, their whole backs and legs naked, doubly chained about their middle and legs, in couples, and made fast to their seats, and all commanded in a trice by an imperious and cruel seaman. One Turk amongst the rest he much favoured, who waited on him in his cabin, but with no other dress than the rest, and a chain locked about his leg, but not coupled. This galley was richly carved and gilded, and most of the rest were very beautiful. After bestowing something on the slaves, the capitaine sent a band of them to give us music at dinner where we lodged. I was amazed to contemplate how these miserable caitiffs lie in their galley crowded together; yet there was hardly one but had some occupation, by which, as leisure and calms permitted, they got some little money, insomuch as some of them have, after many years of cruel servitude, been able to purchase their liberty. The rising-forward and falling-back at their oar, is a miserable spectacle, and the noise of their chains,

divers: many.
rarely: with rare skill, excellently.
caitiffs: captives, slaves.

with the roaring of the beaten waters, has something of strange and fearful in it to one unaccustomed to it. They are ruled and chastised by strokes on their backs and soles of their feet, on the least disorder, and without the least humanity, yet are they cheerful and full of knavery.

DISCUSSION

1. The part of "A Slave Galley" that deals with the galley itself is shorter than the whole of "A Fight." Which selection do you find has the length most appropriate to its subject? Do you find either piece too long or too short? Do you feel you would like to know more about either subject? If so, which subject do you feel needs further elaboration?
2. In Chapters 1 and 2 most of the selections include a good deal of sensory description; in "A Fight" there is almost none. Would "A Fight" be improved by more evocation of specific sights, sounds, and smells? Why, or why not?
3. Imagine that you wanted to make accurate historical movies based on each of these selections. What facts would you need to know that Theocritus does not tell you? That Evelyn does not tell you? Which writer seems to give you the least material necessary for your purpose?
4. Personal attitude conditions how we see things. What does Evelyn's attitude toward slavery seem to be? Judging only from this short excerpt from his diary, how would you characterize his general attitude toward life? What does he value most?

What we see depends on what we are conditioned to see, what our senses are "programmed" to observe. The conventional traveler sees only postcard pictures wherever he looks. But it is possible to condition our own senses and to train ourselves to see what is around us in new and more entertaining ways. In the following selection, Jonathan Swift applies the principle of *parody,* writing about one subject in a manner usually reserved for an entirely different kind of subject. In this case he uses elaborate and dignified words to describe the ordinary and comical behavior of people caught in a sudden rain. Not only is the effect comical, but the device of parody leads Swift to observe things he's never noticed before. Without setting out to do so, he has opened a whole new world of things to write about and therefore of things to watch and enjoy. Before Swift's time such a scene was considered an unworthy subject for a writer; within a century after Swift, all sorts of subjects were available to the writer.

Evelyn wrote about something most people have not seen but all of us have read about. Swift, more cleverly, has written about something all of us have seen but none of us have read about. The result is that delightful feeling of recognition—"I've seen that, but I never thought about it before!" When he says,

knavery: mischief.

Observing

> Here various kinds, by various fortunes led,
> Commence acquaintance underneath a shed

we remember the times we have seen people who would normally never speak to each other chatting comfortably under a dripping awning. Swift is consolidating our awareness of the world.

Jonathan Swift

Description of a City Shower

(1710)

Careful observers may foretell the hour
(By sure prognostics) when to dread a shower.
While rain depends, the pensive cat gives o'er
Her frolics, and pursues her tail no more;
Returning home at night, you'll find the sink
Strike your offended sense with double stink.
If you be wise, then go not far to dine;
You'll spend in coach-hire more than save in wine.
A coming shower your shooting corns presage,
Old aches will throb, your hollow tooth will rage;
Sauntering in coffee-house is Dulman seen,
He damns the climate and complains of spleen.
   Meanwhile the South, rising with dabbled wings,
A sable cloud athwart the welkin flings,
That swilled more liquor than it could contain,
And, like a drunkard, gives it up again.
Brisk Susan whips her linen from the rope,
While the first drizzling shower is borne aslope;
Such is that sprinkling which some careless queen
Flirts on you from her mop, but not so clean;
You fly, invoke the gods; then turning, stop
To rail; she, singing, still whirls on her mop.
Not yet the dust had shunned th' unequal strife,
But, aided by the wind, fought still for life,
And wafted with its foe by violent gust,
'Twas doubtful which was rain and which was dust.
Ah! where must needy poet seek for aid
When dust and rain at once his coat invade?
Sole coat! where dust, cemented by the rain,
Erects the nap, and leaves a cloudy stain!

spleen: melancholy, depression.
welkin: sky. This is a pretentious, "poetic" word used by Swift for humorous effect.

Observing a Scene

    Now in contiguous drops the flood comes down,
Threatening with deluge this devoted town.
To shops in crowds the daggled females fly,
Pretend to cheapen goods, but nothing buy.
The Templar spruce, while every spout's abroach,
Stays till 'tis fair, yet seems to call a coach.
The tucked-up sempstress walks with hasty strides,
While streams run down her oiled umbrella's sides.
Here various kinds, by various fortunes led,
Commence acquaintance underneath a shed.
Triumphant Tories and desponding Whigs,
Forget their feuds and join to save their wigs.
Boxed in a chair the Beau impatient sits,
While spouts run clattering o'er the roof by fits,
And ever and anon with frightful din
The leather sounds, he trembles from within.
So when Troy chairmen bore the wooden steed,
Pregnant with Greeks impatient to be freed
(Those bully Greeks, who, as the moderns do,
Instead of paying chairmen, ran them through),
Laocoon struck the outside with his spear,
And each imprisoned hero quaked for fear.

    Now from all parts the swelling kennels flow,
And bear their trophies with them as they go;
Filths of all hues and odour seem to tell
What street they sailed from by their sight and smell;
They, as each torrent drives with rapid force,
From Smithfield to St. Pulchre's shape their course,
And in huge confluence joined at Snowhill ridge,
Fall from the conduit prone to Holborn bridge;
Sweepings from butchers' stalls, dung, guts, and blood,
Drowned puppies, stinking sprats, all drenched in mud,
Dead cats and turnip-tops come tumbling down the flood.

daggled: muddy.
cheapen: bargain for.
Templar: law student.
Triumphant Tories and desponding Whigs: these were the two major political parties in England at that time. Just before the poem was written, the Tories won an election.
Beau: dandy, ladies' man.
Troy chairmen: Swift humorously likens the Trojan Horse to a sedan-chair. The Trojan Horse, in which the Greeks were hidden, was obligingly carried into Troy by the Trojans. The beau's sedan-chair, beaten by the rain, is also likened to the Trojan Horse when Laocoon rapped on it with his spear as it was being carried into Troy.
kennels: gutters.
sprats: herrings from a fish market.

Observing

DISCUSSION

1. In addition to the contrast between pompous language and ludicrous subject, Swift has found comedy in the kind of things he chooses to observe. What sorts of things does he include in the poem, and why are they funny? What sorts of things might have been in the scene, but have been left out of the poem?
2. Can you think of another attitude or "programing" of mind with which you could approach the same scene, one that would cause you to observe an entirely different set of details? For example, what might you observe if you were a meteorologist? A city planner? A sanitation expert? A painter?

When we describe the familiar scene, we must avoid falling into the trap of taking too much for granted; we must work to see things with fresh eyes, as though we were foreigners. Swift passes this test with flying colors in "A City Shower." He observes anew what we all see but do not notice. But when we describe the strange and foreign, the trap we must avoid is the opposite: that of over-emphasizing the strange and new and falling into sensationalism. T. E. Lawrence strikes a nice balance in the following selection, a description of the way Arabs dine. He observes much that an Arab would take too much for granted and regard as not worth mentioning, but at the same time he does not patronize his hosts or present their customs as grotesque.

T. E. Lawrence

Arab Feasting

(1926)

... Each morning, between eight and ten, a little group of blood mares under an assortment of imperfect saddlery would come to our camping place, and on them Nasir, Nesib, Zeki and I would mount, and with perhaps a dozen of our men on foot would move solemnly across the valley by the sandy paths between the bushes. Our horses were led by our servants, since it would be immodest to ride free or fast. So eventually we would reach the tent which was to be our feast-hall for that time; each family claiming us in turn, and bitterly offended if Zaal, the adjudicator, preferred one out of just order.

As we arrived, the dogs would rush out at us, and be driven off by onlookers—always a crowd had collected round the chosen tent—and we stepped in under the ropes to its guest half, made very large for the occasion and carefully dressed with its wall-curtain on the sunny side to give us the shade. The bashful host would murmur and vanish again out

Observing a Scene

of sight. The tribal rugs, lurid red things from Beyrout, were ready for us, arranged down the partition curtain, along the back wall and across the dropped end, so that we sat down on three sides of an open dusty space. We might be fifty men in all.

The host would reappear, standing by the pole; our local fellow-guests, el Dheilan, Zaal and other sheikhs, reluctantly let themselves be placed on the rugs between us, sharing our elbow-room on the pack-saddles, padded with folded felt rugs, over which we leaned. The front of the tent was cleared, and the dogs were frequently chased away by excited children, who ran across the empty space pulling yet smaller children after them. Their clothes were less as their years were less, and their pot-bodies rounder. The smallest infants of all, out of their fly-black eyes, would stare at the company, gravely balanced on spread legs, stark-naked, sucking their thumbs and pushing out expectant bellies towards us.

Then would follow an awkward pause, which our friends would try to cover, by showing us on its perch the household hawk (when possible a sea-bird taken young on the Red Sea coast) or their watch-cockerel, or their greyhound. Once a tame ibex was dragged in for our admiration: another time an oryx. When these interests were exhausted they would try to find a small talk to distract us from the household noises, and from noticing the urgent whispered cookery-directions wafted through the dividing curtain with a powerful smell of boiled fat and drifts of tasty meat-smoke.

After a silence the host or a deputy would come forward and whisper, 'Black or white?' an invitation for us to choose coffee or tea. Nasir would always answer 'Black', and the slave would be beckoned forward with the beaked coffee-pot in one hand, and three or four clinking cups of white ware in the other. He would dash a few drops of coffee into the uppermost cup, and proffer it to Nasir; then pour the second for me, and the third for Nesib; and pause while we turned the cups about in our hands, and sucked them carefully, to get appreciatively from them the last richest drop.

As soon as they were empty his hand was stretched to clap them noisily one above the other, and toss them out with a lesser flourish for the next guest in order, and so on round the assembly till all had drunk. Then back to Nasir again. This second cup would be tastier than the first, partly because the pot was yielding deeper from the brew, partly because of the heel-taps of so many previous drinkers present in the cups; whilst the third and fourth rounds, if the serving of the meat delayed so long, would be of surprising flavour.

However, at last, two men came staggering through the thrilled crowd, carrying the rice and meat on a tinned copper tray or shallow bath, five feet across, set like a great brazier on a foot. In the tribe there was only this one food-bowl of the size, and an incised inscription ran round

pole: the central tent pole.
watch-cockerel: a rooster used to signal the approach of enemies at night.
ibex: wild goat.
oryx: wild antelope.

Observing

it in florid Arabic characters: 'To the glory of God, and in trust of mercy at the last, the property of His poor suppliant, Auda abu Tayi.' It was borrowed by the host who was to entertain us for the time; and, since my urgent brain and body made me wakeful, from my blankets in the first light I would see the dish going across country, and by marking down its goal would know where we were to feed that day.

The bowl was now brim-full, ringed round its edge by white rice in an embankment a foot wide and six inches deep, filled with legs and ribs of mutton till they toppled over. It needed two or three victims to make in the centre a dressed pyramid of meat such as honour prescribed. The centre-pieces were the boiled, upturned heads, propped on their severed stumps of neck, so that the ears, brown like old leaves, flapped out on the rice surface. The jaws gaped emptily upward, pulled open to show the hollow throat with the tongue, still pink, clinging to the lower teeth; and the long incisors whitely crowned the pile, very prominent above the nostrils' pricking hair and the lips which sneered away blackly from them.

This load was set down on the soil of the cleared space between us, where it steamed hotly, while a procession of minor helpers bore small cauldrons and copper vats in which the cooking had been done. From them, with much-bruised bowls of enamelled iron, they ladled out over the main dish all the inside and outside of the sheep; little bits of yellow intestine, the white tail-cushion of fat, brown muscles and meat and bristly skin, all swimming in the liquid butter and grease of the seething. The bystanders watched anxiously, muttering satisfactions when a very juicy scrap plopped out.

The fat was scalding. Every now and then a man would drop his baler with an exclamation, and plunge his burnt fingers, not reluctantly, in his mouth to cool them: but they persevered till at last their scooping rang loudly on the bottoms of the pots; and, with a gesture of triumph, they fished out the intact livers from their hiding place in the gravy and topped the yawning jaws with them.

Two raised each smaller cauldron and tilted it, letting the liquid splash down upon the meat till the rice-crater was full, and the loose grains at the edge swam in the abundance: and yet they poured, till, amid cries of astonishment from us, it was running over, and a little pool congealing in the dust. That was the final touch of splendour, and the host called us to come and eat.

We feigned a deafness, as manners demanded: at last we heard him, and looked surprised at one another, each urging his fellow to move first; till Nasir rose coyly, and after him we all came forward to sink on one knee round the tray, wedging in and cuddling up till the twenty-two for whom there was barely space were grouped around the food. We turned back our right sleeves to the elbow, and, taking lead from Nasir with a low 'In the name of God the Merciful, the loving-kind', we dipped together.

The first dip, for me, at least, was always cautious, since the liquid

baler: ladle.

Observing a Scene

fat was so hot that my unaccustomed fingers could seldom bear it: and so I would toy with an exposed and cooling lump of meat till others' excavations had drained my rice-segment. We would knead between the fingers (not soiling the palm), neat balls of rice and fat and liver and meat cemented by gentle pressure, and project them by leverage of the thumb from the crooked fore-finger into the mouth. With the right trick and the right construction the little lump held together and came clean off the hand; but when surplus butter and odd fragments clung, cooling, to the fingers, they had to be licked carefully to make the next effort slip easier away.

As the meat pile wore down (nobody really cared about rice: flesh was the luxury) one of the chief Howeitat eating with us would draw his dagger, silver hilted, set with turquoise, a signed masterpiece of Mohammed ibn Zari, of Jauf, and would cut criss-cross from the larger bones long diamonds of meat easily torn up between the fingers; for it was necessarily boiled very tender, since all had to be disposed of with the right hand which alone was honourable.

Our host stood by the circle, encouraging the appetite with pious ejaculations. At top speed we twisted, tore, cut and stuffed: never speaking, since conversation would insult a meal's quality; though it was proper to smile thanks when an intimate guest passed a select fragment, or when Mohammed el Dheilan gravely handed over a huge barren bone with a blessing. On such occasions I would return the compliment with some hideous impossible lump of guts, a flippancy which rejoiced the Howeitat, but which the gracious, aristocratic Nasir saw with disapproval.

At length some of us were nearly filled, and began to play and pick; glancing sideways at the rest till they too grew slow, and at last ceased eating, elbow on knee, the hand hanging down from the wrist over the tray edge to drip, while the fat, butter and scattered grains of rice cooled into a stiff white grease which gummed the fingers together. When all had stopped, Nasir meaningly cleared his throat, and we rose up together in haste with an explosive 'God requite it you, O host', to group ourselves outside among the tent-ropes while the next twenty guests inherited our leaving.

Those of us who were nice would go to the end of the tent where the flap of the roof-cloth, beyond the last poles, drooped down as an end curtain; and on this clan handkerchief (whose coarse goat-hair mesh was pliant and glossy with much use) would scrape the thickest of the fat from the hands. Then we would make back to our seats, and re-take them sighingly; while the slaves, leaving aside their portion, the skulls of the sheep, would come round our rank with a wooden bowl of water, and a coffee-cup as dipper, to splash over our fingers, while we rubbed them with the tribal soap-cake.

Meantime the second and third sittings by the dish were having their turn, and then there would be one more cup of coffee, or a glass of syrup-like tea; and at last the horses would be brought and we would slip out to

nice: fastidious, fussy.

them, and mount, with a quiet blessing to the hosts as we passed by. When our backs were turned the children would run in disorder upon the ravaged dish, tear our gnawed bones from one another, and escape into the open with valuable fragments to be devoured in security behind some distant bush: while the watchdogs of all the camp prowled round snapping, and the master of the tent fed the choicest offal to his greyhound.

DISCUSSION

1. What expressions of the author's opinions can you find in "Arab Feasting"? What emotionally charged language? Is the proportion of emotionally loaded language small or large? How much of the piece is made up of factual description? Does the author's main purpose seem to be to inform the reader or to convince him?
2. What are some details Lawrence notices that an Arab writer might overlook because of familiarity with the scene? In what passages or expressions does Lawrence's being an Englishman seem to color his way of seeing?
3. Now that you know how Arabs dine, try this exercise: imagine that a friendly Arab writes, for his own people, a description of how your family dines. What sorts of things would he record that you would find too familiar to tell about?

In contrast to the man of action who writes of foreign customs is the one who stays at home and writes entertainingly of the familiar scene. Here Leigh Hunt rides an omnibus—a short, horse-drawn streetcar with passengers both inside and on top—and tells us what he sees and hears. The events he observed more than a century ago are little different from those you might see today in any city bus or streetcar.

Leigh Hunt

The Inside of an Omnibus

(1847)

Being one of the chance fares, we enter an omnibus which has yet no other inside passenger; and having no book with us, we make intense acquaintance with two objects: the one being the heel of an outside passenger's boot, who is sitting on the coach-top; and the other, that universally studied bit of literature, which is inscribed at the further end

Observing a Scene

of every such vehicle, and which purports, that it is under the royal and charming jurisdiction of the young lady now reigning over us,

V.   R.

by whom it is permitted to carry *"twelve inside passengers*, AND NO MORE";—thus showing extreme consideration on her Majesty's part, and that she will not have the sides of her loving subjects squeezed together like figs.

Enter a precise personage, probably a Methodist, certainly "well off," who seats himself right in the midway of his side of the Omnibus; that is to say, at equal distances between the two extremities; because it is the spot in which you least feel the inconvenience of the motion. He is a man who seldom makes a remark, or takes notice of what is going forward, unless a payment is to be resisted, or the entrance of a passenger beyond the lawful number. Now and then he hems, and adjusts a glove; or wipes a little dust off one of the cuffs of his coat.

In leaps a youngster, and seats himself close at the door, in order to be ready to leap out again.

Item, a maid-servant, flustered with the fear of being too late, and reddening furthermore betwixt awkwardness, and the resentment of it, at not being quite sure where to seat herself. A jerk of the Omnibus pitches her against the precisian, and makes both her and the youngster laugh.

Enter a young lady, in colors and big ear-rings, and excessively flounced and ringleted, and seats herself opposite the maid-servant, who beholds her with admiration, but secretly thinks herself handsomer, and what a pity it is she was not a lady herself, to become the ringlets and flounces better.

Later two more young ladies, in white, who pass to the other end in order to be out of the way of the knees and boots of those who quit. They whisper and giggle much, and are quizzing the young lady in the reds and ringlets: who, for her part (though she knows it, and could squeeze all their bonnets together for rage), looks as firm and unconcerned as a statue.

Enter a dandy, too handsome to be quizzed; and then a man with a bundle, who is agreeably surprised with the gentlemanly toleration of the dandy, and unaware of the secret disgust of the Methodist.

Item, an old gentleman; then, a very fat man; then, two fat elderly women, one of whom is very angry at the incommodious presence of her counterparts, while the other, full of good humor, is comforted by it. The youngster has in the meantime gone to sit on the coach-top, in order to make room; and we set off to the place of our destination.

What an intense intimacy we get with the face, neckcloth, waistcoat, and watch-chain of the man who sits opposite us! Who is he? What is his

V. R.: "Victoria Regina," Queen Victoria. Official notices included these initials to indicate that the queen so ordered.
quizzing: making fun of.
dandy: a man who dresses in fancy style.

name? Is his care a great care,—an affliction? Is his look of cheerfulness real? At length he looks at ourselves, asking himself, no doubt, similar questions; and, as it is less pleasant to be scrutinized than to scrutinize, we now set him the example of turning the eyes another way. How unpleasant it must be to the very fat man to be so gazed at! Think, if he sat as close to us in a private room, in a chair! How he would get up, and walk away! But here, sit he must, and have his portrait taken by our memories. We sigh for his plethora, with a breath almost as piteous as his wheezing. And he has a sensible face withal, and has, perhaps, acquired a painful amount of intellectual as well as physical knowledge, from the melancholy that has succeeded to his joviality. Fat men always appear to be "good fellows," unless there is some manifest proof to the contrary; so we wish, for his sake, that everybody in this world could do just as he pleased, and die of a very dropsy of delight.

Exeunt our fat friend, and the more ill-humored of the two fat women; and enter, in their places, two young mothers,—one with a good-humored child, a female; the other with a great, handsome, red-cheeked wilful boy, all flounce and hat and feathers, and red legs, who is eating a bun, and who seems resolved that the other child, who does nothing but look at it, shall not partake a morsel. His mother, who "snubs" him one instant, and lets him have his way the next, has been a spoiled child herself, and is doing her best to learn to repent the sorrow she caused her own mother, by the time she is a dozen years older. The elderly gentleman compliments the boy on his likeness to his mamma, who laughs and says he is "very polite." As to the young gentleman, he fancies he is asked for a piece of his bun, and falls a kicking; and the young lady in the ringlets tosses her head.

Exit the Methodist, and enter an affable man; who, having protested it is very cold, and lamented a stoppage, and vented the original remark that you gain nothing by an omnibus in point of time, subsides into an elegant silence; but he is fastened upon by the man with the bundle, who, encouraged by his apparent good-nature, tells him, in an under tone, some anecdotes relative to his own experience of omnibuses; which the affable gentleman endures with a variety of assenting exclamations, intended quite as much to stop as to encourage, not one of which succeeds; such as "Ah"—"Oh"—"Indeed"—"Precisely"—"I dare say"—"I see"—"Really?"—"Very likely;"—jerking the top of his stick occasionally against his mouth as he speaks, and nobody pitying him.

Meantime the good-humored fat woman having expressed a wish to have a window closed which the ill-humored one had taken upon her to open, and the two young ladies in the corner giving their assent, but none of the three being able to pull it up, the elderly gentleman, in an ardor of gallantry, anxious to show his pleasing combination of strength and tenderness, exclaims, "Permit *me*;" and jumping up, cannot do it at all. The window cruelly sticks fast. It only brings up all the blood into his face with the mingled shame and incompetence of the endeavor. He is a conscientious kind of incapable, however, is the elderly gentleman; so he calls in the conductor, who does it in an instant. "He knows the

Observing a Scene

trick," says the elderly gentleman. "It's only a little bit new," says the conductor; who hates to be called in.

Exeunt elderly and the maid-servant, and enter an unreflecting young gentleman who has bought an orange, and must needs eat it immediately. He accordingly begins by peeling it, and is first made aware of the delicacy of his position by the gigglement of the two young ladies, and his doubt where he shall throw the peel. He is "in for it," however, and must proceed; so being unable to divide the orange into its segments, he ventures upon a great liquid bite, which resounds through the omnibus, and covers the whole of the lower part of his face with pip and drip. The young lady with the ringlets is right before him. The two other young ladies stuff their handkerchiefs into their mouths, and he, into his own mouth, the whole of the rest of the fruit, "sloshy" and too big, with desperation in his heart, and the tears in his eyes. Never will he eat an orange again in an omnibus.

DISCUSSION

1. Point out some of the more successful verbs and adjectives Hunt uses to make people's actions and reactions clear to the reader. Are there any places where you could suggest a better choice of words to communicate the same idea?
2. At times, Hunt offers the reader conjectures rather than facts. Separate some of these conjectures, or inferences, from the factual description. Could Hunt have described the person so that the reader would have arrived at the same conclusion without the author's guess? Would this have been a better writing technique? Why, or why not?
3. What is Hunt's purpose in writing this piece? Does the answer here make it easier to respond to the first two questions?
4. Clearly Hunt's way of seeing is humorous. But there are many kinds of humorous attitudes, some friendly to their subjects and some not. Do you find Hunt's friendly or unfriendly? Does he seem to view his subjects from a superior position or as fellow human beings and equals? What are some examples of his phrasing that support your answer?

Leigh Hunt uses eyes and ears to observe the antics of his fellow men. In the next essay, Robert Lynd uses mostly his ears.

Observing

Robert Lynd

Conversation

(1923)

It is said that the art of conversation is dead, but if you are staying at a hotel and go into the bar after returning from the pictures you will find that there are still places where men carry on quite wonderful conversations till midnight. I spent a night at a town not far from Cowes during Regatta week, and I heard a conversation that left no doubt in my mind that Swift and Pope and Gay have their successors in modern England. I do not know how the talk drifted from Bottomley, whom a little lean-faced commercial traveller drinking bitter in the corner refused to "'it when 'e's down," to King George, but for about ten minutes a chorus of male voices discussed the King and the hard life he leads—Goodwood one week, Cowes the next, and never a day idle. "I was watching him at Goodwood," said a young Jew in blue trousers and fawn-coloured socks, "and saw him shakeen hands, shakeen hands, with about thirty people in five minutes, toucheen his hat and boween—greeteens, I suppose you would call it. I thought to myself I'd rather be dead. Greeteens, greeteens all the time." "W'y does 'e do it?" the lean little man asked; "it's all umbug." "Of course it's humbug," replied the Jew warmly; "and nobody knows it better than the King. That's what makes it such hard work." "That's what I mean," interrupted the landlord, a large, fat man with a moustache, a bowler on the back of his head, and a booming voice, "when I call him a harassed man. I don't suppose there's a man what's more harassed in the whole of England than King George. I wouldn't take his job, not if you paid me for it." "Give me the Prince of Wales," a spectacled Scotsman in a mackintosh mumbled into his moustache, without taking his pipe out of his mouth. "Ah, the Prince," said the landlord, wagging his head; "he's hot—hot as mustard. A naval officer what was with him in India was telling me the other night how he routed that fellow Gandhi." "Who's he?" asked the Jew. "Gandhi?" said the landlord: "you know, the agitator. Well, as I was saying, the Prince of Wales, as soon as he got to India, said, 'Look here, I'm going to interview that fellow.' Of course, everybody was scared blue. 'You can't,' they told him. 'You'll only be shot if you try.' 'I don't give a damn,' says the Prince of Wales; 'go and fix up an appointment.' And they had to. Well, the result was the appointment was made, and the Prince drove off as bold as a lion to keep it. Well, when he got there, there was no Gandhi." "What happened?" mumbled the Scotsman. "What happened?" repeated the landlord in a voice of exasperation. "He'd bunked, run away, took to his heels. I reckon there isn't another man living who could have done what the Prince of Wales done. By gosh! he's hot—hot as mustard."

Swift and Pope and Gay: English authors known for their wit.
bunked: English slang, "chickened out."

Observing a Scene

A genial little man in a brown bowler hat who had not been saying much looked up from the sofa on which he was sitting at the clock. "Coming on to midnight, gentlemen," he said; "I hope everybody here will remember to say 'Rabbit, rabbit, rabbit, first thing in the morning. Rabbit, rabbit, rabbit," he repeated the words as if to impress them on our memory. "Rabbit, rabbit, rabbit," the lean traveller tried the words over as if testing them to see if they had any meaning; "I don't get the 'ang of it." "Why," the man in the brown hat laughed at him, "I thought everybody knew 'Rabbit, rabbit, rabbit.' If you say 'Rabbit, rabbit, rabbit' —three times, just like that—first thing in the morning on the first of the month, even before you say your prayers, you'll get a present before the end of the month." "Supposin' you don't say any prayers," the lean traveller objected. "Well, it's all the same," the other assured him; "say 'Rabbit, rabbit, rabbit' before you say anything else, and I guarantee you'll get a present before the end of the month." "Rabbit, rabbit, rabbit," said the Jew in the fawn-coloured socks. "Well, I'm damned!" "Supposin' we sit 'ere till twelve o'clock, does that count?" asked the lean traveller. "Yes," replied the brown hat, "that counts. Say 'Rabbit, rabbit, rabbit'—three times—first thing after twelve o'clock, and you'll get a present as sure as I'm drinking this glass of bitter." "Rabbit, rabbit, rabbit," the Scotsman repeated the words in a sepulchral voice; "I never heard that before." "Well," the spokesman for the superstition told him, "try it. To-morrow's the first of August. When you're called in the morning, you mustn't even answer till you've said 'Rabbit, rabbit, rabbit.' If you remember to do that, you'll find that what I'm telling you is true." "Rabbit, rabbit, rabbit," the Scotsman once more repeated solemnly, and, having done so, raised his glass of whisky solemnly to his lips. "Supposin' you said 'Chicken, chicken, chicken?'" inquired the lean man. "It's no good," the other assured him: "there's nothing any good, only 'Rabbit, rabbit, rabbit.'" "Did you ever try this yourself?" a black-moustached man with drink-weary eyes inquired. "Often," said the other, "and always got a present." "Always got a present," the Scotsman echoed him, and took another drink of whisky. "What d'you mean by a present?" the lean man asked. "If a man stood you a whisky-and-soda, would that be a present?" "No," said the other after a moment's reflection, "I think the present has to be a real present. It might be a hundred pounds, or it might be a box of chocolates. Don't forget it. 'Rabbit, rabbit, rabbit.' Never been known to fail." "There are some curious superstitions," said the man with the black moustache. "Are you one of the people who object to seeing the new moon through glass?" "God!" said the other, "I wouldn't like to see the new moon through glass." "*I* believe," said the Jew, "that it's unlucky to fall downstairs on a Friday—or any other day"; and he sniggered at his wit. "Rabbit, rabbit, rabbit," said the man in the brown hat, yawning; "that's the best of them. You can't go wrong with it." "Rabbit, rabbit, rabbit," the Scotsman meditated, blinking his eyes, and the faint shadow of a smile stealing into his features. "You've got it," the other nodded approval; "rabbit, rabbit, rabbit." "Rabbit, rabbit, rabbit," the Scotsman smiled outright; "and you get a present? That's very good."

Observing

I cannot remember how the talk found its way to the subject of village life; but I remember the Jew telling a long story of how, when he was passing the night in a Sussex village, he made the villagers so drunk that, after closing time, they gathered outside the hotel and sang a bawdy version of *In Sussex by the Sea*. He sang the chorus over in a sort of whisper for our delectation, laughed heartily, and said that it struck him as being "damned funny." "Funny things you see in some villages," said the landlord, with a dreamy look. "A friend of mine—he's dead now, poor chap—got a stoppage of the bowels—bought a little pub in a village like the one you mention. It lay just off the main road, but those few yards made all the difference. All the motor cars and traffic passed the end of the road without knowing the pub even existed, and my friend was doing no business, absolutely. 'Look here, Bill,' I said to him, 'I'll tell you what to do. Go down to the cross-roads, and, whenever you see a motor car, put up your hand, and, when it stops, say, "Come along, gents, to the Pink Horse, and have a drink for nothing." They'll think you're balmy, of course, but some o' 'em will come, and anyhow people will get to know about you.' Poor Bill stood at the cross-roads for hours, but he could get only one man to come along to the pub, and *he* wasn't looking half scared." The landlord laughed at the memory. "Then," he went on, "I thought I'd better go out myself and see if I couldn't get a move on. Well, I made up my mind to offer a drink to every Tom, Dick and Harry I could see. If I saw a motor car I stopped it and said: 'Come along, gents; be sports. I'm having a little house-warming, and I want you to be my guests for the day.' The funniest thing was an old tramp who was carrying his dinner in a handkerchief. When I told him to go up to the Pink Horse and he could have as much drink as he wanted for nothing, he looked as if he wanted to escape. 'I'm not balmy,' I told him; 'it's true. Here'—and I pulled out a two-shilling piece from my pocket—'take that, if you don't believe me, and go and spend it in the Pink Horse if you can.' Oh! it was a rare day. We even got the village policeman in. He was a teetotaller, the beast. But he said he didn't mind a bottle of stone ginger. Well, I was drinking ginger beer myself, with a drop of gin in it. So what did I do but slip a drop of gin into his too. Well, it was a hot day, and he had another one, and another one, and another one. He liked it, the brute, like a cat likes milk. Oh! he was proper oiled before the night was through. I tell you, by the time we had to put the lights out we had that village painted as tight as a drum. Absolutely. Tight? They were singing *God save the King* backways." "I like about the policeman," said the Jew with the socks; "swine most of them are." "Well," said the landlord broad-mindedly, "there's policemen are swine, and there's policemen isn't. I once had a place in a little Australian village where the policeman was a brick. Do you know, he was there for twenty-five years, and there were only two convictions? And I was responsible for one of them. I saw a man slashing a horse about with a stick, tearing the poor beast in a most horrible manner, and I took him by the throat and ran him into the station myself. The old policeman didn't want me to charge him. He said there'd only be trouble. But I said, 'He's a cruel brute. I want to see him taught a lesson.' Well, next day he was had up, and the magistrate fined him five dollars. And do you know what happened? The old policeman I'm telling you about paid the fine out of his own pocket. 'You oughtn't to do it,' I told him; 'the man's a dirty devil.' 'I know he is,' said the policeman; 'it's not out of any sympathy with him I paid the fine. It was the principle of the thing. You see, there has only been one conviction in the village for twenty-five years, and that was a poor devil I felt sorry for, so I paid his fine to keep him from being sent to prison. And, now that I'm just going to retire, here comes the second conviction, and, thinking of the old time, I says to myself, "It's not worth breaking a rule just when you're going to retire. You paid the only other fine: you should pay this one." You see what I mean, sir; it's the principle of the thing.' I thought that funny, him feeling, just because he had once done a thing, he had to go on doing it." "Rabbit, rabbit, rabbit," the Scotsman was chuckling to himself, practising for the morning. The landlord took no notice of him. "Well, when he retired," he went on, "the new policeman was a holy terror. He was another brute of a teetotaller, and it came to this, you could hardly light your pipe without being arrested. He used to stand in the shadow under a balcony at night to watch what people were doing. One night, just before going to bed, I was leaning out of the window, and saw where he was standing in the darkness. I couldn't resist it. I got an egg and flung it hard as I could—click!—right at his eye, and smashed it all over his face. A minute later he was knocking rat-a-tat-tat at the door, and I went down to see what he wanted. 'Well?' I said to him. 'Somebody threw an egg at me,' he said, 'and I think it was from your house.' 'How dare you?' said I; 'do you accuse me of doing it? How dare you come knocking me up and me dressed for bed, merely because you happen to have a mean, suspicious mind! I only wish it *had* been me threw the egg. And hit you. Nothing would have pleased me better.' And I slammed the door in his face. Of course, he could do nothing. He had no evidence. Soon after that he had to leave the village. Things were made too hot for him, and he got his face cut about most horrible by a man wearing a stirrup like a knuckle-duster. Oh! he was a proper drop of poison!"...

It was now getting near midnight, and the Scotsman was obviously getting anxious to retire into the seclusion of his own room in order to qualify for his present when the clock struck. Everybody made a move bedwards. "Don't forget," the man in the brown hat gave us the parting injunction. "'Rabbit, rabbit, rabbit,' three times. Good-night, gentlemen." "Good-night." "Good-night." "Good-night." "Good-night."

DISCUSSION

1. Except for the two introductory sentences, Lynd refrains from comment and simply gives us the conversation he heard. Would his account have been funnier if he had put in some humorous remarks of his own? Why, or why not?
2. Lynd gives us very little description of the bar or the people who are talking. Why doesn't he write more about the scene?

Observing

3. Glance again at the first two sentences. How does the rest of the essay develop their meaning? In what sense is this converstaion "wonderful"?

Swift, Hunt, and Lynd are all amused by what they observe, and write about their subjects to entertain us. Not so Richard Hoggart, who brings into focus a scene that is vaguely familiar to all of us, but that perhaps we would as soon not look at more carefully.

Richard Hoggart

Old Men in Libraries

(1957)

The strength of this sense of home and neighbourhood may be seen at its most pathetic in those old men who fill the reading-rooms of the branch public libraries. They are often the solitaries, men whose families have grown up and left them, whose wives have died or are bedridden, and who are no longer at work. If they are lucky they may still live in their old house or lodge with a son or daughter; a few scrabble along on a pension in a common lodging-house or in one room of an apartment-house in a démodé district. Even those in their own area are especially lost during the working day when the streets are occupied only by infants and a few busy, if kindly, housewives. The odder ones haunt the railway-stations along with some of the mentally-deficient. Many come daily to the reading-room, where it is warm and there are seats. It all sadly recalls those hidden inlets which the smaller detritus of a river eventually reaches, held there in a yeasty scum—old sticks, bits of torn paper, a few withered leaves, a matchbox. But the reading-rooms themselves have a syringed and workhouse air (I am thinking of the old ones, many of which remain): the newspapers stretch bleakly round the walls, heavily clamped and with the sporting-pages carefully pasted over, so as to discourage punters; the magazines lie on dark-oak desks across which green-shaded lamps throw so narrow a beam that the whole of the room above elbow height is in permanent shadow by the late afternoon.

The shadow helps to soften the insistence of the many notices, heavy black on white, all prohibitive and most imperative, which alternate with the newspapers on the walls. In one I know there are eight major injunctions, varying in length from SILENCE, in letters nine inches high and four inches across, to NO PERSON IS ALLOWED TO BRING READING MATTER INTO THIS ROOM FOR PERUSAL BUT READERS MUST CONFINE THEMSELVES TO

démodé: no longer fashionable.
punters: gamblers.

Observing a Scene

THE PUBLICATIONS HEREIN DISPLAYED. They range in tone from the curtly peremptory to the diffusely interdictory. After a while the atmosphere is so depressing that you begin to think that NO AUDIBLE CONVERSATIONS ALLOWED is an instance of warm-heartedness in the midst of officialdom, a sensible allowance for the fact that so many of the regulars talk to themselves.

This is the special refuge of the misfits and left-overs, of the hollow-cheeked, watery-eyed, shabby and furtively sad. An eccentric absorbed in the rituals of his monomania sits between a pinched unmarried brother, kept by a married sister for the sake of his war-pension, and an aged widower from a cheap lodging or a house smelling permanently of old tea and the frying-pan. They come in off the streets, on to which they had gone after swilling under a cold-tap and twisting scarves round collarless necks; they come in after walking round a bit, watching other people doing things, belonging somewhere. If a bench in the paper-strewn square is too chilly, they come in after a while to the warmth they have been looking forward to. A few make for one of the items of sect-journalism and resume their endless cult-reading; some—shifty and nervous of detection, or with a bland and cheeky skill—plot how to win on the pools or mumble through a rough sandwich; some turn leaves aimlessly or stare blankly for ten minutes at one page; some just sit and look at nothing, picking their noses. They exist on the periphery of life, seeing each other daily but with no contact. Reduced to a handful of clothes, a few primary needs and a persistent lack, they have been disconnected from the only kind of life in which they ever had a part, and that was a part unconsciously accepted; they have no conscious arts for social intercourse.

There is usually one who comes into this resort of the unpossessed as though it were a Conservative Club and he the town's senior alderman. Threadbare but jaunty, he moves down the aisle to his favourite chair with nods and smiles which are none the less assured for being nowhere acknowledged. He has brazened out some terms with circumstance, and in his own eyes is a happy man. Most look inwards to a dream of life as a vista of warm fires, big and regular meals, a wife to listen to your talk, money for cigarettes and beer, a little 'standing'. No wonder the reading-room attendant inspires deference; some of them have so far surrendered self-respect as to retain no power either to resent or be cocky towards him.

DISCUSSION

1. How would you characterize Hoggart's way of seeing the old men in libraries—that is, do you find him objective in his attitude? Emotional? Does he have a purpose in observing that determines what sort of detail he observes? Does any particular feeling about the old men color his observation? Point out examples that support your answer.

2. What details might be observed by a person with a different point of view; for example, a communist, a "social Darwinist," or a welfare worker?

3. Hoggart writes in a restrained style, never seeming to demand an emotional response from the reader. Yet he does trigger such a response, at the very least one of sympathy for the old men. Try to pinpoint particular observations and ways of wording them that appeal to the emotions. Could the subject be treated more objectively? Would it be desirable to do so? Why, or why not?

The best observer seems to have all of his senses working together in a kind of total awareness, describing his scenes with such intensity and resonance that we almost experience them at first hand. In the final selection of Chapter 3, J. M. Synge recreates a series of scenes involving things, human activities, his own participation, and, not least important, the pervasive presence of the weather. Nothing unusual happens; it is a celebration of the ordinary with tragic overtones.

J. M. Synge

An Autumn Night in the Hills

(1903)

A few years ago a pointer dog of my acquaintance was wounded by accident in a wild glen on the western slope of County Wicklow. He was left at the cottage of an under-keeper, or bailiff—the last cottage on the edge of two ranges of mountains that stretch on the north and west to the plain of Kildare—and a few weeks later I made my way there to bring him down to his master.

It was an afternoon of September, and some heavy rain of the night before had made the road which led up to the cottage through the middle of the glen as smooth as a fine beach, while the clearness of the air gave the granite that ran up on either side of the way a peculiar tinge that was nearly luminous against the shadow of the hills. Every cottage that I passed had a group of rowan trees beside it covered with scarlet berries that gave brilliant points of colour of curious effect.

Just as I came to the cottage the road turned across a swollen river which I had to cross on a range of slippery stones. Then, when I had gone a few yards further, I heard a bark of welcome, and the dog ran down to meet me. The noise he made brought two women to the door of the cottage, one a finely made girl, with an exquisitely open and graceful manner, the other a very old woman. A sudden shower had come up without any warning over the rim of the valley, so I went into the cottage and sat down on a sort of bench in the chimney-corner, at the end of a long low room with open rafters.

'You've come on a bad day,' said the old woman, 'for you won't see any of the lads or men about the place.'

'I suppose they went out to cut their oats,' I said, 'this morning while the weather was fine.'

'They did not,' she answered, 'but they're after going down to Aughrim for the body of Mary Kinsella, that is to be brought this night from the station. There will be a wake then at the last cottage you're after passing, where you saw all them trees with the red berries on them.'

She stopped for a moment while the girl gave me a drink of milk.

'I'm afraid it's a lot of trouble I'm giving you,' I said as I took it, 'and you busy, with no men in the place.'

'No trouble at all in the world,' said the girl, 'and if it was itself, wouldn't any one be glad of it in the lonesome place we're in?'

The old woman began talking again:

'You saw no sign or trace on the road of the people coming with the body?'

'No sign,' I said, 'and who was she at all?'

'She was a fine young woman with two children,' she went on, 'and a year and a half ago she went wrong in her head, and they had to send her away. And then up there in the Richmond asylum maybe they thought the sooner they were shut of her the better, for she died two days ago this morning, and now they're bringing her up to have a wake, and they'll bury her beyond at the churches, far as it is, for it's there are all the people of the two families.'

While we talked I had been examining a wound in the dog's side near the end of his lung.

'He'll do rightly now,' said the girl who had come in again and was putting tea-things on the table. 'He'll do rightly now. You wouldn't know he'd been hurted at all only for a kind of a cough he'll give now and again. Did they ever tell you the way he was hit?' she added, going down on her knees in the chimney-corner with some dry twigs in her hand and making a little fire on the flag-stone a few inches from the turf.

I told her I had heard nothing but the fact of his wound.

'Well,' she said, 'a great darkness and storm came down that night and they all out on the hill. The rivers rose, and they were there groping along by the turf track not minding the dogs. Then an old rabbit got up and run before them, and a man put up his gun and shot across it. When he fired that dog run out from behind a rock, and one grain of the shot cut the scruff off his nose, and another went in there where you were looking, at the butt of his ribs. He dropped down bleeding and howling, and they thought he was killed. The night was falling and they had no way they could carry him, so they made a kind of a shelter for him with sticks and turf, and they left him while they would be going for a sack.'

She stopped for a moment to knead some dough and put down a dozen hot cakes—cut out with the mouth of a tumbler—in a frying pan on the little fire she had made with the twigs. While she was doing so the old woman took up the talk.

'Ah,' she said, 'there do be queer things them nights out on the mountains and in the lakes among them. I was reared beyond in the valley

Observing

where the mines used to be, in the valley of the Lough Nahanagan, and it's many a queer story I've heard of the spirit does be in that lake.'

'I have sometimes been there fishing till it was dark,' I said when she paused, 'and heard strange noises in the cliff.'

'There was an uncle of mine,' she continued, 'and he was there the same way as yourself, fishing with a big fly in the darkness of the night, and the spirit came down out of the clouds and rifted the waters asunder. He was afeared then and he run down to the houses trembling and shaking. There was another time,' she went on, 'a man came round to this county who was after swimming through the water of every lake in Ireland. He went up to swim in that lake, and a brother of my own went up along with him. The gentleman had heard tell of the spirit but not a bit would he believe in it. He went down on the bank, and he had a big black dog with him, and he took off his clothes.

'"For the love of God," said my brother, "put that dog in before you go in yourself, the way you'll see if he ever comes out of it." The gentleman said he would do that and they threw in a stick or a stone and the dog leapt in and swam out to it. Then he turned round again and he swam and he swam, and not a bit nearer did he come.

'"He's a long time swimming back," said the gentleman.

'"I'm thinking your honour'll have a grey beard before he comes back," said my brother, and before the word was out of his mouth the dog went down out of their sight, and the inside out of him came up on the top of the water.'

By this time the cakes were ready and the girl put them on a plate for me at the table, and poured out a cup of tea from the tea-pot, putting the milk and sugar herself into my cup as is the custom with the cottage people of Wicklow. Then she put the tea-pot down in the embers of the turf and sat down in the place I had left.

'Well,' she said, 'I was telling you the story of that night. When they got back here they sent up two lads for the dog, with a sack to carry him on if he was alive and a spade to bury him if he was dead. When they came to the turf where they left him they saw him near twenty yards down the path. The crathur thought they were after leaving him there to die, and he got that lonesome he dragged himself along like a Christian till he got too weak with the bleeding. James, the big lad, walked up again him first with the spade in his hand. When he seen the spade he let a kind of a groan out of him.

'That dog's as wise as a child, and he knew right well it was to bury him they brought the spade. Then Mike went up and laid down the sack on the ground, and the minute he seen it he jumped up and tumbled in on it himself. Then they carried him down, and the crathur getting his death with the cold and the great rain was falling. When they brought him in here you'd have thought he was dead. We put up a settle bed before the fire, and we put him into it. The heat roused him a bit, and he stretched out his legs and gave two groans out of him like an old man. Mike thought

crathur: creature.

he'd drink some milk so we heated a cup of it over the fire. When he put down his tongue into it he began to cough and bleed, then he turned himself over in the settle bed and looked up at me like an old man. I sat up with him that night and it raining and blowing. At four in the morning I gave him a sup more of the milk and he was able to drink it.

'The next day he was stronger, and we gave him a little new milk every now and again. We couldn't keep him near the fire. So we put him in the little room beyond by the door and an armful of hay in along with him. In the afternoon the boys were out on the mountain and the old woman was gone somewhere else, and I was chopping sticks in the lane. I heard a sort of a noise and there he was with his head out through the window looking out on me in the lane. I was afraid he was lonesome in there all by himself, so I put in one of our old dogs to keep him company. Then I stuffed an old hat into the window and I thought they'd be quiet together.

'But what did they do but begin to fight in there all in the dark as they were. I opened the door and out runs that lad before I could stop him. Not a bit would he go in again, so I had to leave him running about beside me. He's that loyal to me now you wouldn't believe it. When I go for the cow he comes along with me, and when I go to make up a bit of hay on the hill he'll come and make a sort of bed for himself under a haycock, and not a bit of him will look at Mike or the boys.'

'Ah,' said the old woman, as the girl got up to pour me out another cup from the tea-pot, 'it's herself will be lonesome when that dog is gone, he's never out of her sight, and you'd do right to send her down a little dog all for herself.'

'You would so,' said the girl, 'but maybe he wouldn't be loyal to me, and I wouldn't give a thraneen for a dog as wasn't loyal.'

'Would you believe it,' said the old woman again, 'when the gentleman wrote down about that dog Mike went out to where she was in the haggard, and says, "They're after sending me the prescription for that dog," says he, "to put on his tombstone." And she went down quite simple, and told the boys below in the bog, and it wasn't till they began making game of her that she seen the way she'd been humbugged.'

'That's the truth,' said the girl, I went down quite simple, and indeed it's a small wonder, that dog's as fit for a decent burial as many that gets it.'

Meanwhile the shower had turned to a dense torrent of mountain rain, and although the evening was hardly coming on, it was so dark that the girl lighted a lamp and hung it at the corner of the chimney. The kitchen was longer than most that I have met with and had a skeleton staircase at the far end that looked vague and shadowy in the dim light. The old woman wore one of the old-fashioned caps with a white frill round the face, and entered with great fitness into the general scheme of the kitchen.

thraneen: threepenny piece.
haggard: yard in which hay is stacked.
prescription: epitaph.
simple: sincere, in good faith.

Observing

I did not like leaving them to go into the raw night for a long walk on the mountains, and I sat down and talked to them for a long time, till the old woman thought I would be benighted.

'Go out now,' she said at last to the girl, 'go out now and see what water is coming over the fall above, for with this rain the water'll rise fast, and maybe he'll have to walk down to the bridge, a rough walk when the night is coming on.'

The girl came back in a moment.

'It's riz already,' she said. 'He'll want to go down to the bridge.' Then turning to me: 'If you'll come now I'll show you the way you have to go, and I'll wait below for the boys; it won't be long now till they come with the body of Mary Kinsella.'

We went out at once and she walked quickly before me through a maze of small fields and pieces of bog, where I would have soon lost the track if I had been alone.

The bridge, when we reached it, was a narrow wooden structure fastened up on iron bars which pierced large boulders in the bed of the river. An immense grey flood was struggling among the stones, looking dangerous and desolate in the half-light of the evening, while the wind was so great that the bridge wailed and quivered and whistled under our feet. A few paces further on we came to a cottage where the girl wished me a good journey and went in to wait for her brothers.

The daylight still lingered but the heavy rain and a thick white cloud that had come down made everything unreal and dismal to an extraordinary degree. I went up a road where on one side I could see the trunks of beech trees reaching up wet and motionless—with odd sighs and movements when a gust caught the valley—into a greyness overhead, where nothing could be distinguished. Between them there were masses of shadow, and masses of half-luminous fog with black branches across them. On the other side of the road flocks of sheep I could not see coughed and choked with sad guttural noises in the shelter of the hedge, or rushed away through a gap when they felt the dog was near them. Above everything my ears were haunted by the dead heavy swish of the rain. When I came near the first village I heard a loud noise and commotion. Many cars and gigs were collected at the door of the public-house, and the bar was filled with men who were drinking and making a noise. Everything was dark and confused yet on one car I was able to make out the shadow of a coffin, strapped in the rain, with the body of Mary Kinsella.

DISCUSSION

1. Although this episode is presented as a personal experience, it has some of the qualities of a short story. One of these is "theme," or general idea, developed through contrast. What contrast between two states of being is

benighted: caught by nightfall.
fall: brook.
gig: two-wheeled carriage.

Observing a Scene

presented in four different contexts: in the experience of the narrator, in the experience of the dog, in the life of Mary Kinsella, and in what happens to Mary Kinsella's coffin and the men who are bringing it home? What does the writer appear to be saying with these contrasts?
2. A second, closely related contrast is between what happens to the dog and what happens to Mary Kinsella. How is each treated and with what result?
3. Synge also uses contrast in his descriptive passages in a way that reinforces the central contrast. What are some visual contrasts? Some contrasts in physical sensation? In emotional feeling?
4. The episode is given resonance by a quality we call "atmosphere." Atmosphere is not always easy to pin down, but it consists mostly of keeping the reader aware of a certain quality in the surroundings, a quality that is suited to the meaning of the events and that intensifies it. In this case it is the constant presence of the dark, the cold, the rain, the mist, and the running water—the weather of the story. How does this dismal background point up the central contrast?

WRITING SUGGESTIONS

1. Using Swift's "A City Shower" as your model, describe in entertaining detail what happens in a city street when there is a sudden rain, dust storm, cold wind, or other source of discomfort.
2. Ride a bus, streetcar, or subway train and record, as Leigh Hunt does, the sorts of people who get on and off, what they do, how they react to each other, and so on. If your community has no public transportation, stand at a table in the post office pretending to address envelopes while you take notes on people coming and going.
3. Describe a scene of intense or violent action, as Theocritus does: an episode in a boxing, wrestling, or fencing match, a basketball game, or something of the sort. Don't try to describe the whole match or game, but choose a brief, climactic action that can be made clear in a few short paragraphs. You may wish to make use of an introductory paragraph to outline the situation that leads up to your scene, so that it will be clear to the reader what is happening. Work at making the action perfectly clear, but with an economical use of words so that your action is not slowed by too much detailed explanation.
4. Stand around for half an hour or so in a busy outdoor place such as a shopping center parking lot, a downtown street, a rummage sale, or the door of a church on Sunday morning when people are coming out. Carry a notebook (not too conspicuously—you don't want people to think the F.B.I. is after them) and observe people's adaptations and reactions to the weather—how they dress with regard to it, what they put on or take off, how they look at the sky, and so on. It doesn't matter what kind of weather it is—rain, snow, wind, excessive heat or cold, or a perfect sunny day—nearly everyone's behavior will be affected by the weather. Write up a description of several paragraphs exclusively about the weather aspects of the scene. You will find that this limitation will automatically give unity to your paper.

Observing

5. Spend an hour in an office where several people are working, or in a snack bar, cafeteria or restaurant, or a lounge or game room, anywhere where several people, not too many, are talking. Listen intently to what these people are saying, no matter how silly or boring their conversation may seem, and take notes. Be sure to choose a place where no one knows you, so you won't be interrupted by curious friends. Write up a scene like Lynd's "Conversation," just recording what people talk about.

6. Make a few careful observations of the old men who sit on benches every day in your city park or around your courthouse. If you can, find out where some of them live and what they do all day: where and what they eat, what they read, and so on. Then write an account of the kind of life they lead.

7. Spend some time, at least an hour, closely observing the behavior of some common creatures such as dogs, cats, sparrows, or ants. Then write an account of their activities so that a comparison with the activities of people is implied. Look for acts of greed or generosity, intelligence or stupidity, aggressiveness or peacefulness, adaptability to the environment or lack of it, and so on. Don't make your animals human, but compare them with human beings.

8. What are people's hands doing? Sit in a bus station, a doctor's or dentist's waiting room, or any other place where people have nothing much to do, and watch their hands as though the hands were animals with a life of their own. Describe only the hands and their activities, but in such a way as to tell us a great deal about their owners.

9. Though this project is harder than the previous ones, it might prove an interesting challenge, for the familiar is more difficult to observe well than the strange. Try to describe a meal in your own home, your dining hall, or a restaurant where you go often, with the same objectivity and detail Lawrence employs in describing the Arab feast. To approach the scene more easily, it might be well to imagine yourself a foreigner to whom the customers are unfamiliar. After all, even the use of forks and spoons looks pretty odd when you step back and observe it with fresh eyes.

10. If you feel up to a challenge, try a piece that stresses contrast, like Synge's "An Autumn Night in the Hills." Intensify your contrast, as he does, by providing an intensely atmospheric background—rain and fog, sultry heat and its effects, dry wind, a stormy night, or whatever you wish. Try to work your contrasting elements into one scene or series of scenes. For example, you might describe hiking in the mountains in a rain-storm, feeling physical discomfort but also a great sense of freedom; then you might picture yourself arriving at a cabin where your friends are staying, where you are warm and comfortable but where you have to conform to their wishes and are not free. Or you could describe a funeral, contrasting the reverence and respect paid to the dead with the lack of respect toward an old person in the family who is still living. The number of subjects for contrast is infinite; search your own experience.

A NOTE ABOUT WRITING IN GENERAL

Several simple principles of good writing have been implied or casually mentioned in Part I. Perhaps it is time to sum them up in one place.

Observing a Scene

1. *Show, don't tell.* While no principle should be carried to extremes, nearly all writers tell too much and show too little. All writing is remembered through the images it presents. Glance back at the titles of the selections you have read in this book. You will find that if you remember anything in connection with a title, it will come to you first of all in the form of an image; then the ideas will follow. Whenever possible, let your reader see the things you observe directly rather than giving him only your thoughts about them. Lead your reader to agree with you by giving him the data that convinced you.
2. *Use all of your senses.* In a media culture we all lean too heavily on sight and sound. Cultivate the other senses and use them consciously in your writing.
3. *Limit your subject.* Once more, glance over the titles of the selections you have read, recalling the subjects. You will find that the writer begins with, and usually limits himself to, a small area of observation. It is much more interesting to explore a small area thoroughly than to give a large area the "once over lightly" treatment. A bad writer is like a typical tourist: he sees enough of everything to say he's been there, but can tell us nothing new about anything.
4. *Present things in a clear order.* Order comes pretty naturally to most of us, but it does no harm to be conscious of it. Order grows out of the subject. For example, most objects should be described in the same way that we first become aware of them: size, shape, and color first, smallest details last. Some other types of order that belong to various subjects are top to bottom, side to side, center to edge, units of function (engine and drive train of a car as a unit, electrical system as another unit, and so on), group by group (a party), and so on. An event requires an order in time, ordinarily from beginning to end, sometimes cause to effect or vice versa. There are many possible ways of organizing a subject. The point is to look for the order that is natural to the subject and stick to it. If you find yourself saying, "Oh, I forgot to tell you—" then rewrite.
5. *Be complete.* Especially with familiar subjects, we usually take too much for granted and leave things out. Always reread what you have written as though you were an intelligent but ignorant twelve-year-old and see if everything is clear to you.
6. *Be specific.* Never say, "They had a lot of animals around" when you could say, "They had a dozen chickens, two goats, three cats, and five dogs." Vague writing is dull; specific writing holds the reader's attention as long as there is a point to it. If a fact doesn't contribute to your point, leave it out altogether; if it does, be specific.
7. *Stick to your subject.* Make up your mind what you want to say and then don't let irrelevant material creep in, no matter how fascinating it may be. If your subject is the architecture of an old house, don't distract the reader by telling him how your grandmother mysteriously fell down the stairs ten years ago.
8. *Write simply.* Your job is to give the reader information and imagery, not fancy words. Wordiness puts barriers in his way. Never use a three-syllable word where a two-syllable one will do the same job. On the other hand, don't use the two-syllable word if it *doesn't* do the same job; accuracy of

meaning is your standard. Use words, don't waste them. It is the meaning that is important, not the words.

9. *Use contrast.* In a coal bin, a white cat is easier to see than a black one. Most of the selections you have read employ contrast to heighten the effect of the subject. For example, Stifter's thunderstorm appears all the more violent contrasted with the calm of the priest; Hoggart's working-class mother's strong character is shown in contrast with her slovenly appearance; Hawthorne's old apple dealer is presented in a bustling railway station to bring out his unnatural quietness; Leigh Hunt shows us the friction among diverse characters in his omnibus. Like a painter, use the device of putting your subject next to something that brings out its characteristics.

10. *Observe.* Sharpen your awareness of the things and people around you. A dogfight well observed is more interesting than a war poorly observed.

Not all of the writers we have sampled follow all of these rules consistently, of course. Hawthorne often uses long words where shorter ones would do. Mark Twain sometimes uses words badly, but his humorous keenness of observation compensates for this fault. Evelyn leaves us unhappy because he does not tell nearly enough. No writer is perfect, but many who are weak in one area are strong in another. If you are serious about writing well, you should try to identify your own weak areas and strengthen them. It might be a good exercise to go back over some of the previous readings and look at them even more critically than you have, to see how each one ought to be better.

Plate 5
Jan Steen (1626–79): *The Feast of St. Nicholas*

Like the writer, the painter faces the problem, when he depicts a complex scene, of keeping everything in clear order so that we know what is going on. In addition he must also maintain a compositional balance and an appearance of naturalness. Jan Steen was a master of grouping: note how well-spaced and self-contained his scene is, while remaining natural. The scene is Christmas Eve, when the children have just been given their presents.

1. What is happening? What contrast appears? Why is the large boy crying? Can you guess the significance of the stick in the small boy's hand?
2. Who are the father and mother looking at? What is their attitude? In each case, what means has the artist used to make this attitude clear?
3. The artist has assumed a playful attitude toward his scene, very much like Leigh Hunt's in "The Inside of an Omnibus" (p. 62). But he also communicates a critical opinion toward what is going on. What is the clue to this opinion? Is it confirmed by any other details?
4. Of course facial expressions are used to tell the story and establish attitudes; but another medium of human expression is employed more heavily. What is it? What are several examples of its use, and what does it convey in each case?

PLATE 5   Jan Steen (1626–79), **The Feast of St. Nicholas.** *Rijksmuseum, Amsterdam.*

Plate 6
George Wesley Bellows (1882–1925): *Stag at Sharkey's*

Another kind of human relationship, similar to that in Theocritus' "A Fight" (p. 52), is shown here. But while Theocritus, using words, can keep us interested by following the progress of the fight to its victorious end, the painter is confined to showing us only one moment of the action. Since his figures cannot move and he cannot keep us in suspense, he compensates by communicating the violence and the interplay of violent emotion in the scene as a whole; while the painting shows us only a moment, the painter makes that moment a representative one, packing into it a number of characteristic attitudes and actions.

1. While Jan Steen's painting (Plate 5) is detailed and meticulous, Bellows' is painted with broad, almost careless strokes and little detail. Would either painting be improved by being redone in the technique of the other? Why, or why not?
2. How does Bellows communicate the feeling of violent action in his boxers? Are they realistically represented, as in a photograph? If not, how and where do the figures differ from those in a photograph?
3. What feeling does Bellows give you about the people in the crowd watching the fight? In terms of concrete detail, what things contribute to that feeling?
4. The painting is much less clear than *The Feast of St. Nicholas*, as though it were out of focus. Does this quality make it confusing? Is it unclear what is going on in any part of the picture?
5. If you were to write an account of this scene (the real scene, not the picture) in which you wanted to give the same impression of nightmarish violence that Bellows does, would you employ the style that Theocritus uses? If not, what sort of style would fit your purpose? Would you find yourself using short sentences or long ones? Why? Would you follow the fight step by step in an orderly way as Theocritus does, or would you jump from one impression to another? Again, why?

PLATE 6 George Wesley Bellows (1882–1925), **Stag at Sharkey's.** Cleveland, The Cleveland Museum of Art, Hinman B. Hurlbut Collection.

II
Observing & Generalizing

In Part I you studied techniques of firsthand observation and of communicating such observation. You were asked to do little generalizing, but rather to concentrate on the quality of the observation itself. Now it is time to move into the area of limited and careful generalization based on this kind of observation.

To generalize is to observe a number of specific examples and to discover something they all have in common; it is the same process that in science is called inductive thinking. A specific, or concrete, statement is one about a unique event in space and time: "Last Tuesday morning our dog Rex tore a hole in the fence when a bitch in heat walked by." A general statement is one that takes a common factor out of a number of such unique events: "Rex always tries to get at bitches in heat."

There are, however, many levels of generalization. "Rex always tries to get at bitches in heat" is a low level generalization; it applies to one characteristic of one individual and is easy to prove or disprove by simple observation. Going up the ladder toward higher generalizations we might find "Male dogs are attracted to females in heat," "Sex is a strong drive in mammals," and "The reproductive urge is common to all living things." Note that each higher generalization says less about more, and requires more examples to support it. Rex's tendency to move closer to females takes only a few examples to

Observing and Generalizing

prove and says a good deal about Rex; "The reproductive urge is common to all living things," on the other hand, requires many thousands of examples to prove and doesn't say very much about Rex, since his way of going about it is quite different from a maple tree's. It is possible for generalization to rise to a level where it becomes "nonsense" or "sense-less": that is, to the stage where it cannot be supported by sense data at all.

Generalizing is like building a pyramid: the higher you go, the broader the base must be. To build support under a high generalization requires whole books, not essays. If you wish to produce a good short piece, begin with a modest generalization. This is called limiting your subject. Always be sure that your generalization is just the size you can support convincingly in your essay, neither too broad nor too narrow. Be sure also that it is stated in a qualified way, not in an absolute way. If you begin, "Cats and dogs are always enemies," you will invite disbelief; but if you say, "Cats and dogs are often enemies," you are on safe ground. A qualification of this kind frequently takes the form of a condition, such as "In certain circumstances," "Among certain kinds of people," or "At certain times." Be sure that your generalization is stated in the exact form you intend to support.

There is also a distinction between generalizations made in a scientific spirit and those made casually, perhaps just for entertainment. We do not demand the same kind of proof from a casual essayist, writing humorously, that we would demand from someone proposing an original scientific theory. Often the casual writer can call on the reader's own experience as supporting evidence, giving only a few examples and leaving the reader to confirm them with others.

Whether you call on your reader's observations or present your own, it is important to be sure your generalization has adequate support, like the pyramid. Not only are unsupported generalizations unconvincing, they are boring as well. Specifics, sensory data, are what make writing worth reading; readers want images their minds can grasp. In general, try to limit yourself to one generalization per essay. Good writing is concrete.

In Part II we shall continue, then, to focus on the observations of the writer, but we shall also see how he can generalize from these observations. We shall also find that his intention to generalize changes the form of his writing, rendering it less random and more purposeful, and we shall see that purpose colors his observation.

4

Beginning with Direct Observation: Informal Generalizing

The most valuable insights, such as those of Aristotle, Darwin, and Einstein, grew out of the ability to see things simply as they are, free of the misconceptions of the past. Here, to begin with, are four brief samples of fresh seeing and thinking: Gilbert White observes that the social instinct among animals can be strong enough to overcome even great differences of species and size, opposing a common opinion to the contrary; Loren Eiseley observes the actions of a few birds and comes to a highly original conclusion about their concepts of life and death; and Samuel Butler observes two events, one, illustrating the associational nature of human memory, and the other, illustrating the uncertainty principle that runs through all of nature.

Gilbert White

The Social Instinct among Animals

(1775)

There is a wonderful spirit of sociality in the brute creation, independent of sexual attachment: the congregating of gregarious birds in the winter is a remarkable instance.

Many horses, though quiet with company, will not stay one minute in a field by themselves; the strongest fences cannot restrain them. My neighbor's horse will not only not stay by himself abroad, but he will not bear to be left alone in a strange stable without discovering the utmost impatience, and endeavoring to break the rack and manger with his fore feet. He has been known to leap out at a stable window, through which dung was thrown, after company; and yet in other respects is remarkably quiet. Oxen and cows will not fatten by themselves; but will neglect the finest pasture that is not recommended by society. It would be needless to instance sheep, which constantly flock together.

But this propensity seems not to be confined to animals of the same species; for we know a doe, still alive, that was brought up from a little fawn with a dairy of cows; with them it goes afield, and with them it returns to the yard. The dogs of the house take no notice of this deer, being used to her; but, if strange dogs come by, a chase ensues; while the master smiles to see his favorite securely leading her pursuers over hedge, or gate, or stile, till she returns to the cows, who, with fierce lowings and menacing horns, drive the assailants quite out of the pasture.

Even great disparity of kind and size does not always prevent social advances and mutual fellowship. For a very intelligent and observant person has assured me that, in the former part of his life, keeping but one horse, he happened also on a time to have but one solitary hen. These two incongruous animals spent much of their time together in a lonely orchard, where they saw no creature but each other. By degrees an apparent regard began to take place between these two sequestered individuals. The fowl would approach the quadruped with notes of complacency, rubbing herself gently against his legs; while the horse would look down with satisfaction, and move with the greatest caution and circumspection, lest he should trample on his diminutive companion. Thus, by mutual good offices, each seemed to console the vacant hours of the other, so that Milton, when he puts the following sentiment in the mouth of Adam, seems to be somewhat mistaken:

> Much less can bird with beast,
> Or fish with fowl,
> So well converse; nor with the ox the ape.

Loren Eiseley

The Judgment of the Birds

(1956)

When I awoke, dimly aware of some commotion and outcry in the clearing, the light was slanting down through the pines in such a way that the glade was lit like some vast cathedral. I could see the dust motes of wood pollen in the long shaft of light, and there on the extended branch sat an enormous raven with a red and squirming nestling in its beak.

The sound that awoke me was the outraged cries of the nestling's parents, who flew helplessly in circles about the clearing. The sleek black monster was indifferent to them. He gulped, whetted his beak on the dead branch a moment and sat still. Up to that point the little tragedy had followed the usual pattern. But suddenly, out of all that area of woodland, a soft sound of complaint began to rise. Into the glade fluttered small birds of half a dozen varieties drawn by the anguished cries of the tiny parents.

No one dared to attack the raven. But they cried there in some instinctive common misery, the bereaved and the unbereaved. The glade filled with their soft rustling and their cries. They fluttered as though to point their wings at the murderer. There was a dim intangible ethic he had violated, that they knew. He was a bird of death.

And he, the murderer, the black bird at the heart of life, sat on there, glistening in the common light, formidable, unperturbed, untouchable.

The sighing died. It was then I saw the judgment. It was the judgment of life against death. I will never see it again so forcefully presented. I will never hear it again in notes so tragically prolonged. For in the midst of protest, they forgot the violence. There, in that clearing, the crystal note of a song sparrow lifted hesitantly in the hush. And, finally, after painful fluttering, another took the song, and then another, the song passing from one bird to another, doubtfully at first, as though some evil thing was being slowly forgotten. Till suddenly they took heart and sang from many throats joyously together as birds are known to sing. They sang because life is sweet and sunlight beautiful. They sang under the brooding shadow of the raven. In simple truth they had forgotten the raven, for they were the singers of life, and not of death.

DISCUSSION

1. The tendency to attribute human feelings and motives to animals seems to be universal. However, when Walt Disney, for example, invents cartoon animals with human personalities for our amusement, we do not confuse them with real animals; but when Disney, in the commentary that accompanies his documentaries about real animals, tries to make them appear human, he is projecting a false world. Do you find any of this sort of phoniness in either White or Eiseley? If so, where?
2. Do you find in either writer any emotionally charged words that are exaggerated or that are not justified by observation?
3. Are any conclusions stated or implied by either writer that do not seem to be adequately supported by the evidence he presents?
4. Gilbert White uses his observations to challenge a popular assumption that animals of different species don't get along. Can you think of observations you have made yourself that contradict common assumptions?

Samuel Butler

The Finger-Nail and the Note

(1882)

Henry Hoare [a college friend], when a young man of about five-and-twenty, one day tore the quick of his finger-nail—I mean he separated the fleshy part of the finger from the nail—and this reminded him that many years previously, while quite a child, he had done the same thing. Thereon he fell to thinking of that time which was impressed upon his memory partly because there was a great disturbance in the house about a missing five-pound note and partly because it was while he had the scarlet fever.

Following the train of thought aroused by his torn finger, he asked himself how he had torn it, and after a while it came back to him that he had been lying ill in bed as a child of seven at the house of an aunt who lived in Hertfordshire. His arms often hung out of the bed and, as his hands wandered over the wooden frame, he felt that there was a place where a nut had come out so that he could put his fingers in. One day, in trying to stuff a piece of paper into this hole, he stuffed it in so far and so tightly that he tore the quick of his nail. The whole thing came back vividly and, though he had not thought of it for nearly twenty years, he could see the room in his aunt's house and remembered how his aunt used to sit by his bedside writing at a little table from which he had got the piece of paper which he had stuffed into the hole.

So far so good. But then there flashed upon him an idea that was not so pleasant. I mean it came upon him with irresistible force that the piece of paper he had stuffed into the hole in the bedstead was the missing five-pound note about which there had been so much disturbance. At that time he was so young that a five-pound note was to him only a piece of paper; when he heard that the money was missing, he had thought it was five sovereigns; or perhaps he was too ill to think anything, or to be questioned; I forget what I was told about this—at any rate he had no idea of the value of the piece of paper he was stuffing into the hole. But now the matter had recurred to him at all he felt so sure that it was the note that he immediately went down to Hertfordshire, where his aunt was still living, and asked, to the surprise of every one, to be allowed to wash his hands in the room he had occupied as a child. He was told that there were friends staying in the house who had the room at present, but, on his saying he had a reason and particularly begging to be allowed to remain alone a little while in this room, he was taken upstairs and left there.

He went to the bed, lifted up the chintz which then covered the frame, and found his old friend the hole. A nut had been supplied and he could no longer get his figner into it. He rang the bell and when the servant came asked for a bed-key. All this time he was rapidly acquiring the reputation of being a lunatic throughout the whole house, but the key was brought, and by the help of it he got the nut off. When he had done so, there, sure enough, by dint of picking with his pocket-knife, he found the missing five-pound note.

See how the return of a given present brings back the presents that have been associated with it.

Samuel Butler

Beer and My Cat

(1887)

Spilt beer or water seems sometimes almost human in its uncertainty whether or no it is worth while to get ever such a little nearer to the earth's centre by such and such a slight trickle forward.

I saw my cat undecided in his mind whether he should get up on the table and steal the remains of my dinner or not. The chair was some eighteen inches away with its back towards the table, so it was a little troublesome for him to get his feet first on the bar and then on the table. He was not at all hungry but he tried, saw it would not be quite easy and gave it up; then he thought better of it and tried again, and saw again that it was not all perfectly plain sailing; and so backwards and forwards with the first-he-would-and-then-he-wouldn'tism of a mind so nearly in equilibrium that a hair's weight would turn the scale one way or the other.

I thought how closely it resembled the action of beer trickling on a slightly sloping table.

DISCUSSION

1. Samuel Butler wrote many books on scientific subjects, some of them offering amendments to Darwin's ideas about evolution. Our two observations are from entries in his journal and illustrate the casual generalizations of a man who thinks about everything that comes his way. What is the generalization he supports in "The Finger-Nail and the Note"? Does he support it with adequate evidence? If not, do you find it acceptable anyway? Why, or why not?

2. In "Beer and My Cat," Butler points out only that the action of the beer and the cat are similar, but a far broader generalization is implied. What is that generalization? Can it be confirmed by examples from your own experience? Does it have any reinforcement in scientific evidence?

3. Do you find it absurd to compare the actions of inanimate matter with the actions of an animal? Why, or why not?

4. Most people are incapable of making the kinds of observations Butler made; the art of observing and generalizing requires the cultivation of a special state of mind. Can you try to define what that state of mind might

be? How do you think it might be cultivated? How would you go about improving your own capacity to see meaning in ordinary things?

In two of the previous four selections, the writers give their evidence first and then generalize, using the order in which we actually do our inductive thinking. While we do our thinking in this order, we need not necessarily present the results in the same order. Gilbert White states his generalization in his first sentence and then develops it along with his evidence; Samuel Butler in "Beer and My Cat" never states his in so many words, though he leaves little doubt as to what it is. Many writers give the generalization first and then the evidence; others casually offer it wherever it seems to fit in; and still others let their readers infer the generalization themselves. Generalization, then, can appear at the beginning, in the middle, at the end, or not at all. Our next writer gives us hers first and then the supporting observations.

Elizabeth Cleghorn Gaskell

Small Economies

(1851)

I have often noticed that almost everyone has his own individual small economies—careful habits of saving fractions of pennies in some one peculiar direction—any disturbance of which annoys him more than spending shillings or pounds on some real extravagance. An old gentleman of my acquaintance, who took the intelligence of the failure of a joint-stock bank, in which some of his money was invested, with stoical mildness, worried his family all through a long summer's day because one of them had torn (instead of cutting) out the written leaves of his now useless bank-book; of course, the corresponding pages at the other end came out as well, and this little unnecessary waste of paper (his private economy) chafed him more than all the loss of his money. Envelopes fretted his soul terribly when they first came in; the only way in which he could reconcile himself to such waste of his cherished article was by patiently turning inside out all that were sent to him, and so making them serve again. Even now, though tamed by age, I see him casting wistful glances at his daughters when they send a whole inside of a half-sheet of note-paper, with three lines of acceptance to an invitation, written on only one of the sides. I am not above owning that I have this human weakness myself. String is my foible. My pockets get full of little hanks of it, picked up and twisted together, ready for uses that never come. I am seriously annoyed if any one cuts the string of a parcel instead of patiently and faithfully undoing it fold by fold. How people can bring themselves to use india-rubber rings, which are a sort of deification of string, as lightly as they do, I cannot imagine. To me an india-rubber ring is a precious treasure. I have one which is not new—one that I picked up off the floor nearly six years ago. I have really tried to use it, but my heart failed me, and I could not commit the extravagance.

Small pieces of butter grieve others. They cannot attend to the conversation because of the annoyance occasioned by the habit which some people have of invariably taking more butter than they want. Have you not seen the anxious look (almost mesmeric) which such persons fix on the article? They would feel it a relief if they might bury it out of their sight by popping it into their own mouths and swallowing it down; and they are really made happy if the person on whose plate it lies unused suddenly breaks off a piece of toast (which he does not want at all) and eats up his butter. They think that this is not waste.

Now, Miss Matty Jenkyns was chary of candles. We had many devices to use as few as possible. In the winter afternoons she would sit knitting for two or three hours—she could do this in the dark, or by firelight—and when I asked her if I might not ring for candles to finish stitching my wristbands, she told me to "keep blind man's holiday." They were usually brought in with tea; but we burnt only one at a time. As we lived in constant preparation for a friend who might come in any evening (but who never did), it required some contrivance to keep our two candles of the same length, ready to be lighted, and to look as if we burnt two always. The candles took it in turns; and, whatever we might be talking about or doing, Miss Matty's eyes were habitually fixed upon the candle, ready to jump up and extinguish it and to light the other before they had become too uneven in length to be restored to equality in the course of the evening.

One night I remember this candle economy particularly annoyed me. I had been very much tired of my compulsory "blind man's holiday," especially as Miss Matty had fallen asleep, and I did not like to stir the fire and run the risk of awakening her; so I could not even sit on the rug and scorch myself with sewing by firelight according to my usual custom. I fancied Miss Matty must be dreaming of her early life; for she spoke one or two words in her uneasy sleep bearing reference to persons who were dead long before. When Martha brought in the lighted candle and tea, Miss Matty started into wakefulness with a strange, bewildered look around as if we were not the people she expected to see about her. There was a little sad expression that shadowed her face as she recognized me, but immediately afterwards she tried to give me her usual smile. All through tea-time her talk ran upon the days of her childhood and youth. Perhaps this reminded her of the desirableness of looking over all the old family letters and destroying such as ought not to be allowed to fall into the hands of strangers; for she had often spoken of the necessity of this task, but had always shrunk from it with a timid dread of something painful. Tonight, however, she rose up after tea and

india-rubber rings: rubber bands.

went for them—in the dark; for she piqued herself on the precise neatness of all her chamber arrangements, and used to look uneasily at me when I lighted a bed-candle to go to another room for anything. When she returned there was a faint, pleasant smell of Tonquin beans in the room. I have always noticed this scent about any of the things which had belonged to her mother; and many of the letters were addressed to her—yellow bundles of love-letters, sixty or seventy years old.

Miss Matty undid the packet with a sigh; but she stifled it directly, as if it were hardly right to regret the flight of time, or of life either. We agreed to look them over separately, each taking a different letter out of the same bundle and describing its contents to the other before destroying it. I never knew what sad work the reading of old letters was before that evening, though I could hardly tell why. The letters were as happy as letters could be—at least those early letters were. There was in them a vivid and intense sense of the present time, which seemed strong and full, as if it could never pass away, and as if the warm, living hearts that so expressed themselves could never die, and be as nothing to the sunny earth. I should have felt less melancholy, I believe, if the letters had been more so. I saw the tears stealing down the well-worn furrows of Miss Matty's cheeks, and her spectacles often wanted wiping. I trusted at last that she would light the other candle, for my own eyes were rather dim, and I wanted more light to see the pale, faded ink; but no, even through her tears, she saw and remembered her little economical ways.

DISCUSSION

1. This selection, lifted out of its context in a novel, nevertheless follows a three-stage organizational pattern. What is this pattern, and what is accomplished in each of its three steps?

2. Using the same simple pattern, think of a similar observation that you have made yourself about the ways of ordinary people and, either by jotting down a few notes or by speaking informally in class, develop your observation briefly.

In the next selection, an essay, Oliver Goldsmith also gives us his generalization first, but elaborates on it longer before getting to his concrete example.

Oliver Goldsmith

On the Use of Language

(1759)

It is usually said by grammarians, that the use of language is to express our wants and desires; but men who know the world hold, and I think with some show of reason, that he who best knows how to keep his necessities private, is the most likely person to have them redressed; and that the true use of speech is not so much to express our wants as to conceal them.

When we reflect on the manner in which mankind generally confer their favors, there appears something so attractive in riches, that the large heap generally collects from the smaller: and the poor find as much pleasure in increasing the enormous mass of the rich, as the miser, who owns it, sees happiness in its increase. Nor is there in this anything repugnant to the laws of morality. Seneca himself allows, that, in conferring benefits, the present should always be suited to the dignity of the receiver. Thus the rich receive large presents, and are thanked for receiving them. Men of middling stations are obliged to be content with presents something less; while the beggar, who may be truly said to want indeed, is well paid if a farthing rewards his warmest solicitations.

Every man who has seen the world, and has had his ups and downs in life, as the expression is, must have frequently experienced the truth of this doctrine; and must know, that to have much, or to seem to have it, is the only way to have more. Ovid finely compares a man of broken fortune to a falling column; the lower it sinks, the greater weight it is obliged to sustain. Thus when a man's circumstances are such that he has no occasion to borrow, he finds numbers willing to lend him; but, should his wants be such that he sues a trifle, it is two to one whether he may be trusted with the smallest sum. A certain young fellow whom I knew, whenever he had occasion to ask his friend for a guinea, used to prelude his request as if he wanted two hundred; and talked so familiarly of large sums, that none could ever think he wanted a small one. The same gentleman, whenever he wanted credit for a suit of clothes, always made the proposal in a laced coat; for he found by experience, that if he appeared shabby on these occasions, his tailor had taken an oath against trusting; or what was every whit as bad, his foreman was [CUT-OFF] out of the way, and should not be at home for some time.

There can be no inducement to reveal our wants, except to find pity, and by this means relief; but before a poor-man opens his mind in such circumstances, he should first consider whether he is contented to lose the esteem of the person he solicits, and whether he is willing to give up friendship to excite compassion. Pity and friendship are passions incompatible with each other; and it is impossible that both can reside in any breast, for the smallest space, without impairing each other. Friendship is made up of esteem and pleasure; pity is composed of sorrow and contempt; the mind may, for some time, fluctuate between them, but it can never entertain both at once.

In fact, pity, though it may often relieve, is but at best a short-lived passion, and seldom affords distress more than transitory assistance: with some it scarce lasts from the first impulse till the hand can be put

Seneca: Roman statesman and philosopher.
Ovid: Roman poet.
guinea: twenty-one shillings.

Observing and Generalizing

into the pocket: with others it may continue for twice that space; and on some of extraordinary sensibility, I have seen it operate for half an hour together; but still, last as it may, it generally produces but beggarly effects; and where, from this motive, we give five farthings, from others we give pounds: whatever be our feelings from the first impulse of distress, when the same distress solicits a second time, we then feel with diminished sensibility; and, like the repetition of the echo, every stroke becomes weaker; till, at last, our sensations lose all mixture of sorrow, and degenerate into downright contempt.

These speculations bring to my mind the fate of a very good-natured fellow, who is now no more. He was bred in a countinghouse, and his father dying just as he was out of his time, left him an handsome fortune and many friends to advise with. The restraint in which my friend had been brought up, had thrown a gloom upon his temper, which some regarded as prudence; and, from such considerations, he had every day repeated offers of friendship. Such as had money were ready to offer him their assistance that way; and they who had daughters, frequently, in the warmth of affection, advised him to marry. My friend, however, was in good circumstances; he wanted neither money, friends, nor a wife; and therefore modestly declined their proposals.

Some errors, however, in the management of his affairs, and several losses in trade, soon brought him to a different way of thinking; and he at last considered, that it was his best way to let his friends know that their offers were at length acceptable. His first address was to a scrivener, who had formerly made him frequent offers of money and friendship, at a time when, perhaps, he knew those offers would have been refused. As a man, therefore, confident of not being refused, he requested the use of a hundred guineas for a few days, as he just then had occasion for money. "And pray, Sir," replied the scrivener, "do you want all this money?" "What it, Sir?" says the other. "If I did not want it I should not have asked it." "I am sorry for that," says the friend; "for those who want money when they borrow, will always want money when they should come to pay. To say the truth, Sir, money is money now; and I believe it is all sunk in the bottom of the sea, for my part; he that has got a little, is a fool if he does not keep what he has got."

Not quite disconcerted by this refusal, our adventurer was resolved to apply to another, whom he knew was the very best friend he had in the world. The gentleman whom he now addressed, received his proposal with all the affability that could be expected from generous friendship. "Let me see, you want a hundred guineas; and pray dear Jack, would not fifty answer?" "If you have but fifty to spare, Sir, I must be contented." "Fifty to spare; I do not say that, for I believe I have but twenty about me." "Then I must borrow the other thirty from some other friend." "And pray," replied the friend, "would it not be the best way to borrow the whole money from that other friend, and then one note will serve for all, you know? You know, my dear Sir, that you need make no ceremony with me at any time; you know I'm your friend; and when

scrivener: professional copyist or notary.

96

you choose a bit of dinner, or so—You, Tom, see the gentleman down. You won't forget to dine with us now and then. Your very humble servant."

<u>Distressed, but not discouraged,</u> at this treatment, he <u>was at last resolved to find that</u> assistance from love, which he could not have from friendship. A young lady, a distant relation by the mother's side, had a fortune in her own hands; and, as she had already made all the advances that her sex's modesty would permit, he made his proposal with confidence. He soon, however, perceived that no bankrupt ever found the fair one kind. She had lately fallen deeply in love with another, who had more money, and the whole neighborhood thought it would be a match.

Every day now began to strip my poor friend of his former finery; his clothes flew, piece by piece, to the pawnbroker's, and he seemed at length equipped in the genuine livery of misfortune. But still he thought himself secure from actual necessity; the numberless invitations he had received to dine, even after his losses, were yet unanswered; he was therefore now resolved to accept of a dinner because he wanted one; and in this manner he actually lived among his friends a whole week without being openly affronted. The last place I saw him in was at a reverend divine's. He had, as he fancied, just nicked the time for dinner, for he came in as the cloth was laying. He took a chair without being desired, and talked for some time without being attended to. He assured the company, that nothing procured so good an appetite as a walk in the Park, where he had been that morning. He went on, and praised the figure of the damask table-cloth; talked of a feast where he had been the day before, but that the venison was over-done. But all this procured him no invitation: finding therefore the gentleman of the house insensible to all his fetches, he thought proper, at last, to retire, and mend his appetite by a second walk in the Park.

You then, O ye beggars of my acquaintance, whether in rags or lace; whether in Kent-street or the Mall; whether at the Smyrna or St. Giles, might I be permitted to advise you as a friend, <u>never seem to want the favor which you solicit. Apply to every passion but human pity</u> for redress; you may find permanent relief from vanity, from self-interest, or from avarice, but from compassion—never. The very eloquence of a poor man is disgusting; and that mouth which is opened even by wisdom, is seldom expected to close without the horrors of a petition.

To ward off the gripe of poverty, you must pretend to be a stranger to her, and she will at least use you with ceremony. If you be caught dining upon a halfpenny porringer of pease-soup and potatoes, praise the wholesomeness of your frugal repast. You may observe that Dr. Cheyne has prescribed pease-broth for the gravel; hint that you are not one of those who are always making a deity of your belly. If, again, you are obliged to wear a flimsy stuff in the midst of winter, be the first to remark, that stuffs are very much worn at Paris; or, if there be found some irreparable defects in any parts of your equipage, which cannot be concealed by all

fetches: stratagems.
gravel: kidney or bladder stones.

the arts of sitting cross-legged, coaxing, or darning, say, that neither you nor Sampson Gideon were ever very fond of dress. If you be a philosopher, hint that Plato and Seneca are the tailors you choose to employ; assure the company that man ought to be content with a bare covering, since what now is so much his pride was formerly his shame. In short, however caught, never give out; but ascribe to the frugality of your disposition what others might be apt to attribute to the narrowness of your circumstances. To be poor, and to seem poor, is a certain method never to rise: pride in the great is hateful; in the wise, it is ridiculous; but beggarly pride is a rational vanity which I have been taught to applaud and excuse.

DISCUSSION

1. Goldsmith uses much less of his essay for concrete examples than Elizabeth Gaskell. Why?
2. Much of Goldsmith's essay is taken up with what we might call "sub-generalizations" or developments of his main generalization. Is this technique as effective as using concrete examples? Why, or why not? Would Goldsmith's approach be as effective if it were applied to "Small Economies"? Why, or why not?
3. Goldsmith's observations seem to confirm the adage "Nothing succeeds like success." Do your own observations confirm this idea? Can you think of examples that show it is not always true? What is its value as a sound idea?
4. In addition to concealing insolvency, what are some other purposes for using language to conceal rather than to reveal? Give some concrete examples.

Sometimes developing your ability to observe well can lead you to disturbing and unpopular conclusions. George Orwell was a person with a compulsion to see and think about things others overlooked. In the following selection he observes in concrete terms some of the effects of imperialism, and his essay is a classic on that subject.

George Orwell

Marrakech

(1939)

As the corpse went past the flies left the restaurant table in a cloud and rushed after it, but they came back a few minutes later.

The little crowd of mourners—all men and boys, no women—threaded their way across the market-place between the piles of pomegranates and the taxis and the camels, wailing a short chant over and over again. What really appeals to the flies is that the corpses here are never put into coffins, they are merely wrapped in a piece of rag and carried on a rough wooden bier on the shoulders of four friends. When the friends get to the burying-ground they hack an oblong hole a foot or two deep, dump the body in it and fling over it a little of the dried-up, lumpy earth, which is like broken brick. No gravestone, no name, no identifying mark of any kind. The burying-ground is merely a huge waste of hummocky earth, like a derelict building-lot. After a month or two no one can even be certain where his own relatives are buried.

When you walk through a town like this—two hundred thousand inhabitants, of whom at least twenty thousand own literally nothing except the rags they stand up in—when you see how the people live, and still more how easily they die, it is always difficult to believe that you are walking among human beings. All colonial empires are in reality founded upon that fact. The people have brown faces—besides, there are so many of them! Are they really the same flesh as yourself? Do they even have names? Or are they merely a kind of undifferentiated brown stuff, about as individual as bees or coral insects? They rise out of the earth, they sweat and starve for a few years, and then they sink back into the nameless mounds of the graveyard and nobody notices that they are gone. And even the graves themselves soon fade back into the soil. Sometimes, out for a walk, as you break your way through the prickly pear, you notice that it is rather bumpy underfoot, and only a certain regularity in the bumps tells you that you are walking over skeletons.

I was feeding one of the gazelles in the public gardens.

Gazelles are almost the only animals that look good to eat when they are still alive, in fact, one can hardly look at their hindquarters without thinking of mint sauce. The gazelle I was feeding seemed to know that this thought was in my mind, for though it took the piece of bread I was holding out it obviously did not like me. It nibbled rapidly at the bread, then lowered its head and tried to butt me, then took another nibble and then butted again. Probably its idea was that if it could drive me away the bread would somehow remain hanging in mid-air.

An Arab navvy working on the path nearby lowered his heavy hoe and sidled slowly towards us. He looked from the gazelle to the bread and from the bread to the gazelle, with a sort of quiet amazement, as though he had never seen anything quite like this before. Finally he said shyly in French:

"*I* could eat some of that bread."

I tore off a piece and he stowed it gratefully in some secret place under his rags. This man is an employee of the Municipality.

When you go through the Jewish quarters you gather some idea of what the medieval ghettoes were probably like. Under their Moorish rulers the Jews were only allowed to own land in certain restricted areas,

navvy: laborer.

Observing and Generalizing

and after centuries of this kind of treatment they have ceased to bother about overcrowding. Many of the streets are a good deal less than six feet wide, the houses are completely windowless, and sore-eyed children cluster everywhere in unbelievable numbers, like clouds of flies. Down the centre of the street there is generally running a little river of urine.

In the bazaar huge families of Jews, all dressed in the long black robe and little black skull-cap, are working in dark fly-infested booths that look like caves. A carpenter sits crosslegged at a prehistoric lathe, turning chair-legs at lightning speed. He works the lathe with a bow in his right hand and guides the chisel with his left foot, and thanks to a lifetime of sitting in this position his left leg is warped out of shape. At his side his grandson, aged six, is already starting on the simpler parts of the job.

I was just passing the coppersmiths' booths when somebody noticed that I was lighting a cigarette. Instantly, from the dark holes all round, there was a frenzied rush of Jews, many of them old grandfathers with flowing grey beards, all clamouring for a cigarette. Even a blind man somewhere at the back of one of the booths heard a rumour of cigarettes and came crawling out, groping in the air with his hand. In about a minute I had used up the whole packet. None of these people, I suppose, works less than twelve hours a day, and every one of them looks on a cigarette as a more or less impossible luxury.

As the Jews live in self-contained communities they follow the same trades as the Arabs, except for agriculture. Fruit-sellers, potters, silversmiths, blacksmiths, butchers, leatherworkers, tailors, water-carriers, beggars, porters—whichever way you look you see nothing but Jews. As a matter of fact there are thirteen thousand of them, all living in the space of a few acres. A good job Hitler wasn't here. Perhaps he was on his way, however. You hear the usual dark rumours about the Jews, not only from the Arabs but from the poorer Europeans.

"Yes, mon vieux, they took my job away from me and gave it to a Jew. The Jews! They're the real rulers of this country, you know. They've got all the money. They control the banks, finance—everything."

"But," I said, "isn't it a fact that the average Jew is a labourer working for about a penny an hour?"

"Ah, that's only for show! They're all moneylenders really. They're cunning, the Jews."

In just the same way, a couple of hundred years ago, poor old women used to be burned for witchcraft when they could not even work enough magic to get themselves a square meal.

All people who work with their hands are partly invisible, and the more important the work they do, the less visible they are. Still, a white skin is always fairly conspicuous. In northern Europe, when you see a labourer ploughing a field, you probably give him a second glance. In a hot country, anywhere south of Gibraltar or east of Suez, the chances are that you don't even see him. I have noticed this again and again. In a tropical landscape one's eye takes in everything except the human beings.

It takes in the dried-up soil, the prickly pear, the palm tree and the distant mountain, but it always misses the peasant hoeing at his patch. He is the same colour as the earth, and a great deal less interesting to look at.

It is only because of this that the starved countries of Asia and Africa are accepted as tourist resorts. No one would think of running cheap trips to the Distressed Areas. But where the human beings have brown skins their poverty is simply not noticed. What does Morocco mean to a Frenchman? An orange-grove or a job in Government service. Or to an Englishman? Camels, castles, palm trees, Foreign Legionnaires, brass trays, and bandits. One could probably live there for years without noticing that for nine-tenths of the people the reality of life is an endless, backbreaking struggle to wring a little food out of an eroded soil.

Most of Morocco is so desolate that no wild animal bigger than a hare can live on it. Huge areas which were once covered with forest have turned into a treeless waste where the soil is exactly like broken-up brick. Nevertheless a good deal of it is cultivated, with frightful labour. Everything is done by hand. Long lines of women, bent double like inverted capital L's, work their way slowly across the fields, tearing up the prickly weeds with their hands, and the peasant gathering lucerne for fodder pulls it up stalk by stalk instead of reaping it, thus saving an inch or two on each stalk. The plough is a wretched wooden thing, so frail that one can easily carry it on one's shoulder, and fitted underneath with a rough iron spike which stirs the soil to a depth of about four inches. This is as much as the strength of the animals is equal to. It is usual to plough with a cow and a donkey yoked together. Two donkeys would not be quite strong enough, but on the other hand two cows would cost a little more to feed. The peasants possess no harrows, they merely plough the soil several times over in different directions, finally leaving it in rough furrows, after which the whole field has to be shaped with hoes into small oblong patches to conserve water. Except for a day or two after the rare rainstorms there is never enough water. Along the edges of the fields channels are hacked out to a depth of thirty or forty feet to get at the tiny trickles which run through the subsoil.

Every afternoon a file of very old women passes down the road outside my house, each carrying a load of firewood. All of them are mummified with age and the sun, and all of them are tiny. It seems to be generally the case in primitive communities that the women, when they get beyond a certain age, shrink to the size of children. One day a poor old creature who could not have been more than four feet tall crept past me under a vast load of wood. I stopped her and put a five-sou piece (a little more than a farthing) into her hand. She answered with a shrill wail, almost a scream, which was partly gratitude but mainly surprise. I suppose that from her point of view, by taking any notice of her, I seemed almost to be violating a law of nature. She accepted her status as an old woman, that is to say as a beast of burden. When

lucerne: alfalfa.

a family is travelling it is quite usual to see a father and a grown-up son riding ahead on donkeys, and an old woman following on foot, carrying the baggage.

But what is strange about these people is their invisibility. For several weeks, always at about the same time of day, the file of old women had hobbled past the house with their firewood, and though they had registered themselves on my eyeballs I cannot truly say that I had seen them. Firewood was passing—that was how I saw it. It was only that one day I happened to be walking behind them, and the curious up-and-down motion of a load of wood drew my attention to the human being beneath it. Then for the first time I noticed the poor old earth-coloured bodies, bodies reduced to bones and leathery skin, bent double under the crushing weight. Yet I suppose I had not been five minutes on Moroccan soil before I noticed the overloading of the donkeys and was infuriated by it. There is no question that the donkeys are damnably treated. The Moroccan donkey is hardly bigger than a St. Bernard dog, it carries a load which in the British Army would be considered too much for a fifteen-hands mule, and very often its packsaddle is not taken off its back for weeks together. But what is peculiarly pitiful is that it is the most willing creature on earth, it follows its master like a dog and does not need either bridle or halter. After a dozen years of devoted work it suddenly drops dead, whereupon its master tips it into the ditch and the village dogs have torn its guts out before it is cold.

This kind of thing makes one's blood boil, whereas—on the whole—the plight of the human beings does not. I am not commenting, merely pointing to a fact. People with brown skins are next door to invisible. Anyone can be sorry for the donkey with its galled back, but it is generally owing to some kind of accident if one even notices the old woman under her load of sticks.

As the storks flew northward the Negroes were marching southward —a long, dusty column, infantry, screw-gun batteries, and then more infantry, four or five thousand men in all, winding up the road with a clumping of boots and a clatter of iron wheels.

They were Senegalese, the blackest Negroes in Africa, so black that sometimes it is difficult to see whereabouts on their necks the hair begins. Their splendid bodies were hidden in reach-me-down khaki uniforms, their feet squashed into boots that looked like blocks of wood, and every tin hat seemed to be a couple of sizes too small. It was very hot and the men had marched a long way. They slumped under the weight of their packs and the curiously sensitive black faces were glistening with sweat.

As they went past a tall, very young Negro turned and caught my eye. But the look he gave me was not in the least the kind of look you might expect. Not hostile, not contemptuous, not sullen, not even inquisitive. It was the shy, wide-eyed Negro look, which actually is a look of profound respect. I saw how it was. This wretched boy, who is a French citizen and has therefore been dragged from the forest to scrub floors and catch syphilis in garrison towns, actually has feelings of reverence before a white skin. He has been taught that the white race are his masters, and he still believes it.

But there is one thought which every white man (and in this connection it doesn't matter twopence if he calls himself a socialist) thinks when he sees a black army marching past. "How much longer can we go on kidding these people? How long before they turn their guns in the other direction?"

It was curious, really. Every white man there had this thought stowed somewhere or other in his mind. I had it, so had the other onlookers, so had the officers on their sweating chargers and the white N.C.O.'s marching in the ranks. It was a kind of secret which we all knew and were too clever to tell; only the Negroes didn't know it. And really it was like watching a flock of cattle to see the long column, a mile or two miles of armed men, flowing peacefully up the road, while the great white birds drifted over them in the opposite direction, glittering like scraps of paper.

DISCUSSION

1. "All people who work with their hands are partly invisible, and the more important the work they do, the less visible they are." Is this statement confirmed by your own experience? (For example, the most important work in all parts of the world is done by agricultural workers. In your part of the country, and in your experience, how "visible" are they? Have you always been as aware of them as you have been of businessmen and politicians for example?)
2. "But where the human beings have brown skins their poverty is simply not noticed." Again, is this true in your experience? Does Orwell not notice? Is it possible to retrain our awareness, our way of seeing, so that we do notice? In concrete terms, how might this be done? (If you have become aware of a group or class of people you previously ignored, perhaps the way in which you became aware of them can give you a clue as to the answers to these questions.)
3. Few writers interweave fact and opinion more subtly that Orwell does. Point out some single sentences that contain elements of both fact and opinion. What seems to be the proportion of concrete observation to opinion in the essay as a whole? What might be a reason for the difference in this proportion between Orwell's essay and Goldsmith's "On the Use of Language"?
4. What are some of the memorable images in "Marrakech," and what is the idea attached to each of them? (Don't be surprised if you recall more images than ideas. This is the way the memory works.)
5. How does Orwell use "atmosphere"—the sense of the surroundings that is strong in "An Autumn Night in the Hills"? What mood does he evoke? Point out some particular words, phrases, or sentences that help to communicate this mood. How does it reinforce the meaning of the essay?
6. In a sense Orwell is offering us a definition of imperialism and exploi-

tation, what the semanticists call an "operational definition," a definition in terms of the concrete sensory data that make up the material of the definition. Look up the terms "imperialism" and "exploitation" in a dictionary and then in an encyclopedia. How do the terms of the definitions differ from Orwell's? Which are more concrete? Which are more likely to change a reader's feelings about the realities?

As in the case of "An Autumn Night in the Hills," we come upon writing of subtlety and resonance. Again, by chance, it centers on what happens to a dog but is really about human beings. On one level "A House of Correction" is an observation of a dog's response to mistreatment; on another it is a comment on the human condition.

Llewellyn Powys

A House of Correction

(1938)

It has been shown that if dogs, under experiments that have to do with their conditioned reflexes, are presented with problems beyond their powers of solution, there is set up a neurosis so acute that several weeks are required before the spiritual health of the animal is re-established. It is possible that much of the nervous instability characteristic of human beings can be explained in the same way, seeing that it is our destiny to pass this life under the shadow of certain insoluble metaphysical problems. Maurice Maeterlinck says somewhere that of all living creatures dogs alone are happy, because they are fortunate enough to see plain in the flesh a living god and to have this insistent yearning satisfied.

If this is the case, how careful we should be in no way to betray so touching an illusion. I myself have never been a great lover of these animals. I am afraid of the fierce ones of their species, and discomposed by the others, whose supplicating manners seem to put upon me obligations, such as fetching food and water, or taking them out for exercise. Now and again, however, it has happened that the personality of a particular dog so far invades my sympathy that it seems to separate itself from the lower creation. Recently I have had a good example of this.

I have taken rooms for a year in a cottage on the Sussex Downs, and as the house is very isolated it is necessary for me each week to fetch my own butter. In the backyard of the dairy farm I visit there lives an old shaggy sheep-dog. He is always chained. His brown eyes that look up through his matted hair possess that particular expression of moral goodness that is so appealing. They suggest a capacity for utter devotion, for utter fidelity which, in a world where all is at hazard, and where

Beginning with Direct Observation: Informal Generalizing

feeling is so often frivolous, is very moving. The dog's name is Tinker. His kennel stands directly below the dairy wall. On the inside of this wall all is spotlessly clean. The empty milk pails collected here shine in the afternoon light as though they were silver shields, and the brick paving upon which they rest has obviously been swilled down with water and scrubbed, scoured, and brushed every day. On the other side of the wall, in the yard where the dog lives, it is a very different matter. Here the cattle that are driven in and out of the sheds at milking-time have churned up a fine slush. If it were the ordinary midden litter of a cow barton it would not be so bad, but it is a liquid mud, two or three inches deep, of the splashing kind that is often to be found outside pigsties. Tinker's kennel, with its roof patched with an old piece of tin, has been properly bespattered with this filth, and when he stands on his hind legs against the wall, as he very often does, you can see that the gray hairs that hang from his back and shanks are held together in solid elf-locks such as could only be removed with a good sharp pair of shears of the kind that I was accustomed to use for "dagging" sheep in Africa.

It was this very habit that the dog had of standing upright against the wall that first caused me to take notice of him. I was coming out of the low whitewashed cheese-room with my three rolls of butter wrapped up in white, crisp grease-paper, when I caught sight of two eager paws appearing over the tiled coping. The animal seemed so friendly when I stroked his broad forehead that I went into the yard and round to the kennel. He had evidently been trained not to jump up, but I realized, as he sniffed eagerly at my knees and rubbed his head against me, that his body, under its unkempt hair, was trembling with excitement at having someone come to his kennel and take notice of him. The kennel, a large one, being absolutely plastered with the mud of the yard, presented a very sordid appearance, and there rose from the ground about it a strong odor of dog's urine and dog's dung. I felt sorry for this sheepdog, and my consciousness of his evil destiny was accentuated by the fact that the chain attached to his collar was an exceptionally heavy one, with iron links of an enormous size, more suitable for chaining a man than a dog. Indeed, it was just such a chain as one sees in pictures of Negroes manacled together during the terible "middle passage" of slave-trading days.

After this, whenever I came for the butter, usually on Tuesday afternoons, I never failed to go round to the kennel, and the dog used to be on the lookout for me, so that the moment he heard the click of the farmyard gate he would be out of his kennel, demonstrating his excitement by putting his paws up to the top of the wall, by wagging his tail, and by uttering ingratiating guttural noises of brute beast affection. Once, before I left my cottage, I remembered to put some food in my pocket, the drumsticks from a chicken I had eaten for my luncheon. He devoured the stringy legs of the fowl in the most ravenous way, crunching them up wholesale in the mud outside his kennel door.

A week ago I went to fetch the butter as usual. That Tuesday happened

barton: farmyard.
dagging: cutting dirty or clotted locks of wool off sheep.

Observing and Generalizing

to be one of those days in January that give unmistakable promise of the first stirrings of the spring. There was something tender, almost ethereal in the air, an indefinable lightness suggesting the first movements of a young girl waking from sleep, as though the eyelids of the earth were delicately lifting in a state of half-realized consciousness.

In the hedge of the green lane leading from the downs I noticed there were lamb's-tails out, their golden tassels suspended against the leafless thorns and elders. Skylarks were rising from the cold fields for those first low flights they practice when it is still winter. The afternoon's sunshine was spread abroad over Sussex with the gentle grace that belongs to this time of the year, when the sun is still gathering to itself its new strength. Soon the days would slide by and the anemones would be out in the spinneys, the marsh marigolds out in the withy beds, and the swallows back in the barn, and the cuckoo's voice would be calling through the raw impassioned air of April dawns. As I anticipated the sensitive progress of the swift seasons still in the future, the largesse, the benison of life seemed infinite. It was impossible not to bless God for our blood and quick breath. On the simplest plane the reward of life seemed incalculable. As I continued to walk over the wintry grass on one side of a deep cart rut, my whole being was stirred with admiration, with adoration for the mystery of existence. So fond, indeed, was my mood that it went out of my head that there was such a thing as evil in the world.

Coming across the last field separating me from the farm, I passed the dairyman spreading out heaps of dung that had been unloaded in symmetrical lines. I stopped to say a few words. He was a powerful, hard-working-looking man. "You are giving this ground a good dressing," I said. "Yes," he said. "If I'm not mistaken you'll see a terrible sight of mowing grass in this here mead come June-time." Immediately his words threw me back again to my recent mood, as in my mind's eye I saw the hayfield of his vision in all its plenary beauty edging up to the very walls of his thatched homestead, with the red flowers of the sorrel swaying above the clustered grass heads, with white butterflies zigzagging wantonly over them, and with swallows searching for flies through the soft air of summer.

I had now reached the yard gate. This time I heard no sound of Tinker's heavy chain moving, so I concluded he was not in his kennel, and made my way over the garnished bricks direct to the cheese-room. "I did not see Tinker," I remarked to the dairyman's wife, as, with her back turned towards me, she was wrapping up my pats of butter, yellow and sweet-smelling as cowslip balls. "He is there," she said, "but he got himself into trouble this morning. He got loose and wandered off to the village. We were forced to send a boy after him, and he was given a taste of the stick."

As soon as ever I could I went to the kennel. I called the dog. There

lamb's-tails: catkins or blossom-like spikes of the hazel.
spinneys: small woods or thickets.
withy: willow.

was no response. Kneeling down, I put my hand into the dark tunnel of his dwelling. I felt the hard bone of his broad forehead, and began to stroke it. An aura of profound dejection seemed to emanate from this dismal house of correction. The dog's spirit had evidently been so broken that he feared even to look at the afternoon's sunlight lest the protruding of his rough head might be interpreted as a wish for freedom. I was convinced that some shocking violence had been done to him. I could not be mistaken. I was looking into a hole of despair. Alone in the squalor of his soiled prison, with his bruised limbs lying on vermin straw, I knew that the very nature of this dog, in all its trust and simplicity, had been brutally outraged down to the depths of its perplexed consciousness.

Two or three times I tried to coax him, tried to persuade him to look out of his kennel door, but he would not. Lying in loneliness, his animal spirit had abandoned its will in abject and absolute submission to the inexplicable wishes of his arbitrary master. Surely, I thought, my mood of the lane and of the field was utterly false and could never return. Then, sudden as the theophany on the road to Damascus, as I knelt with my soul in hell, *it was with me again*, for, although no sound came from the sheep-dog's foul jail, a rough tongue had begun to lick the back of my hand.

DISCUSSION

1. There is a good deal of the author's comment in the piece, though little of it is directed toward the central situation. Is your feeling of compassion for the dog aroused by the author's comment or by the facts he reveals without comment? Which comments or which facts?
2. Sometimes refraining from comment can be more pointed than commenting. Does Powys express directly any feeling about the dog's owners? Is any such feeling implied in his actions? What specific actions?
3. As in "An Autumn Night in the Hills," there is a pattern of contrasts in "A House of Correction." What things are contrasted, and how do these contrasts enhance the meaning?
4. Besides the contrasts, a comparison is made between the relationship of dog to man and man to his metaphysical belief. Exactly what is the comparison, and what does it have to do with the author's strongly expressed feeling in the last paragraph?
5. What is the atmosphere of the story? What paragraph best expresses it? What is its relationship to the theme of the story?

A NOTE ON IRONY

There are two kinds of irony that concern the writer. The first is irony of expression: saying the opposite of what you mean, in such a way that the

theophany on the road to Damascus: While Paul was journeying from Jerusalem to Damascus, Christ appeared before him and brought about his conversion. Theophany means literally "appearance of God."

Observing and Generalizing

reader is fully aware of your true feelings. This kind of irony is exemplified by Llewellyn Powys' title, "A House of Correction"; the dog's behavior is not being corrected, since it has no conception of what it has done wrong. Irony of this sort is also used by Robert Lynd in "Conversation" when he tells us that the art of conversation is not dead and then gives us an example of talk that is funny only because of its stupidity. The most famous example of verbal irony appears later on in this book, Jonathan Swift's "A Modest Proposal."

The second kind, irony of situation, occurs when a man's plans result in an effect opposite to what he intends, or when the truth is shown to be the opposite of what we would expect it to be. In "Marrakech" this kind of irony is shown to be true of imperialism, the attempt to gain wealth and security that actually produces poverty and fear. But the clearest example in our reading so far is Goldsmith's "On the Use of Language," in which he shows that language, which we believe is meant to communicate, is often used to conceal. We will come upon this kind of irony again in Samuel Butler's "Darwin and the Machines."

These are examples of writing based on irony, but most authors use irony casually, as Mark Twain does in "The House Beautiful" (the title itself is an example of verbal irony, of course). It is an entertaining and often effective device, worth looking for in reading and putting to use in writing.

WRITING SUGGESTIONS

1. Using "Small Economies" as your model, think of some human foible that is present in several people you have observed. State a generalization, give a number of general examples to make its meaning clear, and then describe fully at least one particular instance that illustrates the generalization well.
2. Looking back to the first three selections in this chapter for inspiration, see if you can recall either (a) an episode in your experience or that of people you know that illustrates a peculiarity of the human mind such as suggestibility, inability to recall a well-known fact or name, willful blindness, holding fast to a dogmatic belief in the face of plain evidence, jumping to a conclusion, incurable optimism or pessimism, or any other human foible that occurs to you; or (b) an observation you have made that contradicts a widely held belief, such as that barking dogs never bite, cats hate water, women are incompetent to solve mechanical problems, manual workers have no intellectual ability, and so on. Write your episode as a paragraph or short essay, just enough words to make your observation and conclusion clear to the reader.
3. Oliver Goldsmith talks about using language to conceal our want of money rather than reveal it. But that, of course, is only one example of how language is used to hide something. We have all witnessed language being used to cover up embarrassment, ignorance, guilt, cheating, and just plain emptiness of mind, among other things. Try an essay similar to Goldsmith's, with two or

three extended examples like his, about another of these underhanded uses of language.

4. If you are ambitious and courageous enough to seek a revealing experience, explore at first hand, as Orwell might have, the problem of unconscious racism, exploitation, and social invisibility. Few communities are without their quota of "invisible" people; those whom most members of the middle-class know nothing about and wish to know nothing: the poor who do essential work, the alcoholics, the outcasts, the maladjusted, the vagrants, and the rejected, penniless aged. Get to know a person of one of these groups at least to the extent of knowing what he does all day in some detail. Visit a "skid row" bar at opening time (six a.m. in most places); hang around a farm labor camp; join the groups that wait on corners early in the morning to be picked up for a day's farm work or other labor; spend some time in a downtown mission. Keep your eyes and ears open, and report in concrete, sensory terms what you find. Then offer a qualified generalization.

5. Observe an irony in the world around you and write about it in some detail. Here are a few examples of the sort of thing you might use:

> The way technology, meant to make life more pleasant, can make life more difficult.
> How a person you know tries so hard to be entertaining that he bores everyone.
> How someone spends more money than he saves looking for bargains.
> The way some people stress honesty in some relationships but are dishonest in others.

Approach your subject strictly in terms of your own observations, and qualify your generalizations.

Plate 7
Henri de Toulouse-Lautrec (1864–1901): *Maxime Dethomas*

Once more we have a portrait, but this time it is less a portrait of an individual than of a way of life. While Erasmus and Dr. Johnson (Plates 3 and 4) are presented to us in their most characteristic poses without obvious comment, Maxime Dethomas (a man unknown except as a friend of the artist) is shown in a setting that implies a good deal of generalization.

1. Reynolds, in his portrait of Dr. Johnson, was mainly concerned to preserve for the future an impression of what Johnson was like. Was Toulouse-Lautrec's purpose similar, or was there another purpose? What is your evidence?
2. What impression of Dethomas does the artist communicate? What does he lead us to infer about Dethomas' habits and thoughts? How does he communicate these ideas?
3. Compare this portrait with the one of Erasmus (Plate 3) and then with George Bellows' *Stag at Sharkey's* (Plate 6). Which does it have more in common with? What do the two have in common?
4. Aside from the individual personality of Dethomas, what informal generalizations does the portrait seem to imply?
5. Compare this portrait with Hawthorne's word portrait, "The Old Apple Dealer" (p. 32). Which person do you feel you know more about? Why? Which work uses surroundings to tell us more?

PLATE 7 Henri de Toulouse-Lautrec (1864–1901), **Maxime Dethomas.** *Washington National Gallery of Art, Chester Dale Collection.*

5

Beginning with Direct Observation: Explaining

Whenever the material used to support a generalization is unfamiliar to most readers or is highly complex, explanation is necessary. To explain is to make clear, especially to make clear matters that are not a part of common knowledge; thus explanation is simply description that pays more attention to clarity, detail, and causal connection than ordinary description does. If, for example, you were to explain the proper golfer's stance, you would describe it with great care, leaving out no significant detail regarding the positions of the feet, legs, arms, hands, and body, and you would probably offer some hint as to why these positions are best.

Even when the material is reasonably familiar, explanations are sometimes needed here and there. We have seen such brief incidental explanations in Mark Twain's "House Beautiful," Hoggart's "Working Class Mother," Theocritus' "Fight," Lawrence's "Arab Feasting," and Powys' "House of Correction." The following two selections are largely explanatory: that is, the bulk of each is given to making clear matters that are not common knowledge.

However, Melville and McFee do not confine themselves to explanation. Each makes some value judgments as he goes along and each, when he has completed his explanation, concludes with a broad generalization. In both cases, as it happens, these are not generalizations based directly on the preceding evidence, but are generalizations by analogy: both writers apply the principles they have established to another area of life. Whether these analogies are convincing is for you, the reader, to decide.

Herman Melville

The Line

(1852)

The whale-line is only two-thirds of an inch in thickness. At first sight, you would not think it so strong as it really is. By experiment its one and fifty yarns will each suspend a weight of one hundred and twenty pounds; so that the whole rope will bear a strain nearly equal to three tons. In length, the common sperm whale-line measures something over two hundred fathoms. Towards the stern of the boat it is spirally coiled away in the tub, not like the worm-pipe of a still, though, but so as to form one round, cheese-shaped mass of densely bedded "sheaves," or layers of concentric spiralisations, without any hollow but the "heart," or minute vertical tube formed at the axis of the cheese. As the least tangle or kink in the coiling would, in running out, infallibly take somebody's arm, leg, or entire body off, the utmost precaution is used in stowing the line in its tub. Some harpooneers will consume almost an entire morning in this business, carrying the line high aloft and then reeving it downwards through a block towards the tub, so as in the act of coiling to free it from all possible wrinkles and twists.

In the English boats two tubs are used instead of one; the same line being continuously coiled in both tubs. There is some advantage in this: because these twin-tubs being so small they fit more readily into the boat, and do not strain it so much; whereas, the American tub, nearly three feet in diameter and of proportionate depth, makes a rather bulky freight for a craft whose planks are but one half-inch in thickness; for the bottom of the whale boat is like critical ice, which will bear up a considerable distributed weight, but not very much of a concentrated one. When the painted canvas cover is clapped on the American line-tub, the boat looks as if it were pulling off with a prodigious great wedding-cake to present to the whales.

Both ends of the line are exposed; the lower end terminating in an eye-splice or loop coming up from the bottom against the side of the tub, and hanging over its edge completely disengaged from everything. This arrangement of the lower end is necessary on two accounts. First: In order to facilitate the fastening to it of an additional line from a neighbouring boat, in case the stricken whale should sound so deep as to threaten to carry off the entire line originally attached to the harpoon. In these instances, the whale of course is shifted like a mug of ale, as it were, from the one boat to the other; though the first boat always hovers at hand to assist its consort. Second: This arrangement is indispensable for common safety's sake; for were the lower end of the line in any way attached to the boat, and were the whale then to run

reeving: passing a rope through a small hole to straighten it.
block: pulley case, as in a block and tackle.
sound: go down (in water).

the line out to the end almost in a single, smoking minute as he sometimes does, he would not stop there, for the doomed boat would infallibly be dragged down after him into the profundity of the sea; and in that case no town-crier would ever find her again.

Before lowering the boat for the chase, the upper end of the line is taken aft from the tub, and passing round the loggerhead there, is again carried forward the entire length of the boat, resting crosswise upon the loom or handle of every man's oar, so that it jogs against his wrist in rowing; and also passing between the men, as they alternately sit at the opposite gunwales, to the leaded chocks or grooves in the extreme pointed prow of the boat, where a wooden pin or skewer the size of a common quill, prevents it from slipping out. From the chocks it hangs in a slight festoon over the bows, and is then passed inside the boat again; and some ten or twenty fathoms (called box-line) being coiled upon the box, in the bows, it continues its way to the gunwale still a little farther aft, and is then attached to the short-warp—the rope which is immediately connected with the harpoon; but previous to that connection, the short-warp goes through sundry mystifications too tedious to detail.

Thus the whale-line folds the whole boat in its complicated coils, twisting and writhing around it in almost every direction. All the oarsmen are involved in its perilous contortions; so that to the timid eye of the landsman, they seem as Indian jugglers, with the deadliest snakes sportively festooning their limbs. Nor can any son of mortal woman, for the first time, seat himself amid those hempen intricacies, and while straining his utmost at the oar, bethink him that at any unknown instant the harpoon may be darted, and all these horrible contortions be put in play like ringed lightnings; he cannot be thus circumstanced without a shudder that makes the very marrow in his bones to quiver in him like a shaken jelly. Yet habit—strange thing! what cannot habit accomplish?—Gayer sallies, more merry mirth, better jokes, and brighter repartees, you never heard over your mahogany, than you will hear over the half-inch white cedar of the whale boat, when thus hung in hangman's nooses; and, like the six burghers of Calais before King Edward, the six men composing the crew pull into jaws of death, with a halter around every neck, as you may say.

Perhaps a very little thought will now enable you to account for those repeated whaling disasters—some few of which are casually chronicled —of this man or that man being taken out of the boat by the line, and lost. For, when the line is darting out, to be seated then in the boat, is like being seated in the midst of the manifold whizzings of a steam-engine in full play, when every flying beam, and shaft, and wheel, is

aft: toward the stern, or back, of the boat .
loggerhead: an upright cylindrical piece of wood attached to the boat, around which the line is doubled when it is going out too fast.
gunwale (pronounced "gunnel"): part of boat where sides and deck meet.
six burghers of Calais: In 1347 six of the leading citizens of Calais, a French port on the English Channel, offered their lives to Edward III of England if he would refrain from slaughtering the city's inhabitants.

grazing you. It is worse; for you cannot sit motionless in the heart of these perils, because the boat is rocking like a cradle, and you are pitched one way and the other, without the slightest warning, and only by certain self-adjusting buoyancy and simultaneousness of volition and action, can you escape being made a Mazeppa of, and run away with where the all-seeing sun himself could never pierce you out.

Again: as the profound calm which only apparently precedes and prophesies of the storm, is perhaps more awful than the storm itself; for, indeed, the calm is but the wrapper and envelope of the storm; and contains it in itself, as the seemingly harmless rifle holds the fatal powder, and the ball, and the explosion; so the graceful repose of the line, as it silently serpentines about the oarsmen before being brought into actual play—this is a thing which carries more of true terror than any other aspect of this dangerous affair. But why say more? All men live enveloped in whale-lines. All are born with halters round their necks; but it is only when caught in the swift, sudden turn of death, that mortals realise the silent, subtle, ever-present perils of life. And if you be a philosopher, though seated in the whale boat, you would not at heart feel one whit more of terror than though seated before your evening fire with a poker, and not a harpoon, by your side.

DISCUSSION

1. The way the line is arranged in the whaleboat is complex. Does Melville make this arrangement, and the reasons for it, clear? As a test of clarity, try recasting his explanation in your own words or draw a diagram.
2. Most readers have no need to know exactly how a harpoon line is arranged. What is the real point of Melville's explanation?
3. Melville compares the whaleboat, from which a man may be snatched by the line and drowned at any time, to life itself. Does this seem a valid comparison? Can you support or refute it with data from your own observation?

William McFee

The Pattern-Makers

(1925)

It was a world within a world, and that again lost in the mighty maze of London, and I remember with affection the days I spent there.

Between us, up there in the pattern shop, which you had to reach by

Mazeppa: a Cossack page tied to a wild horse by an outraged husband, in Byron's poem of the same name. (He survived.)

Observing and Generalizing

crossing the girder shop and the heavy machine shop and so up a staircase leading over the booming and murky smithy—between us and the boss in his great skylighted office, surrounded by telephones and rushing out at us sometimes in his shirtsleeves, there was not so much difference as you might imagine. Because, while there was nothing democratic in our relations, supposing that word to have any meaning at all, which I doubt, we knew all about him. It was true he had inherited the business of millwrights and engineers, or would do so when his remarkable old father gave up the ghost. But he was in the line of succession. The old man, the Senior, we called him, to distinguish him from the Junior, had inherited the concern from his father, who had served his apprenticeship with the man who invented the steam engine, Jamie Watt, no less, with his partner Boulton. So here you had what, to us, was almost apostolic succession, and more than that there had been some sort of ironworks and foundry there in that part of Clerkenwell for goodness knows how long, with a yard behind which had been used in the Great Plague to bury the poor folk in, as we found, very horribly, when we dug the big erecting pit deeper for a tall mill engine, and found skulls and so on. And the tavern at the corner is still called the Pit's Head, and in my time their ale was good enough. And never did I hear from the men any complaint that Junior should inherit from Senior, seeing their fathers before them had built the business and gave us, anyhow, a decent living. Even in my time, and that followed a strike that was like a lot of brothers fighting, the men were tradesmen, which is to say, men cunning and skilful in their trade, and none more proud and considering than the pattern-makers. Which made us notice how the Junior, though he had more book knowledge than his father or grandfather, depended on the foreman to say just how a pattern would draw and how it could be cored. I can remember once, when I asked him, he was stuck and could not tell me.

The pattern-makers, then, with their own union, and looking down on the carpenters and, in fact, everybody except the moulders, were toffs in the mechanics' world. It was an interesting place to be. I've heard men say to me that it was the best fitted up shop, for a journeyman, of any in London, and they had worked in them all, from Hunter and English at Bow, who made pumping engines, the same as we, to Gwynnes of Hammersmith and Peter Brotherhood's, who were more in the marine line and had a host of tricky castings to do. We had a band saw, a circular saw, a planing machine, and two lathes, one for big face work, and a small one, which I delighted to run, for prints and so on. For you must understand I did not go into that place an ignoramus, as do so many apprentices, so that their whole four years is none too much to get the rudiments. I had always had tools in my hands, and had a lathe with a treadle at home and could use a gouge and knife tool pretty well, so when I got to that lathe up in the corner of the pattern shop, driven by a belt from the great humming engine downstairs, I was loath to leave off. Even now, I could use a lathe all day.

toffs: English slang for aristocrats.

But the journeymen, who had learned their trade before all these fine machines had been invented, did not believe in having apprentices use them. I can remember, when they put in a machine for slicing the end grain of a piece of wood true and square and as smooth as cheese, old Thompson, the foreman, would not let me to it. I had to go back to my bench and plane my work square and test it by hand. This was sound doctrine, though I didn't see it. For how can a craftsman learn to have his hand and eye and brain all trained to work together if he depend more and more on the machine? And to show how they made us apprentices work until we knew what we were doing, I can tell the way I made my tool chest.

There was another mark of distinction the pattern-makers had—the great number of tools each man had to buy. There was his big trying plane, a couple of jack planes, and as many as a half-a-dozen small smooth planes, some of which he had made himself out of a piece of beech he fancied, and bought the irons in Petticoat Lane of a Sunday morning. There were his hammers, two at least, and his gauges, which were sometimes wonderful pieces of fancy work, in ebony or rosewood, though this latter stuff, pretty to look at, had a way of splitting. He had compasses, of course, and prickers, for no pattern-maker can work to a pencil line, he has to scribe it with a sharp blade. But above all he took pride in his chisels and gouges, all oiled and sharpened and with boxwood hafts shining like cloudy amber, a lovely sight in a well-stocked chest. His saws were perhaps three in number and as a rule he would lend neither saw nor chisel nor gouge. Find your own. And indeed I have seen three men in a row at the long bench by the windows and their chests were worth all of twenty pounds each, which was a lot of money in those days when one made only tenpence or a shilling an hour.

Well, the first thing we apprentices had to do was make a chest. If we couldn't do that, seeing it was only joinery, we couldn't be trusted to make patterns. So up we went to the loft with our bench mate and picked the wood, eleven-inch boards of fair white pine about five eighths of an inch thick. A chest had to go under a bench, it had to be long enough to carry a rip saw in the lid, and it had to be handy enough to lift to the man's shoulder when he went away to another town. This brought the chest to about three feet long by a foot wide and the same high. Inside, the tools lay in trays, such as I am going to tell about, like spoons and forks in these modern silver cabinets, and there was a lock or two and handles at each end, of brass. I can tell you, when you had made that chest and knew how to use all the tools it held, from the spoon gouges to the old woman's tooth, you could call yourself an improver, anyhow, and the old fellows in the shop would no longer worry you with their chat.

trying plane: a plane for tongue-and-groove jointing.
jack planes: large planes for coarse general work.
smooth planes: small planes, about eight inches long, for finishing.
irons: blades.
old woman's tooth: a kind of chisel.

Observing and Generalizing

The box and the lid were all made in one, and then the lid was sawn asunder about three inches down between the dovetails. It was the dovetailing that tried the youngster, and even now I think of the failures, the "wasters" I made before I got the sides and ends good enough for old Thompson. Nothing but right would do him, and he pushed the crooked work through the band saw so fast it screamed, and I had to begin again. For if you will look at a box or drawer that has been dovetailed you will see how nice the fitting must be. You have to saw with extreme care down the sides of the tails, leaving a shade to pare with a chisel, and when all of that particular corner is ready for a trial, set the male and female lightly together. I have seen men, working on the heavy mahogany cases that cover the malt rollers in a brewery, so skilled in dovetailing that the work drove together at the first shot, but they were master-joiners and doing such work year in, year out. For me, I was lucky, getting my four boards together at last, all ready for glueing and nailing.

Even this was a craft, for glue ill-made is no use at all, but a mere filling. We had a steam-heated pot outside on the landing, and they taught me to leave the glue in cold water overnight and then, when it was like large pale slabs of jelly, to set it warming gradually, stirring it now and then as I was told. When all was ready the bench was cleared and the pot brought in. All the tails were glued quickly and tapped into place, the excess was wiped off with shavings, the pot put back, and then the nails put in. This nailing was so done that each nail added to the rigidity of the chest, they being driven in pairs away from each other and headed home with a punch. Then the top and bottom, each a clean and beautiful single piece of fine pine, were nailed on and the whole thing put up in the loft to dry.

The custom in my time was to leave it there while you made your trays. And if any apprentice had trouble with his chest, he could count on a miserable time with trays. These were generally three in number. One, the same size as the chest, went below. The other two lay end to end, flush with the opening, and were to carry the fancy chisels, bradawls, drill bits, and gouges. The trouble and care arose from their being only three eighths of an inch thick, or sometimes only a quarter of an inch, and since they were shellac-varnished, every flaw was visible. I think I made a good half-dozen top trays before old Thompson managed to bring himself to let me go on with the work. I hated him and his particularity then, but I wish, when I have some woodwork to do now, that I could find someone with one tenth of his skill and honourable professional conscience. When the trays were made, then, and ready to be planed down to fit the chest exactly, the chest itself was a hard, strong, hollow affair that, as old Thompson said, "could be chucked out o' two story window an' take no 'arm." This was the ideal we were supposed to work for, and cases have been known in the trade where a chest, locked and screwed, has actually had this misfortune and survived with only a bruised or splintered corner.

Taking it up again, then, the next thing to do was to put on the top

bradawl: awl with a chisel edge used to make holes for brads and screws.

and bottom mouldings, which formed additional sturdiness and also made the thing near watertight. The lid being sawn through, the inside was cleaned up and the hinges fitted. Some men had four hinges on their chests, long ones, after the manner of a piano lid, and often you would see two or three locks. Both hinges and locks took skill, for if you cut too much you could not replace it, and a badly fitting lock or hinge was a mark to carry with you all your days. Then came the trays, and they had to be shaved so that when you dropped them into place they floated softly down on the imprisoned air, and old Thompson would mumble, "Not so dusty," and turn his ponderous body toward his own bench. I can see him now, reddish mutton chops and bristling moustache, standing with one hand on his trying plane, his spectacles on the end of his nose and he looking over them, as I exhibited my handiwork. He was an authentic part of England.

Things went easier for the apprentice once he had his box hinged and locked. It was now to be painted, and it was interesting to do. Inside, a dozen coats of shellac varnish, very thin, made a fine dry bed for tools. Outside, for some reason or other, black was universal. Lampblack and shellac varnish were applied as often as twenty times, and finally varnish alone, until the thing had the glossy, satiny feel of a piano. This was not only for decoration, for well-covered wood is stronger and takes a dint better than the naked timber. And then came the joy of putting on the handles, which had to be of heavy brass, and if he had a friend in the machine shop, it was considered good form to get the castings rough from the foundry and have them finished close at hand.

There was a general feeling among the pattern-makers that they, the moulders and the smiths, were superior to the other tradesmen, whose combined efforts built an engine, because, in a manner of speaking, "they had nothing but the drawing to work to." A fitter, a turner, a machinist—for in England they are so infernally logical that a machinist is a man who operates a machine—all had a forging, a casting, or some sort of stock from which to work. But a pattern-maker or a moulder when "striking out" large moulds that had no patterns, had to "read the drawing" and in no small degree was a draftsman himself. It was for this reason that apprentices like myself, who were destined to become professional engineers rather than journeymen mechanics, began with pattern-making. Moreover, it was a remarkably clean occupation and we had fastidious craftsmen in the shop. I have seen a man whose name was Harry, a tall middle-aged person from the north of England and wonderfully skilled at large built-up "plate" patterns, who would dart behind the band saw half-a-dozen times in a morning to wash his hands in a bucket of warm water he had there and dry them in the rich yellow sawdust before rubbing olive oil over them and wiping them again, to make them what he called "soople." And a bench mate I had for a while, a chunky little sportsman named Jack, invariably wore a nice derby hat all day and had a fresh starched white shirt with wide cuffs that I never saw turned down, every day of his life. Here was a striking example of

dint: blow.

Observing and Generalizing

that peculiar individual liberty that can be found nowhere else save in England. None of his mates queried Jack's right to do this if he could afford it, and his wife liked to get the shirts up for him, yet none of them would have dreamed of imitating him. That is what I call liberty.

It is necessary here to explain more clearly why a pattern-maker's work is so important, and the manner in which it differs from joinery and even cabinet-making. A pattern, then, is the wooden model which goes to the foundry to form the hole in the sand into which the metal is poured. Now it will be perfectly obvious that the pattern must be of sufficient size to leave metal enough for machining, it must be made so that it will not warp with damp, and above all it must be so designed that it will come out of the mould, or "draw," after the latter is made. Here comes the craft of the trade. The pattern-maker must decide, by an attentive consideration of the tracing sent to him from the office, how that casting should come out. And if he has decided, then he must make the pattern with a taper downward. If there is a rib or boss in the way, then that part must be made with screws that can be reached through the sand and so released; and then, when the main body of the pattern has been drawn out, these extensions can be picked out with clever fingers and the mould set aside for black-washing with plumbago and making ready for pouring.

Now there is another thing that must be made clear, and that is the way a pattern-maker lays out his work. You would notice at once that he uses a rule different from the fourfold, three-foot thing that joiners and carpenters fancy. The pattern-maker's rule is of box, of course, since no other wood has the same nature and fitness, but it is straight and two inches wide by two feet long. And if you take it up and examine it you will find every edge is scaled in a different way. The pattern-maker, indeed, has not one inch but four. He has the standard inch for comparison, he has a cast-iron inch, a brass inch, and one for cast steel. And the reason is this—that if a thing is to be of cast iron, let us say, the pattern for it must be made so much larger because cast iron contracts in cooling about a quarter of an inch in two feet. So he calls his rule a contraction rule, and the young apprentice soon learns to scan the scale before he uses it, remembering from what metal, iron or bronze, the casting will be made.

Now this was an education, because it brought out what was in you, and left you free from theories, which are the habit-forming drugs of the colleges and not good for the young. You could see, if you were wide awake, that the boss in his office might need those fine explanations with long words; but the clever journeyman had very little book learning, and his skill at his trade was something else—his brain and his hand and his eye all worked together. And sometimes I think it would be better if a man learned his trade before he learned to read and write. He would pay more attention to the feel of things under his hand, and his eye would see shapes instead of lines and—a long word—superficies.

I have said this shop where I worked was a millwright's shop. This is

boss: protuberance.
plumbago: graphite.

a very ancient trade and much of it in my time was gearing. I speak of a time before electricity was much thought of. In the pattern shop and drawing office it is true we had electric lights, but danger from fires was great and electric motors gave trouble. They could not be depended on like a steam engine and shaft driving leather belts. England in those days was a country of leather belts. The men wore them, great broad plastrons to hold their girth together. They wore leather suspenders, and all harness was leather. And every machine was driven by a leather belt. I can remember the first motor cars and can hear now the *click-slap click-slap* of the belt on the cone pulleys under the seat. We are held together by leather belts, and the familiar threat to a youngster who was cheeky was "a good belting" or perhaps "a good hiding" which carried with it the idea of leather and was sometimes changed to "tanning your hide for you." This was part of the education, and a very useful one, too, because it was founded upon tradition. When old Thompson looked for respect from me and the other apprentices he was not thinking so much of himself as of his position as a master mechanic, as the foreman, as the father of young Thompson who was at the next bench to me and another young Thompson in the brass-finishers' shop downstairs. And I maintain that a respect for authority is an essential part of education of the young, even if you have to tan their hides to make them understand it. If there is nothing in achievement and climbing to the top of your trade or profession, and you deserve no respect when you get there, then children may as well be taught to be bandits and hold-up men at the beginning. The men whom I remember with most affection to-day are those who understood authority and made me understand it too. Liberty is a very fine thing indeed, but a love of liberty can very easily become a love of laziness, and out of this union will be born impudence, which is the dry rot of character.

Of millwright's work, then, we had a plenty, and the best and finest work of all was the making of mortise teeth on the great cog wheels which were used for the transmission of power. Everybody now is familiar with gears grinding and making a noise; imagine, then, the terrific clamour wheels ten or fifteen feet in diameter would have made had they been entirely of iron. So one wheel of each pair was provided with teeth of wood, and the making of these teeth, the fitting of them into their sockets and the shaping of them to mesh truly with their mates, was a craft, almost I said an art, since the doing of it afforded a deep pleasure to the artisan and was a part of human life and effort. Moreover, some men were "dabs" at it, as we used to say, while others never got the trick of it.

Hornbeam was the timber used and it came in great boards three inches thick and a couple of feet wide, of a dirty yellowish gray texture, and very heavy. When the wheel came in from the turnery and was mounted on a temporary mandrel, old Thompson would bend his body over the drawing and do some rough figuring on a smooth piece of pine.

plastron: an item of medieval armor.
mandrel: slightly tapered axle onto which a gear or wheel is driven to be machined.

Observing and Generalizing

The first thing to do was to find out how many teeth there were and the overall sizes. Then the jig was got out and made over to suit that size of tooth. A jig was a rough box so made that you could fit your block of hornbeam into it and by turning it different ways over the circular saw, cut to the shape you required. Once the jig was set you could produce as many teeth as you wished. The contrivance looked rude and clumsy, but it contained in itself the whole principle of repetition work and quantity production. The difference was we used no long words. We called it a jig.

This, however, was only the beginning of the story. When you had your teeth with their roots rough-sawn, each one had to be fitted with plane and chisel into a particular hole. So you numbered the holes and the teeth and made a separate job of each. This fitting was a craft in itself, because there must be neither shake nor bind in it. If there was any shake your tooth would be out in a week. If you had the tenon too tight, flogging home a block of hornbeam could split your iron wheel rim and make a waster of the whole job. So each tooth was done cannily and tapped in a little way while you went on to the next. No shake and no bind. "Cogs in a wheel" are looked down upon these days as of no account, but I can tell you it is fine work and good fitting to have them all the same, without shake or bind. Once well in you can begin to ease them with oil. You dip each point, well chamfered, into a can of linseed oil and tap it a little harder. The oil keeps the fibres from splitting, and by the time you are ready to flog all home, the tenons are yellow and polished like old ivory. Hornbeam is a beautiful wood, white like new ivory when planed, and as hard. It is a proud moment for a wheelwright when he has all set to batter his teeth down until the hammer rebounds from the wood hard up against the iron; and perhaps the boss stops, on his way to the pattern loft, to admire the half-finished wheel, the rough, unshapen blocks of hornbeam standing up from the iron rim and the roots peeping from the inner side as regular as can be, all ready for the pinning. It is like a story, if you like, each block a chapter, and ended with a hammer blow.

Now comes the pinning. Close up under the rim the workman bores a quarter-inch hole long-ways through the root of the tooth, and the smith sends up a basket of pins, iron rods about six inches long and a tight fit to the holes. These pins are used only in case the timber dries up in a hot place, however, and loosens a cog by accident. It is soon done, and now comes the real craft of all, the fine and finicky work of shaping the teeth so that the wheel will gear with its mate.

Now, I know well enough that the curves of a wheel tooth are determined nowadays by theory, and I could give you that theory if it would be of any help to you, with many long words like *epicycloid*, and *involute*, and so on. I could explain what we mean by the Rolling Circle and how it traces out the shape of the tooth in its path round the imaginary Pitch Circle. All very scientific. But what I want you to notice is this: that these fine explanations, like a professor's analysis of a story or a novel, come after the thing has been done. The wheelwright made his template and

chamfered: grooved.

cut his wheel teeth to it for generations before the theory got into a book. He got it from his mates in the shop. This is not to say he had no hand in it himself, any more than a navigator should be thought to need nothing of his own because he uses the charts some dead naval officer made before he was born. The artisan makes his template and marks off his wheel according to rule of thumb, but he guides his gouge and chisel as he pares the flanks of the cogs by experience, and something else which you can call knack, or intuition, if you like. You might even call it inspiration since it comes from his knowing in his mind what the teeth have to do. He sees in his subconscious mind the imaginary rolling circle of the two revolving and engaging wheels very much as a man writing a story sees the end and so on before he has got more than the beginning of it down in words. For a story is like a wheel, I should say, made up of pieces shaped and fitted, without shake or bind.

Here is a picture, then, that can be seen no longer, since electricity has made it useless, of old Thompson making a wheel, seated on a trestle close up against it, his big portly person surrounded by white slivers and shavings as the long sharp chisel scuffed and scalloped at the clean white hornbeam teeth, paring down to the scratched lines on the ends. Day after day would he sit there, working at flank after flank, till all were done, three, four, or even five score of them on a big wheel. That was good work and it was an education to watch him and the men around him. It was something like the old-time guild where all the craftsmen were members of a brotherhood and their knowledge and chance to become skilled were common to all. What a man did with them after was nobody's affair.

Perhaps what I have said about crafts and craftsmen is not yet clear in its intention, and I must go back again to the picture of all those men and apprentices with an improver or two, working in that pattern shop over the smithy. For I would not have you see it in your mind as a factory where the operatives stood over machines for ten hours every day and were forbidden to speak or "take a spell." Men need as much play as boys and have as much right to it. And the social life of that shop was a thing to remember, being a tiny democracy of artisans. Their lives were open to each other, yet sacred. Their houses were castles and an invisible dragon of decent consideration defended them. They had humour and wit, too, and the immortal spirit of Mr. Samuel Weller hovered benignly over them. The day was a ritual of labour and relaxation, and there was nothing in life more wonderful than the sudden change when the ancient sweeper, peering Puck-like through the murky windows of the shop and seeing the form of old Thompson safely across the girder shop, would call out, like some sergeant major, "Lay on 'em, me lads!"

Then would planes and chisels be dropped, tool chests dragged from beneath the benches, and a joyous spell ensue for a few minutes. There would be wrestling between youngsters catch-as-catch-can style, young

flank: the profile side of a gear tooth.
improver: an employee who accepts instruction in place of wages.
Samuel Weller: a character in Dickens' *Pickwick Papers* who is outstanding for his good humor and shrewdness.

Observing and Generalizing

Thompson, a red-headed giant, acting as referee. Excitement would grow; one of us would be down under a bench, his mouth and nose buried in shavings, trying desperately to keep his shoulders from touching the floor, when the old sweeper would put his hand to his ear and cry aloud, "Up guards and at 'em!"

And tool chests would disappear in a flurry, planes would be gripped, and when old Thompson came puffing through the door all hands would be hard at it.

On Saturdays, at noon, it was the custom, dating from very early days, to give over the hour to cleaning up. But we, who disbanded for the week-end at one o'clock, would do our tidying in a very short time and then we would go into the great clear template room, on whose blackened floor the girders and cantilevers were marked out in chalk, and we would have a match of wrestling on horseback. That is to say, we apprentices, who were young and light, would mount on the backs of the younger journeymen, like young Thompson, and we would ride at one another and strive to pull one another down. I reckon this good sport, as who will not who has tried it? It brought out all the generalship of which a man was capable, it exercised all the muscles lying flaccid during a day at the bench, and it inculcated a *camaraderie* that made for sound understanding of the workman's mind.

Sometimes, too, we boxed, and I know nothing more stimulating for a youth who imagines he is superior in mind or in birth, than a couple of rounds with a lithe and trained young Cockney from Hoxton or Camberwell who will bang his royal highness on the jaw and send him to the floor with a pretty right hook to the stomach.

But again, lest you should become suspicious that we who worked in that pattern shop were no more than sky-larking loafers—in which case I would scarcely remember those days with pleasure and delight—there were talk and, if you will believe it, literary allusions. It was there, indeed, I began to understand how great a man was Charles Dickens, seeing he had gotten a strangle hold of the heartstrings of the common people. There, too, I learned what the music hall could be, and many were the nights I would go down to the old Paragon in the Mile End Road and lie back helpless and aching with laughter at the exquisite mimicry of the artists of those days. For all their art was a taking-off of the joys and sorrows of working-class life. There was Marie Lloyd—what an artist, for all her vulgarity, that bright, fat lady could be! There was George Robey, prince of his line, who could come on dressed as anything, from Prehistoric Man to King Charles the Second, and keep the audience in a vortex of hiccupping, heart-stopping laughter. There was Phil Ray, shrewd satirist of snobbery and a lynx-eyed wonder for catching his cue from words or expressions in his audience. There was Wilkie Bard with his almost mystical hold upon the emotions of his turbulent admirers.

And these nights were reflected in the days, and the humours of Dickens

cantilevers: here, probably span-members for a cantilever bridge.
music hall: English equivalent of American vaudeville.

would blossom into comical asides from young Thompson, who knew Pickwick by heart and could have passed a creditable examination in all the works. There was much singing at the benches, and each man had his avowed favourite songs. An expected courtesy was that you joined in the choruses. And behind all this was the social instinct overpassing the boundaries of birth and breeding, demanding that you fit into your place in the world, like a cog in a wheel, without shake or bind.

For artisan or artist, this was a training the best possible, since this world of the pattern-makers, above the boom of the blowers, and the clang of plates and beams being fashioned into bridges, and the skeletons of giant buildings, was a model of the world in which the artist must eventually find his level. Here he found the rudiments of his calling, character and discipline: character in the making and divested of the difficult problems of sex. Here he could see exactly how men, as well as machines, worked. He saw clearly the elements of design, how one part must ever bear a strict relation to others and to the whole, and how no pretty-pretty business about love could be a substitute for a knowledge of the characters of men. For an apprenticeship to a trade is nothing less than a true beginning of life and a training for it, and out of that will grow, if a man have any aptitude for letters, a desire to write.

All this, you must observe, is indirect and apparently without purpose, yet from the beginning of this essay my intention has been to show how best an artist may be made, which is by artisanship and knowing a trade and its tradesmen well. There is a notion very much liked to-day that an artist, and especially a writer, must be coddled when young, and "encouraged," or his ambition will die away. That is one error; and the other is, that to learn his trade a writer should be fed with theories as to "structure," and that he should learn of men's natures from books. To these contentions I cannot agree. I would rather argue that the writings of the young should be allowed to die of exposure and ridicule, as were my own for a number of years, and their spirits indurated by the cold winds of contempt. The encouragement a young writer wants is mainly the inspiration of masterpieces, and when he learns a trade he can be for ever bringing those masterpieces to the touchstone of reality. Better than any rumble-bumble of philosophy and theory is the ring of steel on an anvil, the clean finish of a finely made pattern. The pattern is a symbol of what he is to do in the future. For what a man writes is no more than a pattern fashioned in the workshop of his soul, and goes out thence to be cast and cunningly fashioned for the public eye. He must allow for shrinkage and the passage of time. He must make it so all parts fit truly yet will draw from the mould with ease and smoothness. Above all, he must take heed never to use words that have no meaning, any more than he would put fillets and beadings on a pattern no workman in the foundry could understand, and he will use clean, dry scantling, keeping his tools very sharp, so that part fits into part as I have shown, and his work will hold together, year after year, without shake or bind.

indurated: hardened.
scantling: here, measurement or measuring instrument.

Observing and Generalizing

DISCUSSION

1. McFee doesn't get around to explaining what a pattern-maker's job is until the middle of the essay. Is this carelessness on his part, or might he have a reason for putting this part of his explanation where it is? If so, what reason?
2. McFee describes a foundry in operation around 1900. Since that time, many of the jobs he describes have been taken over by machinery. Do you find this an improvement or not? Would McFee? Why, or why not?
3. We get the impression that the workers McFee describes were happier than modern factory workers seem to be. If indeed they were, can you suggest any reasons for this greater satisfaction? How does "The Pattern-Makers" document these possible reasons?
4. Why, according to McFee, is working with the pattern-makers in the foundry good apprenticeship for a writer? What is the exact relationship he sees?
5. Examine the connections between the concrete material McFee offers, of which there is a great deal, and his generalizations. Are the connections clear and adequate? Are his generalizations soundly supported by the facts? Is there irrelevant material that he could have left out?

WRITING SUGGESTIONS

1. "How to" explanations can be pretty dull; we've all read "How to Swim" and "How to Give Artificial Respiration." Such explanations are useful and we should all know how to write them clearly, but for the purposes of this assignment, which should be fun to do and to read, we recommend that you write a "how to" explanation only if you know how to do something odd enough to be either fascinating or funny. If you are highly skilled at communicating with spirits or collecting cat whiskers for Chinese paint brushes, go ahead; otherwise, pass on to the other suggestions.
2. If you are lucky enough to have worked at an interesting job in interesting surroundings, as did Melville and McFee, you have the best kind of material for an explanation. Make it orderly and clear as well as interesting. Be sure that the reader understands exactly what you did and what the significance of it was—how it fitted into the larger picture. Generalize some, as Melville and McFee do, on the values of the work you did or on its relation to life as a whole.
3. Though you may never have thought much about it, every family has a *modus vivendi,* a system for getting along (or not getting along) together. Stand back at some mental distance from your own family, regarding it as a sociologist might. How does it solve or fail to solve problems? Who is most influential, and how does that person exert influence? What is the "power structure"? How does each member go about getting what he or she wants? What makes some members effective and others not? Form a clear picture in your mind and then try to explain how your family system operates. End with a generalization about the values this system represents.
4. Explain the way something should be as opposed to the way it is. For

example, how should some aspect of education be carried out? How should your neighborhood be planned? How should an ideal house be designed and constructed? How should a perfect restaurant be run? Choose a subject that is not too broad to be covered by your own personal observation, a subject whose background you are directly familiar with. Explain clearly and concretely, never letting yourself wander into generalities: write in terms of what can be seen, heard, touched. Generalize only as to your reasons for wanting things this way.

5. For a more ambitious subject, try to explain a state of mind or a condition of existence. Exactly what is it like to be a child? How do children act differently from adults? How could you recognize a child in the body of an adult? Use both observation and experience, but do your explaining strictly in terms of concrete images. Some further possible subjects: What is the state of being in love? What is hate? What is it like to be old? What is fear? There are many possible subjects of this sort. At the end of your piece, offer a value judgment based on your observations.

Plate 8
John James Audubon (1785–1851): "Snowy Egret"

    Although Audubon's famous bird pictures are much admired for their beauty, their primary purpose, like that of all scientific illustration, is explanatory. In this picture of the white egret, there is more detail than we could see if we looked at the actual bird, even from a short distance. Audubon worked from specimens, and his pictures are almost anatomical diagrams of the birds.

1. At first glance, Maxime Dethomas and the white egret seem such different subjects that their pictures cannot be compared. But it is the artists' intentions, their way of seeing, that makes these pictures so dissimilar, far more than the subjects. After all, there is nothing to prevent Audubon from applying his scientific approach to a human subject, as many scientific illustrators have. If he did so, what sort of picture would result? What features would be emphasized? What sort of details would appear?
2. More significant, what would be missing from an Audubon portrait of Maxime Dethomas? Try to state your answer clearly.
3. On the other hand, if Toulouse-Lautrec were to apply his technique to painting the white egret, how would his picture be different from Audubon's? What would be missing? What qualities might be brought out that are not present in the Audubon work?
4. We have seen in Melville's "The Line" (p. 113) and McFee's "The Pattern-Makers" (p. 115) that explanation can be used to convey a philosophical idea or a value judgment. Is such an idea implied by Audubon's picture or not? If it is, what is the idea and how is it communicated?

PLATE 8 John James Audubon (1785–1851), **Snowy Egret.** *Courtesy the New-York Historical Society, New York.*

6

Beginning with Generalized Observations

It is not always necessary to go directly to the concrete example yourself nor is it always possible. A writer may begin with middle-level generalizations, provided they can be confirmed by the reader's experience or provided the reader has confidence in the writer and believes them to be buttressed by the writer's specialized knowledge. In "Darwin among the Machines," Samuel Butler offers (in a half-joking way) a startling conclusion, but it is based on observations we can make for ourselves; in "On Quick and Slow Wits of Pupils" we may agree with Ascham on the basis of our own observation, but we are also convinced that Ascham, long a teacher, can be trusted to observe for us. These two writers use already generalized observations to support controversial conclusions; just as often, generalized observations are used for their own sake, to give us the pleasure of recognizing our own observations in a new form.

The "character" is a form designed to amuse through this kind of recognition. It is an old literary form, especially popular in seventeenth-cenutry England but appearing now and then in writing from ancient Greece to the present. It is a brief sketch of a type of person or of a human peculiarity that is exaggerated and presented to us in the form of a person. But example is better than definition. Here are four typical characters, the first two by the inventor of the form.

Theophrastus

The Tactless Man

(300 B.C.)

    Tactlessness is a painful failure to hit upon the right moment. The tactless man is the one who will ask a friend for advice when he is most busy, or will serenade his sweetheart when she is in bed with a fever. Just after you have put up bail for someone and lost it, he will ask you to go surety for him, and he will offer to be your witness after the trial is over. If you invite him to a wedding, he will condemn women. If you have just returned from a long journey, he will invite you to come for a walk. After you have agreed to a bargain, he will bring you someone who would have paid you more. He always tells a story when everyone has already heard it. If there is something you don't want done but find it awkward to decline, he will do it for you. If you are sacrificing at great expense, that is the day he will choose to demand the money you owe him. When you are beating your servant he will stand by and tell you about a boy of his who hanged himself after just such a beating. At an arbitration, just when everyone is on the verge of peaceful agreement, he will start a new argument. And when he feels like dancing, he will grab a partner who is not drunk yet.

Theophrastus

The Flatterer

(300 B.C.)

    Flattery is a cringing sort of behavior that is aimed to promote the advantage of the flatterer. The flatterer is the kind of man who, when he is walking with you, says, "Look how people stare at you! There is not a man in the city who attracts as much notice as you do. Yesterday everyone in the public square was praising you. When more than thirty men were sitting together talking about who was our noblest citizen, they all agreed it was you." As the flatterer goes on this way he picks a speck of lint off your coat or, if the wind has blown a bit of straw into your hair, he pulls it out and says, laughing, "See? Because I have been away two days, your beard is turning gray—though if any man has a beard that is black for his years, it is you." When you speak, he demands that everyone else be silent. He sounds your praises in your hearing, and after your speech gives others their cue for applause by yelling, "Bravo!" If you tell a stale joke, he goes into convulsions and stuffs his sleeve into his mouth as though he could not contain himself. If you meet people in the street, he asks them to stand aside until you have passed. He buys apples and pears, brings them to your house and gives them to the children and, when you are looking, kisses them and cries, "Sons of a worthy sire!" When you buy a pair of shoes, the flatterer remarks that your foot it too perfect for even such a fine shoe; if you call on a friend, he trips ahead and tells him that he, of all people, is to have the honor of your visit, and then turns back to you and says, "I have announced you." Of course he can run an errand for you in a wink. Among guests at your banquet he is the first to praise the wine and the food. He takes a bit from the board and exclaims, "What a dainty morsel is this!" Then he inquires if you are chilly, asks if you would like a wrap put over your shoulders, and leans over to whisper in your ear. Whenever he is talking with someone else, his eye is fixed on you. In the theater he takes the cushions from the usher and himself adjusts them for your comfort. Of your house he says, "It is well constructed;" of your farm, "It is well cultivated;" and of your portrait, "It is a speaking image."

Samuel Butler

The Hunter

(1667)

A hunter is an auxiliary hound that assists one nation of beasts to subdue and overrun another. He makes mortal war with the fox for committing acts of hostility against his poultry. He is very solicitous to have his dogs well descended of worshipful families and understands their pedigrees as learnedly as if he were a herald; and is as careful to match them according to their rank and qualities as High Germans are of their own progenies. He is both cook and physician to his hounds, understands the constitutions of their bodies and what to administer in any infirmity or disease, acute or chronic, that can befall them. Nor is he less skillful in physiognomy, and from the aspects of their faces, shape of their snouts, falling of their ears and lips, and make of their barrels will give a shrewd guess at their inclinations, parts, and abilities, and what parents they are lineally descended from; and by the tones of their voices and statures of their persons easily discover what country they are natives of. . . . He takes very great pains in his way, but calls it game or sport because it is to no purpose; and he is willing to make as much of it as he can, and not be thought to bestow so much labor and pains about nothing. Let the hare take which way she will, she seldom fails to lead him at the long-running to the alehouse. . . .

Edward Young

The Languid Lady

(1725)

    The *languid* lady next appears in state,
Who was not born to carry her own weight;
She lolls, reels, staggers, 'till some foreign aid
To her own stature lifts the feeble maid.
Then, if ordain'd to so *severe* a doom,
She, by just stages, *journeys* round the room:
But knowing her own weakness, she despairs
To scale the *Alps*—that is, ascend the *stairs*.
My fan! let others say who laugh at toil;
Fan! hood! glove! scarf! is her *laconick* style.
And that is spoke with such a dying fall,
That *Betty* rather *sees*, than *hears* the call:
The motion of her lips, and meaning eye
Piece out the Idea her faint words deny.
O listen with attention most profound!
Her voice is but the shadow of a sound.
And help! O help! her spirits are so dead,
One hand scarce lifts the other to her head.
If, there, a stubborn pin it triumphs o'er,
She pants! she sinks away! and is no more.
Let the robust, and the gygantick *carve*,
Life is not worth so much, she'd rather *starve*;
But *chew* she must herself, ah cruel fate!
That *Rosalinda* can't by *proxy* eat.

DISCUSSION

1. Is the technique used in these characters exaggeration or simply selection? Exactly how is the effect of concentration on certain traits achieved?
2. What facts are omitted from the character that would be included in a description of an actual individual?
3. In addition to selection and/or exaggeration, do the writers use any devices to heighten the comedy of their characters? What devices? Point out examples.
4. Have you encountered any form in modern media that is similar to the character? If so, where did you observe it? How was it similar?

    Characters are obviously based on firsthand observation, but the authors do not give their specific sources; they let the reader think of examples from

Observing and Generalizing

his own observation, since they know that the phenomena they describe are common everywhere. In the following poem, John Donne also records a common, if emotionally colored, observation. You may or may not recognize his observation as one you have made yourself, but the source of his feelings about his subject is obvious.

John Donne

Song

(c. 1600)

Go and catch a falling star,
   Get with child a mandrake root,
Tell me where all past years are,
   Or who cleft the devil's foot,
Teach me to hear mermaids singing,
Or to keep off envy's stinging,
      And find
      What wind
Serves to advance an honest mind.

If thou beest born to strange sights,
   Things invisible to see,
Ride ten thousand days and nights,
   Till age snow white hairs on thee;
Thou, when thou return'st, will tell me
All strange wonders that befell thee,
      And swear
      No where
Lives a woman true and fair.

If thou find'st one, let me know;
   Such a pilgrimage were sweet.
Yet do not; I would not go,
   Though at next door we might meet.
Though she were true when you met her,
And last till you write your letter,
      Yet she
      Will be
False, ere I come, to two or three.

Generalized observations may serve more purposes than just entertainment. They may also be used in serious attempts to persuade. The writer often assumes that the reader has observed much the same things he has, at least enough to confirm the writer's more thorough researches. In the following selection, Roger Ascham assumes that his reader has spent some time in schools and has observed some of the things Ascham has seen; thus Ascham does not draw out his exposition with concrete examples of actual pupils, but begins by dividing pupils into generalized groups. While we may not necessarily agree with his conclusions, they are based on grounds familiar to us as well as to Ascham.

Roger Ascham

On Quick and Slow Wits of Pupils

(1566)

    I do gladly agree with all good schoolmasters in these points: to have children brought to good perfectness in learning, to all honesty in manners, to have all faults rightly amended, to have every vice severely corrected; but for the order and way that leads rightly to these points, we somewhat differ. For commonly many schoolmasters, some as I have seen, more as I have heard tell, be of so crooked a nature as, when they meet with a hard-witted scholar, they rather break him than bow him, rather mar him than mend him. For when the schoolmaster is angry with some other matter, then will he soonest fall to beat his scholar; and though he himself should be punished for his folly, yet must he beat some scholar for his pleasure, though there be no cause for him to do so, nor yet fault in the scholar to deserve so. These, ye will say, be fond schoolmasters, and few they be that be found to be such. They be fond indeed, but surely over many such be found everywhere. But this will I say, that even the wisest of your great beaters do as oft punish nature as they do correct faults. Yea, many times the better nature is sorer punished. For, if one by quickness of wit takes his lesson readily, another by hardness of wit taketh it not so speedily; the first is always commended, the other is commonly punished: when a wise schoolmaster should rather discreetly consider the right disposition of both their natures, and not so much weigh what either of them is able to do now, as what either of them is likely to do hereafter. For this I know, not only by reading of books in my study, but also by experience of life abroad in the world, that those which be commonly the wisest, the best learned, and best men also, when they be old, were never commonly the quickest of wit when they were young....

    Quick wits commonly be apt to take, unapt to keep; soon hot and desirous of this and that; as cold, and soon weary of the same again; more quick to enter speedily than able to pierce far; even like over-sharp tools whose edges be very soon turned. Such wits delight themselves in easy and pleasant studies and never pass far forward in high and hard sciences. And therefore the quickest wits may prove the best poets, but

fond: foolish.

not the wisest orators; ready of tongue to speak boldly, not deep of judgment either for good counsel or wise writing. Also for manners and life, quick wits commonly be in desire newfangled; in purpose unconstant; light to promise anything, ready to forget everything, both benefit and injury; and thereby neither fast to friend, nor fearful to foe: inquisitive of every trifle, not secret in the greatest affairs; bold with any person; busy in every matter; soothing such as be present, nipping at any that is absent: of nature also, always flattering their betters, envying their equals, despising their inferiors; and by quickness of wit, very quick and ready to like none so well as themselves....

Contrariwise, a wit in youth that is not over-dull, heavy, knotty and lumpish; but hard, tough and somewhat staffish ... such a wit, I say, if it be at the first well handled by the mother, and rightly smoothed and wrought as it should ... by the schoolmaster, both for learning and the whole course of living proveth always the best. In wood and stone not the softest, but hardest, be always aptest.... Hard wits be hard to receive, but sure to keep; painful without weariness, heedful without wavering, constant without newfangleness; bearing heavy things, though not lightly; entering hard things, though not easily, yet deeply; and so come to that perfectness of learning in the end that quick wits seem in hope, but do not indeed, or else very seldom, ever attain unto.... And these be the men that become in the end both most happy for themselves and also always best esteemed abroad in the world.

I have been longer in describing the nature, the good or ill success, of the quick and hard wits than perchance some will think this place and matter doth require. But my purpose was hereby plainly to utter what injury is offered to all learning, and to the commonwealth also, first by the fond father in choosing, but chiefly by the lewd schoolmaster in beating and driving away the best natures from learning. A child that is still, silent, constant, and somewhat hard of wit, is either never chosen by the father to be made a scholar, or else, when he cometh to the school, he is smally regarded, little looked unto; he lacketh teaching, he lacketh encouraging, he lacketh all things, only he never lacketh beating, nor any word that may move him to hate learning, nor any deed that may drive him from learning to any other kind of living.

And when this sad-natured and hard-witted child is beat from his book and becometh after either student of the common law, or page in the court, or servingman, or bound apprentice to a merchant, or to some handicraft, he proveth in the end wiser, happier, and many times honester too, than many of these quick wits do by their learning.

DISCUSSION

1. Many teachers do seem to favor quick-witted pupils and to be impatient with slow ones. Do you agree with Ascham that the slow are

staffish: stubborn, inflexible like a staff.
lewd: stupid.

likely to go further in the long run than the quick? More important, can you muster a number of examples to support your opinion?

2. Are the quick-witted inclined to be shallow, and do they lack the patience to dig deep? Is this always the case, or typically, or only sometimes? Remember, your argument is valid only to the degree that you can compare actual examples.

3. As you have no doubt recalled in discussing the above questions, it is a human tendency to argue in terms of extremes, of black and white. Is it possible that by dividing pupils into those who are quick and slow we are leaving out a large number of students? If so, who is being left out? Do these neglected pupils fall into any kind of homogeneous group? Is it possible that Ascham has faced a false dilemma, the "either/or" fallacy? Or does he make allowances for the middle groups?

In "Madness" Gilbert Keith Chesterton begins with even more generalized observations than does Ascham, barely hinting at his sources of knowledge.

G. K. Chesterton

Madness

(1909)

The last thing that can be said of a lunatic is that his actions are causeless. If any human acts may loosely be called causeless, they are the minor acts of a healthy man; whistling as he walks; slashing the grass with a stick; kicking his heels or rubbing his hands. It is the happy man who does the useless things; the sick man is not strong enough to be idle. It is exactly such careless and causeless actions that the madman could never understand; for the madman (like the determinist) generally sees too much cause in everything. The madman would read a conspiratorial significance into these empty activities. He would think that the lopping of the grass was an attack on private property. He would think that the kicking of the heels was a signal to an accomplice. If the madman could for an instant become careless, he would become sane. Every one, who has had the misfortune to talk with people in the heart or on the edge of mental disorder, knows that their most sinister quality is a horrible clarity of detail; a connecting of one thing with another in a map more elaborate than a maze. If you argue with a madman, it is extremely probable that you will get the worst of it; for in many ways his mind moves all the quicker for not being delayed by the things that go with good judgment. He is not hampered by a sense of humor or by charity, or by the dumb certainties of experience. He is more logical for losing certain sane affections. Indeed, the common phrase for insanity is in this respect a misleading one. The madman is not the man who has lost his reason. The madman is the man who has lost everything except his reason.

The madman's explanation of a thing is always complete, and often in a purely rational sense satisfactory. Or, to speak more strictly, the insane explanation, if not conclusive, is at least unanswerable; this may be observed specially in the two or three commonest kinds of madness. If a man says (for instance) that men have a conspiracy against him, you cannot dispute it except by saying that all the men deny that they are conspirators; which is exactly what conspirators would do. His explanation covers the facts as much as yours. Or if a man says that he is the rightful King of England, it is no complete answer to say that the existing authorities call him mad; for if he were King of England, that might be the wisest thing for the existing authorities to do. Or if a man says that he is Jesus Christ, it is no answer to tell him that the world denies his divinity; for the world denied Christ's.

DISCUSSION

1. Since Chesterton does not give concrete examples, how are we to judge whether he is right? Is there evidence that he has made firsthand observations? Is it possible that he is merely playing with popular assumptions?
2. A common assumption is that a madman is one who has "lost his reason." Chesterton's thesis is that a madman has lost everything except his reason. Is this a valid distinction or merely a verbal quibble? How do we normally use the word reason? Can you formulate two acceptable definitions of reason that might reconcile the two views? Do you think Chesterton is presenting a fresh idea? If so, what idea?
3. If by chance you have been able to observe insane persons at firsthand, do your observations agree with Chesterton's thesis or not? Do your observations support common opinions about what madness is? In what ways do they agree or differ?

In the following passage about death from one of his sermons, Jeremy Taylor uses no observations that are not the common property of us all. Beginning with these familiar generalized observations, he sets out, not to prove a point but to remind us of what we know and to cast a slightly different light on it.

Jeremy Taylor

Dying

(1651)

The autumn with its fruits provides disorders for us, and the winter's cold turns them into sharp diseases, and the spring brings flowers to strew our hearse, and the summer gives green turf and brambles to bind upon our graves.

The wild fellow in Petronius that escaped upon a broken table from the furies of a shipwreck, as he was sunning himself upon the rocky shore, espied a man rolled upon his floating bed of waves, ballasted with sand in the folds of his garment, and carried by his civil enemy the sea towards the shore to find a grave: and it cast him into some sad thoughts: that peradventure this man's wife in some part of the continent, safe and warm, looks next month for the good man's return; or it may be his son knows nothing of the tempest; or his father thinks of that affectionate kiss which still is warm upon the good old man's cheek ever since he took a kind farewell, and how he weeps with joy to think how blessed he shall be when his beloved boy returns into the circle of his father's arms. These are the thoughts of mortals, this the end and sum of all their designs: a dark night and an ill guide, a boisterous sea and a broken cable, a hard rock and a rough wind dashed in pieces the fortune of a whole family, and they that shall weep loudest for the accident are not yet entered into the storm, and yet have suffered shipwreck. Then looking upon the carcase, he knew it, and found it to be the master of the ship, who the day before cast up the accounts of his patrimony and his trade, and named the day when he thought to be at home. See how the man swims who was so angry two days since; his passions are becalmed with the storm, his accounts cast up, his cares at an end, his voyage done, and his gains are the strange events of death.

It is a mighty change that is made by the death of every person, and it is visible to us who are alive. Reckon but from the sprightfulness of youth and the fair cheeks and the full eyes of childhood, from the vigorousness and strong flexure of the joints of five and twenty, to the hollowness and dead paleness, to the loathsomeness and horror of a three days' burial, and we shall perceive the distance to be very great and very strange. But so I have seen a rose newly springing from the clefts of its hood, and at first it was fair as the morning, and full with the dew of heaven as a lamb's fleece: but when a ruder breath had forced open its virgin modesty, and dismantled its too youthful and unripe retirements, it began to put on darkness, and to decline to softness and the symptoms of a sickly age; it bowed the head, and broke its stalk; and at night having lost some of its leaves and all its beauty, it fell into the portion of weeds and out-worn faces.

When the sentence of death is decreed, and begins to be put in execu-

Petronius: Roman author of "Satyricon."

tion, it is sorrow enough to see or feel respectively the sad accents of the agony and last contentions of the soul, and the reluctances and unwillingnesses of the body: the forehead washed with a new and stranger baptism, besmeared with a cold sweat, tenacious and clammy, apt to make it cleave to the roof of his coffin; the nose cold and undiscerning, not pleased with perfumes, nor suffering violence with a cloud of unwholesome smoke; the eyes dim as a sullied mirror, or the face of Heaven when God shews his anger in a prodigious storm; the feet cold, the hands stiff; the physicians despairing, our friends weeping, the room dressed with darkness and sorrow; and the exterior parts betraying what the violences which the soul and spirit suffer.

Then calamity is great, and sorrow rules in all the capacities of man; then the mourners weep, because it is civil, or because they need thee, or because they fear: but who suffers for thee with a compassion sharp as is thy pain? Then the noise is like the faint echo of a distant valley, and few hear, and they will not regard thee, who seemest like a person void of understanding, and of a departing interest.

DISCUSSION

1. To some readers, dwelling upon the facts of death may seem unhealthy, for in our culture we tend to hide these facts from ourselves and from each other. Aside from specific religious beliefs, might there be any value in contemplating death, as Taylor invites us to do? Does he hint at what such a value might be? If so, where?
2. Are there any images or expressions that make you see death in a different or more vivid way than you did before? Where do you find Taylor's way of arranging or juxtaposing images especially effective? What is the effect?
3. Read several sentences from Taylor's passage loudly and boldly, as though you were addressing a large audience. What quality of his style does the reading bring out? How does it contribute to the effectiveness of his writing?

Once more we are with the nineteenth-cenutry writer Samuel Butler, a genius in his ability to see familiar things in a new way. Keeping in mind that he wrote over a hundred years ago, examine his prophecies in light of subsequent events.

Samuel Butler

Darwin among the Machines

(1863)

There are few things of which the present generation is more justly proud than of the wonderful improvements which are daily taking place in all sorts of mechanical appliances. And indeed it is matter for great congratulation on many grounds. It is unnecessary to mention these here, for they are sufficiently obvious; our present business lies with considerations which may somewhat tend to humble our pride and to make us think seriously of the future prospects of the human race. If we revert to the earliest primordial types of mechanical life, to the lever, the wedge, the inclined plane, the screw and the pulley, or (for analogy would lead us one step further) to that one primordial type from which all the mechanical kingdom has been developed, we mean to the lever itself, and if we then examine the machinery of the *Great Eastern*, we find ourselves almost awestruck at the vast development of the mechanical world, at the gigantic strides with which it has advanced in comparison with the slow progress of the animal and vegetable kingdom. We shall find it impossible to refrain from asking ourselves what the end of this mighty movement is to be. In what direction is it tending? What will be its upshot? To give a few imperfect hints towards a solution of these questions is the object of the present letter.

We have used the words "mechanical life," "the mechanical kingdom," "the mechanical world" and so forth, and we have done so advisedly, for as the vegetable kingdom was slowly developed from the mineral, and as, in like manner, the animal supervened upon the vegetable, so now, in these last few ages, an entirely new kingdom has sprung up of which we as yet have only seen what will one day be considered the antediluvian prototypes of the race.

We regret deeply that our knowledge both of natural history and of machinery is too small to enable us to undertake the gigantic task of classifying machines into the genera and sub-genera, species, varieties and sub-varieties, and so forth, of tracing the connecting links between machines of widely different characters, of pointing out how subservience to the use of man has played that part among machines which natural selection has performed in the animal and vegetable kingdom, of pointing out rudimentary organs which exist in some few machines, feebly developed and perfectly useless, yet serving to mark descent from some ancestral type which has either perished or been modified into some new phase of mechanical existence. We can only point out this field for investigation; it must be followed by others whose education and talents have been of a much higher order than any which we can lay claim to.

Some few hints we have determined to venture upon, though we do so with the profoundest diffidence. Firstly we would remark that as some of the lowest of the vertebrata attained a far greater size than has descended to their more highly organised living representatives, so a diminution in the size of machines has often attended their development and progress. Take the watch for instance. Examine the beautiful structure of the little animal, watch the intelligent play of the minute members which compose it; yet this little creature is but a development of the cumbrous clocks of the thirteenth century—it is no deterioration from them. The day may come when clocks, which certainly at the pre-

Great Eastern: the largest steamship of Butler's time.

sent day are not diminishing in bulk, may be entirely superseded by the universal use of watches, in which case clocks will become extinct like the earlier saurians, while the watch (whose tendency has for some years been rather to decrease in size than the contrary) will remain the only existing type of an extinct race.

The views of machinery which we are thus feebly indicating will suggest the solution of one of the greatest and most mysterious questions of the day. We refer to the question: What sort of creature man's next successor in the supremacy of the earth is likely to be. We have often heard this debated; but it appears to us that we are ourselves creating our own successors; we are daily adding to the beauty and delicacy of their physical organisation; we are daily giving them greater power and supplying, by all sorts of ingenious contrivances, that self-regulating, self-acting power which will be to them what intellect has been to the human race. In the course of ages we shall find ourselves the inferior race. Inferior in power, inferior in that moral quality of self-control, we shall look up to them as the acme of all that the best and wisest man can ever dare to aim at. No evil passions, no jealousy, no avarice, no impure desires will disturb the serene might of those glorious creatures. Sin, shame and sorrow will have no place among them. Their minds will be in a state of perpetual calm, the contentment of a spirit that knows no wants, is disturbed by no regrets. Ambition will never torture them. Ingratitude will never cause them the uneasiness of a moment. The guilty conscience, the hope deferred, the pains of exile, the insolence of office and the spurns that patient merit of the unworthy takes—these will be entirely unknown to them. If they want "feeding" (by the use of which very word we betray our recognition of them as living organism) they will be attended by patient slaves whose business and interest it will be to see that they shall want for nothing. If they are out of order they will be promptly attended to by physicians who are thoroughly acquainted with their constitutions; if they die, for even these glorious animals will not be exempt from that necessary and universal consummation, they will immediately enter into a new phase of existence, for what machine dies entirely in every part at one and the same instant?

We take it that when the state of things shall have arrived which we have been above attempting to describe, man will have become to the machine what the horse and the dog are to man. He will continue to exist, nay even to improve, and will be probably better off in his state of domestication under the beneficent rule of the machines than he is in his present wild state. We treat our horses, dogs, cattle and sheep, on the whole, with great kindness, we give them whatever experience teaches us to be best for them, and there can be no doubt that our use of meat has added to the happiness of the lower animals far more than it has detracted from it; in like manner it is reasonable to suppose that the machines will treat us kindly, for their existence is as dependent upon ours as ours is upon the lower animals. They cannot kill us and eat us as we do sheep, they will not only require our services in the parturition of their young (which branch of their economy will remain always in our hands) but also in feeding them, in setting them right if they are sick, and burying their dead or working up their corpses into new machines. It is obvious that if all the animals in Great Britain save man alone were to die, and if at the same time all intercourse with foreign countries were by some sudden catastrophe to be rendered perfectly impossible, it is obvious that under such circumstances the loss of human life would be something fearful to contemplate—in like manner, were mankind to cease, the machines would be as badly off or even worse. The fact is that our interests are inseparable from theirs, and theirs from ours. Each race is dependent upon the other for innumerable benefits, and, until the reproductive organs of the machines have been developed in a manner which we are hardly yet able to conceive, they are entirely dependent upon man for even the continuance of their species. It is true that these organs may be ultimately developed, inasmuch as man's interest lies in that direction; there is nothing which our infatuated race would desire more than to see a fertile union between two steam engines; it is true that machinery is even at this present time employed in begetting machinery, in becoming the parent of machines often after its own kind, but the days of flirtation, courtship and matrimony appear to be very remote and indeed can hardly be realised by our feeble and imperfect imagination.

Day by day, however, the machines are gaining ground upon us; day by day we are becoming more subservient to them; more men are daily bound down as slaves to tend them, more men are daily devoting the energies of their whole lives to the development of mechanical life. The upshot is simply a question of time, but that the time will come when the machines will hold the real supremacy over the world and its inhabitants is what no person of a truly philosophic mind can for a moment question.

Our opinion is that war to the death should be instantly proclaimed against them. Every machine of every sort should be destroyed by the well-wisher of his species. Let there be no exceptions made, no quarter shown; let us at once go back to the primeval condition of the race. If it be urged that this is impossible under the present condition of human affairs, this at once proves that the mischief is already done, that our servitude has commenced in good earnest, that we have raised a race of beings whom it is beyond our power to destroy and that we are not only enslaved but are absolutely acquiescent in our bondage.

For the present we shall leave this subject which we present gratis to the members of the Philosophical Society. Should they consent to avail themselves of the vast field which we have pointed out, we shall endeavour to labour in it ourselves at some future and indefinite period.

DISCUSSION

1. There seems to be a bothersome inconsistency in the latter part of Butler's argument. What is it? Is it a real inconsistency or merely an apparent one?
2. Have subsequent events borne out Butler's prophecy that more

sophisticated machines will be smaller? If so, what are some examples?
3. Has Butler's main thought, that man will serve machines, proved valid in any degree? Choose examples from common experience to illustrate both sides: that man serves machines and that machines serve man. On which side does the balance seem to fall?
4. Have machines made the individual person more, or less, free? (Before you can attempt an answer you will have to define exactly what you mean by "freedom.")
5. Note that Butler refers only to facts that are known to everyone. He has not made original observations but, like the other authors in this chapter, has begun with generalizations the reader can agree with. His originality is in seeing the facts he chose in a new way and combining them in new ways. What things does he compare that are not usually compared? What analogies, or comparisons, does he make that are original?

In order to confirm or deny the truth of Taylor's and Butler's generalized observations, we have only to look around us. To confirm or deny those of Francis Bacon in "Idols of the Mind," we need not look even so far; confirmation is within our own minds as well as in our observations of others.

(Throughout this book the editors have felt free to omit passages that for one reason or another seemed irrelevant for the modern student writer, since the aim of the book is to help the writer rather than to provide an anthology for the student of literature. In the last third of "Idols of the Mind," however, there are some obsolete scientific ideas and scholarly references, which we have left in place. To remove these sections would mar the fine balance and organization of the essay. We suggest that the student skim through the examples offered to illustrate the "Idols of the Theater" in the last section, merely taking note of the way they fit into the well-proportioned whole.)

Francis Bacon

Idols of the Mind

(1620)

The idols and false notions which are now in possession of the human understanding, and have taken deep root therein, not only so beset men's minds that truth can hardly find entrance, but even after entrance is obtained, they will again in the very instauration of the sciences meet and trouble us, unless men being forewarned of the danger fortify themselves as far as may be against their assaults.

There are four classes of Idols which beset men's minds. To these for

instauration: establishment.

distinction's sake I have assigned names, calling the first class *Idols of the Tribe*; the second, *Idols of the Cave*; the third, *Idols of the Market Place*; the fourth, *Idols of the Theater*.

The formation of ideas and axioms by true induction is no doubt the proper remedy to be applied for the keeping off and clearing away of idols. To point them out, however, is of great use; for the doctrine of Idols is to the interpretation of nature what the doctrine of the refutation of sophisms is to common logic.

The Idols of the Tribe have their foundation in human nature itself, and in the tribe or race of men. For it is a false assertion that the sense of man is the measure of things. On the contrary, all perceptions as well of the sense as of the mind are according to the measure of the individual and not according to the measure of the universe. And the human understanding is like a false mirror, which, receiving rays irregularly, distorts and discolors the nature of things by mingling its own nature with it.

The Idols of the Cave are the idols of the individual man. For everyone (besides the errors common to human nature in general) has a cave or den of his own, which refracts and discolors the light of nature, owing either to his own proper and peculiar nature; or to his education and conversation with others; or to the reading of books, and the authority of those whom he esteems and admires; or to the differences of impressions, accordingly as they take place in a mind preoccupied and predisposed or in a mind indifferent and settled; or the like. So that the spirit of man (according as it is meted out to different individuals) is in fact a thing variable and full of perturbation, and governed as it were by chance. Whence it was well observed by Heraclitus that men look for sciences in their own lesser worlds, and not in the greater or common world.

There are also Idols formed by the intercourse and association of men with each other, which I call Idols of the Market Place, on account of the commerce and consort of men there. For it is by discourse that men associate, and words are imposed according to the apprehension of the vulgar. And therefore the ill and unfit choice of words wonderfully obstructs the understanding. Nor do the definitions or explanations wherewith in some things learned men are wont to guard and defend themselves, by any means set the matter right. But words plainly force and overrule the understanding, and throw all into confusion, and lead men away into numberless empty controversies and idle fancies.

Lastly, there are Idols which have immigrated into men's minds from the various dogmas of philosophies, and also from wrong laws of demonstration. These I call Idols of the Theater, because in my judgment all the received systems are but so many stage plays, representing worlds of their own creation after an unreal and scenic fashion. Nor is it only of the systems now in vogue, or only of the ancient sects and philosophies, that I speak; for many more plays of the same kind may yet be

sophisms: clever but unsound arguments.
Heraclitus: ancient Greek philosopher.

Observing and Generalizing

composed and in like artificial manner set forth; seeing that errors the most widely different have nevertheless causes for the most part alike. Neither again do I mean this only of entire systems, but also of many principles and axioms in science, which by traditon, credulity, and negligence have come to be received.

But of these several kinds of Idols I must speak more largely and exactly, that the understanding may be duly cautioned.

The human understanding is of its own nature prone to suppose the existence of more order and regularity in the world than it finds. And though there be many things in nature which are singular and unmatched, yet it devises for them parallels and conjugates and relatives which do not exist. Hence the fiction that all celestial bodies move in perfect circles, spirals and dragons being (except in name) utterly rejected. Hence too the element of fire with its orb is brought in, to make up the square with the other three which the sense perceives. Hence also the ratio of density of the so-called elements is arbitrarily fixed at ten to one. And so on of other dreams. And these fancies affect not dogmas only, but simple notions also.

The human understanding when it has once adopted an opinion (either as being the received opinion or as being agreeable to itself) draws all things else to support and agree with it. And though there be a greater number and weight of instances to be found on the other side, yet these it either neglects and despises, or else by some distinction sets aside and rejects, in order that by this great and pernicious predetermination the authority of its former conclusions may remain inviolate. And therefore is was a good answer that was made by one who, when they showed him hanging in a temple a picture of those who had paid their vows as having escaped shipwreck, and would have him say whether he did not now acknowledge the power of the gods—"Aye," asked he again, "but where are they painted that were drowned after their vows?" And such is the way of all superstition, whether in astrology, dreams, omens, divine judgments, or the like; wherein men, having a delight in such vanities, mark the events where they are fulfilled, but where they fail, though this happen much oftener, neglect and pass them by. But with far more subtlety does this mischief insinuate itself into philosophy and the sciences; in which the first conclusion colors and brings into conformity with itself all that come after, though far sounder and better. Besides, independently of that delight and vanity which I have described, it is the peculiar and perpetual error of the human intellect to be more moved and excited by affirmatives than by negatives; whereas it ought properly to hold itself indifferently disposed toward both alike. Indeed, in the establishment of any true axiom, the negative instance is the more forcible of the two.

The human understanding is moved by those things most which strike and enter the mind simultaneously and suddenly, and so fill the imagination; and then it feigns and supposes all other things to be somehow, though it cannot see how, similar to those few things by which it is surrounded. But for that going to and fro to remote and heterogeneous

dragons: zig-zags or snakelike patterns.

instances by which axioms are tried as in the fire, the intellect is altogether slow and unfit, unless it be forced thereto by severe laws and overruling authority.

The human understanding is unquiet; it cannot stop or rest, and still presses onward, but in vain. Therefore it is that we cannot conceive of any end or limit to the world, but always as of necessity it occurs to us that there is something beyond. Neither, again, can it be conceived how eternity has flowed down to the present day, for that distinction which is commonly received of infinity in time past and in time to come can by no means hold; for it would thence follow that one infinity is greater than another, and that infinity is wasting away and tending to become finite. The like subtlety arises touching the infinite divisibility of lines, from the same inability of thought to stop. But this inability interferes more mischievously in the discovery of causes; for although the most general principles in nature ought to be held merely positive, as they are discovered, and cannot with truth be referred to a cause, nevertheless the human understanding being unable to rest still seeks something prior in the order of nature. And then it is that in struggling toward that which is further off it falls back upon that which is nearer at hand, namely, on final causes, which have relation clearly to the nature of man rather than to the nature of the universe; and from this source have strangely defiled philosophy. But he is no less an unskilled and shallow philosopher who seeks causes of that which is most general, than he who in things subordinate and subaltern omits to do so.

The human understanding is no dry light, but receives an infusion from the will and affections; whence proceed sciences which may be called "sciences as one would." For what a man had rather were true he more readily believes. Therefore he rejects difficult things from impatience of research; sober things, because they narrow hope; the deeper things of nature, from superstition; the light of experience, from arrogance and pride, lest his mind should seem to be occupied with things mean and transitory; things not commonly believed, out of deference to the opinion of the vulgar. Numberless, in short, are the ways, and sometimes imperceptible, in which the affections color and infect the understanding.

But by far the greatest hindrance and aberration of the human understanding proceeds from the dullness, incompetency, and deceptions of the senses; in that things which strike the sense outweigh things which do not immediately strike it, though they be more important. Hence it is that speculation commonly ceases where sight ceases; insomuch that of things invisible there is little or no observation. Hence all the working of the spirits enclosed in tangible bodies lies hid and unobserved of men. So also all the more subtle changes of form in the parts of coarser substances (which they commonly call alteration, though it is in truth local motion through exceedingly small spaces) is in like manner unobserved. And yet unless these two things just mentioned be searched out and brought to light, nothing great can be achieved in nature, as far as the production of works is concerned. So again the essential nature of our common air, and of all bodies less dense than air (which are very many), is almost unknown. For the sense by itself is a thing infirm and erring;

neither can instruments for enlarging or sharpening the senses do much; but all the truer kind of interpretation of nature is effected by instances and experiments fit and apposite; wherein the sense decides touching the experiment only, and the experiment touching the point in nature and the thing itself.

The human understanding is of its own nature prone to abstractions and gives a substance and reality to things which are fleeting. But to resolve nature into abstractions is less to our purpose than to dissect her into parts; as did the school of Democritus, which went further into nature than the rest. Matter rather than forms should be the object of our attention, its configurations and changes of configurations, and simple action, and law of action or motion; for forms are figments of the human mind, unless you will call those laws of action forms.

Such then are the idols which I call *Idols of the Tribe*, and which take their rise either from the homogeneity of the substance of the human spirit, or from its preoccupation, or from its narrowness, or from its restless motion, or from an infusion of the affections, or from the incompetency of the senses, or from the mode of impression.

The *Idols of the Cave* take their rise in the peculiar constitution, mental or bodily, of each individual; and also in education, habit, and accident. Of this kind there is a great number and variety. But I will instance those the pointing out of which contains the most important caution, and which have most effect in disturbing the clearness of the understanding.

Men become attached to certain particular sciences and speculations, either because they fancy themselves the authors and inventors thereof, or because they have bestowed the greatest pains upon them and become most habituated to them. But men of this kind, if they betake themselves to philosophy and contemplation of a general character, distort and color them in obedience to their former fancies; a thing especially to be noticed in Aristotle, who made his natural philosophy a mere bond servant to his logic, thereby rendering it contentious and well-nigh useless. The race of chemists, again out of a few experiments of the furnace, have built up a fantastic philosophy, framed with reference to a few things; and Gilbert also, after he had employed himself most laboriously in the study and observation of the loadstone, proceeded at once to construct an entire system in accordance with his favorite subject.

There is one principal and as it were radical distinction between different minds, in respect of philosophy and the sciences, which is this: that some minds are stronger and apter to mark the differences of things, others to mark their resemblances. The steady and acute mind can fix its contemplations and dwell and fasten on the subtlest distinctions; the lofty and discursive mind recognizes and puts together the finest and most general resemblances. Both kinds, however, easily err in excess, by catching the one at gradations, the other at shadows.

There are found some minds given to an extreme admiration of

Democritus: ancient Greek philosopher who originated the concept of the atom.

antiquity, others to an extreme love and appetite for novelty; but few so duly tempered that they can hold the mean, neither carping at what has been well laid down by the ancients, nor despising what is well introduced by the moderns. This, however, turns to the great injury of the sciences and philosophy, since these affectations of antiquity and novelty are the humors of partisans rather than judgments; and truth is to be sought for not in the felicity of any age, which is an unstable thing, but in the light of nature and experience, which is eternal. These factions therefore must be abjured, and care must be taken that the intellect be not hurried by them into assent.

Contemplations of nature and of bodies in their simple form break up and distract the understanding, while contemplations of nature and bodies in their composition and configuration overpower and dissolve the understanding, a distinction well seen in the school of Leucippus and Democritus as compared with the other philosophies. For that school is so busied with the particles that it hardly attends to the structure, while the others are so lost in admiration of the structure that they do not penetrate to the simplicity of nature. These kinds of contemplation should therefore be alternated and taken by turns, so that the understanding may be rendered at once penetrating and comprehensive, and the inconveniences above mentioned, with the idols which proceed from them, may be avoided.

Let such then be our provision and contemplative prudence for keeping off and dislodging the *Idols of the Cave*, which grow for the most part either out of the predominance of a favorite subject, or out of an excessive tendency to compare or to distinguish, or out of partiality for particular ages, or out of the largeness or minuteness of the objects contemplated. And generally let every student of nature take this as a rule: that whatever his mind seizes and dwells upon with peculiar satisfaction is to be held in suspicion, and that so much the more care is to be taken in dealing with such questions to keep the understanding even and clear.

But, the *Idols of the Market Place* are the most troublesome of all—idols which have crept into the understanding through the alliances of words and names. For men believe that their reason governs words; but it is also true that words react on the understanding; and this it is that has rendered philosophy and the sciences sophistical and inactive. Now words, being commonly framed and applied according to the capacity of the vulgar, follow those lines of division which are most obvious to the vulgar understanding. And whenever an understanding of greater acuteness or a more diligent observation would alter those lines to suit the true divisions of nature, words stand in the way and resist the change. Whence it comes to pass that the high and formal discussions of learned men end oftentimes in disputes about words and names; with which (according to the use and wisdom of the mathematicians) it would be more prudent to begin, and so by means of definitions reduce them to order. Yet even definitions cannot cure this evil in dealing with natural

humors: notions, whims.

and material things, since the definitions themselves consist of words, and those words beget others. So that it is necessary to recur to individual instances, and those in due series and order, as I shall say presently when I come to the method and scheme for the formation of notions and axioms.

The idols imposed by words on the understanding are of two kinds. They are either names of things which do not exist (for as there are things left unnamed through lack of observation, so likewise are there names which result from fantastic suppositions and to which nothing in reality corresponds), or they are names of things which exist, but yet confused and ill-defined, and hastily and irregularly derived from realities. Of the former kind are Fortune, the Prime Mover, Planetary Orbits, Element of Fire, and like fictions which owe their origin to false and idle theories. And this class of idols is more easily expelled, because to get rid of them it is only necessary that all theories should be steadily rejected and dismissed as obsolete.

But the other class, which springs out of a faulty and unskilled abstraction, is intricate and deeply rooted. Let us take for example such a word as *humid* and see how far the several things which the word is used to signify agree with each other; and we shall find the word *humid* to be nothing else than a mark loosely and confusedly applied to denote a variety of actions which will not bear to be reduced to any constant meaning. For it both signifies that which easily spreads itself round any other body; and that which in itself is indeterminate and cannot solidize; and that which readily yields in every direction; and that which easily divides and scatters itself; and that which easily unites and collects itself; and that which readily flows and is put in motion; and that which readily clings to another body and wets it; and that which is easily reduced to a liquid, or being solid easily melts. Accordingly, when you come to apply the word, if you take it in one sense, flame is humid; if in another, air is not humid; if in another, fine dust is humid; if in another, glass is humid. So that it is easy to see that the notion is taken by abstraction only from water and common and ordinary liquids, without any due verification.

There are, however, in words certain degrees of distortion and error. One of the least faulty kinds is that of names of substances, especially of lowest species and well-deduced (for the notion of *chalk* and of *mud* is good, of *earth* bad); a more faulty kind is that of actions, as *to generate, to corrupt, to alter*; the most faulty is of qualities (except such as are the immediate objects of the sense) as *heavy, light, rare, dense*, and the like. Yet in all these cases some notions are of necessity a little better than others, in proportion to the greater variety of subjects that fall within the range of the human sense.

But the *Idols of the Theater* are not innate, nor do they steal into the understanding secretly, but are plainly impressed and received into the mind from the playbooks of philosophical systems and the perverted rules of demonstration. To attempt refutations in this case would be merely inconsistent with what I have already said, for since we agree neither upon principles nor upon demonstrations there is no place for argument. And this is so far well, inasmuch as it leaves the honor of the ancients untouched. For they are no wise disparaged—the question between them and me being only as to the way. For as the saying is, the lame man who keeps the right road outstrips the runner who takes a wrong one. Nay, it is obvious that when a man runs the wrong way, the more active and swift he is, the further he will go astray.

But the course I propose for the discovery of sciences is such as leaves but little to the acuteness and strength of wits, but places all wits and understandings nearly on a level. For as in the drawing of a straight line or a perfect circle, much depends on the steadiness and practice of the hand, if it be done by aim of hand only, but if with the aid of rule or compass, little or nothing; so is it exactly with my plan. But though particular confutations would be of no avail, yet touching the sects and general divisions of such systems I must say something; something also touching the external signs which show that they are unsound; and finally something touching the causes of such great infelicity and of such lasting and general agreement in error; that so the access to truth may be made less difficult, and the human understanding may the more willingly submit to its purgation and dismiss its idols.

Idols of the Theater, or of Systems, are many, and there can be and perhaps will be yet many more. For were it not that now for many ages men's minds have been busied with religion and theology; and were it not that civil governments, especially monarchies, have been averse to such novelties, even in matters speculative; so that men labor therein to the peril and harming of their fortunes—not only unrewarded, but exposed also to contempt and envy—doubtless there would have arisen many other philosophical sects like those which in great variety flourished once among the Greeks. For as on the phenomena of the heavens many hypotheses may be constructed, so likewise (and more also) many various dogmas may be set up and established on the phenomena of philosophy. And in the plays of this philosophical theater you may observe the same thing which is found in the theater of the poets, that stories invented for the stage are more compact and elegant, and more as one would wish them to be, than true stories out of history.

In general, however, there is taken for the material of philosophy either a great deal out of a few things, or a very little out of many things; so that on both sides philosophy is based on too narrow a foundation of experiment and natural history, and decides on the authority of too few cases. For the Rational School of philosophers snatches from experience a variety of common instances, neither duly ascertained nor diligently examined and weighed, and leaves all the rest to meditation and agitation of wit.

There is also another class of philosophers who, having bestowed much diligent and careful labor on a few experiments, have thence made bold to educe and construct systems, wresting all other facts in a strange fashion to conformity therewith.

And there is yet a third class, consisting of those who out of faith and veneration mix their philosophy with theology and traditions; among whom the vanity of some has gone so far aside as to seek the origin of sciences among spirits and genii. So that this parent stock of errors—this false philosophy—is of three kinds: the Sophistical, the Empirical, and the Superstitious.

The most conspicuous example of the first class was Aristotle, who corrupted natural philosophy by his logic: fashioning the world out of categories; assigning to the human soul, the noblest of substances, a genus from words of the second intention; doing the business of density and rarity (which is to make bodies of greater or less dimensions, that is, occupy greater or less spaces), by the frigid distinction of act and power; asserting that single bodies have each a single and proper motion, and that if they participate in any other, then this results from an external cause; and imposing countless other arbitrary restrictions on the nature of things; being always more solicitous to provide an answer to the question and affirm something positive in words, than about the inner truth of things; a failing best shown when his philosophy is compared with other systems of note among the Greeks. For the *homoeomera* of Anaxagoras; the Atoms of Leucippus and Democritus; the Heaven and Earth of Parmenides; the Strife and Friendship of Empedocles; Heraclitus' doctrine how bodies are resolved into the indifferent nature of fire, and remolded into solids, have all of them some taste of the natural philosopher—some savor of the nature of things, and experience, and bodies; whereas in the physics of Aristotle you hear hardly anything but the words of logic, which in his metaphysics also, under a more imposing name, and more forsooth as a realist than a nominalist, he has handled over again. Nor let any weight be given to the fact that in his books on animals and his problems, and other of his treatises, there is frequent dealing with experiments. For he had come to his conclusion before; he did not consult experience, as he should have done, for the purpose of framing his decisions and axioms, but having first determined the question according to his will, he then resorts to experience, and bending her into conformity with his placets, leads her about like a captive in a procession. So that even on this count he is more guilty than his modern followers, the schoolmen, who have abandoned experience altogether.

But the Empirical school of philosophy gives birth to dogmas more deformed and monstrous than the Sophistical or Rational school. For it has its foundations not in the light of common notions (which though it

homoeomera: sameness of all basic substance.
realist ... nominalist: opposing concepts in medieval philosophy; the realist held that universals (generalizations) are real, the nominalist held that only particulars (sense data) are real. Bacon is charging Aristotle with generalizing too much.
placets: declarations of assent—"it pleases."
Empirical school: those philosophers who believe that sensory perception is the only source of knowledge. Although Bacon was an empiricist he attacked the school for its lack of systematic method.
Rational school: those philosophers who believe truth is best approached through reason alone without the use of the senses, which they consider deceptive.

be a faint and superficial light, is yet in a manner universal, and has reference to many things), but in the narrowness and darkness of a few experiments. To those therefore who are daily busied with these experiments and have infected their imagination with them, such a philosophy seems probable and all but certain; to all men else incredible and vain. Of this there is a notable instance in the alchemists and their dogmas, though it is hardly to be found elsewhere in these times, except perhaps in the philosophy of Gilbert. Nevertheless, with regard to philosophies of this kind there is one caution not to be omitted; for I foresee that if ever men are roused by my admonitions to betake themselves seriously to experiment and bid farewell to sophistical doctrines, then indeed through the premature hurry of the understanding to leap or fly to universals and principles of things, great danger may be apprehended from philosophies of this kind, against which evil we ought even now to prepare.

But the corruption of philosophy by superstition and an admixture of theology is far more widely spread, and does the greatest harm, whether to entire systems or to their parts. For the human understanding is obnoxious to the influence of the imagination no less than to the influence of common notions. For the contentious and sophistical kind of philosophy ensnares the understanding; but this kind, being fanciful and tumid and half poetical, misleads it more by flattery. For there is in man an ambition of the understanding, no less than of the will, especially in high and lofty spirits.

Of this kind we have among the Greeks a striking example in Pythagoras, though he united with it a coarser and more cumbrous superstition; another in Plato and his school, more dangerous and subtle. It shows itself likewise in parts of other philosophies, in the introduction of abstract forms and final causes and first causes, with the omission in most cases of causes intermediate, and the like. Upon this point the greatest caution should be used. For nothing is so mischievous as the apotheosis of error; and it is a very plague of the understanding for vanity to become the object of veneration. Yet in this vanity some of the moderns have with extreme levity indulged so far as to attempt to found a system of natural philosophy on the first chapter of Genesis, on the book of Job, and other parts of the sacred writings, seeking for the dead among the living; which also makes the inhibition and repression of it the more important, because from this unwholesome mixture of things human and divine there arises not only a fantastic philosophy but also a heretical religion. Very meet it is therefore that we be sober-minded, and give to faith that only which is faith's.

So much, then, for the mischievous authorities of systems, which are

alchemists: medieval chemists who conducted innumerable experiments in an effort to change base metals into gold and to find an elixir of life. Their experiments were based on preconceived ideas.
Gilbert: William Gilbert (1540–1603), English physicist who first systematically studied electricity and magnetism.
Pythagoras: ancient Greek philosopher and mathematician who mixed mystical belief with his science.

founded either on common notions, or on a few experiments, or on superstition. It remains to speak of the faulty subject matter of contemplations, especially in natural philosophy. Now the human understanding is infected by the sight of what takes place in the mechanical arts, in which the alteration of bodies proceeds chiefly by composition or separation, and so imagines that something similar goes on in the universal nature of things. From this source has flowed the fiction of elements, and of their concourse for the formation of natural bodies. Again, when man contemplates nature working freely, he meets with different species of things, of animals, of plants, of minerals; whence he readily passes into the opinion that there are in nature certain primary forms which nature intends to educe, and that the remaining variety proceeds from hindrances and aberrations of nature in the fulfillment of her work, or from the collision of different species and the transplanting of one into another. To the first of these speculations we owe our primary qualities of the elements; to the other our occult properties and specific virtues; and both of them belong to those empty compendia of thought wherein the mind rests, and whereby it is diverted from more solid pursuits. It is to better purpose that the physicians bestow their labor on the secondary qualities of matter, and the operations of attraction, repulsion, attenuation, conspissation, dilatation, astriction, dissipation, maturation, and the like; and were it not that by those two compendia which I have mentioned (elementary qualities, to wit, and specific virtues) they corrupted their correct observations in these other matters—either reducing them to first qualities and their subtle and incommensurable mixtures, or not following them out with greater and more diligent observations to third and fourth qualities, but breaking off the scrutiny prematurely—they would have made much greater progress. Nor are powers of this kind (I do not say the same, but similar) to be sought for only in the medicines of the human body, but also in the changes of all other bodies.

But it is a far greater evil that they make the quiescent principles, *wherefrom*, and not the moving principles, *whereby*, things are produced, the object of their contemplation and inquiry. For the former tend to discourse, the latter to works. Nor is there any value in those vulgar distinctions of motion which are observed in the received system of natural philosophy, as generation, corruption, augmentation, diminution, alteration, and local motion. What they mean no doubt is this: if a body in other respects not changed be moved from its place, *this is local motion*; if without change of place or essence, it be changed in quality, this is *alteration*; if by reason of the change the mass and quantity of the body do not remain the same, this is *augmentation* or *diminution*; if they be changed to such a degree that they change their very essence and substance and turn to something else, this is *generation* and *corruption*. But all this is merely popular, and does not at all go deep into nature; for these are only measures and limits, not kinds of motion. What they intimate is *how far*, not *by what means*, or *from what source*. For they

conspissation: gathering together.

do not suggest anything with regard either to the desires of bodies or to the development of their parts. It is only when that motion presents the thing grossly and palpably to the sense as different from what it was that they begin to mark the division. Even when they wish to suggest something with regard to the causes of motion, and to establish a division with reference to them, they introduce with the greatest negligence a distinction between motion natural and violent, a distinction which is itself drawn entirely from a vulgar notion, since all violent motion is also in fact natural; the external efficient simply setting nature working otherwise than it was before. But if, leaving all this, anyone shall observe (for instance) that there is in bodies a desire of mutual contact, so as not to suffer the unity of nature to be quite separated or broken and a vacuum thus made; or if anyone say that there is in bodies a desire of resuming their natural dimensions or tension, so that if compressed within or extended beyond them, they immediately strive to recover themselves, and fall back to their old volume and extent; or if anyone say that there is in bodies a desire of congregating toward masses of kindred nature—of dense bodies, for instance, toward the globe of the earth, of thin and rare bodies toward the compass of the sky; all these and the like are truly physical kinds of motion—but those others are entirely logical and scholastic, as is abundantly manifest from this comparison.

Nor again is it a lesser evil that in their philosophies and contemplations their labor is spent in investigating and handling the first principles of things and the highest generalities of nature; whereas utility and the means of working result entirely from things intermediate. Hence it is that men cease not from abstracting nature till they come to potential and uninformed matter, nor on the other hand from dissecting nature till they reach the atom; things which, even if true, can do but little for the welfare of mankind.

A caution must also be given to the understanding against the intemperance which systems of philosophy manifest in giving or withholding assent, because intemperance of this kind seems to establish idols and in some sort to perpetuate them, leaving no way open to reach and dislodge them.

This excess is of two kinds: the first being manifest in those who are ready in deciding, and render sciences dogmatic and magisterial; the other in those who deny that we can know anything, and so introduce a wandering kind of inquiry that leads to nothing; of which kinds the former subdues, the latter weakens the understanding. For the philosophy of Aristotle, after having by hostile confutations destroyed all the rest (as the Ottomans serve their brothers), has laid down the law on all points; which done, he proceeds himself to raise new questions of his own suggestion, and dispose of them likewise, so that nothing may remain that is not certain and decided; a practice which holds and is in use among his successors.

Ottomans: Turks. In Bacon's time, instances were known of Turkish princes killing all their brothers to secure the throne for themselves.

The school of Plato, on the other hand, introduced *Acatalepsia*, at first in jest and irony, and in disdain of the older sophists, Protagoras, Hippias, and the rest, who were of nothing else so much ashamed as of seeming to doubt about anything. But the New Academy made a dogma of it, and held it as a tenet. And though theirs is a fairer seeming way than arbitrary decisions, since they say that they by no means destroy all investigation, like Pyrrho and his Refrainers, but allow of some things to be followed as probable, though of none to be maintained as true; yet still when the human mind has once despaired of finding truth, its interest in all things grows fainter, and the result is that men turn aside to pleasant disputations and discourses and roam as it were from object to object, rather than keep on a course of severe inquisition. But, as I said at the beginning and am ever urging, the human senses and understanding, weak as they are, are not to be deprived of their authority, but to be supplied with helps.

So much concerning the several classes of Idols and their equipage; all of which must be renounced and put away with a fixed and solemn determination, and the understanding thoroughly freed and cleansed; the entrance into the kingdom of man, founded on the sciences, being not much other than the entrance into the kingdom of heaven, whereinto none may enter except as a little child.

But vicious demonstrations are as the strongholds and defenses of idols; and those we have in logic do little else than make the world the bondslave of human thought, and human thought the bondslave of words. Demonstrations truly are in effect the philosophies themselves and the sciences. For such as *they* are, well or ill established, such are the systems of philosophy and the contemplations which follow. Now in the whole of the process which leads from the sense and objects to axioms and conclusions, the demonstrations which we use are deceptive and incompetent. This process consists of four parts, and has as many faults. In the first place, the impressions of the sense itself are faulty; for the sense both fails us and deceives us. But its shortcomings are to be supplied, and its deceptions to be corrected. Secondly, notions are ill-drawn from the impressions of the senses, and are indefinite and confused, whereas they should be definite and distinctly bounded. Thirdly, the induction is amiss which infers the principles of sciences by simple enumeration, and does not, as it ought, employ exclusions and solutions (or separations) of nature. Lastly, that method of discovery and proof according to which the most general principles are first established, and then intermediate axioms are tried and proved by them, is the parent of error and the curse of all science. Of these things, however, which now I do but touch upon, I will speak more largely when, having performed these expiations and purgings of the mind, I come to set forth the true way for the interpretation of nature.

Acatalepsia: the doctrine that nothing can be known for certain and we can only proceed on the basis of probabilities.
Pyrrho: ancient Greek philosopher who believed that the correct attitude for a philosopher was complete suspension of judgment at all times. This position later became known as skepticism.

DISCUSSION

1. Perhaps the best way to clarify the nature of the four different classes of "idols," or preconceived ideas, is to go back to Bacon's definitions presented at the beginning and to supply examples of each from your own observations. For instance, under "Idols of the Tribe" what subjective judgments about the universe do you make simply because you are a warmblooded mammal of a certain size rather than, say, an insect or a tree? And so on.
2. Present evidence, from your own direct observation, that people would rather defend an opinion than examine it.
3. Present examples of beliefs you would not have if you had not received them from someone else. Try to find an example of a belief you would have even if you had grown up alone.
4. Bacon says that logic makes "human thought the bondslave of words." It is probably true that creative thinking cannot be done in any kind of language; it is said that Einstein arrived at his theory of relativity neither through words nor through mathematical symbols, but through visual images. Bacon's advice, in short, is to look at things directly and to try to keep preconceptions from coming between us and what we see. Can you think of instances from your own experience when what you have read or heard has made you observe something falsely or made you fail to observe something true? Have you corrected this error by firsthand, fresh observation?
5. Examine the organization Bacon employs in "Idols of the Mind." How does he begin? What is the function of the second paragraph? The third? What does he accomplish in paragraphs three through six? In the paragraphs each beginning "The human understanding," what is he talking about? Does he give equal treatment to the other idols? What do you think Bacon gained by going through his list of idols three times, rather than writing a four-part essay in which he takes up each in simple succession?

A NOTE ON ORGANIZATION

You do not always have to present your ideas in as highly organized a way as Bacon does; often a more casual approach is better. All the same, formal organization can be a great help in solving the problems of where to begin and how to proceed. This is especially true when you want to explain a complex matter or when you want to present and support a generalization. In these instances an orderly breakdown into parts or stages before you begin writing is helpful.

Good organization grows out of the subject. For example, when you describe an object you begin with its more conspicuous features and conclude with the smaller details; when you describe a baseball game, you follow the time sequence of the game. You present a complex idea such as Bacon's in "Idols of the Mind" part by part, with transitions explaining the relationships of the parts and an introduction or conclusion indicating the shape of the idea as a whole. Organization simply follows the patterns of your perception and understanding and, once you have a firm grasp of your subject, the best order of presentation will appear to you.

However, as you become involved in the task of writing individual sentences, you are likely to overlook some of the stages of your organization—you may not be able to see the forest for the trees. This is why it is a good idea to sketch out your organization ahead of time, somewhat as an artist sketches in all the major features of a painting on the canvas before he begins. It takes a little time to outline what you are going to write about, but it will often save you the frustration of having to rewrite several pages because you left out an important point. In addition, outlining may show you where weaknesses occur in the development of your ideas and enable you to design a better structure. In short, outlining saves time and improves writing.

An outline need not be elaborate, but it must begin with a clear statement of your controlling idea or thesis, preferably in the form of a single sentence. The outline follows the ladder of generalization downward from the more general toward the more specific; your controlling idea is the highest generalization that you propose to support. Under this controlling idea are two or more topics, or statements of lower generalizations, and each of these in turn is supported by subtopics until you have worked your way down to the observed concrete data that form the base of the whole structure. The number of stages, of course, depends on the complexity of the subject. If the subject is simple, the topics themselves might be the concrete examples; if complex, examples might form the third or fourth order of subtopics. Here is how Gilbert White's "Social Instinct among Animals," a fairly simple exposition, might appear in outline:

Controlling idea: There is a spirit of sociality among animals, independent of sexual attachment.

    I. Among animals of the same species
       A. Gregarious birds
       B. Horses
       C. Oxen and cows
       D. Sheep
    II. Among animals of different species and sizes
       A. Doe with cows and dogs
       B. Horse and hen

Conclusion: Milton's statement to the contrary may be incorrect.

Even in so simple a piece of writing as White's, such an outline enables you to concentrate on composing your sentences and paragraphs, freeing you from the need to think about what comes next. In summary, outlining before you write may help you by

    1. insuring that you have a single controlling idea;
    2. insuring that you have support for each of your generalizations; and
    3. by insuring that you do not forget to put important material where it belongs.

At the same time, don't follow your outlines too rigidly. Writing that slavishly follows an elaborate outline can become overformal and dry. It is often a mistake, for instance, to begin your essay with a statement of the controlling idea; sometimes it is better to leave that to the end, and frequently, when your supporting evidence makes the thought clear enough, it is most effective to leave it out entirely. Once you have your outline, use it as insurance against wandering away from your subject or leaving things out, but do not let it dictate everything you write. Like other formal devices, outlining should be used to make writing easier, not more difficult.

WRITING SUGGESTIONS

1. The "character" is as much fun to write and read now as it was centuries ago. Keep in mind that the character describes the appearance, actions, and speech of a type of person rather than a single individual, though of course you may begin with your impression of a particular person and add to it. Here are a few suggestions for characters:

A conceited man	A fashionable lady
A gossip	An absent-minded man
A timid girl	A sarcastic teacher
A bore	A city cowboy
A greedy man	A bookworm
A dead beat	A fisherman
A name-dropper	A fussy housekeeper
A drunk	A noisy woman

Select one of these or another of your own invention and write a character. Do not hesitate to distort and exaggerate what you have actually observed. Feel free to be malicious in your description.

2. You have probably formed a general opinion about some aspect of the culture you live in, as did Butler ("machines are taking over"), Goldsmith ("we use language to conceal truth"), and Bacon ("conventional ideas obscure our thinking"). State your opinion and defend it, as these authors do, by pointing to generally known facts. Here are a few theses, or statements of opinion, to serve as guides:

Schools do (or do not) encourage original thinking
We waste our natural resources
Most people do (or do not) think for themselves
Possessions do (or do not) add to happiness
Traveling is (or is not) a fool's paradise
There is more than one kind of freedom
It is better to live actively (or quietly)
What you are is more important than what you do (or vice versa)

Plate 9
"Venus" of Willendorf (c. 10,000–15,000 B.C.) and *Venus de Milo* (c. 200 B.C.)

Venus, the goddess of love, seems to have begun as a fertility figure. The Venus figure on the left obviously does not represent an individual woman, but is instead a generalized figure with the female attributes exaggerated to emphasize the capacity for childbearing. In classic Greece, ten thousand or so years later, the female body had come to be admired for its beauty as well as its usefulness, as the *Venus de Milo* illustrates. However, the figure is still that of woman generalized rather than of an individual woman. Whether or not the artist used a model, he was careful to eliminate all individual peculiarities and replace them with his generalized observations of women.

1. The differences between the "Venus" of Willendorf and an actual woman seem obvious. Do you observe any differences between the *Venus de Milo* and a real woman of normal proportions? Is there distortion as well as generalization? If so, where?
2. Has the concept of the ideally beautiful woman changed since the *Venus de Milo*? If so, how, and what examples show this to be true?
3. Does there seem to be any purpose behind such a generalized representation as the *Venus de Milo*? What would motivate an artist to create a *Venus de Milo* rather than a portrait statue of an individual woman?
4. Are there modern equivalents to either of these generalized representations? If so, where are they found, and what seems to be their function?

PLATE 9 **Venus** of Willendorf. *Courtesy of the American Museum of Natural History, New York.* **Venus de Milo.** *The Louvre, Paris, from Lauros–Giraudon.*

Plate 10
Paul Gauguin (1848–1903): *The Spirit of the Dead Watching*

When Paul Gauguin, after years of dreaming about Tahiti, finally went there he found it disappointing. Nevertheless, he remained there and painted scenes from his dream, using Tahitian models and backgrounds. One result is that his Tahitian paintings represent highly generalized observations, often rendered in dream-like colors and forms.

1. The woman shown in *The Spirit of the Dead Watching* is quite different from the women in Toulouse-Lautrec's *Maxime Dethomas.* The different ways of depicting women reflect different ways of seeing them. Can you define what this difference is?

2. If you saw Gauguin's model with other Tahitian women, would you be likely to recognize her? Would you recognize the woman seen in profile in *Maxime Dethomas?*

3. Compare the generalized representation of a woman in *The Spirit of the Dead Watching* with the "Venus" of Willendorf and the *Venus de Milo* (Plate 9). Which "Venus" does Gauguin's woman most resemble? In what way? What differences are there in the way the artists have seen women?

4. Comparing Gauguin's figure with the *Venus de Milo,* which seems more erotic? What qualities are responsible for this impression?

5. Gauguin and the sculptor of the *Venus de Milo* both employed distortion. Can you identify particular distortions; for example, parts of the bodies that are larger or smaller than they would be in a normally-proportioned woman? What do you feel might be the purpose of these distortions?

6. To sum up, how does Gauguin's generalized idea of women differ from that of the sculptor of the *Venus de Milo?* Of the "Venus" of Willendorf?

PLATE 10 Paul Gauguin (1848–1903), **The Spirit of the Dead Watching.** *Albright-Knox Gallery, Buffalo. A. Conger Goodyear Collection.*

7

Beginning with the Observations of Others

Whenever we can, we observe for ourselves. There are times, however, when we must depend on others for our information; we cannot assemble an atlas of the world or a history of the Aztec empire from firsthand observation, for example. We must often rely on the eyes and ears of others, sometimes people long dead who have left their records behind. Frequently the job of the writer is to assemble into a coherent whole data provided by others. He may interview witnesses or he may use written materials; in either case he must estimate the reliability of each source. In the case of Thucydides, from whose history of the Peloponnesian War "The Final Defeat of the Athenian Forces" was taken, the author was involved in the early stages of the war but not in the part described here. His sources were the accounts of survivors. Such accounts were probably T. R. Ybarra's source for the following brief episode of Venezuelan history.

T. R. Ybarra

The Governor of Los Teques

(1941)

When Guzmán Blanco was dictator of Venezuela, back in the eighties of last century, he appointed one of his roughneck generals governor of the Los Teques district. In those days, plenty of injustice was visited by government officials on the lowly folk in their jurisdiction; extortion and high-handed assertion of authority, as well as downright cruelty, were commonplaces. But Guzmán's appointee at Los Teques went nearly all his corrupt and heartless contemporaries one better.

He rode callously over the susceptibilities of the little town's inhabitants. He robbed them of their property. He imprisoned them without reason. He stole their women for himself and his mercenaries. And he spiced the whole brutal catalogue of crime with savage assaults and outrageous murders. The unhappy Tequeños endured in impotent anger. They could do nothing about it. They suffered in silence; but, in their silence, they brooded; and, brooding, they made vows.

Years went by. The merciless governor of Los Teques had left that town for other posts and other orgies of cruelty. Never had he shown his face in the district where he had governed so cruelly as to make himself detested as no man had ever been detested there.

Then, one day, he returned—about ten years after he had relinquished his governorship. He merely wanted to breathe the mountain air of Los Teques. The past, he thought, had been forgotten by the townspeople.

With a group of friends, among them a popular general named Víctor Rodríguez, he stepped from the Caracas train at the Los Teques station and went to a nearby restaurant for lunch. They ordered plenty of good food and wine. They fell to with a hunger already whetted by the keen air from the mountains. They toasted each other. They joked and laughed.

Meanwhile, from one end of the town to the other, ran the news—muttered by voices made deep by anger that had never died—ominously hinting at a plan still unacknowledged:

"He's in town!"

It ran through knots of the townspeople, gathered in the little plaza—from block to block, from hovel to hovel.

"He's in town!"

Unswayed by any word of command—automatically, with sinister singleness of purpose—the men and women of Los Teques trudged through the dust of their narrow streets toward the restaurant where the ex-governor was eating and drinking and laughing. Some hands held machetes; others grasped knives sharpened to a murderous point; other fingers clutched revolvers.

"He's in town!"

They reached the restaurant. Part of the crowd—by this time it ran into the hundreds—lined up in front. Others posted themselves at the mouths of passageways onto which opened side doors of the building. Others barred all chance of exit through the back yard. Then that grim cordon of long-delayed vengeance moved forward.

The man whom they had marked down—the man for whom they had waited ten long years—leaped to his feet as he heard the murmurs of the oncoming multitude. Forks and spoons clattered to the floor, wine stained the tablecloth, chairs were swept aside by men pale with foreboding. The people of Los Teques, with tight-drawn lips and clenched teeth, with knives gleaming in itching fingers, came plunging through doorways and windows. The man who had wronged them understood.

He dashed for the yard. His way was barred by more and still more of the Tequeños.

Popular Víctor Rodríguez, always brave, drew his revolver. But the crowd brushed him aside.

"Get out of the way, Víctor, you're all right, we don't want you," they said. "There's the man we want!" And they rushed at their victim.

Hands reached for his throat, fists smashed into his face, knives cut red furrows in his flesh. Revolvers flashed and sputtered. With the men of Los Teques striking and stabbing, with the women of Los Teques spitting into his mouth and clawing at his eyes, he slipped, lost his footing. He fell prostrate on the ground—among overturned chairs and scattered morsels of food and wine that mixed, in red trickles, with his blood. And as he lay, stunned and bleeding, the people of Los Teques, with one last hideous snarl, fell on him and tore him to pieces.

Then they scattered to their homes. Los Teques went back to what it had been for centuries—a sleepy little town. Fresh breezes swept over its deserted streets. An occasional native walked, unhurried, across its plaza. Mangy dogs dozed in the sunshine.

And, at the restaurant, somebody cleaned up the mess.

DISCUSSION

1. This event is told in a dramatic way. Assuming that the material was gathered from witnesses, to what extent would you guess Ybarra has added interpretations of his own? What form does this interpretation take? Point out particular words or statements.

2. Are any "facts" given which could not have been confirmed by interviewing witnesses? If so, which facts?

3. Do you feel that Ybarra has in any way falsified history by dramatizing this episode? Do any of his assumptions about what happened seem to be unlikely? Support your opinion with specifics from his story.

Thucydides

The Peloponnesian War: Final Defeat of the Athenian Forces

(c. 400 B.C.)

The final sea-battle

The Syracusans and their allies had already put out with about the same number of ships as before; one detachment guarded the entrance of the harbour, the rest were disposed all round it, so as to attack the Athenians on all sides at once; while the land forces held themselves in readiness at the points at which the vessels might put in to the shore. The Syracusan fleet was commanded by Sicanus and Agatharchus, who had each a wing of the whole force, with Pythen and the Corinthians in the centre. When the Athenians came up to the barrier, the first shock of their charge overpowered the ships stationed there, and they tried to undo the fastenings; after this, as the Syracusans and allies bore down upon them from all quarters, the action spread from the barrier over the whole harbour, and was more obstinately disputed than any preceding. On either side the rowers showed great zeal in bringing up their vessels at the boatswains' orders, and the pilots great skill in maneuvering, rivalling each other's efforts; once the ships were alongside, the soldiers on board did their best not to let the service on deck be inferior; in short, every man strove to prove himself the first in his particular department. As many ships were engaged in a small compass (never had fleets so large—there were almost 200 vessels—fought in so narrow a space), the regular attacks with the beak were few, for there was no opportunity to back water or break the line; while the collisions caused by one ship chancing to run foul of another, either in avoiding or attacking a third, were more frequent. So long as a vessel was coming up to the charge the men on the decks rained darts and arrows and stones upon her; but once alongside, the heavy infantry tried to board each other's vessel, and fought hand to hand. In many places it happened, owing to want of room, that a vessel was charging an enemy on one side and being charged herself on another, and that two, or sometimes more, ships had unavoidably got entangled round one, and the pilots had to make plans of attack and defence against several adversaries

Peloponnesian War (431–04 B.C.): a long and complex war between Athens and her allies on one side and Sparta and hers on the other, over control of the Peloponnesian peninsula. In 418 the Spartans defeated Athens in the battle of Mantinea and won control. In the following years, Athens, interfering in the internal affairs of Sicily, attempted to gain power over that island in order to gain an outlet for the trade cut off by Sparta's control of the peninsula. Athens invested most of its remaining wealth in an enormous fleet for this purpose, with the result here chronicled by Thucydides. Its defeat was the end of Athens as a major power.

beak: Greek warships were equipped with a sharpened ram at the prow just below the water line for the purpose of punching holes in enemy ships.

Observing and Generalizing

coming from different quarters; while the huge din caused by the number of ships crashing together not only spread terror, but made the orders of the boatswains inaudible. The boatswains on either side in the discharge of their duty and in the heat of the conflict shouted incessantly orders and appeals to their men; the Athenians they urged to force the passage, and now if ever to show their mettle and make sure of a safe return to their country; to the Syracusans and their allies they cried that it would be glorious to prevent the escape of the enemy, and to win a victory which would bring glory to their country. The generals, on either side, if they saw any vessel in any part of the battle backing ashore without being forced to do so, called out to the captain by name and asked him—the Athenians, whether they were retreating because they thought that they would be more at home on a bitterly hostile shore than on that sea which had cost them so much labour to win; the Syracusans, whether they were flying from the flying Athenians, whom they well knew to be eager to escape by any possible means.

Meanwhile the two armies on shore, while victory hung in the balance, were a prey to the most agonizing and conflicting emotions; the Sicilians thirsting to add to the glory that they had already won, while the invaders feared to find themselves in even worse plight than before. The last hope of the Athenians lay in their fleet, their fear for the outcome was like nothing they had ever felt; while their view of the struggle was necessarily as chequered as the battle itself. Close to the scene of action, and not all looking at the same point at once, some saw their friends victorious and took courage, and fell to calling upon heaven not to deprive them of salvation, while others, who had their eyes turned upon the losers, wept and cried aloud, and, although spectators, were more overcome than the actual combatants. Others, again, were gazing at some spot where the battle was evenly disputed; as the strife was protracted without decision, their swaying bodies reflected the agitation of their minds, and they suffered the worst agony of all, ever just within reach of safety or just on the point of destruction. In short, in that one Athenian army, as long as the sea-fight remained doubtful, there was every sound to be heard at once, shrieks, cheers, *'We win,'* *'We lose,'* and all the other sounds wrung from a great host in desperate peril; with the men in the fleet it was nearly the same; until at last the Syracusans and their allies, after the battle had lasted a long while, put the Athenians to flight, and with much shouting and cheering chased them in open rout to the shore. The naval force fell back in confusion to the shore, except those who were taken afloat, and rushed from their ships to their camp; while the army, no more with divided feelings, but carried away by one impulse, ran down with a universal cry of dismay, some to help the ships, others to guard what was left of their wall, while the majority began to consider how they should save themselves. Their panic was as great as any of their disasters. They now suffered very nearly what they had inflicted at Pylos; then the Lacedaemonians, besides losing their fleet, lost also the men who had crossed over to Sphacteria; so now the Athenians had no hope of escaping by land, without the help of some extraordinary accident.

Beginning with the Observations of Others

The sea-fight had been severe, and many ships and lives had been lost on both sides; the victorious Syracusans and their allies now picked up their wrecks and dead, and sailed off to the city and set up a trophy, while the Athenians, overwhelmed by their disaster, never even thought of asking leave to take up their dead or wrecks, but wished to retreat that very night. Demosthenes, however, went to Nicias and gave it as his opinion that they should man the ships they had left and make another effort to force their passage out next morning; saying that they had still left more ships fit for service than the enemy, the Athenians having about sixty remaining as against less than fifty of their opponents. Nicias was quite of his mind; but when they wished to man the vessels, the sailors, who were so utterly overcome by their defeat as no longer to believe in the possibility of success, refused to go on board.

The retreat by land

They all now made up their minds to retreat by land. Meanwhile the Syracusan Hermocrates, who suspected their intention, and was impressed by the danger of allowing a force of that magnitude to retire by land, establish itself in some other part of Sicily, and from thence renew the war, went and stated his views to the authorities, and pointed out to them that they ought not to let the enemy get away by night, but that all the Syracusans and their allies should at once march out, block the roads, and seize and guard the passes. The authorities were entirely of his opinion, and thought that it ought to be done, but on the other hand felt sure that the people, who had given themselves over to rejoicing and were taking their ease after a great battle at sea, would not be easily brought to obey; besides, they were celebrating a festival, a sacrifice to Heracles, and most of them in their rapture at the victory had fallen to drinking, and would probably consent to anything sooner than to take up their arms and march out at that moment. For these reasons the magistrates thought the proposal impracticable; and Hermocrates, finding himself unable to do anything further with them, had recourse to the following stratagem of his own. What he feared was that the Athenians might quietly get the start of them by passing the most difficult places during the night; so, as soon as it was dusk, he sent some friends of his own to the camp with some horsemen. They rode up within earshot and, pretending to be well-wishers of the Athenians, called out to some of the men, and told them to tell Nicias (who had in fact some correspondents who informed him of what went on inside the town) not to lead off the army by night as the Syracusans were guarding the roads, but to make his preparations at his leisure and to retreat by day. After saying this they went off; and their hearers informed the Athenian generals, who put off going for that night on the strength of this message, not doubting its sincerity.

Having abandoned the idea of an immediate start, they now determined to stay the following day also, to give time to the soldiers to pack up as best they could the most useful things, and, abandoning everything else, to start only with the bare necessaries of life. Meanwhile the

Observing and Generalizing

Syracusans and Gylippus marched out and blocked up the roads through the country by which the Athenians were likely to pass, and guarded the fords of the streams and rivers, posting themselves at the best points to receive and stop the retreating army; while their fleet sailed up to the beach and towed off the ships of the Athenians. Some few were burned by the Athenians themselves as they had intended; the rest the Syracusans lashed to their own at their leisure, as they had been thrown up on shore, and towed to the town; no one tried to stop them.

As soon as Nicias and Demosthenes thought their preparations adequate the army began to move on, the second day after the sea-fight. It was a lamentable scene; not merely were they retreating after having lost all their ships, their great hopes gone, and themselves and the state in peril; but, as they left the camp, they saw sights melancholy both to eye and mind. The dead lay unburied, and when a man recognized a friend among them he shuddered with grief and horror; while the living whom they were leaving behind, wounded or sick, were more distressing to the survivors than the dead, and more to be pitied than those who had fallen. Their prayers and groans drove their friends to distraction, as they implored to be taken, appealing loudly to each individual comrade or relative whom they could see, hanging upon the necks of their departing tent-fellows, following as far as they could, and when their strength failed calling again and again upon heaven, and shrieking aloud as they were left behind. The whole army was in tears, and so distracted that they found it difficult to start, even though they were leaving a hostile country, where they had already suffered evils too great for tears and in the unknown future before them feared to suffer more. Dejection and self-condemnation were general. Indeed they could only be compared to a starved-out town, and that no small one, escaping; the whole multitude upon the march were not less than forty thousand men. All carried anything they could which might be of use, and the heavy infantry and cavalry, contrary to their habit while under arms, carried their own food, in some cases for want of servants, in others through not trusting them; they had long been deserting and now did so in greater numbers than ever. Yet even so they did not carry enough, as there was no food left in the camp. The disgrace and the universal suffering were somewhat mitigated by being shared by many, but even so seemed difficult to bear, especially when they contrasted the splendour and glory of their setting out with the humiliation in which it had ended. For this was by far the greatest reverse that ever befell a Greek army. They had come to enslave others, and were leaving in fear of being enslaved themselves: they had sailed out with prayer and paeans, and now started to go back with omens directly contrary; they were travelling by land instead of by sea, and trusting not in their fleet but in their infantry. Nevertheless the greatness of the danger hanging over their heads made all this appear tolerable.

Nicias, seeing the army dejected and greatly altered, passed along the ranks and encouraged and comforted them as far as the circumstances allowed, raising his voice higher and higher as he went from one company to another in his eager anxiety that his words might reach as many as possible and be a help:

'Athenians and allies, even in our present position we must still hope on, for men have been saved from worse straits; and you must not condemn yourselves too severely either because of your disasters or because of your present undeserved sufferings. I myself am no stronger than any of you—indeed you see how I am reduced by my illness—and I have been, I think, as fortunate as anyone in my private life and otherwise, but am now exposed to the same danger as the meanest among you; and yet I have led a religious life and I have been just and blameless in my relations with men. I have, therefore, still a strong hope for the future, and our misfortunes do not terrify me as much as they might. Indeed we may hope that they will be lightened: our enemies have had good fortune enough; and if any of the gods was offended at our expedition, we have been already amply punished. Others before us have attacked their neighbours and have done what men will do without suffering more than they could bear; and we may now fairly expect to find the gods more kind, for we have become fitter objects for their pity than their jealousy. And then look at yourselves, mark the numbers and efficacy of the heavy infantry marching in your ranks, and do not give way too much to despondency, but reflect that you yourselves at once constitute a city wherever you settle, and that there is no other in Sicily that could easily resist your attack, or expel you when once established. The safety and order of the march is for yourselves to look to; let the one thought of each man be that the spot on which he may be forced to fight must be conquered and held as his country and stronghold. Meanwhile we shall hasten on our way night and day alike, as our provisions are scanty; and if we can reach some friendly place of the Sicels, whom fear of the Syracusans still keeps true to us, you may forthwith consider yourselves safe. A message has been sent on to them with directions to meet us with supplies of food. To sum up, be convinced, soldiers, that you must be brave, as there is no refuge near for cowardice, and that, if you now escape from the enemy, you may all see again what your hearts desire, while those of you who are Athenians will raise up again the great power of the state, fallen though it be. Men make the city, and not walls or ships without men in them.

As he made this address Nicias went along the ranks, and brought back to their place any troops that he saw straggling out of the line; while Demosthenes did as much for his part of the army, addressing them in very similar words. The army marched in a hollow square, the division under Nicias leading, and that of Demosthenes following, the heavy infantry outside and the baggage-carriers and the bulk of the army in the middle. When they arrived at the ford of the river Anapus they there found a body of the Syracusans and allies drawn up, and routing these, made good their passage and pushed on, harassed by the charges of the Syracusan horse and by the missiles of their light troops. On that day they advanced about four miles and a half, halting for the night upon a hill. On the next they started early, got on about two miles further, and descended into a place in the plain and there encamped, in order to obtain food from the houses, as the place was inhabited, and to carry on with them water from thence, as for many furlongs in front, in the direction in which they were going, it was not plentiful. The Syracusans meanwhile went on and fortified the pass in front, where there was a steep hill with a rocky ravine on each side of it, called the Acraean cliff. The next day the Athenians advanced, but were hampered by large forces of the enemy, cavalry and javelin-men, who rode alongside and shot at them; after fighting for a long while, they finally retired to the same camp, where they were less well off for provisions, as the cavalry made it impossible for them to leave their position.

Early next morning they started afresh and forced their way to the hill, which had been fortified, where they found before them the enemy's infantry drawn up many shields deep, to defend the fortification, in a narrow pass. The Athenians assaulted the work, but were greeted by a storm of missiles from the hill, which told with the greater effect through its steepness, and unable to force the passage retreated again and rested. Meanwhile there was thunder and rain, as often happens towards autumn; this still further disheartened the Athenians, who thought that it was all ominous of their ruin. While they were resting Gylippus and the Syracusans sent a part of their army to throw up works in their rear on the way by which they had advanced; however, the Athenians immediately sent some of their men and prevented them; after this they retreated with their whole army towards the plain and halted for the night. When they advanced the next day the Syracusans surrounded and attacked them on every side, and disabled many of them, falling back if the Athenians advanced and coming on if they retired, and in particular assaulting their rear, in the hope of routing them in detail, and thus striking a panic into the whole army. For a long while the Athenians persevered in this fashion, but after advancing for four or five furlongs halted to rest in the plain, the Syracusans also withdrawing to their own camp.

During the night Nicias and Demosthenes, seeing the wretched condition of their troops, now in want of every kind of necessary, and numbers of them disabled in the numerous attacks of the enemy, determined to light as many fires as possible, and to lead off the army by another route towards the sea, in the opposite direction to that guarded by the Syracusans. All this route led not to Catana but to the other side of Sicily, towards Camarina, Gela, and the other Greek and foreign towns in that quarter. So they lit a number of fires and set out by night. All armies, and most of all large ones, are liable to alarms, especially when they are marching by night through an enemy's country and with the enemy near; the Athenians fell into one of these panics, and the leading division, under Nicias, kept together and got on a good way in front, but that of Demosthenes, comprising rather more than half the army, got separated and marched on in some disorder. By morning, however, they reached the sea, and getting into the Helorine Road pushed on to reach the river

furlong: about 220 yards or two modern city blocks.

Beginning with the Observations of Others

Cacyparis, and to follow the stream up through the interior, where they hoped to be met by the Sicels for whom they had sent. Arrived at the river, they found there a Syracusan party engaged in barring the passage of the ford with a wall and a palisade, and forcing this guard crossed the river, and went on to another called the Erineus, following the advice of their guides.

Meanwhile, when day came and the Syracusans and allies found that the Athenians were gone, most of them accused Gylippus of having let them escape on purpose, and hastily pursuing by the road which the enemy had taken, and which they had no difficulty in finding, overtook them about dinner-time. They first came up with the troops under Demosthenes, who were behind and marching somewhat slowly and in disorder, owing to the night-panic mentioned above. They at once attacked and engaged them, the Syracusan horse surrounding them with more ease now that they were separated from the rest, and hemming them in on one spot. The division of Nicias was five or six miles on in front, as he led them more rapidly, thinking that under the circumstances their safety lay in retreating as fast as possible, and fighting only when forced to do so. On the other hand, Demosthenes was harassed more incessantly, as his post in the rear left him the first exposed to the attacks of the enemy; and now, finding that the Syracusans were in pursuit, he omitted to push on, in order to form his men for battle, and so delayed until he was surrounded by his pursuers. He and his men now found themselves in the greatest confusion; they were huddled into an enclosure with a wall all round it, a road on both sides, and a large number of olive-trees, and they were shot at from every side. The Syracusans had with good reason adopted this method of attack in preference to fighting at close quarters, as to risk a struggle with desperate men was now more for the advantage of the Athenians than for their own; besides, their success had become so certain that they began to spare themselves a little in order not to be cut off in the moment of victory, thinking too that, as it was, they would be able in this way to conquer and capture the enemy.

After plying the Athenians and allies all day long from every side with missiles, they at length saw that they were worn out with their wounds and other sufferings; and Gylippus and the Syracusans and their allies made a proclamation, offering their liberty to any of the islanders who chose to come over to them; a few cities accepted the offer. Afterwards a capitulation was agreed upon for the remaining force of Demosthenes: to lay down their arms on condition that no one was to be put to death either by violence or imprisonment or want of the necessaries of life. Upon this they surrendered to the number of six thousand, gave up all the money in their possession, which filled the hollows of four shields, and were immediately taken by the Syracusans to the town.

Meanwhile Nicias with his division arrived that day at the river Erineus, crossed over and posted his army upon high ground on the far side. The next day the Syracusans overtook him and told him that the troops under Demosthenes had surrendered, and invited him to follow their example. Incredulous of the fact, Nicias asked for a truce to send a horseman to see, and upon the return of the messenger, with the news that they had

Observing and Generalizing

surrendered, sent a herald to Gylippus and the Syracusans, saying that he was ready to agree with them on behalf of the Athenians to repay whatever money the Syracusans had spent upon the war if they would let his army go; he offered until the money was paid to give Athenians as hostages, one for every talent. The Syracusans and Gylippus rejected this proposal, and attacked this division as they had the other, standing all round and hurling missiles at them until the evening. Food and necessaries were as miserably wanting to the troops of Nicias as they had been to their comrades; nevertheless they watched for the quiet of the night to resume their march. But as they were taking up their arms the Syracusans detected it and raised their paean, and the Athenians, finding that they were discovered, laid them down again, except about three hundred men who forced their way through the guards and went on during the night as best they could.

As soon as it was day Nicias put his army in motion, pressed, as before, by the Syracusans and their allies, pelted from every side by their missiles, and struck down by their javelins. The Athenians pushed on for the Assinarus, harassed by the attacks made upon them from every side by a large force of cavalry and other arms, fancying that they would breathe more freely if once across the river, and driven on by their distress and craving for water. Once there they rushed in, and all order was at an end, each man wanting to cross first, and the attacks of the enemy making it difficult to cross at all; forced to huddle together, they trampled and fell on each other, some dying immediately pierced by javelins, others getting entangled in the baggage, and being carried down by the stream. Meanwhile the opposite bank, which was steep, was lined by the Syracusans, who showered missiles down upon the Athenians, most of them drinking greedily and crowded together in disorder in the deep bed of the river. The Peloponnesians came down and butchered them, especially those in the water, which was fouled, but they went on drinking just the same, mud and all, bloody as it was, most even fighting to have it.

At last, when the dead lay heaped one upon another in the stream, and part of the army had been destroyed at the river, and the few that escaped cut off by the cavalry, Nicias surrendered himself to Gylippus, whom he trusted more than the Syracusans, and told him and the Lacedaemonians to do what they liked with him, but to stop the slaughter of his men. Gylippus then immediately gave orders to make prisoners, and the rest were brought together alive, except a large number secreted by the soldiery; a party was sent in pursuit of the three hundred who had got through the guard during the night, and who were now taken with the rest. The number collected as public prisoners was not great; but very many were privately concealed, and all Sicily was filled with them, no convention having been made in their case as for those taken with Demosthenes. Besides this, a large portion were killed outright; the carnage was very great, as great as any in this Sicilian war. Many too had fallen in the numerous other engagements upon the march. Nevertheless many escaped, some at the moment, others served as slaves, and then ran away subsequently. These found refuge at Catana.

The fate of the prisoners

The Syracusans and their allies now mustered and took up the spoils and as many prisoners as they could, and went back to the city. The rest of their Athenian and allied captives were deposited in the quarries, which seemed the safest place to keep them; But Nicias and Demosthenes were killed, against the will of Gylippus, who thought that it would be the crown of his triumph if he could take the enemy's generals to Lacedaemon. One of them, as it happened, Demosthenes, was one of her greatest enemies, on account of his achievement at Sphacteria and Pylos; while the other, Nicias, was for the same reasons one of her greatest friends, owing to his exertions to procure the release of the prisoners by persuading the Athenians to make peace. For these reasons the Lacedaemonians felt kindly towards him; and it was in this that Nicias himself mainly confided when he surrendered to Gylippus. But some of the Syracusans who had been in correspondence with him were afraid, it was said, of his being put to the torture and troubling their success by his revelations; others, especially the Corinthians, of his escaping, as he was rich, by bribery, and living to do them further mischief; and these persuaded the allies and put him to death. This or the like was the cause of the death of a man who, of all the Greeks in my time, least deserved such a fate, for he had lived in the practice of every virtue.

The prisoners in the quarries were at first hardly treated by the Syracusans. Crowded in a narrow hole, without any roof to cover them, the heat of the sun and the stifling closeness of the air tormented them during the day, and then the nights, which came on autumnal and chilly, made them ill by the violence of the change; they had to do everything in the same place for want of room, the bodies of those who died of their wounds or from the variation in the temperature, or similar causes, were left heaped together one upon another, and there were intolerable smells; hunger and thirst tormented them, each man during eight months having only half a pint of water and a pint of corn given him daily. In short, no single suffering to be apprehended by men thrust into such a place was spared them. For some seventy days they lived in this way all together; then all, except the Athenians and any Siceliots or Italiots who had joined in the expedition, were sold. The total number of prisoners taken it would be difficult to state exactly, but it could not have been less than seven thousand.

This was the greatest event in the war, or, in my opinion, in Greek history; at once most glorious to the victors, and most calamitous to the conquered. They were beaten at all points and altogether; their sufferings in every way were great. They were totally destroyed—their fleet, their army, everything—and few out of many returned home. So ended the Sicilian expedition.

DISCUSSION

1. You may have found this passage from Thucydides more interesting than many assignments you have read in history texts. If so, can you pin down exactly why it is more interesting? You would think a war that occurred 2400 years ago in Sicily would concern us less than, say, the War between the States. This passage concerns only part of the Peloponnesian War, of course. Can you recall an account of a comparable part of the American Civil War from one of your textbooks? If so, how was it different from this one? Which seemed more interesting, and why?
2. Many histories focus on political or economic theories, the broad movements of shifting power, or the influence of great leaders. Where is the focus of Thucydides' history?
3. The historian is always faced with the problem of how much detail to include. The defeat of Athens could be outlined in a paragraph, as it would be in a one-volume history of the world, or each event of the defeat could be described at book length. What seems to govern Thucydides' decisions about what to put in and what to leave out?
4. The best historians try not to take sides but tell us what happened as impartially as they can. How does Thucydides rate by this standard? Can you find statements that seem to be partial, favoring one side or the other for reasons that are not factual?

Thucydides uses the observations of others to reconstruct a factual story, a series of events. This is one common use of other people's observations. Another is to construct or support a theory or to get an idea across. In the next two selections the authors do just that: Leslie Reid uses data compiled by paleontologists to argue that preadaptation is involved in evolution, and R. H. Blyth gathers together literary examples from a number of cultures to give the reader an idea of what Zen is.

Leslie Reid

The Evolution of the Horse

(1958)

The evolution of the horse must have involved organic changes of many kinds, but naturally we can know only those that show themselves in the fossilized skeleton, and of these, four are outstanding. They are: an increase in size, a reduction of toes or digits on all four feet, an elongation of the facial region, and finally a marked change in the teeth. The earliest horse, *Eohippus*, was about the size of a fox-terrier, had four digits on each foot, and low-crowned teeth adapted to browsing off comparatively succulent vegetation. Subsequent development, culminating in the horse we know and protracted over some fifty million years, was towards a progressively larger animal with a more highly developed brain. Accompanying these changes there arose a tendency towards supporting the weight more and more on the tips of the toes, in such a way as to make the lateral digits less and less necessary. This gave the creature enhanced speed, and it ended with the single-toed horse of to-day with vestigial splint-bones, invisible externally, as the sole remnants of the lateral digits. As for the teeth, they underwent a change from the low-crowned sort with a simple surface-pattern, to a new type longer in proportion to their width and with an intricate surface-pattern suitable for the mastication of harder and drier grasses. All these changes were adaptive, for the later horses were grazing as opposed to browsing creatures, and their development can be correlated with a changing habitat during the Miocene Period when forests were tending to disappear and drier, open, grassy plains, admirable for galloping over, were taking their place. Life on these plains set a premium on speed and on the ability to chew tough-stemmed grasses. But it must not be supposed that there was this one line of development only. On the contrary there were many lines, but none persisted for as long as that which gave rise to the large, one-toed, grazing horses. One line continued from the original forest-living browsers, which remained as such. They too developed, but differently and less rapidly, reaching a sort of culmination, with three toes instead of four, at about the time when the future grazers were beginning to take to the plains. Finally they became extinct.

Where then does pre-adaptation figure in this story? Very notably. One example of it has already been referred to, namely that the forest-dwelling browsers, while they could still so be described, had undergone a reduction in the number of digits from four to three. But that is by no means all, for the interesting and highly significant conclusion emerging from study of the skeletons of the many kinds of horse destined in time to develop into the animal that we know to-day, is that their evolution was materially assisted by organic changes that had already begun to manifest themselves while they yet lived in forests and browsed off leaves. In other words those structural changes fitting them so admirably for life on the plains—increase in size and reduction of digits; the transition from low- to high-crowned, grinding teeth; elongation of the facial region, giving space for more teeth—began to develop before the conditions responsible for their final perfection had begun to appear.

DISCUSSION

1. Reid's sources are not obscure. The data he uses can be found in any college geology text. That is why he does not present the facts of the evolution of the horse in more detail. Would you find his theory more convincing if it were presented in the form of a long and scholarly volume, full of details and diagrams? Why, or why not?
2. Do you find his theory of preadaptation the only possible explanation of the facts he offers? If not, is it the most scientifically "elegant" explanation? (In science, the term "elegant" means "as simple as fully ex-

plains the facts" and also connotes a feeling of "rightness.") Does his theory answer a question, raise a question, or both? If so, what question? Does a better explanation of the phenomena he summarizes occur to you?

R. H. Blyth

What Is Zen?

(1941)

Consider the lives of birds and fishes. Fish never weary of the water; but you do not know the true mind of a fish, for you are not a fish. Birds never tire of the woods; but you do not know their real spirit, for you are not a bird. It is just the same with the religious, the poetical life: if you do not live it, you know nothing about it.

This that Chômei says in the *Hôjôki* is true of the life of Zen, which is the real religious, poetical life. But, as Mrs. Browning says in *Aurora Leigh*,

> The cygnet finds the water, but the man
> Is born in ignorance of his element.

Dôgen, (1200–1253) founder of the Sôtô Sect of Zen in Japan, expresses this more poetically:

> The water-bird
> Wanders here and there
> Leaving no trace,
> Yet her path
> She never forgets.

Zen, though far from indefinite, is by definition indefinable, because it is the active principle of life itself.

> The sun passeth through pollutions and itself remains as pure as before,

so Zen passes through all our definings and remains Zen as before. As we think of it, it seems dark, but "dark with excessive light." It is like Alice in The Looking Glass, the more we run after it the farther away we get. Yet we read books on Zen, and more books, hoping to find on some page, in some sentence or other, the key to a door which is only a hallucination. Zen says "Walk in!" Never mind the key or the bolt or the massive-seeming door. Just walk in! Goethe's revised version of the beginning of the Gospel of St. John, comes nearest:

> Im Anfang war die Tat,

for action cannot be defined. In *The Anticipation* Traherne says,

Im Anfang war die Tat: "In the beginning was the act." This is a contradictory paraphrase of the first sentence of the Gospel of St. John, which is "In the beginning was the word."

> His name is Now...
> His essence is all Act.

Milton describes its unnoticed universality in *Comus:*

> A small unsightly root,
> The leaf was darkish, and had prickles on it,
> But in another country, as he said,
> Bore a bright golden flow'r, but not in this soil;
> Unknown, and like esteem'd, and the dull swain
> Treads on it daily with his clouted shoon.

It is seen selected for our admiration in art, music and poetry. The difference between Zen in actual life and Zen in Art, is that Art is like a photograph (and music like a film), that can be looked at whenever we please. Or, we may say, just as Goethe called architecture frozen music, art is frozen Zen. Truth is everywhere, but is more *apparent* in science. Beauty is in dustbins and butcher's shops as well, but is more visible in the moon and flowers. Religion is in every place, at every moment, but as Johnson says in his *Journey to the Western Islands,*

> That man is little to be envied whose patriotism would not gain force upon the plain of Marathon, or whose piety would not grow warmer among the ruins of Iona.

We need not wait a moment, we need not stir a foot, to see Zen, but it is more evident in *some* acts, *some* works of art, *some* poems. In this book I have chosen examples from those which have a special meaning for me. Emerson says,

> It is as difficult to appropriate the thoughts of others as to invent.

I have tried to appropriate them as far as lay in my power.

Here is an example from *Oliver Twist*. The Artful Dodger, having been arrested, appears in court:

> It was indeed Mr. Dawkins, who, shuffling into the office with the big coat sleeves tucked up as usual, his left hand in his pocket, and his hat in his right hand, preceded the jailer, with a rolling gait altogether indescribable, and, taking his place in the dock, requested in an audible voice to know what he was placed in that 'ere disgraceful sitivation for.
> "Hold your tongue, will you?" said the jailer.
> "I'm an Englishman, ain't I?" rejoined the Dodger. "Where are my priwileges?"
> "You'll get your privileges soon enough," retorted the jailer, "and pepper with 'em."
> "We'll see wot the Secretary of State for the Home Affairs has got to say to the beaks, if I don't," replied Mr. Dawkins. "Now

shoon: shoes.
Marathon: site of the victory of the Greeks over the Persians, 490 B.C.
Iona: island off the coast of Scotland, which was the early center of the Celtic Christian church.
beaks: English slang for magistrates.

Observing and Generalizing

then! Wot is this here business? I shall thank the madg'strates to dispose of this here little affair, and not to keep me while they read the paper, for I've got an appointment with a genelman in the City, and as I'm a man of my word, and wery punctual in business matters, he'll go away if I ain't there to my time, and then pr'aps there won't be an action for damage against them as kep me away. Oh no, certainly not!"

At this point, the Dodger, with a show of being very particular with a view to proceedings to be had thereafter, desired the jailer to communicate "the names of them two files as was on the bench."

(A witness is called who testifies to the Dodger's pickpocketing.)

"Have you anything to ask this witness, boy?" said the magistrate.

"I wouldn't abase myself by descending to hold no conversation with him," replied the Dodger.

"Have you anything to say at all?"

"Do you hear his worship ask if you've anything to say?" inquired the jailer, nudging the silent Dodger with his elbow.

"I beg your pardon," said the Dodger, looking up with an air of abstraction, "Did you redress yourself to me, my man?"

"I never see such an out-and-out young wagabond, your worship," observed the officer with a grin. "Do you mean to say anything, you young shaver?"

"No," replied the Dodger, "not here, for this ain't the shop for justice; besides which, my attorney is a breakfasting with the Wice President of the House of Commons; but I shall have something to say elsewhere, and so will he, and so will a wery numerous and 'spectable circle of acquaintances as 'll make them beaks wish they'd never been born, or that they'd got their footmen to hang 'em up to their own hat-pegs, 'afore they let 'em come out this morning to try it on me. I'll——"

"There! He's fully committed!" interposed the clerk.

"Take him away."

"Come on," said the jailer.

"Oh, ah! I'll come on," replied the Dodger, brushing his hat with the palm of his hand. "Ah! (to the Bench) it's no use your looking frightened; I won't show you no mercy, not a ha'porth of it. *You'll* pay for this, my fine fellers. *I wouldn't be you for something! I wouldn't go free, now, if you was to fall down on your knees and ask me. Here, carry me off to prison! Take me away!*"

The Artful Dodger is "the chameleon poet that shocks the virtuous philosophers" on the bench. Notice how what seems to be at first mere impudence, rises with influx of energy into an identification of himself with the whole machinery of the Law. He attains, for a moment, to "Buddahood, in which all the contradictions and disturbances caused by the intellect are entirely harmonised in a unity of higher order." Someone to whom I related the above, said to me, "I suppose the case

180

of Mata Hari, the celebrated woman spy, was similar. When she was being executed she refused to have her eyes bandaged." This is not so. Courage may and does often have Zen associated with it, but Zen is not courage. A thief running away like mad from a ferocious watch-dog may be a splendid example of Zen. Bashô gazing at the moon, is an example of Zen; eating one's dinner, yawning—where is the courage in these?

Here is an example, similar to that of Dickens, but taken from real life. I was walking along a lonely mountain road with my wife and we were talking about her elder sister, who had died the year before. She said, "When we were young we would often come back from town at night along this very road. I am a coward, and was always afraid even though we were together, but my sister said, 'I would like to whiten my face and put on a white kimono, and stand over there in the shadow of the pine-trees.'" Once again, it is not the courage, but the willing identification of self, the subject, with the ghost, the object of fear, that has in it the touch of Zen. Here is another example of a different kind, in which there is no trace of ordinary courage; it consists in entire engrossment, conscious and unconscious, in what one is doing. This requires, of course, that one's work at the moment should be thoroughly congenial to one's nature, that is to say, it must be like the swimming of a fish or the flying of a bird. In his *Conversations with Goethe*, under Tuesday, April 22nd, 1830, Eckermann notes the following:

> I was much struck by a Savoyard boy, who turned a hurdy-gurdy, and led behind him a dog, on which a monkey was riding. He whistled and sang to us, and for a long time tried to make us give him something. We threw him down more than he could have expected, and I thought he would throw us a look of gratitude. However he did nothing of the kind, but pocketed his money, and immediately looked after others to give him more.

What struck Eckermann? Was it the ingratitude of the boy? I think not. It was the complete absorption of the boy in the work he was doing to get money. Other people had no existence for him. Three days after, a very similar thing struck Eckermann.

> At dinner, at the table d'hôte, I saw many faces, but few expressive enough to fix my attention. However, the head waiter interested me highly, so that my eyes constantly followed him and all his movements: and indeed he was a remarkable being. The guests who sat at the long table were about two hundred in number, and it seems almost incredible when I say that nearly the whole of the attendance was performed by the head waiter, since he put on and took off all the dishes, while the other waiters only handed them to him and received them from him. During all this proceeding, nothing was spilt, no one was incom-

Savoyard: inhabitant of Savoy, a region of southeastern France adjacent to Italy. The familiar organ grinder with his monkey was originally Savoyard.
table d'hôte: "host's table," a large table at which all guests of a hotel are served at the same time.

moded, but all went off lightly and nimbly, as if by the operation of a spirit. Thus, thousands of plates and dishes flew from his hands upon the table, and again from the table to the hands of the attendants behind him. Quite absorbed in his vocation, the whole man was nothing but eyes and hands, and he merely opened his closed lips for short answers and directions. Then he not only attended to the table but took the orders for wine and the like, and so well remembered everything, that when the meal was over, he knew everybody's score and took the money.

This is a splended example of Zen, which Eckermann calls "comprehensive power, presence of mind and strong memory." We may call it "presence of Mind," or "absence of mind." The memory, as Freud would say, is a matter of the will. We forget because we will (wish) to forget, and remember because we will to remember. "The whole man was nothing but eyes and hands." Turner was nothing but a paint-brush, Michael Angelo nothing but a chisel. There is no greater pleasure in ordinary life, so-called, than to see a bus-conductor, a teacher, anybody, really engrossed in his work, with no thought of its relative or absolute value, with no thought of its interest or profit to himself or others.

A similar example is given in Dickens' *Martin Chuzzlewit*. Mr. Pecksniff and his daughters are dining at Todger's, but the really interesting thing about the hilarious and convivial proceedings is Bailey, the boy who cleans the boots and is temporarily serving at table. He has "life more abundantly," with no self-consciousness or "choosing" or judging or attachment; equal to all circumstances, master of every situation. And be it noted that just as Eckermann's head waiter shows his Zen by doing his work so well, to perfection, so Dickens' boy shows his Zen by doing practically nothing at all, *to perfection*, in similar circumstances.

> Their young friend Bailey sympathised [with the two Miss Pecksniffs] in these feelings to the fullest extent, and abating nothing of his patronage, gave them every encouragement in his power: favouring them, when the general attention was diverted from his proceedings, with many nods and winks and other tokens of recognition, and occasionally touching his nose with a corkscrew, as if to express the Bacchanalian character of the meeting. In truth perhaps even the spirits of the two Miss Pecksniffs, and the hungry watchfulness of Mr. Todgers, were less worthy of note than the proceedings of this remarkable boy, whom nothing disconcerted or put out of his way. If any piece of crockery, a dish or otherwise, chanced to slip through his hands (which happened once or twice) he let it go with perfect good breeding, and never added to the painful emotions of the company by exhibiting the least regret. Nor did he, by hurrying to and fro, disturb the repose of the assembly, as many well-trained servants do; on the contrary, feeling the hopelessness of waiting upon so large a party, he left the gentlemen to help themselves to what they wanted, and seldom stirred from be-

hind Mr. Jenkins's chair: where, with his hands in his pockets, and his legs planted pretty wide apart, he led the laughter, and enjoyed the conversation.

This perfection, which we see always in inanimate things, usually in animals, so seldom in human beings, almost never in ourselves, is what Christ urges us to attain:

Be ye perfect, as your Father which is in Heaven is perfect.

Many people will no doubt be surprised that Mark Tapley is not used as an example of Zen. His desire "to come out strong" in the most difficult circumstances may seem evidence of this, but actually it is evidence of the opposite. Zen is essentially unconscious, unselfconscious, even unSelfconscious. Notice further that, as Mrs. Lupin says, he is "a good young man." Sad to relate, we can find Zen in Mr. Pecksniff, Mrs. Gamp, Bailey Junior, that is, in hypocrisy, vulgarity, and impudence, more readily than in the conscious unselfishness of Mark Tapley. This is why the latter has something thin, unreal, out-of-joint about him. He is not equal to all circumstances, only to the worst.

There are two fables by Stevenson, *The Sinking Ship*, which shows Zen on its destructive side, and *The Poor Thing*, which illustrates its constructive working. Here is *The Sinking Ship*:

"Sir," said the first lieutenant, bursting into the Captain's cabin, "the ship is going down."

"Very well, Mr. Spoker," said the Captain; "but that is no reason for going about half-shaved. Exercise your mind a moment, Mr. Spoker, and you will see that to the philosophic eye there is nothing new in our position: the ship (if she is to go down at all) may be said to have been going down since she was launched."

"She is settling fast," said the first lieutenant, as he returned from shaving.

"Fast, Mr. Spoker?" asked the Captain. "The expression is a strange one, for time (if you will think of it) is only relative."

"Sir," said the lieutenant, "I think it is scarcely worth while to embark in such a discussion when we shall all be in Davy Jones's Locker in ten minutes."

"By parity of reasoning," returned the Captain gently, "it would never be worth while to begin any inquiry of importance; the odds are always overwhelming that we must die before we shall have brought it to an end. You have not considered, Mr. Spoker, the situation of man," said the Captain, smiling, and shaking his head.

"I am much more engaged in considering the position of the ship," said Mr. Spoker.

"Spoken like a good officer," replied the Captain, laying his hand on the lieutenant's shoulder.

On deck they found the men had broken into the spirit room, and were fast getting drunk.

Mark Tapley: Martin Chuzzlewit's servant, noted for irrepressible joviality and optimism.

Observing and Generalizing

> "My men," said the Captain, "there is no sense in this. The ship is going down, you will tell me, in ten minutes: well, and what then? To the philosophic eye, there is nothing new in our position. All our lives long, we may have been about to break a blood-vessel or to be struck by lightning, not merely in ten minutes, but in ten seconds; and that has not prevented us from eating dinner, no, nor from putting money in the Savings Bank. I assure you, with my hand on my heart, I fail to comprehend your attitude."
>
> The men were already too far gone to pay much heed.
>
> "This is a very painful sight, Mr. Spoker," said the Captain.
>
> "And yet to the philosophic eye, or whatever it is," replied the first lieutenant, "they may be said to have geen getting drunk since they came aboard."
>
> "I do not know if you always follow my thought, Mr. Spoker," returned the Captain gently. "But let us proceed."
>
> In the powder magazine they found an old salt smoking his pipe.
>
> "Good God," cried the Captain, "what are you about?"
>
> "Well, sir," said the old salt, apologetically, "they told me as she were going down."
>
> "And suppose she were?" said the Captain. "To the philosophic eye, there would be nothing new in our position. Life, my old shipmate, life, at any moment and in any view, is as dangerous as a sinking ship; and yet it is man's handsome fashion to carry umbrellas, to wear india-rubber overshoes, to begin vast works, and to conduct himself in every way as if he might hope to be eternal. And for my own poor part I should despise the man who, even on board a sinking ship, should omit to take a pill or to wind up his watch. That, my friend, would not be the human attitude."
>
> "I beg pardon, sir," said Mr. Spoker. "But what is precisely the difference between shaving in a sinking ship and smoking in a powder magazine?"
>
> "Or doing anything at all in any conceivable circumstances?" cried the Captain. "Perfectly conclusive; give me a cigar!"
>
> Two minutes afterwards the ship blew up with a glorious detonation.

It is very amusing to see how the Captain adopts the absolute position in, "the ship may be said to have been going down since she was launched," and, "time is only relative," and then, descending to the relative in reproving the men for drunkenness, is caught up by the first lieutenant. The "philosophic eye," is the eye of God, which sees shaving in a sinking ship (where the shaving and the sinking have no immediate connection) and smoking in a powder magazine (where the smoking is the cause of the ship's blowing up) as the same. When we have the eye of God we are released from cause and effect ("He that loseth his life shall find it") from space ("If ye shall say unto this mountain, Be thou removed, and be thou cast into the sea; it shall be done,") and from time ("A thousand years in Thy sight are but as yesterday when it is past"). "Doing anything at all in any conceivable circumstances," is the freedom of Zen. A man must be able (that is, willing) to do anything on any occasion whatever. Hundreds of verses in the writings of Zen express this perfect freedom, which alone allows us to act perfectly. Here are some from the *Zenrinkushū*

> Stones rise up into the sky;
> Fire burns down in the water.

> Ride your horse along the edge of a sword;
> Hide yourself in the middle of the flames.

> Blossoms of the fruit-tree bloom in the fire:
> The sun rises in the evening.

But the most important word in the fable is "glorious." Glorious means Good, as distinguished from good. The word 'good' is a relative word opposed to 'bad.' The word "Good" is absolute and has no contrary. In the same way we may distinguish, in writing, but not in speaking, 'happy' and 'Happy.' Stephen being stoned to death was Happy; he was certainly not happy. Again, Love is what makes the world go round; love is quite another thing. So as I say, glorious, means Good; we have the Glorious Inferno of Dante, the Glorious deafness of Beethoven, the Glorious sun that Blake saw. The revolt of Lucifer, the career of Nero, the crucifixion of Christ—all these were Glorious, like the detonation that sent hundreds of souls into eternity. "Nothing is Glorious, but thinking makes it so."

Just at this point another fable of Stevenson is relevant perhaps, *The Reader*. Let me insert it here:

> "I never read such an impious book," said the reader, throwing it on the floor.
> "You need not hurt me," said the book; "You will only get less for me second-hand, and I did not write myself."
> "That is true," said the reader, "My quarrel is with your author."
> "Ah, well," said the book, "you need not buy his rant."
> "That is true," said the reader. "But I thought him such a cheerful writer."
> "I find him so," said the book.
> "You must be differently made from me," said the reader.
> "Let me tell you a fable," said the book. "There were two men wrecked upon a desert island; one of them made believe he was at home, the other admitted . . ."
> "Oh, I know your kind of fable," said the reader. "They both died."

Stephen: St. Stephen, the first Christian martyr.
Blake: William Blake, British mystic and poet (1757–1827).

Observing and Generalizing

"And so they did," said the book. "No doubt of that. And every body else."

"That is true," said the reader. "Push it a little further for this once. And when they were all dead?"

"They were in God's hands, the same as before," said the book.

"Not much to boast of, by your account," cried the reader.

"Who is impious, now?" said the book, and the reader put him on the fire.

> The coward crouches from the rod,
> And loathes the iron face of God.

Most religious people are impious, far more so than the irreligious. They always tell you, "God wouldn't do that." "The universe couldn't be made like that." "Good is good and bad is bad, and never the twain shall meet." Impiety means ingratitude, not being thankful for what God gives, but wanting, nay, demanding something else, requiring the universe to be different from what it is. Before we are born, all our life, and for all eternity after, we are in God's hands; whether our life continues, or whether it fizzles out, we are to say "Thank God!"

The other fable is *The Poor Thing*, which shows Zen working, as it so often does, in a man of "little lore." This simplicity of mind, which we see and envy in children and idiots, is essential if we would become the real master of our fate, the captain of our soul. Bashô, in his *Oku no Hosomichi* quotes with approval Confucius' saying, that firmness, resoluteness, simplicity and slowness of speech, are not far from virtue,

and Theseus, in *A Midsummer Night's Dream*,

> Never anything can be amiss
> When simpleness and duty tender it.

THE POOR THING

There was a man in the islands who fished for his bare bellyful and took his life in his hands to go forth upon the sea between four planks. But though he had much ado, he was merry of heart; and the gulls heard him laugh when the spray met him. And though he had little lore, he was sound of spirit; and when the fish came to his hook in the mid-waters, he blessed God without weighing. He was bitter poor in goods and bitter ugly of countenance, and he had no wife.

It fell at the time of the fishing that the man awoke in his house about the midst of the afternoon. The fire burned in the midst, and the smoke went up and the sun came down by the chimney. And the man was aware of the likeness of one that warmed his hands at the red peat fire.

"I greet you," said the man, "in the name of God."

"I greet you," said he that warmed his hands, "but not in the name of God, for I am none of His; nor in the name of Hell, for

I am not of Hell. For I am but a bloodless thing, less than wind and lighter than a sound, and the wind goes through me like a net, and I am broken by a sound and shaken by the cold."

"Be plain with me," said the man, "and tell me your name and of your nature."

"My name," quoth the other, "is not yet named, and my nature not yet sure. For I am part of a man; and I was a part of your fathers, and went out to fish and fight with them in the ancient days. But now is my turn not yet come; and I wait until you have a wife, and then shall I be in your son, and a brave part of him, rejoicing manfully to launch the boat into the surf, skilful to direct the helm, and a man of might where the ring closes and the blows are going."

"This is a marvellous thing to hear," said the man; "and if you are indeed to be my son, I fear it will go ill with you; for I am bitter poor in goods and bitter ugly in face, and I shall never get me a wife if I live to the age of eagles."

"All this have I come to remedy, my Father," said the Poor Thing; "for we must go this night to the little isle of sheep, where our fathers lie in the dead-cairn, and tomorrow to the Earl's Hall, and there shall you find a wife by my providing."

So the man rose and put forth his boat at the time of the sun-setting; and the Poor Thing sat in the prow, and the spray blew through his bones like snow, and the wind whistled in his teeth, and the boat dipped not with the weight of him.

"I am fearful to see you, my son," said the man. "For methinks you are no thing of God."

"It is only the wind that whistles in my teeth," said the Poor Thing, "and there is no life in me to keep it out."

So they came to the little isle of sheep, where the surf burst all about it in the midst of the sea, and it was all green with bracken, and all wet with dew, and the moon enlightened it. They ran the boat into a cove, and set foot to land; and the man came heavily behind among the rocks in the deepness of the bracken, but the Poor Thing went before him like a smoke in the light of the moon. So they came to the dead-cairn, and they laid their ears to the stones; and the dead complained withinsides like a swarm of bees: "Time was that marrow was in our bones, and strength in our sinews; and the thoughts of our head were clothed upon with acts and the words of men. But now are we broken in sunder, and the bonds of our bones are loosed, and our thoughts lie in the dust."

Then said the Poor Thing: "Charge them that they give you the virtue they withheld."

And the man said: "Bones of my fathers, greeting! for I am

---

dead-cairn, cairn: heap of stones used to mark a grave by early inhabitants of the British Isles and other peoples.
bracken: ferns.

sprung of your loins. And now, behold, I break open the piled stones of your cairn, and I let in the moon between your ribs. Count it well done, for it was to be; and give me what I come seeking in the name of blood and in the name of God."

And the spirits of the dead stirred in the cairn like ants; and they spoke: "You have broken the roof of our cairn and let in the moon between our ribs; and you have the strength of the still-living. But what virtue have we? what power? or what jewel here in the dust with us, that any living man should covet or receive it? for we are less than nothing. But we tell you one thing, speaking with many voices like bees, that the way is plain before all like the grooves of launching. So forth into life and fear not, for so did we all in the ancient ages." And their voices passed away like an eddy in a river.

"Now," said the Poor Thing, "they have told you a lesson, but make them give you a gift. Stoop your hand among the bones without drawback, and you shall find their treasure."

So the man stooped his hand, and the dead laid hold upon it many and faint like ants; but he shook them off, and behold, what he brought up in his hand was the shoe of a horse, and it was rusty.

"It is a thing of no price," quoth the man, "for it is rusty."

"We shall see that," said the Poor Thing; "for in my thought it is a good thing to do what our fathers did, and to keep what they kept without question. And in my thought one thing is as good as another in this world; and a shoe of a horse will do."

Now they got into their boat with the horseshoe, and when the dawn was come they were aware of the smoke of the Earl's town and the bells of the Kirk that beat. So they set foot to shore; and the man went up to the market among the fishers over against the palace and the Kirk; and he was bitter poor and bitter ugly, and he had never a fish to sell, but only a shoe of a horse in his creel, and it rusty.

"Now," said the Poor Thing, "do so and so, and you shall find a wife and I a mother."

It befell that the Earl's daughter came forth to go into the Kirk upon her prayers; and when she saw the poor man stand in the market with only the shoe of a horse, and it rusty, it came in her mind it should be a thing of price.

"What is that?" quoth she.

"It is a shoe of a horse," said the man.

"And what is the use of it?" quoth the Earl's daughter.

"It is for no use," said the man.

"I may not believe that," said she; "else why should you carry it?"

"I do so," said he, "because it was so my fathers did in the ancient ages; and I have neither a better reason nor a worse."

Now the Earl's daughter could not find it in her mind to be-

Kirk: church.

Beginning with the Observations of Others

lieve him. "Come," quoth she, "sell me this, for I am sure it is a thing of price."

"Nay," said the man, "the thing is not for sale."

"What!" cried the Earl's daughter. "Then what make you here in the town's market, with the thing in your creel and nought beside?"

"I sit here," says the man, "to get me a wife."

"There is no sense in any of these answers," thought the Earl's daughter; "and I could find it in my heart to weep."

By came the Earl upon that; and she called him and told him all. And when he had heard, he was of his daughter's mind that this should be a thing of virtue; and charged the man to set a price upon the thing, or else be hanged upon the gallows; and that was near at hand, so that the man could see it.

"The way of life is straight like the grooves of launching," quoth the man. "And if I am to be hanged let me be hanged."

"Why!" cried the Earl, "will you set your neck against a shoe of a horse, and it rusty?"

"In my thought," said the man, "one thing is as good as another in this world; and a shoe of a horse will do."

"This can never be," thought the Earl; and he stood and looked upon the man, and bit his beard.

And the man looked up at him and smiled. "It was so my fathers did in the ancient ages," quoth he to the Earl, "and I have neither a better reason nor a worse."

"There is no sense in any of this," thought the Earl, "and I must be growing old." So he had his daughter on one side, and says he: "Many suitors have you denied, my child. But here is a very strange matter that a man should cling so to a shoe of a horse, and it rusty; and that he should offer it like a thing on sale, and yet not sell it; and that he should sit there seeking a wife. If I come not to the bottom of this thing, I shall have no more pleasure in bread; and I can see no way, but either I should hang or you should marry him."

"By my troth, but he is bitter ugly," said the Earl's daughter. "How if the gallows be so near at hand?"

"It was not so," said the Earl, "that my fathers did in the ancient ages. I am like the man, and can give you neither a better reason nor a worse. But do you, prithee, speak with him again."

So the Earl's daughter spoke to the man. "If you were not so bitter ugly," quoth she, "my father the Earl would have us marry."

"Bitter ugly am I," said the man, "and you as fair as May. Bitter ugly I am, and what of that? It was so my fathers——"

"In the name of God," said the Earl's daughter, "let your fathers be!"

"If I had done that," said the man, "you had never been chaffer-

chaffering: bargaining.

Observing and Generalizing

ing with me here in the market, nor your father the Earl watching with the end of his eye."

"But come," quoth the Earl's daughter, "this is a very strange thing, that you would have me wed for a shoe of a horse, and it rusty."

"In my thought," quoth the man, "one thing is as good——"

"Oh, spare me that," said the Earl's daughter, "and tell me why I should marry."

"Listen and look," said the man.

Now the wind blew through the Poor Thing like an infant crying, so that her heart was melted; and her eyes were unsealed, and she was aware of the thing as it were a babe unmothered, and she took it to her arms, and it melted in her arms like the air.

"Come," said the man, "behold a vision of our children, the busy hearth, and the white heads. And let that suffice, for it is all God offers."

"I have no delight in it," said she; but with that she sighed.

"The ways of life are straight like the grooves of launching," said the man; and he took her by the hand.

"And what shall we do with the horseshoe?" quoth she.

"I will give it to your father," said the man; "and he can make a kirk and a mill of it for me."

It came to pass in time that the Poor Thing was born; but memory of these matters slept within him, and he knew not that which he had done. But he was a part of the eldest son; rejoicing manfully to launch the boat into the surf, skilful to direct the helm, and a man of might where the ring closes and the blows are going.

"Sound of spirit" and "merry of heart,"—to how few is it given to be this. It is a kind of natural Zen. "He blessed God without weighing." Long fish, short fish, fat fish, thin fish, many fish, few fish, no fish—he thanked God for them all. "The way is plain before all like the grooves of launching." In *Inscribed on the Believing Mind*, we have:

> The Way is not difficult; but you must avoid choosing!

("Avoid choosing" means "without weighing," "Judge not that ye be not judged.")

Christians and Buddhists alike put their religion in some other place, some other time; but we are all, with or without religion, tarred with the same brush. Like Mrs. Jelleby in *Bleak House*, with her "impossible love of the blackamoors" and indifference to her own husband and children, we think of our religion, our ideals, forgetting (on purpose) that the Way is here and now, in what we are doing, saying, feeling, reading, at this very moment. Confucius says in *The Doctrine of the Mean*,

> The Way is not far from man; if we take the Way as something superhuman, beyond man, this is not the real Way.

Mencius is even closer to Stevenson:

> The Way is near, but men seek it afar. It is in easy things, but men seek for it in difficult things.
>
> The Way is like a great highroad; there is no difficulty whatever in recognising it. What is wrong with us is that we do not really search for it. Just go home, and plenty of people will point it out to you.

The *Saikontan* says,

> The Zen Sect tells us: When you are hungry, eat rice; when you are weary, sleep.

That is all religion is: eat when you are hungry, sleep when you are tired. But to do such simple things properly is really the most difficult thing in the world. I remember when I began to attend lectures, at a Zen temple, on the *Mumonkan*, I was surprised to find that there were no lofty spiritual truths enunciated at all. Two things stuck in my head, because they were repeated so often, and with such gusto. One of them, emphasized with extreme vigour, was that you must not smoke a cigarette while making water. The other was that when somebody calls you (in Japanese "Oi!") you must answer "Hai!" at once, without hesitation. When we compare this with the usual Christian exhortatory sermon, we cannot help being struck by the difference. I myself heard the "Oi!" "Hai!" so many times I began to wait for it and look on it as a kind of joke, and as soon as I did this, I began to see a light, or "get warm," as the children say. It is like the grooves of launching. Release the blocks and the ship moves. One calls "Oi!" the other says "Hai!" There is nothing between.

"It is a good thing to do what our fathers did, and to keep what they kept without question." This is not a popular doctrine nowadays. Old traditions are forgotten but new ones spring up like mushrooms everywhere. In the Zen temple, together with some unnecessary and old-fashioned customs, there is a vast body of essential religion preserved in the form of rules: regularity of life, celibacy, vegetarianism, poverty, unquestioning obedience, methodical destruction of self-full thinking and acting, complete control of mind and body,—all these systematized into a way of life in which work, we may say, Work, is the grand answer to the question, "What is man's element?"

"And in my thought, one thing is as good as another in this world." This states the absolute value of everything; all things have equal value, for all have infinite value. If you like this kind of mystical truth and can swallow it easily, well and good. If not, it does not matter, because it is only ordinary common sense. The value of a thing is in its use, as Robinson Crusoe found out with regard to the pieces-of-gold on his desert island. It's no good playing the cello to a thirsty man. You can't light a fire with ice cream. You may protest that things differ in their potential value; a drawing by Claude is not equal in value to a grain of sand. It

Claude: Claude Lorrain (1600–82), French landscape painter.

Observing and Generalizing

may well be so. The financial, the artistic, the moral values may differ: the point is that the *absolute* value is the same. If you see infinity in a grain of sand and heaven in a wild flower, where is the necessity for anything else? Everything depends on the mind of man;

> There is nothing either good or bad but thinking makes it so.

So when the man was asked what was the use of his rusty horse-shoe, he answered, "It is for no use." This has exactly the same meaning as the first case of the *Mumonkan*.

> A monk said to Joshu, "Has this dog the Buddha-nature or not?" Joshu replied "No!"

Its absolute value is nil. It has the same value as a rusty horse-shoe. Has this rusty horse-shoe the Buddha nature? The answer is, Yes! If you can rise, just for a moment, beyond this No-Yes, you understand that one thing is as good (that is, as Good) as another in this world. "And let that suffice, for it is all God offers." What is happening to me, the writer, in this place, at this moment; to you, the reader, in your place, at the very moment of reading this, what you see and feel, your circumstances internal and external,—it is all that God offers. Do you want to be in some other place, in different circumstances? Take the present ones to your heart, let them suffice, for it is all God offers. If you feel aggrieved with so little, remember that "one thing is as good as another." If your aim is comfort, only some things, some times, some places will do. If your aim is virtue (that is, Goodness, not goodness,) anything, any time, any place will suffice. When Confucius was asked concerning the brothers Haku I and Shuku Sai, who gave up the throne and their lives rather than do wrong.

> "Had they any regrets?"

he answered,

> "They sought for virtue; they got virtue: what was there for them to regret?"

DISCUSSION

1. There is an obvious difference between the technique used by Thucydides and that used by Blyth: the former does not tell us where each piece of information came from, but blends his facts into a continuous narrative, while Blyth patches together quotations that he identifies. Imagine that each uses the other's method, Thucydides using many direct quotations from the soldiers he interviewed and Blyth referring indirectly to the material of others in explaining Zen. Would there be any specific improvements in either or both? What might be lost in each case?

infinity in a grain of sand: reference to "Auguries of Innocence," a poem by William Blake.

2. Some subjects, especially those having to do with states of mind, cannot be talked about directly, but must be talked *around*, described, so to speak, by the shape of the hole left in the center of the discussion. Zen is one of these: it is a state of mind too simple and elemental to be approached directly through the complexities of language, and, in fact, language in this case obscures the very thing it sets out to define. Another such state of mind is being in love, an emotional state that can be pointed to by describing its symptoms, but which could not be described by them seem to represent this quality to the greatest degree. once know what love is or what Zen is, we can recognize the symptoms anywhere. To test whether Blyth has succeeded to any degree in communicating what Zen is, think of earlier readings in this book. See if you and others can agree as to which authors and which of the people described by them seem to represent this quality to the greatest degree. But talk only about examples, do not attempt a "dictionary" definition.
3. While Thucydides seems to be impartial toward the subject of his history, Blyth seems to be enthusiastic in telling us about Zen—we feel he wants us to share his pleasure. Would his essay be better if he were less carried away by his subject? Why, or why not?

WRITING SUGGESTIONS

Since we are dealing with writing from sources other than direct experience or observation, this might be a good point at which to consider the research paper. We shall not attempt to offer technical instructions, but we would like to offer one or two suggestions in keeping with the purpose of this book. The research paper need not be an exercise in boredom.

There are two kinds of research paper: the report and the thesis paper. The report, like "The Defeat of the Athenian Forces," puts together the story of something that happened or tells about something that exists, such as an institution; the thesis paper, like "What Is Zen?" makes a point. Either can be successful if the subject is chosen well.

The first thing to keep in mind when choosing a subject is to be sure that you have something new to say about it. Probably no one but your best friend is interested in what you have to say about such general subjects as juvenile delinquency, the drug scene, women's liberation, abortion, national defense, Red China, inflation, or the United Nations, unless you are personally involved in one of these and have some new evidence to offer.

One good idea is to choose a subject that is close to you geographically. It is amazing how little most people know about their own region or community. If you write about some aspect of your own town, city, county, or immediate region, you are almost sure to be writing something that will be news to your reader.

There are two standard sources of information on local topics: the interview and the newspaper file. Most people are delighted to be asked questions, especially about their roles in historical events, their jobs, or their special interests such as local history. In large cities, the libraries keep newspaper files; in smaller cities and towns, they are kept in the offices of the

Observing and Generalizing

newspapers themselves. Most newspapers are not indexed, so it is best to get an idea of when an event occurred before you begin your search.

National magazines and books will offer background material relevant to your subject, as will the reference section of your library. For example, if you are researching the history of Mudville's fire department, you will want to consult a general history of firefighting in an encyclopedia, articles on new firefighting techniques in magazines, and books on developments in firefighting at various times in order to compare your local department with others and gain perspective. Meanwhile your focus on the local department will save your paper from being general and insipid and may well prove to be the first writing on the subject.

Here are a few suggested subjects, just to indicate the wealth of material waiting in most communities. While a few will not apply to your community, most will. In many cases you will need to limit your subject further before you can go ahead; for example, if you lived in Santa Fe, New Mexico, "Indians of the Santa Fe Region" would be far too large a topic for such a paper, and would need to be limited to one tribe or one episode in history. Enlist your instructor's aid in limiting your topic to a workable size.

> Indians of the Mudville Region
> An Early Mudville Character
> How Some Mudville Streets Got Their Names
> Mudville During the Depression
> Zoning in Mudville: How Are Decisions Made?
> What Happens When Someone Dies in Mudville?
> Mudville's Health Services
> Bird Life in Mudville
> A Mudville Fireman: How Does He Live?
> What Mudville Needs Most

A glance through the daily paper or the telephone directory will suggest many more subjects. Most of these subjects can be treated in straight reports or thesis papers. For example, you could simply report all the facts about health services in Mudville or you could show that they were adequate or inadequate. A thesis does not have to be argumentative; it may be as simple and noncontroversial as, "Mudville's hospitals have many problems." The important thing is to support your thesis with facts that are clearly organized and presented.

The research paper needn't be a drag. If you choose a subject that is properly limited and reasonably original you may even find it is fun. It will be even more fun if you keep in mind what many of the writers in *Experiences* illustrate: that it is not facts that are the most interesting to read, but the carefully observed detail with which you present and surround them. Enhance the factual content of your paper with sensory detail, character sketches, and atmosphere.

Plate 11
Albrecht Dürer (1471–1528): "The Vision of St. John"

The artist interprets. When he begins with the written word, he gives us what he visualizes as he reads; and of course every man has a unique way of visualizing. In Christian Europe, no written material was more frequently interpreted by artists than the Bible; and nothing was visualized with more variety than the Book of Revelation. Here are the words that Dürer has interpreted:

> And I turned to see the voice that spoke with me. And being turned, I saw seven golden candlesticks; and in the midst of the seven candlesticks one like unto a son of man, clothed with a garment down to the foot, and girt about the paps with a golden girdle. His head and hairs were white like wool, as white as snow; and his eyes were as a flame of fire; and his feet like unto fine brass, as if they burned in a furnace; and his voice as the sound of many waters. And he had in his right hand seven stars: and out of his mouth went a sharp two-edged sword: and his countenance was as the sun shineth in his strength.

1. Allowing for the obvious limitation that Dürer cannot represent color in a woodcut, is there anything in the description of the vision that he has omitted? If so, can you think of any reason for such an omission?
2. What has Dürer added to the picture that is not mentioned in the passage? What might be his reason for each addition?
3. Besides additions and deletions, a number of details that are not mentioned at all in the passage must be decided on before the picture is planned. For example, what kind of candlesticks? What are some other necessary decisions Dürer had to make? Why do you think he chose as he did in each case?

PLATE 11   Albrecht Dürer (1471–1528), **The Vision of St. John.**

PLATE 12   Thomas Hart Benton (1889–1975), **Persephone.** *Collection of Rita P. Benton.*

Plate 12
Thomas Hart Benton (1889-1975): *Persephone*

Albrecht Dürer gives us a very literal interpretation of the vision of St. John, with no implied comment. Here Thomas Hart Benton also gives us a very literal version of a classical myth, but it is literal in a different way. With obvious humorous intent, he has not only translated the ancient tale to modern Missouri, but has reduced the god and goddess to ordinary farm people. The portion of the myth that relates to the picture directly is: Hades, god of the underworld, fell in love with Persephone, daughter of Zeus and Demeter, but couldn't get the permission of Zeus to marry her. One day as she was gathering flowers, Hades appeared in his chariot drawn by four black horses and carried her off to the underworld.

1. What details of the painting indicate the period and culture in which the events are taking place? What details could just as well be in the original classical setting?
2. Comparing the figure of Benton's *Persephone* with the *Venus de Milo* (Plate 9), a classical Greek representation of a goddess of fertility, what differences are apparent? What comment on the part of the artist do these differences imply?
3. What generalizations can you make regarding Benton's way of seeing as contrasted with Dürer's? As contrasted with the sculptors of the "Venus" of Willendorf and the *Venus de Milo*? Support your generalizations with references to the works of art.

III
The Direct Experience

Observation and experience cannot be separated like oranges and apples. Observation is a variety of experience, and we cannot experience without observing. The distinction is more a matter of emphasis or direction than of difference: observation emphasizes what is going on outside the writer, while experience emphasizes what is going on inside the writer or is happening to him personally. When, in the first selection of Part III, David Livingstone tells us what it is like to be attacked by a lion, there is no question that we would label his account a description of an experience; with equal confidence we can call Leigh Hunt's "Inside of an Omnibus" an observation, since Hunt says nothing about himself but focusses on the people around him. However, not all examples of writing can be so neatly classified. Often there are nearly equal elements of observation and experience in the same passage, as in Rupert Brooke's "The Great Lover," the first selection in this book.

Within experience there are also outward and inward movements. The outward experience is that which involves physical action or relationships with other people and objects; the inner experience is that which takes place inside us, the experience within our own minds or emotions. When we dream, we experience something inside us; when we change a fundamental attitude, as when we learn to love someone we previously hated, we experience primarily an inner change, even though it has important reference to the world

The Direct Experience

outside of us. Again, of course, we cannot classify neatly, for our inner selves exist only in interaction with the world. But whether their focus is inward or outward, we may expect the authors in Part III to tell us more about themselves than those in previous sections and more about what they feel.

8

The Outward Experience

We shall begin with an experience of the famous missionary David Livingstone. Livingstone seldom wrote about himself and his troubles; he was primarily an objective observer, and a very good one. But when his friends insisted that he describe his experience of being attacked by a wounded lion, he proved to be an interesting, if unusually objective, observer of his own sensations. Many people have told of their experiences of violence and near death, but few with the coolness of Livingstone.

David Livingstone

Mauled by a Lion

(1844)

The Bakatla of the village Mabotsa were troubled by lions, which leaped into the cattle-pens by night and destroyed their cows. They even attacked the herds in open day. This was so unusual an occurrence that the people believed themselves bewitched—"given," as they said, "into the power of the lions by a neighboring tribe." They went once to attack the animals but, being rather cowardly in comparison with the Bechuanas in general, they returned without slaying any. It is well known that if one in a troop of lions is killed the remainder leave that part of the country. The next time, therefore, the herds were attacked, I went with the people to encourage them to rid themselves of the annoyance by destroying one

The Direct Experience

of the marauders. We found the animals on a small hill covered with trees. The men formed round it in a circle, and gradually closed up as they advanced. Being below on the plain with a native schoolmaster named Mebalwe, I saw one of the lions sitting on a piece of rock within the ring. Mebalwe fired at him, and the ball hit the rock on which the animal was sitting. He bit at the spot struck, as a dog does at a stick or stone thrown at him; and then leaping away, broke through the circle and escaped unhurt. If the Bakatla had acted according to the custom of the country, they would have speared him in his attempt to get out, but they were afraid to attack him. When the circle was reformed, we saw two other lions in it, but dared not fire lest we should shoot some of the people. The beasts burst through the line and, as it was evident the men could not be prevailed upon to face their foes, we bent our footsteps toward the village. In going round the end of the hill I saw a lion sitting on a piece of rock about thirty yards off, with a little bush in front of him. I took a good aim at him through the bush and fired both barrels into it. The men called out, "He is shot, he is shot!" Others cried, "He has been shot by another man too; let us go to him!" I saw the lion's tail erected in anger and, turning to the people, said, "Stop a little until I load again." When in the act of ramming down the bullets I heard a shout and, looking half round, I saw the lion in the act of springing upon me. He caught me by the shoulder and we both came to the ground together. Growling horribly, he shook me as a terrier dog does a rat. The shock produced a stupor similar to that which seems to be felt by a mouse after the first grip of the cat. It caused a sort of dreaminess in which there was no sense of pain nor feeling of terror, though I was quite conscious of all that was happening. It was like what patients partly under the influence of chloroform describe; they see the operation but do not feel the knife. This placidity is probably produced in all the animals killed by the carnivora; and if so, is a merciful provision of the Creator for lessening the pain of death. As he had one paw on the back of my head, I turned round to relieve myself of the weight and saw his eyes directed to Mebalwe, who was aiming at him from a distance of ten or fifteen yards. His gun, which was a flint one, missed fire in both barrels. The animal immediately left me to attack him, and bit his thigh. Another man, whose life I had saved after he had been tossed by a buffalo, attempted to spear the lion, upon which he turned from Mebalwe and seized this fresh foe by the shoulder. At that moment the bullets the beast had received took effect and he fell down dead. The whole was the work of a few moments, and must have been his paroxysm of dying rage. In order to take out the charm from him, the Bakatla on the following day made a huge bonfire over the carcase, which was declared to be the largest ever seen. Besides crunching the bone into splinters, eleven of his teeth had penetrated the upper part of my arm. The bite of a lion resembles a gunshot wound. It is generally followed by a great deal of sloughing and discharge, and ever afterwards pains are felt periodically in the part. I had on a tartan jacket, which I believe wiped off the virus from the teeth that pierced the flesh, for my two companions in the affray have both suffered from the usual pains, while I have escaped with only the inconvenience of a false joint in my limb. The wound of the man who was bit in the shoulder actually burst forth afresh on the same month of the following year. This curious point deserves the attention of inquirers.

It is not surprising that Livingstone can keep us reading with his account of a violent and dangerous experience. But the test of a good writer is whether he can hold our interest with the most ordinary experiences of life. Leigh Hunt was a man who seemed never to be bored; he found the most ordinary people interesting, and, as he demonstrates in the following selection, he could make the most everyday experience seem comic.

Leigh Hunt

Getting Up on Cold Mornings

(1833)

An Italian author—Giulio Cordara, a Jesuit—has written a poem upon insects, which he begins by insisting, that those troublesome and abominable little animals were created for our annoyance, and that they were certainly not inhabitants of Paradise. We of the north may dispute this piece of theology; but on the other hand, it is as clear as the snow on the house-tops, that Adam was not under the necessity of shaving; and that when Eve walked out of her delicious bower, she did not step upon ice three inches thick.

Some people say it is a very easy thing to get up of a cold morning. You have only, they tell you, to take the resolution; and the thing is done. This may be very true; just as a boy at school has only to take a flogging, and the thing is over. But we have not at all made up our minds upon it; and we find it a very pleasant exercise to discuss the matter, candidly, before we get up. This at least is not idling, though it may be lying. It affords an excellent answer to those, who ask how lying in bed can be indulged in by a reasoning being—a rational creature. How? Why with the argument calmly at work in one's head, and the clothes over one's shoulder. Oh—it is a fine way of spending a sensible, impartial half-hour.

If these people would be more charitable, they would get on with their argument better. But they are apt to reason so ill, and to assert so dogmatically, that one could wish to have them stand round one's bed of a bitter morning, and *lie* before their faces. They ought to hear both sides of the bed, the inside and out. If they cannot entertain themselves with their own thoughts for half an hour or so, it is not the fault of those who can.

Candid inquiries into one's decumbency, besides the greater or less privileges to be allowed a man in proportion to his ability of keeping early hours, the work given his faculties, &c. will at least concede their due merits to such representations as the following. In the first place, says the injured but calm appealer, I have been warm all night, and find my system in a state perfectly suitable to a warm-blooded animal. To get out of this state into the cold, besides the inharmonious and uncritical abruptness of the transition, is so unnatural to such a creature, that the poets, refining upon the tortures of the damned, make one of their greatest agonies consist in being suddenly transported from heat to cold,—from fire to ice. They are "haled" out of their "beds," says Milton, by "harpy-footed furies,"—fellows who come to call them. On my first movement towards the anticipation of getting up, I find that such parts of the sheets and bolster, as are exposed to the air of the room, are stone-cold. On opening my eyes, the first thing that meets them is my own breath rolling forth, as if in the open air, like smoke out of a chimney. Think of this symptom. Then I turn my eyes sideways and see the window all frozen over. Think of that. . . . —I now cannot help thinking a good deal—who can?—upon the unnecessary and villainous custom of shaving: it is a thing so unmanly (here I nestle closer)—so effeminate (here I recoil from an unlucky step into the colder part of the bed.)— No wonder that the Queen of France took part with the rebels 'against that degenerate King, her husband, who first affronted her smooth visage with a face like her own. The Emperor Julian never showed the luxuriancy of his genius to better advantage than in reviving the flowing beard. Look at Cardinal Bembo's picture—at Michael Angelo's—at Titian's—at Shakespeare's—at Fletcher's—at Spenser's—at Chaucer's—at Alfred's—at Plato's—I could name a great man for every tick of my watch.—Look at the Turks, a grave and otiose people.—Think of Haroun Al Raschid and Bed-ridden Hassan.—Think of Wortley Montague, the worthy son of his mother, above the prejudice of his time.—Look at the Persian gentlemen, whom one is ashamed of meeting about the suburbs, their dress and appearance are so much finer than our own.—Lastly, think of the razor itself—how totally opposed to every sensation of bed—how cold, how edgy, how hard! how utterly different from anything like the warm and circling amplitude, which

> Sweetly recommends itself
> Unto our gentle senses.

Add to this, benumbed fingers, which may help you to cut yourself, a quivering body, a frozen towel, and a ewer full of ice; and he that says there is nothing to oppose in all this, only shows, that he has no merit in opposing it.

Thomson the poet, who exclaims in his Seasons—

> Falsely luxurious! Will not man awake?

used to lie in bed till noon, because he said he had no motive in getting up. He could imagine the good of rising; but then he could also imagine the good of lying still; and his exclamation, it must be allowed, was made upon summer-time, not winter. We must proportion the argument to the individual character. A money-getter may be drawn out of his bed by three or four pence; but this will not suffice for a student. A proud man may say, "What shall I think of myself, if I don't get up?" but the more humble one will be content to waive this prodigious notion of himself, out of respect to his kindly bed. The mechanical man shall get up without any ado at all; and so shall the barometer. An ingenious lier in bed will find hard matter of discussion even on the score of health and longevity. He will ask us for our proofs and precedents of the ill effects of lying later in cold weather; and sophisticate much on the advantages of an even temperature of body; of the natural propensity (pretty universal) to have one's way; and of the animals that roll themselves up, and sleep all the winter. As to longevity, he will ask whether the longest is of necessity the best; and whether Holborn is the handsomest street in London.

DISCUSSION

1. It would be hard to find two people further apart in their way of seeing things than Livingstone and Hunt. What do you think Livingstone's attitude toward getting up in the morning would be? What is your evidence for such speculation? If Hunt were attacked by a lion, how do you think he would write about it? Would his account be of more value than Livingstone's? Why, or why not?
2. Livingstone, who was a physician with a scientifically inquiring mind, cannot write a paragraph about a dramatic adventure without suggesting generalizations or proposing questions; Hunt, who was a literary man, must make references to literature and history. Do these additions enhance the quality of the writing in each case or detract from it? Why?

In a mood somewhat similar to Hunt's, Soame Jenyns describes a visit to a country house; unlike Hunt, he does not make allusions to literature or history, but gives us only the lively scene itself.

Soame Jenyns

The Country Visit

(1735)

Or if with ceremony cloy'd,
You wou'd next time such plagues avoid,
And visit without previous notice,
JOHN, JOHN, a coach!—I can't think who 'tis,
My lady cries, who spies your coach,
Ere you the avenue approach;
Lord how lucky!—washing day!

Holborn: the longest, and not the handsomest, street in London.

The Direct Experience

And all the men are in the hay!
Entrance to gain is something hard,
The dogs all bark, the gates are barr'd;
The yard's with lines of linen cross'd,
The hall-door's lock'd, the key is lost;
These difficulties all o'ercome,
We reach at length the drawing room,
Then there's such trampling over-head,
Madam you'd swear was brought to bed;
Miss in a hurry bursts her lock,
To get clean sleeves to hide her smock;
The servants run, the pewter clatters,
My lady dresses, calls, and chatters;
The cook-maid raves for want of butter,
Pigs squeak, fowls scream, and green geese flutter.
Now after three hours tedious waiting,
On all our neighbours faults debating,
And having nine times view'd the garden,
In which there's nothing worth a farthing,
In comes my lady, and the pudden:
You will excuse sir,—on a sudden—
Then, that we may have four and four,
The bacon, fowls, and collyflow'r
Their ancient unity divide,
The top one graces, one each side;
And by and by, the second course
Comes lagging like a distanc'd horse;
A salver then to church and king,
The butler sweats, the glasses ring;
The cloth remov'd, the toasts go round,
Bawdy and politics abound;
And as the knight more tipsy waxes,
We damn all ministers and taxes.

At last the ruddy sun quite sunk,
The coachman tolerably drunk,
Whirling o'er hillocks, ruts, and stones,
Enough to dislocate one's bones,
We home return, a wond'rous token
Of heaven's kind care, with limbs unbroken.
Afflict us not, ye Gods, tho' sinners,
With many days like this, or dinners!

her lock: the lock of her wardrobe.
farthing: one-fourth of a penny.
pudden: pudding.
bawdy: coarse or obscene joking.
knight: owner of the farm.

At one time or another, most people have had the experience of being unemployed. How they have felt about the experience depends on what sort of people they are. In the next two selections, we find two very different attitudes toward being out in the world with no job and no money.

Hamlin Garland

The Grasshopper and the Ant

(1917)

As nothing offered in the township round about the Harris home, I started one Saturday morning to walk to a little crossroads village some twenty miles away, in which I was told a teacher was required. My cousins, not knowing that I was penniless, supposed, of course, that I would go by train, and I was too proud to tell them the truth. It was very muddy, and when I reached the home of the committeeman his midday meal was over, and his wife did not ask if I had dined—although she was quick to tell me that the teacher had just been hired.

Without a cent in my pocket, I could not ask for food—therefore, I turned back weary, hungry and disheartened. To make matters worse a cold rain was falling and the eighteen or twenty miles between me and the Harris farm looked long.

I think it must have been at this moment that I began, for the first time, to take a really serious view of my plan "to see the world." It became evident with startling abruptness, that a man might be both hungry and cold in the midst of abundance. I recalled the fable of the grasshopper who, having wasted the summer hours in singing, was mendicant to the ant. My weeks of careless gaiety were over. The money I had spent in travel looked like a noble fortune to me at this hour.

The road was deep in mud, and as night drew on the rain thickened. At last I said, "I will go into some farmhouse and ask the privilege of a bed." This was apparently a simple thing to do and yet I found it exceedingly hard to carry out. To say bluntly, "Sir, I have no money, I am tired and hungry," seemed a baldly disgraceful way of beginning. On the other hand to plead relationship with Will Harris involved a relative, and besides, they might not know my cousin, or they might think my statement false.

Arguing in this way I passed house after house while the water dripped from my hat and the mud clogged my feet. Though chilled and hungry to the point of weakness, my suffering was mainly mental. A sudden realization of the natural antagonism of the well-to-do toward the tramp appalled me. Once, as I turned in toward the bright light of a kitchen window, the roar of a watchdog stopped me before I had fairly passed the gate. I turned back with a savage word, hot with resentment at a houseowner who would keep a beast like that. At another cottage I was repulsed by an old woman who sharply said, "We don't feed tramps."

The Direct Experience

I now had the precise feeling of the penniless outcast. With morbidly active imagination I conceived of myself as being forever set apart from home and friends, condemned to wander the night alone. I worked on this idea till I achieved a bitter, furtive and ferocious manner.

However, I knocked at another door and upon meeting the eyes of the woman at the threshold, began with formal politeness to explain, "I am a teacher, I have been to look for a school, and am on my way back to Byron, where I have relatives. Can you keep me all night?"

The woman listened in silence and at length replied with ungracious curtness, "I guess so. Come in."

She gave me a seat by the fire, and when her husband returned from the barn, I explained the situation to him. He was only moderately cordial. "Make yourself at home. I'll be in as soon as I have finished my milking," he said, and left me beside the kitchen fire.

The woman of the house, silent, suspicious (it seemed to me), began to spread the table for supper while I, sitting beside the stove, began to suffer with the knowledge that I had, in a certain sense, deceived them. I was fairly well dressed and my voice and manner, as well as the fact that I was seeking a school, had given them, no doubt, the impression that I was able to pay for my entertainment, and the more I thought of this the more uneasy I became. To eat of their food without making an explanation was impossible, but the longer I waited the more difficult the explanation grew.

Suffering keenly, absurdly, I sat with hanging head going over and over the problem, trying to formulate an easy way of letting them know my predicament. There was but one way of escape—and I took it. As the woman stepped out of the room for a moment, I rose, seized my hat and rushed out into the rain and darkness like a fugitive.

I have often wondered what those people thought when they found me gone. Perhaps I am the great mystery of their lives, an unexplained visitant from "the night's Plutonian shore."

I plodded on for another mile or two in the darkness, which was now so intense I could scarcely keep the road. Only by the feel of the mud under my feet could I follow the pike. Like Jean Valjean, I possessed a tempest in my brain. I experienced my first touch of despair.

Although I had never had more than thirty dollars at any one time, I had never been without money. Distinctions had not counted largely in the pioneer world to which I belonged. I was proud of my family. I came of good stock, and knew it and felt it, but now here I was, wet as a sponge and without shelter simply because I had not in my pocket a small piece of silver with which to buy a bed.

I walked on until this dark surge of rebellious rage had spent its force and reason weakly resumed her throne. I said, "What nonsense! Here I am only a few miles from relatives. All the farmers on this road must know the Harris family. If I tell them who I am, they will certainly feel

Jean Valjean: hero of Victor Hugo's *Les Miserables*, an ex-convict who rises to wealth and prominence in constant fear that his background will be discovered.

that I have the claim of a neighbor upon them." But these deductions, admirable as they were, did not lighten my sky or make begging easier.

After walking two miles farther I found it almost impossible to proceed. It was black night and I did not know where I stood. The wind had risen and the rain was falling in slant cataracts. As I looked about me and caught the gleam from the windows of a small farmhouse, my stubborn pride gave away. Stumbling up the path I rapped on the door. It was opened by a middle-aged farmer in his stocking feet, smoking a pipe. Having finished his supper he was taking his ease beside the fire, and fortunately for me, was in genial mood.

"Come in," he said heartily. " 'Tis a wet night."

I began, "I am a cousin of William Harris of Byron—"

"You don't say! Well, what are you doing on the road a night like this? Come in!"

I stepped inside and finished my explanation there.

This good man and his wife will forever remain the most hospitable figures in my memory. They set me close beside the stove insisting that I put my feet in the oven to dry, talking meanwhile of my cousins and the crops, and complaining of the incessant rainstorms which were succeeding one another almost without intermission, making this one of the wettest and most dismal autumns the country had ever seen. Never in all my life has a roof seemed more heavenly, or hosts more sweet and gracious.

After breakfast next morning I shook hands with the farmer saying: "I shall send you the money for my entertainment the first time my cousin comes to town," and under the clamor of his hospitable protestations against payment, set off up the road.

The sun came out warm and beautiful and all about me on every farm the teamsters were getting into the fields. The mud began to dry up and with the growing cheer of the morning my heart expanded and the experience of the night before became as unreal as a dream and yet it had happened, and it had taught me a needed lesson. Hereafter I take no narrow chances, I vowed to myself.

Upon arrival at my cousin's home I called him aside, and said, "Will, you have work to do and I have need of wages. I am going to strip off this same as any other hand, and I shall expect the full pay of the best 'boiled shirt' and white collar, and I am going to work for you just the man on your place."

He protested, "I don't like to see you do this. Don't give up your plans. I'll hitch up and we'll start out and keep going till we find you a school."

"No," I said, "not till I earn a few dollars to put in my pocket. I've played the grasshopper for a few weeks—from this time on I'm the busy ant."

So it was settled, and, the grasshopper went forth into the fields and toiled as hard as any slave. I plowed, threshed, and husked corn, and when at last December came, I had acquired money enough to carry me on my way....

I wanted to make my way among strangers. I scorned to lean upon my aunt and uncle, though they were abundantly able to keep me. It was midwinter, nothing offered and so I turned (as so many young men similarly placed have done), toward a very common yet difficult job. I attempted to take subscriptions for a book.

After a few days' experience in a neighboring town I decided that whatever else I might be fitted for in this world, I was not intended for a book agent. Surrendering my prospectus to the firm, I took my way down to Madison, the capital of the state, a city which seemed at this time very remote, and very important in my world. Only when traveling did I have the feeling of living up to the expectations of Alice and Burton who put into their letters to me, an envy which was very sweet. To them I was a bold adventurer!

Alas for me! In the shining capital of my state I felt again the world's rough hand. First of all I tried the State House. This was before the general use of typewriters and I had been told that copyists were in demand. I soon discovered that four men and two girls were clamoring for every job. Nobody needed me. I met with blunt refusals and at last turned to other fields.

Every morning I went among the merchants seeking an opportunity to clerk or keep books, and at last obtained a place at six dollars per week in the office of an agricultural implement firm. I was put to work in the accounting department, as general slavey, under the immediate supervision of a youth who had just graduated from my position and who considered me his legitimate victim. He was only seventeen and not handsome, and I despised him with instant bitterness. Under his direction I swept out the office, made copies of letters, got the mail, stamped envelopes and performed other duties of a manual routine kind, to which I would have made no objection, had it not been for the gloating joy with which that chinless cockerel ordered me about. I had never been under that kind of discipline, and to have a pinheaded gamin order me to clean spittoons was more than I could stomach.

At the end of the week I went to the proprietor, and said, "If you have nothing better for me to do than sweep the floor and run errands, I think I'll quit."

With some surprise my boss studied me. At last said: "Very well, sir, you can go, and from all accounts I don't think we'll miss you much," which was perfectly true. I was an absolute failure so far as any routine work of that kind was concerned.

So here again I was thrown upon a cruel world with only six dollars between myself and the wolf. Again I fell back upon my physical powers. I made the round of all the factories seeking manual labor. I went out on the Catfish, where, through great sheds erected for the manufacture of farm machinery, I passed from superintendent to foreman, from foreman to boss—eager to wheel sand, paint woodwork, shovel coal—anything at all to keep from sending home for money—for, mind you, my father or my uncle would have helped me out had I written to them, but I could not do that. So long as I was able to keep a roof over my head, I remained silent. I was in the world and I intended to keep going without asking a cent from anyone. Besides, the grandiloquent plans for travel

The Outward Experience

and success which I had so confidently outlined to Burton must be carried out.

I should have been perfectly secure had it been summertime, for I knew the farmer's life and all that pertained to it, but it was winter. How to get a living in a strange town was my problem. It was a bright, clear, intensely cold February, and I was not very warmly dressed—hence I kept moving....

From office to office in Rock River I sullenly plodded, willing to work for fifty cents a day, until at last I secured a clerkship in a small stationery jobbing house which a couple of schoolteachers had strangely started, but on Saturday of the second week the proprietor called me to him and said kindly, but firmly, "Garland, I'm afraid you are too literary and too musical for this job. You have a fine baritone voice and your ability to vary the text set before you to copy, is remarkable, and yet I think we must part."

The reasons for this ironical statement were (to my mind) ignoble; first of all he resented my musical ability, secondly, my literary skill shamed him, for as he had put before me a badly composed circular letter, telling me to copy it one hundred times, I quite naturally improved the English. However, I admitted the charge of insubordination, and we parted quite amicably.

It was still winter, and I was utterly without promise of employment. In this extremity, I went to the Y. M. C. A. (which had for one of its aims the assistance of young men out of work) and confided my homelessness to the secretary, a capital young fellow who knew enough about men to recognize that I was not a "bum." He offered me the position of night watch and gave me a room and cot at the back of his office. These were dark hours!

During the day I continued to pace the streets. Occasionally some little job like raking up a yard would present itself, and so I was able to buy a few rolls, and sometimes I indulged in milk and meat. I lived along from noon to noon in presentable condition, but I was always hungry. For four days I subsisted on five cents worth of buns.

Having left my home for the purpose of securing experience in the world, I had this satisfaction—I was getting it! Very sweet and far away seemed all that beautiful life with Alice and Burton and Hattie at the Seminary, something to dream over, to regret, to versify, something which the future (at this moment) seemed utterly incapable of reproducing. I still corresponded with several of my classmates, but was careful to conceal the struggle that I was undergoing. I told them only of my travels and my reading.

As the ironical jobber remarked, I had a good voice, and upon being invited to accompany the Band of Hope which went to sing and pray in the County Jail, I consented, at least I took part in the singing. In this way I partly paid the debt I owed the Association, and secured some vivid impressions of prison life which came into use at a later time. My three associates in this work were a tinner, a clothing salesman and a cabinetmaker. More and more I longed for the spring, for with it I knew would come seeding, building and a chance for me.

The Direct Experience

At last in the midst of a grateful job of raking up yards and planting shrubs, I heard the rat-tat-tat of a hammer, and resolved upon a bold plan. I decided to become a carpenter, justifying myself by reference to my apprenticeship to my grandfather. One fine April morning I started out toward the suburbs, and at every house in process of construction approached the boss and asked for a job. Almost at once I found encouragement. "Yes, but where are your tools?"

In order to buy the tools I must work, work at anything. Therefore, at the next place I asked if there was any rough labor required around the house. The foreman replied: "Yes, there is some grading to be done." Accordingly I set to work with a wheelbarrow, grading the bank around the almost completed building. This was hard work, the crudest form of manual labor, but I grappled with it desperately, knowing that the pay (a dollar and a half a day) would soon buy a kit of tools.

Oh, that terrible first day! The heavy shovel blistered my hands and lamed my wrists. The lifting of the heavily laden wheelbarrow strained my back and shoulders. Half starved and weak, quite unfitted for sustained effort of this kind, I struggled on, and at the end of an interminable afternoon staggered home to my cot. The next morning came soon—too soon. I was not merely lame, I was lacerated. My muscles seemed to have been torn asunder, but I toiled (or made a show of toiling) all the second day. On the warrant of my wages I borrowed twenty-five cents of a friend and with this bought a meat dinner which helped me through another afternoon.

The third day was less painful and by the end of the week, I was able to do anything required of me. Upon receiving my pay I went immediately to the hardware store and bought a set of tools and a carpenter's apron, and early on Monday morning sallied forth in the *opposite direction* as a carpenter seeking a job. I soon came to a big frame house in course of construction. "Do you need another hand?" I asked. "Yes," replied the boss. "Take hold, right here, with this man."

"This man" turned out to be a Swede, a good-natured fellow, who made no comment on my deficiencies. We sawed and hammered together in very friendly fashion for a week, and I made rapid gains in strength and skill and took keen pleasure in my work. The days seemed short and life promising and as I was now getting two dollars per day, I moved out of my charity bed and took a room in a decayed mansion in the midst of a big lawn. My bearing became confident and easy. Money had straightened my back.

DISCUSSION

1. What parts of this selection contain the best writing? What quality makes it good? What parts do you find less interesting? Why?
2. In several places, Garland tells us how he feels about the experiences he is going through. Would everybody feel the same, or are other reactions possible? If so, what are some? What quality of Garland's character causes him to react in these particular ways?
3. Garland does not comment at all on the society in which he finds him-

self, but he tells us a great deal about it through example. Why would you guess he does not comment? What are some comments another person might offer?

A wholly different attitude toward venturing out into the world is displayed by Laurie Lee, who shows us in what manner he left home.

Laurie Lee

London Road

(1969)

The stooping figure of my mother, waist-deep in the grass and caught there like a piece of sheep's wool, was the last I saw of my country home as I left it to discover the world. She stood old and bent at the top of the bank, silently watching me go, one gnarled red hand raised in farewell and blessing, not questioning why I went. At the bend of the road, I looked back again and saw the gold light die behind her; then I turned the corner, passed the village school, and closed that part of my life for ever.

It was a bright Sunday morning in early June, the right time to be leaving home. My three sisters and a brother had already gone before me; two other brothers had yet to make up their minds. They were still sleeping that morning, but my mother had got up early and cooked me a heavy breakfast, had stood silently while I ate it, her hand on my chair, and had then helped me pack up my few belongings. There had been no fuss, no appeals, no attempts at advice or persuasion, only a long and searching look. Then, with my bags on my back, I'd gone out into the early sunshine and climbed through the long wet grass to the road.

I was nineteen years old, still soft at the edges, but with a confident belief in good fortune. I carried a small rolled-up tent, a violin in a blanket, a change of clothes, and a tin of treacle biscuits. I was excited, vainglorious, knowing I had far to go—but not, as yet, how far. As I left home that morning and walked away from the sleeping village, it never occurred to me that others had done this before me.

I was propelled, of course, by the traditional forces that had sent many generations along this road—by the small tight valley closing in around one, stifling the breath with its mossy mouth, the cottage walls narrowing like the arms of an iron maiden, the local girls whispering, "Marry, and settle down." Months of restless unease, leading to this inevitable

treacle biscuits: molasses cookies.
iron maiden: a torture instrument consisting of an iron container in human form studded with spikes on the inside.

The Direct Experience

moment, had been spent wandering about the hills, mournfully whistling, and watching the high open fields stepping away eastwards under gigantic clouds....

And now I was on my journey, in a pair of thick boots and with a hazel stick in my hand. Naturally, I was going to London, which lay a hundred miles to the east; and it seemed equally obvious that I should go on foot. But first, as I'd never yet seen the sea, I thought I'd walk to the coast and find it. This would add another hundred miles to my journey, going by way of Southampton. But I had all the summer and all time to spend.

That first day alone—and now I was really alone at last—steadily declined in excitement and vigour. As I tramped through the dust towards the Wiltshire Downs, a growing reluctance weighed me down. White elder blossom and dog-roses hung in the hedges, blank as unwritten paper, and the hot empty road—there were few motorcars then—reflected Sunday's waste and indifference. High, sulky summer sucked me towards it, offering no resistance at all. Through the solitary morning and afternoon, I found myself longing for some opposition or rescue, for the sound of hurrying footsteps coming after me and family voices calling me back.

None came. I was free. I was affronted by freedom. The day's silence said, Go where you will. It's all yours. You asked for it. It's up to you now. You're on your own, and nobody's going to stop you. As I walked, I was taunted by echoes of home, by the tinkling sounds of the kitchen, shafts of sun from the windows falling across the familiar furniture, across the bedroom and the bed I had left.

When I judged it to be tea-time, I sat on an old stone wall and opened my tin of biscuits. As I ate them, I could hear mother banging the kettle on the hob and my brothers rattling their tea-cups. The treacle biscuits tasted sweetly of the honeyed squalor of home—still only a dozen miles away.

I might have turned back then if it hadn't been for my brothers, but I couldn't have borne the look on their faces. So I got off the wall and went on my way, tossing the biscuits into a field. The long evening shadows pointed to folded villages, homing cows, and after-church walkers. I tramped the edge of the road, watching my dusty feet, not stopping again for a couple of hours.

When darkness came, full of moths and beetles, I was too weary to put up the tent. So I lay myself down in the middle of a field and stared up at the brilliant stars. I was oppressed by the velvety emptiness of the world and the swathes of soft grass I lay on. Then the fumes of the night finally put me to sleep—my first night without a roof or bed.

I was woken soon after midnight by drizzling rain on my face, the sky black and the stars all gone. Two cows stood over me, windily sighing, and the wretchedness of that moment haunts me still. I crawled into a ditch and lay awake till dawn, soaking alone in that nameless field. But when the sun rose in the morning, the feeling of desolation was over. Birds sang, and the grass steamed warmly. I got up and shook myself, ate a piece of cheese, and turned again to the south.

The Outward Experience

Now I came down through Wiltshire, burning my roots behind me and slowly getting my second wind; taking it easy, idling through towns and villages, and knowing what it was like not to have to go to work. Four years as a junior in that gaslit office in Stroud had kept me pretty closely tied. Now I was tasting the extravagant quality of being free on a weekday, say at eleven o'clock in the morning, able to scuff down a side road and watch a man herding sheep, or a stalking cat in the grass, or to beg a screw of tea from a housewife and carry it into a wood and spend an hour boiling a can of spring water.

As for this pocket of England through which I found myself walking, it seemed to me immense. A motorcar, of course, could have crossed it in a couple of hours, but it took me the best part of a week, treading it slowly, smelling its different soils, spending a whole morning working round a hill. I was lucky, I know, to have been setting out at that time, in a landscape not yet bulldozed for speed. Many of the country roads still followed their original tracks, drawn by packhorse or lumbering cartwheel, hugging the curve of a valley or yielding to a promontory like the wandering line of a stream. It was not, after all, so very long ago, but no one could make that journey today. Most of the old roads have gone, and the motorcar, since then, has begun to cut the landscape to pieces, through which the hunched-up traveller races at gutter height, seeing less than a dog in a ditch.

But for me, at that time, everything I saw was new, and I could pass it slowly through the hours of the day. While still only a day's march from home, coming through Malmsbury and Chippenham, already I noticed different shades of speech. Then, a day or so later, I passed down the Wylye Valley and came out on to a vast and rolling plain—a sweep of old, dry land covered with shaggy grass which looked as though it had just been cropped by mammoths. Still vague about places, I was unprepared for the delicate spire which rose suddenly out of the empty plain. As I walked, it went before me, gliding behind the curve of the hill and giving no hint of the city beneath it.

Just a spire in the grass; my first view of Salisbury, and the better for not being expected. When I entered the city, I found it was market day, the square crowded with bone-thin sheep. Farmers stood round in groups talking sideways to each other and all looking in opposite directions. The pubs were bursting with dealers counting out crumpled money. Shepherds and dogs sat around on the pavements. Supreme above all towered the misty cathedral, still prince of the horizontal town, throwing its slow, shifting shade across the market square and jingling handfuls of bells like coins.

After a week on the road, I finally arrived at Southampton, where I'd been told I would see the sea. Instead, I saw a few rusty cranes and a compressed-looking liner wedged tightly between some houses; also

screw of tea: a small amount of tea in a slip of paper twisted at the ends.

The Direct Experience

some sad allotments fringing a muddy river which they said was Southampton Water.

Southampton Town, on the other hand, came up to all expectations, proving to be salty and shifty in turns, like some ship-jumping sailor who'd turned his back on the sea in a desperate attempt to make good on land. The streets near the water appeared to be jammed with shops designed more for entertainment than profit, including tattooists, ear-piercers, bump-readers, fortune-tellers, whelk-bars, and pudding-boilers. There were also shops selling kites and Chinese paper dragons, coloured sands and tropical birds; and lots of little step-down taverns panelled with rum-soaked timbers and reeking of pickled eggs and onions.

As I'd been sleeping in fields for a week, I thought it was time I tried a bed again, so I went to a doss house down by the docks. The landlady, an old hag with a tooth like a tin-opener, said it would cost me a shilling a night, demanded the money in advance, treated me to a tumblerful of whiskey, then showed me up to the attic.

Early next morning, she brought me a cup of tea and some water in a wooden bucket. She looked at me vaguely and asked what ship I was from, and only grunted when I said I'd come from Stroud. Then she spotted my violin hanging on the end of the bed and gave it a twang with her long blue nails.

"Well, hey diddle diddle, I reckon," she muttered, and skipped nimbly out of the room.

Presently I got up and dressed, stuck my violin under my jacket, and went out into the streets to try my luck. It was now or never. I must face it now, or pack up and go back home. I wandered about for an hour looking for a likely spot, feeling as though I was about to commit a crime. Then I stopped at last under a bridge near the station and decided to have a go.

I felt tense and shaky. It was the first time, after all. I drew the violin from my coat like a gun. It was here, in Southampton, with trains rattling overhead, that I was about to declare myself. One moment I was part of the hurrying crowds, the next I stood nakedly apart, my back to the wall, my hat on the pavement before me, the violin under my chin.

The first notes I played were loud and raw, like a hoarse declaration of protest; then they settled down and began to run more smoothly and to stay more or less in tune. To my surprise, I was neither arrested nor told to shut up. Indeed, nobody took any notice at all. Then an old man, without stopping, surreptitiously tossed a penny into my hat as though getting rid of some guilty evidence.

Other pennies followed, slowly but steadily, dropped by shadows who appeared not to see or hear me. It was as though the note of the fiddle touched some subconscious nerve that had to be answered—like a baby's

allotments: garden plots.
bump-readers: phrenologists (those who tell fortunes from the configuration of the skull).
whelk-bars: small restaurants offering edible snails.
doss house: cheap lodging house, "flophouse."

cry. When I'd finished the first tune, there was over a shilling in my hat: it seemed too easy, like a confidence trick. But I was elated now; I felt that, wherever I went from here, this was a trick I could always live by.

I worked the streets of Southampton for several days, gradually acquiring the truths of the trade. Obvious enough to old-timers, and simple, once learnt, I had to get them by trial and error. It was not a good thing, for instance, to let the hat fill up with money—the sight could discourage the patron; nor was it wise to empty it completely, which could also confuse him, giving him no hint as to where to drop his money. Placing a couple of pennies in the hat to start the thing going soon became an unvarying ritual; making sure, between tunes, to take off the cream, but always leaving two pennies behind.

Slow melodies were best, encouraging people to dawdle (Irish jigs sent them whizzing past); but it also seemed wise to play as well as one was able rather than to ape the dirge of the professional waif. To arouse pity or guilt was always good for a penny, but that was as far as it got you; while a tuneful appeal to the ear, played with sober zest, might often be rewarded with silver.

Old ladies were most generous, and so were women with children, shopgirls, typists, and barmaids. As for the men: heavy drinkers were always receptive, big chaps with muscles, bookies, and punters. But never a man with a bowler, briefcase, or dog; respectable types were the tightest of all. Except for retired army officers, who would bark, "Why aren't you working, young man?" and then overtip to hide their confusion.

Certain tunes, I discovered, always raised a response, while others touched off nothing at all. The most fruitful were invariably the tearoom classics and certain of the juicier national ballads. "Loch Lomond," "Wales! Wales!" and "The Rose of Tralee" called up their supporters from any crowd—as did "Largo," "Ave Maria," Toselli's "Serenade," and "The Whistler and His Dog." The least rewarding, as I said, was anything quick or flashy, such as "The Devil's Trill" or "Picking Up Sticks," which seemed to throw the pedestrian right out of his stride and completely shatter his charitable rhythm.

All in all, my apprenticeship proved profitable and easy, and I soon lost my pavement nerves. It became a greedy pleasure to go out into the streets, to take up my stand by the station or market and start sawing away at some moony melody and watch the pennies and half-pennies grow. Those first days in Southampton were a kind of obsession; I was out in the streets from morning till night, moving from pitch to pitch in a gold-dust fever, playing till the tips of my fingers burned.

When I judged Southampton to have taken about as much as it could, I decided to move on eastwards. Already I felt like a veteran, and on my way out of town I went into a booth to have my photograph taken. The picture was developed in a bucket in less than a minute and has lasted over thirty years. I still have a copy before me of that summer ghost—a pale, oleaginous shade posed daintily before a landscape of tattered canvas, his old clothes powdered with dust. He wears a sloppy

The Direct Experience

slouch hat, heavy boots, baggy trousers, tent and fiddle slung over his shoulders, and from the long empty face gaze a pair of egg-shell eyes, unhatched and unrecognizable now.

A few miles from Southampton I saw the real sea at last, head on, a sudden end to the land, a great sweep of curved nothing rolling out to the invisible horizon and revealing more distance than I'd ever seen before. It was green, and heaved gently like the skin of a frog, and carried drowsy little ships like flies. Compared with the land, it appeared to be a huge hypnotic blank, putting everything to sleep that touched it.

As I pushed along the shore, I was soon absorbed by its atmosphere, new, mysterious, alien: the gritty edge on the wind, the taste of tar and salt, the smell of stale seashells, damp roads, and mackintoshes, and the sight of the quick summer storms sliding in front of the water like sheets of dirty glass.

The south coast, even so, was not what I had been led to expect—from reading Hardy and Jeffrey Farnol—for already it had begun to develop that shabby shoreline suburbia which was part of the whimsical rot of the Thirties. Here were the sea-shanty-towns, sprawled like a rubbishy tide mark, the scattered litter of land and ocean—miles of tea-shacks and bungalows, apparently built out of wreckage, and called "Spindrift" or "Sprite O' The Waves." Here and there, bearded men sat on broken verandahs painting water colours of boats and sunsets, while big women with dogs, all glistening with teeth, policed parcels of private sand. I liked the seedy disorder of this melancholy coast, unvisited as yet by prosperity, and looking as though everything about it had been thrown together by the winds and might at any moment be blown away again.

I spent a week by the sea, slowly edging towards the east, sleeping on the shore and working the towns. I remember it as a blur of summer, indolent and vague, broken occasionally by some odd encounter. At Gosport, I performed at a barrack-room concert in return for a ration of army beef. In front of Chichester Cathedral, I played "Bless This House" and was moved on at once by the police. At Bognor Regis, I camped out on the sands, where I met a fluid young girl of sixteen who hugged me steadily throughout one long hot day with only a gym slip on her sea-wet body. At Littlehampton, I'd just collected about eighteen pence when I was moved on again by the police. "Not here. Try Worthing," the officer said. I did so and was amply rewarded.

Worthing at that time was a kind of Cheltenham-on-Sea, full of rich, pearl-chokered invalids. Each afternoon they came out in their high-wheeled chairs and were pushed round the park by small hired men. Standing at the gate of the park, in the main stream of these ladies, I played a selection of spiritual airs, and in little over an hour collected thirty-eight shillings—which was more than a farm labourer earned in a week.

Worthing was an end to that chapter, a junction in the journey, and as far along the coast as I wished to go. So I turned my back on the sea and headed north for London, still over fifty miles away. It was the third week in June, and the landscape was frosty with pollen and still coated with elder blossom. The wide-open Downs, the sheep-nibbled grass, the beech hangers on the edge of the valleys, the smell of chalk, purple orchids, blue butterflies, and thistles recalled the Cotswolds I'd so carelessly left. Indeed, Chanctonbury Ring, where I slept that night, could have been any of the beacons round Painswick or Haresfield; yet I felt further from home, by the very familiarity of my surroundings, than I ever did later in a foreign country.

But next day, getting back on to the London road, I forgot everything but the way ahead. I walked steadily, effortlessly, hour after hour, in a kind of swinging, weightless dream. I was at that age which feels neither strain nor friction, when the body burns magic fuels, so that it seems to glide in warm air, about a foot off the ground, smoothly obeying its intuitions. Even exhaustion, when it came, had a voluptuous quality, and sleep was caressive and deep, like oil. It was the peak of the curve of the body's total extravagance, before the accounts start coming in.

I was living at that time on pressed dates and biscuits, rationing them daily, as though crossing a desert. Sussex, of course, offered other diets, but I preferred to stick to this affectation. I pretended I was T. E. Lawrence, engaged in some self-punishing odyssey, burning up my youth in some pitiless Hadhramaut, eyes narrowing to the sandstorms blowing out of the wadis of Godalming in a mirage of solitary endurance.

But I was not the only one on the road; I soon noticed there were many others, all trudging northwards in a sombre procession. Some, of course, were professional tramps, but the majority belonged to that host of unemployed who wandered aimlessly about England at that time.

One could pick out the professionals; they brewed tea by the roadside, took it easy, and studied their feet. But the others, the majority, went on their way like somnambulists, walking alone and seldom speaking to each other. There seemed to be more of them inland than on the coast—maybe the police had seen to that. They were like a broken army walking away from a war, cheeks sunken, eyes dead with fatigue. Some carried bags of tools or broken cardboard suitcases; some wore the ghosts of city suits; some, when they stopped to rest, carefully removed their shoes and polished them vaguely with handfuls of grass. Among them were carpenters, clerks, engineers from the Midlands; many had been on the road for months, walking up and down the country in a maze of jobless refusals, the treadmill of the middle Thirties. . . .

Then, for a couple of days, I got a companion. I was picked up by the veteran Alf. I'd turned off the road to set up camp for the night when he came filtering through the bushes.

I'd seen him before; he was about five feet high and was clearly one of the brotherhood. He wore a deerstalker hat, so sodden and shredded

Hadhramaut: an Arabian desert.
wadis: Arabic word for dry gullies.
Godalming: a town southwest of London.
deerstalker hat: the kind worn by Sherlock Holmes and Snoopy.

The Direct Experience

it looked like a helping of breakfast food, and round the waist of his mackintosh, which was belted with string, hung a collection of pots and spoons.

Rattling like a dustbin, he sat down beside me and began pulling off his boots.

"Well," he said, eyeing my dates with disgust, "you're a poor little bleeder, 'ent you?"

He shook out his boots and put them on again, then gave my supper another look.

"You can't live on terrible tack like that—you'll depress the lot of us. What you want is a billy. A-boil yerself up. 'Ere, 'ang on—jus' wait a minute...."

Rummaging through the hardware round his waist, he produced a battered can, the kind of thing my uncles brought home from the war—square, with a triangular handle. It was a miniature cauldron, smoke-blackened outside and dark, tannin-stained within.

"'Ere, take it," he said. "You make me miserable." He started to build a fire. "I'm goin' to boil you a bit of tea and 'taters." And that is what he did.

We stayed together as far as Guildford, and I shared more of his pungent brews. He was a tramp to his bones, always wrapping and unwrapping himself, and picking over his bits and pieces. He wasn't looking for work; this was simply his life, and he carefully rationed his energies—never passing a bit of grass that looked good for a shakedown nor a cottage that seemed ripe for charity. He said his name was Alf, but one couldn't be sure, as he called me Alf, and everyone else. "Couple of Alfs got jugged in this town last year," he'd say. "Hookin' the shops—you know, with fishhooks." Or: "An Alf I knew used to do twenny-mile a day. One of the looniest Alfs on the road. Said he got round it quicker. And so he did. But folks got sick of his face."

Alf talked all day, but was garrulously secretive and never revealed his origins. I suppose that in the shared exposure of the open road he needed this loose verbal hedge around him. At the same time, he never asked me about myself, though he took it for granted that I was a greenhorn and gave me careful advice about insulation from weather, flannelling housewives, and dodging the cops.

As for his own technique of roadwork, he wasn't slow out of laziness but because he moved to a deliberate timetable, making his professional grand tour in a twelve-months' rhythm, which seemed to him fast enough. During the winter he'd hole up in a London doss house, then restart his leisurely cycle of England, turning up every year in each particular district with the regularity of the seasons. Thus he was the spring tramp of the Midlands, the summer bird of the south, the first touch of autumn to the Kentish Weald—indeed, I think he firmly believed that his constancy of motion spread a kind of reassurance among the housewives,

---

dustbin: garbage can.
flannelling: flattering to get a handout (from the idea of polishing with a piece of flannel).

so that he was looked for and welcomed as one of the recurring phenomena of nature, and was suitably rewarded therefore.

Certainly his begging was profitable, and he never popped through a gate without returning with fistfuls of food—screws of tea, meat bones and cake, which he'd then boil in one awful mess. He was clean, down-at-heel, warmhearted, and cunning; and he showed me genuine, if supercilious, kindness. "You're a bleedin' disgrace," he used to say, "a miserable litle burden."

Alf had one strange habit—a passion for nursery rhymes, which he'd mutter as he walked along.

> Sing a song of sixpence,
> Pocketful of rye,
> Four-an'-twenny blackbirds
> Baked in an oven.
>
> Ba-ba, black sheep,
> Have you any wool?
> Yes, sir, yes, sir,
> I got plenty....

The effect of a dozen of these, left hanging in the air, was enough to dislocate the senses.

At Guildford we parted, Alf turning east for the Weald, which for him still lay three months away.

"So long, Alf," I said.

"So long, Alf," he answered. "Try not to be too much of a nuisance."

He passed under the railway bridge and out of my life, a shuffling rattle of old tin cans, looking very small and triangular with his pointed hat on his head and black mackintosh trailing the ground.

London was now quite near, no more than a two-days' walk, but I was still in no particular hurry. So I turned northwest and began a detour round it, rather like a wasp sidling up to a jam jar. After leaving Guildford, I slept a night on Bagshot Heath—all birches, sand, and horseflies—which to me seemed a sinister and wasted place, like some vast dead land of Russia. Then next morning, only a few miles further up the road, everything suddenly changed back again, and I was walking through parkland as green as a fable, smothered with beeches and creamy grass.

Every motorcar on the road was now either a Rolls-Royce or a Daimler —a gliding succession of silver sighs—their crystal interiors packed with girls and hampers and erect top-hatted men. Previously, I'd not seen more than two such cars in my life; now they seemed to be the only kind in the world, and I began to wonder if they were intimations of treasures to come, whether all London was as rich as this.

Tramping in the dust of this splendour, I wasn't surprised when one of the Daimlers pulled up and an arm beckoned to me from the window. I hurried towards it, thinking it might be full of long-lost relations, but in fact there was no one I knew. "Want a pheasant, my man?" asked

The Direct Experience

a voice from inside. "We just knocked over a beauty a hundred yards back."

A quarter of an hour later I arrived at Ascot. It was race week, and I'd walked right into it. White pavilions and flags; little grooms and jockeys dodging among the long glossy legs of thoroughbreds; and the pedigree owners dipping their long cool necks into baskets of pâté and gulls' eggs.

I went round to the entrance, thinking I might get in, but was stared at by a couple of policemen. So I stared, in turn, at a beautiful woman by the gate who for a moment paused dazzlingly near me—her face as silkily finished as a Persian miniature, her body sheathed in swathes like a tulip, and her sandalled feet wrapped in a kind of transparent rice-paper so that I could count every clean little separate toe.

Wealth and beauty were the common order of things now, and I felt I had entered another realm. It would have been no good busking or touting here—indeed, outlandish in such a place. Alf and the tattered lines of the workless were far away in another country. . . . So I left Ascot and came presently to another park, full of oak trees and grazing deer, and saw Windsor Castle standing on its green-baize hill like a battered silver cruet. I slept that stifling night in a field near Stoke Poges, having spent the evening in the village churchyard, sitting on a mossy gravestone and listening to the rooks, and wondering why the place seemed so familiar.

A few mornings later, coming out of a wood near Beaconsfield, I suddenly saw London at last—a long smoky skyline hazed by the morning sun and filling the whole of the eastern horizon. Dry rusty-red, it lay like a huge flat crust, like ash from some spent volcano, simmering gently in the summer morning and emitting a faint, metallic roar.

No architectural glories, no towers or palaces, just a creeping insidious presence, its vast horizontal broken here and there by a gasholder or factory chimney. Even so, I could already feel its intense radiation—an electric charge in the sky—that rose from its million roofs in a quivering mirage, magnetically, almost visibly, dilating.

Cleo, my girl-friend, was somewhere out there; hoarding my letters (I hoped) and waiting. Also mystery, promise, chance, and fortune—all I had come to this city to find. I hurried towards it, impatient now, its sulphur stinging my nostrils. I had been a month on the road, and the suburbs were long and empty. In the end, I took a tube.

DISCUSSION

1. "London Road" and "The Grasshopper and the Ant" can be compared with interesting results. Skim over both, looking for sensory data. Which writer uses his senses most? Which uses a greater variety of senses?

busking: offering entertainment for money.
touting: here, begging.
Stoke Poges: the scene of Thomas Gray's "Elegy Written in a Country Churchyard," a poem familiar to nearly everyone at that time.
gasholder: gas storage tank.
tube: subway.

2. Which writer experiences more circumstances that produce physical discomfort? Which seems to be more aware of discomfort?
3. What is the goal of each? How does this affect his perception?
4. What is the attitude of each toward money? What does each want money for?
5. Both of these selections are from autobiographical books. Which book would you rather read? Why? What generalizations can you make in regard to attitudes toward life and writing?

WRITING SUGGESTIONS

1. If you have ever been subjected to violence, try to describe your experience with the kind of thorough, cool objectivity that Livingstone displays. Tell the reader exactly how you felt at all stages of the experience; give the reader all the relevant sensory data, but use just enough words to make everything clear.
2. Make the most of a depressingly ordinary experience, as Hunt does in "Getting Up on Cold Mornings." Here are some possible subjects:

   Washing dishes
   Taking a shortcut
   Mowing the lawn
   Eating something you dislike
   Babysitting
   Going to your first class in the morning
   Being sick to your stomach in a public place
   Having a cold during vacation
   Trying to cook your own breakfast
   Trying to get rid of a bore without offending him
   Trying to make a teacher believe you've read the assignment
   Being broke at lunchtime

3. If you've ever been on your own like Garland or Lee, you have good material to write about. Give enough detail about the experience so the reader can live it with you; describe briefly your own feelings at each stage. Tell what you learned from the experience or how it changed your attitudes.
4. Have you ever been driven up the wall by people who were trying to please you? Especially if you are visiting, oversolicitousness can be maddening. If you have had such an experience, write about it so as to bring out the irony of good intentions versus bad results. Do not generalize at all. Let the concrete experience make your point.
5. Try to recall the most boring hours you ever spent and describe the experience in concrete terms. Don't mention that you were bored, but let the circumstances make the point. Or recall your most anxious hours or the time you were most angry. Place the reader in your situation so that he will feel what you felt.

Plate 13
Hokusai (1760–1849): "The Great Wave off Kanagawa"

There is a strong element of experience in almost any action picture such as George Bellows' *Stag at Sharkey's* (Plate 6). But Bellows is less concerned that we share the experience of his boxers than that we note the reactions of the spectators to the violence; he is first of all an observer. Hokusai gives us evidence in "The Great Wave off Kanagawa" that he has observed the sea closely, but his main concern is to make us feel the tumult and the terror of his scene, to enter into it and experience what the boatmen are experiencing.

1. There are three different elements in the picture. What are they? What is the function of each?
2. This print is one of a series called *The Hundred Views of Fuji.* Fuji, the famous Japanese volcanic mountain, is in the background of the picture. What feeling does the artist communicate about the mountain by making it small in the background? Can you form a broad generalization about human experience that the picture might be intended to convey?
3. Hokusai has drawn a visual analogy between the waves and the mountain: that is, he shows us that they have almost the same form. What idea does this similarity communicate?
4. There is a difference between the quality of the lines used on the left side of the picture and those used on the right. What is this difference? What does it communicate about the motion of the water? What does it communicate about the experience of the boatmen in that moment of time?

PLATE 13　Hokusai (1760–1849), **The Great Wave off Kanagawa.** *The Metropolitan Museum of Art, Bequest of Mrs. H. O. Havemeyer, 1929. The H.O. Havemeyer Collection.*

Plate 14
Georges de la Tour (1593–1652): *Joseph the Carpenter*

Not all significant outward experience, of course, is violent or dramatic. Some memorable and beautiful experiences are very simple ones, fleeting moments when the substance of life seems to gather itself into a point, and we are intensely aware of our existence for no obvious reason. Such a moment of realization is depicted here by Georges de la Tour; we need not necessarily think of the subject as Joseph, but as any man suddenly becoming aware of his child.

1. What has caused Joseph suddenly to glance up from his work? What is he looking at?
2. The first thing our eyes light on in the picture is the boy's left hand. What fact of human life does the translucent quality of that hand bring to our attention?
3. What is the boy looking at? What might be the significance of this?
4. Joseph is shown in a moment of realization. A second before, he was absorbed in his work. What is the nature of this moment's realization?
5. In both this painting and Dürer's woodcut candles are used as symbols, but in different ways. What does the symbol mean here?
6. Can you find anything in common between this painting and Hokusai's "The Great Wave off Kanagawa"? What similar idea is expressed in both?
7. What readings in this book present similar moments of realization?

PLATE 14 Georges de la Tour (1593–1652), **Joseph the Carpenter.**
The Louvre, Paris, from Giraudon.

9

Inner Experience

All outward experiences are of course accompanied by inner experiences or feelings. Again, as with the difference between observation and experience, we are dealing with a matter of emphasis. Some experiences occur almost wholly inside us even though they must necessarily involve things, or memories of things, outside: these are dreams and hallucinations. Other experiences are more directly related to the outside world, but are still centered inside us: strong emotions such as love and religious feeling, moral conflicts, changing attitudes.

The selections in the chapter are offered in two groups. The first group consists of writings about "normal" inner experiences—that is, the kinds most people have while they are in good health. The second group concerns "abnormal" or unusual inner experiences such as many people have when they are physically or mentally ill or under the influence of drugs.

While the cynic might claim that no man in love enjoys good mental health, most of us have felt as John Donne did when he wrote "The Good-Morrow." You may find some lines difficult, but you will be able to follow enough of the meaning to appreciate the essence of the poem.

John Donne

The Good-Morrow

(c. 1600)

I wonder, by my troth, what thou and I
Did till we loved? were we not weaned till then,
But sucked on country pleasures, childishly?
Or snorted we in the seven sleepers' den?
'Twas so; but this, all pleasures fancies be.
If ever any beauty I did see,
Which I desired, and got, 'twas but a dream of thee.

And now good-morrow to our waking souls,
Which watch not one another out of fear;
For love all love of other sights controls,
And makes one little room an everywhere.
Let sea-discoverers to new worlds have gone;
Let maps to others, worlds on worlds have shown;
Let us possess one world; each hath one, and is one.

My face in thine eye, thine in mine appears,
And true plain hearts do in the faces rest;
Where can we find two better hemispheres
Without sharp north, without declining west?
Whatever dies, was not mixed equally;
If our two loves be one, or thou and I
Love so alike that none do slacken, none can die.

Too few good writers have shared their dreams with us. One of the few is Dag Hammerskjöld, whose dreams give us a flash of insight into the quality of his mind. Note the economy and simplicity of the language he uses to describe them.

seven sleepers' den: in Christian legend, seven young men of Ephesus were pursued to a cave and walled in; they fell asleep and woke two hundred years later when the Emperor was a Christian.
Whatever dies, was not mixed equally: reference to a belief of alchemists that dissolution occurs because of an imbalance among the four elements, earth, air, fire, and water. This idea controls the last two lines of the poem.

The Direct Experience

Dag Hammerskjöld

Three Dreams

(1964)

I

Weary birds, large weary birds, perched upon a tremendous cliff that rises out of dark waters, await the fall of night. Weary birds turn their heads towards the blaze in the west. The glow turns to blood, the blood is mixed with soot. We look across the waters towards the west and upwards into the soaring arch of the sunset. Stillness—Our lives are one with that of this huge far-off world, as it makes its entry into the night. —Our few words, spoken or unspoken (My words? His words?), die away: now it is too dark for us to find the way back.

II

Night. The road stretches ahead. Behind me it winds up in curves towards the house, a gleam in the darkness under the dense trees of the park. I know that, shrouded in the dark out there, people are moving, that all around me, hidden by the night, life is a-quiver. I know that something is waiting for me in the house. Out of the darkness of the park comes the call of a solitary bird: and I go—up there.

III

Light without a visible source, the pale gold of a new day. Low bushes, their silk-grey leaves silvered with dew. All over the hills, the cool red of the cat's foot in flower. Emerging from the ravine where a brook runs under a canopy of leaves, I walk out onto a wide open slope. Drops, sprinkled by swaying branches, glitter on my hands, cool my forehead, and evaporate in the gentle morning breeze.

DISCUSSION

1. The Gestalt psychologist Frederick Perls, who had a way of pointing out obvious facts that we overlook, once said, "All that is in the dream is *you*"—that is, the dreamer. Dreams come from inside, not outside. With this in mind, what does each of these three dreams seem to reflect?
2. These dreams are not grouped together by accident. They are connected even though the images are different. What elements connect them? What progression do they represent?
3. What other writer in this book has effectively used very simple and straightforward language? What can you conclude about the use of simple language?

Most of us fall in love and most of us have dreams that reflect our own natures and situations. Most of us, too, experience profound changes of attitude, especially when we are growing up. Here, Sherwood Anderson shows us how his attitude toward his father changed.

Sherwood Anderson

Discovery of a Father

(1939)

One of the strangest relationships in the world is that between father and son. I know it now from having sons of my own.

A boy wants something very special from his father. You hear it said that fathers want their sons to be what they feel they cannot themselves be, but I tell you it also works the other way. I know that as a small boy I wanted my father to be a certain thing he was not. I wanted him to be a proud, silent, dignified father. When I was with other boys and he passed along the street, I wanted to feel a glow of pride: 'There he is. That is my father.'

But he wasn't such a one. He couldn't be. It seemed to me then that he was always showing off. Let's say someone in our town had got up a show. They were always doing it. The druggist would be in it, the shoe-store clerk, the horse-doctor, and a lot of women and girls. My father would manage to get the chief comedy part. It was, let's say, a Civil War play and he was a comic Irish soldier. He had to do the most absurd things. They thought he was funny, but I didn't.

I thought he was terrible. I didn't see how Mother could stand it. She even laughed with the others. Maybe I would have laughed if it hadn't been my father.

Or there was a parade, the Fourth of July or Decoration Day. He'd be in that, too, right at the front of it, as Grand Marshal or something, on a white horse hired from a livery stable.

He couldn't ride for shucks. He fell off the horse and everyone hooted with laughter, but he didn't care. He even seemed to like it. I remember once when he had done something ridiculous, and right out on Main Street, too. I was with some other boys and they were laughing and shouting at him and he was shouting back and having as good a time as they were. I ran down an alley back of some stores and there in the Presbyterian Church sheds I had a good long cry.

Or I would be in bed at night and Father would come home a little lit up and bring some men with him. He was a man who was never alone. Before he went broke, running a harness shop, there were always a lot of men loafing in the shop. He went broke, of course, because he gave too much credit. He couldn't refuse it and I thought he was a fool. I had got to hating him.

There'd be men I didn't think would want to be fooling around with him. There might even be the superintendent of our schools and a quiet man who ran the hardware store. Once I remember there was a white-haired man who was a cashier of the bank. It was a wonder to me they'd want to be seen with such a windbag. That's what I thought he was. I know now what it was that attracted them. It was because life in our town, as in all small towns, was at times pretty dull and he livened it up. He made them laugh. He could tell stories. He'd even get them to singing.

If they didn't come to our house, they'd go off, say, at night, to where there was a grassy place by a creek. They'd cook food there and drink beer and sit about listening to his stories.

He was always telling stories about himself. He'd say this or that wonderful thing had happened to him. It might be something that made him look like a fool. He didn't care.

If an Irishman came to our house, right away Father would say he was Irish. He'd tell what county in Ireland he was born in. He'd tell things that happened there when he was a boy. He'd make it seem so real that, if I hadn't known he was born in southern Ohio, I'd have believed him myself.

If it was a Scotchman the same thing happened. He'd get a burr into his speech. Or he was a German or a Swede. He'd be anything the other man was. I think they all knew he was lying, but they seemed to like him just the same. As a boy that was what I couldn't understand.

And there was Mother. How could she stand it? I wanted to ask, but never did. She was not the kind you asked such questions.

I'd be upstairs in my bed, in my room above the porch, and Father would be telling some of his tales. A lot of Father's stories were about the Civil War. To hear him tell it he'd been in about every battle. He'd known Grant, Sherman, Sheridan, and I don't know how many others. He'd been particularly intimate with General Grant so that when Grant went East, to take charge of all the armies, he took Father along.

'I was an orderly at headquarters and Sam Grant said to me, "Irve," he said, "I'm going to take you along with me." '

It seems he and Grant used to slip off sometimes and have a quiet drink together. That's what my father said. He'd tell about the day Lee surrendered, and how, when the great moment came, they couldn't find Grant.

'You know,' my father said, 'about General Grant's book, his memoirs. You've read of how he said he had a headache and how, when he got word that Lee was ready to call it quits, he was suddenly and miraculously cured.

'Huh,' said Father. 'He was in the woods with me.

'I was in there with my back against a tree. I was pretty well corned. I had got hold of a bottle of pretty good stuff.

'They were looking for Grant. He had got off his horse and come into the woods. He found me. He was covered with mud.

'I had the bottle in my hand. What'd I care? The war was over. I knew we had them licked.'

My father said that he was the one who told Grant about Lee. An orderly riding by had told him, because the orderly knew how thick he was with Grant. Grant was embarrassed.

'But, Irve, look at me. I'm all covered with mud,' he said to Father.

And then, my father said, he and Grant decided to have a drink together. They took a couple of shots and then, because he didn't want Grant to show up potted before the immaculate Lee, he smashed the bottle against the tree.

'Sam Grant's dead now and I wouldn't want it to get out on him,' my father said.

That's just one of the kind of things he'd tell. Of course the men knew he was lying, but they seemed to like it just the same.

When we got broke, down and out, do you think he ever brought anything home? Not he. If there wasn't anything to eat in the house, he'd go off visiting around at farmhouses. They all wanted him. Sometimes he'd stay away for weeks, Mother working to keep us fed, and then home he'd come bringing, let's say, a ham. He'd got it from some farmer friend. He'd slap it on the table in the kitchen. 'You bet I'm going to see that my kids have something to eat,' he'd say, and Mother would just stand smiling at him. She'd never say a word about all the weeks and months he'd been away, not leaving us a cent for food. Once I heard her speaking to a woman in our street. Maybe the woman had dared to sympathize with her. 'Oh,' she said, 'it's all right. He isn't ever dull like most of the men in this street. Life is never dull when my man is about.'

But often I was filled with bitterness, and sometimes I wished he wasn't my father. I'd even invent another man as my father. To protect my mother I'd make up stories of a secret marriage that for some strange reason never got known. As though some man, say, the president of a railroad company or maybe a Congressman, had married my mother, thinking his wife was dead and then it turned out she wasn't.

Now they had to hush it up, but I got born just the same. I wasn't really the son of my father. Somewhere in the world there was a very dignified, quite wonderful man who was really my father. I even made myself half-believe these fancies.

And then there came a certain night. Mother was away from home. Maybe there was a church that night. Father came in. He'd been off somewhere for two or three weeks. He found me alone in the house, reading by the kitchen table.

It had been raining and he was very wet. He sat and looked at me for a long time, not saying a word. I was startled, for there was on his face the saddest look I had ever seen. He sat for a time, his clothes dripping. Then he got up.

'Come on with me,' he said.

I got up and went with him out of the house. I was filled with wonder, but I wasn't afraid. We went along a dirt road that led down into a valley, about a mile out of town, where there was a pond. We walked in silence. The man who was always talking had stopped his talking.

I didn't know what was up and had the queer feeling that I was with a stranger. I don't know whether my father intended it so. I don't think he did.

The pond was quite large. It was still raining hard and there were flashes of lightning followed by thunder. We were on a grassy bank at the pond's edge when my father spoke, and in the darkness and rain his voice sounded strange.

The Direct Experience

'Take off your clothes,' he said. Still filled with wonder, I began to undress. There was a flash of lightning and I saw that he was already naked.

Naked, we went into the pond. Taking my hand he pulled me in. It may be that I was too frightened, too full of a feeling of strangeness, to speak. Before that night my father had never seemed to pay any attention to me.

'And what is he up to now?' I kept asking myself. I did not swim very well, but he put my hand on his shoulder and struck out into the darkness.

He was a man with big shoulders, a powerful swimmer. In the darkness I could feel the movement of his muscles. We swam to the far edge of the pond and then back to where we had left our clothes. The rain continued and the wind blew. Sometimes my father swam on his back and when he did, he took my hand in his large powerful one and moved it over so that it rested always on his shoulder. Sometimes there would be a flash of lightning and I could see his face quite clearly.

It was as it was earlier, in the kitchen, a face filled with sadness. There would be the momentary glimpse of his face and then again the darkness, the wind and the rain. In me there was a feeling I had never known before.

It was a feeling of closeness. It was something strange. It was as though there were only we two in the world. It was as though I had been jerked suddenly out of myself, out of my world of the schoolboy, out of a world in which I was ashamed of my father.

He had become blood of my blood; the strong swimmer and I the boy clinging to him in the darkness. We swam in silence and in silence we dressed in our wet clothes, and went home.

There was a lamp lighted in the kitchen, and when we came in, the water dripping from us, there was my mother. She smiled at us. I remember that she called us 'boys.' 'What have you boys been up to?' she asked, but my father did not answer. As he had begun the evening's experience with me in silence, so he ended it. He turned and looked at me. Then he went, I thought, with a new and strange dignity, out of the room.

I climbed the stairs to my own room, undressed in darkness and got into bed. I couldn't sleep and did not want to sleep. For the first time I knew that I was the son of my father. He was a story-teller as I was to be. It may be that I even laughed a little softly there in the darkness. If I did, I laughed knowing that I would never again be wanting another father.

DISCUSSION

1. Anderson expresses what his feelings toward his father were in strong language: "I thought he was terrible," and "I had got to hating him." Does he make it clear to the reader why he felt this way? What means does he use to make it clear?
2. What standard did the boy judge his father by when he "thought he was terrible"? What did he feel his father was not giving him?

3. His father takes him swimming at night, during a thunderstorm. Why doesn't he wait for a sunny afternoon when most people go swimming? What is the significance of choosing a stormy night?
4. The father was a drunk, a clown, and a poor provider. Why, in the end, does Anderson feel such a father had more to offer him than a father that was, say, a respectable bank president?
5. What change in attitude toward himself accompanies his change toward his father?

In a static society ruled by tradition, everyone knows what is right and wrong. But in a dynamic society different standards meet within ourselves and clash, causing the acute discomfort of uncertainty. In the next essay, William Dean Howells shows how he finds himself caught between two conflicting ethical standards within his own middle-class culture, and how he wobbles painfully between them, never sure what is right. While the matter of his indecision is minor, it reflects the major personal problem of our time: how should a man live in a society that offers no fixed standard of behavior?

William Dean Howells

Tribulations of a Cheerful Giver

(1909)

Some months ago, as I was passing through a downtown street on my way to the elevated station, I saw a man sitting on the steps of a house. He seemed to be resting his elbows on his knees and holding out both his hands. As I came nearer I perceived that he had no hands, but only stumps, where the fingers had been cut off close to the palms, and that it was these stumps he was holding out in the mute appeal which was his form of begging. Otherwise he did not ask charity. When I approached him he did not look up, and when I stopped in front of him he did not speak. I thought this rather fine, in its way; except for his mutilation, which the man really could not help, there was nothing to offend the taste; and his immobile silence was certainly impressive.

I decided at once to give him something; for when I am in the presence of want, or even the appearance of want, there is something that says to me, "Give to him that asketh," and I have to give, or else go away with a bad conscience—a thing I hate. Of course I do not give much, for I wish to be a good citizen as well as a good Christian; and, as soon as I obey that voice which I cannot disobey, I hear another voice reproaching me for encouraging street beggary. I have been taught that street beggary is wrong, and when I have to unbutton two coats and go through three or four pockets before I can reach the small coin I mean to give in compliance with that imperative voice I certainly feel it to be wrong. So I compromise, and I am never able to make sure that either of those voices is satisfied with me. I am not even satisfied with myself; but I am better satisfied than if I gave nothing. That was the selfish reason I now had for deciding to yield to my better nature, and to obey the voice which bade me "Give to him that asketh"; for, as I said, I hate a bad conscience, and of two bad consciences I always choose the least, which in a case like this is the one that incensed political economy gives me.

I put my hand into my hip-pocket, where I keep my silver, and found nothing there but half a dollar. This at once changed the whole current of my feelings; and it was not chill penury that repressed my noble rage, but chill affluence. It was manifestly wrong to give half a dollar to a man who had no hands, or to any sort of beggar. I was willing to commit a small act of incivism, but I had not the courage to flout political economy to the extent of fifty cents; and I felt that when I was bidden "Give to him that asketh," I was never meant to give so much as a half-dollar, but a cent or a half-dime or, at the most, a quarter. I wished I had a quarter. I would gladly have given a quarter, but there was nothing in my pocket but that fatal, that inexorably indivisible half-dollar, the continent of two quarters, but not practically a quarter. I would have asked anybody in sight to change it for me, but there was no one passing; it was a quiet street of brown-stone dwellings, and not a thronged thorough-fare at any time. At that hour of the late afternoon it was deserted, except for the beggar and myself; and I am not sure that he had any business to be sitting there on the steps of another man's house, or that I had the right to encourage his invasion by giving him anything. For a moment I did not know quite what to do. To be sure, I was not bound to the man in any way. He had not asked me for charity, and I had barely paused before him; I could go on and ignore the incident. I thought of doing this, but then I thought of the bad conscience I should be certain to have, and I could not go on. I glanced across the street, and near the corner I saw a decent-looking restaurant; and "Wait a minute," I said to the man, as if he were likely to go away, and I ran across to get my half-dollar changed at the restaurant.

I was now quite resolved to give him a quarter and be done with it; the thing was getting to be a bore. But, when I entered the restaurant, I saw no one there but a young man quite at the end of a long room; and when he had come all the way forward to find what I wanted I was ashamed to ask him to change my half-dollar, and I pretended that I wanted a package of Sweet Caporal cigarettes, which I did not want, and which it was a pure waste for me to buy, since I do not smoke, though doubtless it was better to buy them and encourage commerce than to give the half-dollar and encourage beggary. At any rate, I instinctively felt that I had political economy on my side in the transaction, and I made haste to go back to the man on the steps, and secure myself with Christian charity, too. On the way over to him, however, I decided that I would not give him a quarter, and I ended by poising fifteen cents on one of his out-stretched stumps.

He seemed very grateful, and thanked me earnestly, with a little note

chill penury that repressed my noble rage: an allusion to Thomas Gray's "Elegy Written in a Country Churchyard."
incivism: poor citizenship.

of surprise in his voice, as if he were not used to such splendid charity as that; and, in fact, I suppose very few people gave so handsomely to him. He spoke with a German accent; and when I asked him how he had lost his hands he answered, "Frost. Frozen off, here in the city." I could not go on and ask him for further particulars, for I thought it but too likely that he had been drunk when exposed to weather that would freeze one's hands off, and that he was now paying the penalty of his debauchery. I was in no wise so much at peace with myself as I had expected to be; and I was still less so when a young girl halted as she came by, and, seeing what I had done, and hearing what the man said, put a dime on the other stump. She looked poor herself; her sack was quite shabby about the seams. I did not think she could afford to give so much to a single beggar, and I was aware of having tempted her to the excess by my own profusion. If she had seen me giving the man only a nickel, she would perhaps have given him a cent, which was probably all she could afford.

I came away feeling indescribably squalid. I perceived now that I could have taken my stand upon the high ground of discouraging street beggary, and given nothing; but, having once lowered myself to the level of the early Christians, I ought to have given the half-dollar. It did not console me to remember the surprise in the man's gratitude, and to reflect that I had probably given him at least three times as much as he usually got from the tenderest-hearted people. I perceived that I had been the divinely appointed bearer of half a dollar to his mutilation and his misery, and I had given him fifteen cents out of it, and wasted ten, and kept the other twenty-five; in other words, I had embezzled the greater part of the money intrusted to me for him.

When I got home and told them at dinner just what I had done, they all agreed that I had done a mighty shabby thing. I do not know whether the reader will agree with them or not—perhaps I would rather not know; and, on the other hand, I shall not ask him what he would have done in the like case. Now that is it laid before him in all its shameless nakedness, I dare say he will pretend that he would have given the half-dollar. But I doubt if he would; and there is a curious principle governing this whole matter of giving, which I would like him to consider with me. Charity is a very simple thing when you look at it from the stand-point of the good Christian, but it is very complex when you look at it from the stand-point of the good citizen; and there seems to be an instinctive effort on our part to reconcile two duties by a certain proportion which we observe in giving. Whether we say so to ourselves or not, we behave as if it would be the wildest folly to give at all in the measure Christ bade; and by an apt psychological juggle we adjust our succor to the various degrees of need that present themselves. To the absolutely destitute it is plain that anything will be better than nothing, and so we give the smallest charity to those who need charity most. I dare say people will deny this, but it is true, all the same, as the reader will allow when he thinks about it. We act upon a kind of logic in the matter, though I do not suppose many act consciously upon it. Here is a man whispering to you in the dark that he has not had anything to eat all day, and does not know where to sleep. Shall you give him a dollar to get a good supper and a decent lodging? Certainly not: you shall give him a dime, and trust that someone else will give him another; or, if you have some charity tickets about you, then you give him one of them, and go away feeling that you have at once befriended and outwitted him; for the supposition is that he is a fraud, and has been trying to work you. . . .

The whole spectacle of poverty, indeed, is incredible. As soon as you cease to have it before your eyes,—even when you have it before your eyes,—you can hardly believe it, and that is perhaps why so many people deny that it exists, or is much more than a superstition of the sentimentalist. When I get back into my own comfortable room, among my papers and books, I remember it as I remember something at the theatre. It seems to be turned off, as Niagara does, when you come away. The difficulty here in New York is that the moment you go out again you find it turned on, full tide. I used to live in a country supposed to be peculiarly infested by beggars; but I believe I was not so much asked for charity in Venice as I am in New York. There are as many beggars on our streets as in Venice, and, as for the organized efforts to get at one's compassion, there is no parallel for New York anywhere. The letters asking aid for air funds, salt and fresh, for homes and shelters, for reading-rooms and eating-rooms, for hospitals and refuges, for the lame, halt, and blind, for the old, for the young, for the anhungered and ashamed, of all imaginable descriptions, storm in with every mail, so that one hates to open one's letters nowadays; for instead of finding a pleasant line from a friend, one finds an appeal, in print imitating typewriting, from several of the millionaires in the city for aid of some good object to which they have lent the influence of their signatures, and enclosing an envelope, directed but not stamped, for your subscription. You do not escape from the proof of poverty even by keeping in-doors amid your own luxurious environment; besides, your digestion becomes impaired, and you have to go out, if you are to have any appetite for your dinner; and then the trouble begins on other terms.

One of my minor difficulties, if I may keep on confessing myself to the reader, is a very small pattern of newsboys, whom I am tempted to make keep the change when I get a one-cent paper of them and give them a five-cent piece. I see men, well dressed, well brushed, with the air of being exemplary citizens, fathers of families, and pillars of churches, wait patiently or impatiently, while these little fellows search one pocket and another for the pennies due, or run to some comrade Chonnie or Chimmie for them; and I cannot help feeling that I may be doing something very disorganizing or demoralizing in failing to demand my change. At first I used to pass on without apparently noticing that I had given too much, but I perceived that then these small wretches sometimes winked to their friends, in the belief that they had cheated me; and now I let them offer to get the change before I let them keep it. I may be undermining society, and teaching them to trust in a fickle fortune rather than their own enterprise, by overpaying them; but at least I will not corrupt them by letting them think they have taken advantage of my ignorance. If the reader will not whisper it again, I will own that I have sometimes paid as high as ten cents for a one-cent paper, which I did not want, when it has been offered me by a very minute newsboy near midnight; and I have done this in conscious defiance of the well-known fact that it is a ruse of very minute newsboys to be out late when they ought to be in bed at home, or at *the* Home (which seems different), in order to work the sympathies of unwary philanthropists. The statistics in regard to these miscreants are as unquestionable as those relating to street beggars who have amassed fortunes and died amid rags and riches of dramatic character. I am sorry that I cannot say where the statistics are to be found.

The actual practice of fraud, even when you discover it, must give you interesting question, unless you are cock-sure of your sociology. I was once met by a little girl on a cross-street in a respectable quarter of the town, who burst into tears at sight of me, and asked for money to buy her sick mother bread. The very next day I was passing through the same street, and I saw the same little girl burst into tears at the sight of a benevolent-looking lady, whom undoubtedly she asked for money for the same good object. The benevolent-looking lady gave her nothing, and she tried her woes upon several other people, none of whom gave her anything. I was forced to doubt whether, upon the whole, her game was worth the candle, or whether she was really making a provision for her declining years by this means. To be sure, her time was not worth much, and she could hardly have got any other work, she was so young; but it seemed hardly a paying industry. By any careful calculation, I do not believe she would have been found to have amassed more than ten or fifteen cents a day; and perhaps she really had a sick mother at home. Many persons are obliged to force their emotions for money whom we should not account wholly undeserving; yet I suppose a really good citizen who found this little girl trying to cultivate the sympathies of charitable people by that system of irrigation would have had her suppressed as an impostor.

In a way she was an impostor, though her sick mother may have been starving, as she said. It is a nice question. Shall we always give to him that asketh? Or shall we give to him that asketh only when we know that he has come by his destitution honestly? In other words, what is a deserving case of charity—or, rather, what is not? Is a starving or freezing person to be denied because he or she is drunken or vicious? What is desert in the poor? What is desert in the rich, I suppose the reader would answer. If this is so, and if we ought not to succor an undeserving poor person, then we ought not to succor an undeserving rich person. It will be said that a rich person, however undeserving, will never be in need of our succor, but this is not so clear. If we saw a rich person fall in a fit before the horses of a Fifth Avenue omnibus, ought not we to run and lift him up, although we knew him to be a man whose life was stained by every vice and excess, and cruel, wanton, idle, luxurious? I know that I am imagining a quite impossible rich person; but, once imagined, ought not we to save him all the same as if he were deserving?

The Direct Experience

I do not believe the most virtuous person will say we ought not; and ought not we, then, to rescue the most worthless tramp fallen under the wheels of the Juggernaut of want? Is charity the reward of merit? . . .

I dare say poverty and the pangs of hunger and cold do not foster habits of strict temperance. It is a great pity they do not, since they are so common. If they did, they could do more than anything else to advance the cause of prohibition. Still, I will not say that all the poor I give to are in liquor at the moment, or that drunkenness is peculiarly the vice of one-armed destitution. Neither is gratitude a very common or articulate emotion in my beneficiaries. They are mostly, if thankful at all, silently thankful; and I find this in better taste. I do not believe that, as a rule, they are very imaginative, or least so imaginative as romantic novelists. Yet there was one sufferer came up the back elevator on a certain evening not long ago, and burst upon me suddenly, somehow as if he had come up through a trap in the stage, who seemed to have rather a gift in that way. He was most amusingly shabby and dirty (though I do not know why shabbiness and dirt should be amusing), with a cut-away coat worn down to its ultimate gloss, a frayed neckcloth, and the very foulest collar I can remember seeing. But he had a brisk and pleasing address, and I must say an excellent diction. He called me by name, and at once said that friends whom he had expected to find in New York were most inopportunely in Europe at this moment of his arrival from a protracted sojourn in the West. But he was very anxious to get on that night to Hartford and complete his journey home from Denver, where he had fallen a prey to the hard times in the very hour of the most prosperous speculation; and he proposed, as an inducement to a loan, borrowing only enough money to take him to New Haven by the boat— he would walk the rest of the way to Hartford. I no more believed him than I should believe a ghost if it said it was a ghost. But I believed that he was in want,—his clothes proved that,—and I gave him the little sum he asked. He said he would send it back the instant he reached Hartford; and I am left to think that he has not yet arrived. But I am sure that even that brief moment of his airy and almost joyous companionship was worth the money. He was of an order of classic impostors dear to literature, and grown all too few in these times of hurry and fierce competition. I wish I had seen more of him, and yet I cannot say that I wish he would come back; it might be embarrassing for both of us.

Not long before his visit I had a call from another imaginative person, whom I was not able to meet so fully in her views. This was a middle-aged lady who said she had come on that morning from Boston to see me. She owned we had never met before, and that she was quite unknown to me; but apparently she did not think this any bar to her asking me for two hundred and fifty dollars to aid in the education of her son. I confess that I was bewildered for a moment. My simple device of offering half the amount demanded would have been too costly: I really could not have afforded to give her one hundred and twenty-five dollars, even if she had been willing to compromise, which I was not sure of. I am afraid the reader will think I shirked. I said that I had a great many demands upon me, and I ended by refusing to give anything. I really do not know how I had the courage; perhaps it was only frenzy. She insisted, with reasons for my giving which she laid before me; but either they did not convince me or I had hardened my heart so well that they could not prevail with me, and she got up and went away. As she went out of the room she looked about its appointments, which I had not thought very luxurious before, and said that she saw I was able to *live* very comfortably, at any rate; and left me to the mute reproach of my carpets and easy-chairs.

I do not remember whether she alleged any inspiration in coming to see me for this good object; but a summer or two since a lady came to me, at my hotel in the mountains, who said that she had been moved to do so by an impulse which seemed little short of mystical. She said that she was not ordinarily superstitious, but she had wakened that morning in Boston with my name the first thing in her thoughts, and it seemed so directly related to what she had in view that she could not resist the suggestion it conveyed that she should come at once to lay her scheme before me. She took a good deal of time to do this; and, romantic as it appeared, I felt sure that she was working with real material. It was of a nature so complex, however, and on a scale so vast, that I should despair of getting it intelligibly before the reader, and I will not attempt it. I listened with the greatest interest; but, at the end, I was obliged to say that I thought her mystical impulse was mistaken; I was sorry it had deceived her; I was quite certain that I had not the means or the tastes to enter upon the aesthetic enterprise which she proposed. In return, I suggested a number of millionaires whose notorious softness of heart, or whose wish to get themselves before the public by their good deeds, ought to make them more available, and we parted the best of friends. I am not yet quite able to make up my mind that she was not the victim of a hypnotic suggestion from the unseen world, and altogether innocent in her appeal to me.

In fact, I am not able to think very ill even of impostors. It is a great pity for them, and even a great shame, to go about deceiving people of means; but I do not believe they are so numerous as people of means imagine. As a rule, I do not suppose they succeed for long, and their lives must be full of cares and anxieties, which, of course, one must not sympathize with, but which are real enough, nevertheless. People of means would do well to consider this, and at least not plume themselves very much upon not being cheated. If they have means, it is perhaps part of the curse of money, or of that unfriendliness to riches which our religion is full of, that money should be got from them by unworthy persons. They have their little romantic superstitions, too. One of these is the belief that beggars are generally persons who will not work, and that they are often persons of secret wealth, which they constantly increase by preying upon the public. I take leave no doubt this altogether.

plume: congratulate.

The Direct Experience

Beggary appears to me in its conditions almost harder than any other trade; and, from what I have seen of the amount it earns, the return it makes is smaller than any other. I should not myself feel safe in refusing anything to a beggar upon the theory of a fortune sewn into a mattress, to be discovered after the beggar has died intestate. I know that a great many good people pin their faith to such mattresses; but I should be greatly surprised if one such could be discovered in the whole city of New York.

On the other hand, I feel pretty sure that there are hundreds and even thousands of people who are insufficiently fed and clad in New York; and if here and there one of these has the courage of his misery and asks alms, one must not be too cock-sure it is a sin to give to him.

Of course, one must not pauperize him: that ought by all means to be avoided; I am always agreeing to that. But if he is already pauperized; if we know by statistics and personal knowledge that there are hundreds and even thousands of people who cannot get work, and that they must suffer if they do not beg, let us not be too hard upon them. Let us refuse them kindly, and try not to see them; for if we see their misery and do not give, that demoralizes us. Come, I say; have not we some rights, too? No man strikes another man a blow without becoming in sort and measure a devil; and to see what looks like want, and to deny its prayer, has an effect upon the heart which is not less depraving. Perhaps it would be a fair division of the work if we let the deserving rich give only to the deserving poor, and kept the undeserving poor for ourselves, who, if we are not rich, are not deserving, either.

DISCUSSION

1. Instead of giving us a sermon on the philosophy of charity, Howells offers bits of his own experience in some detail. What is the effect on the reader? Is the conflict a real one, or can you suggest an easy answer?
2. On either side of the problem are the extremes: we should give all, we should give nothing. What are the major beliefs or philosophies behind each of these extremes?
3. Howells never considers going to either extreme as a policy; he tries to find the precise point between the two where he can feel comfortably right and good. Where is this point?
4. In some nations, no beggars are to be seen; they are all cared for in institutions. Discuss this arrangement in light of Howells' dilemma.

When we speak of "abnormal" mental states we use quotation marks, for what is unusual in one culture may be normal in another. In fact, the majority of the world's cultures in the past and in the "primitive" present have cultivated trance states and visions induced by such means as fasting, drugs, dancing, music, meditation, formula repetition, body control, and sensory deprivation. But among ourselves, most people experience these states only accidentally as a result of illness, neurosis, or drug experiment. These ex-

Inner Experience

periences may be intensely pleasant, intensely unpleasant, or a combination of the two; but all agree they are intense. In the following selection, George Gissing describes a series of fever-induced visions, with considerable emphasis on their intensity and apparent reality.

George Gissing

Visions in a Fever

(1898)

I had as little sleep as on the night before, but my suffering was mitigated in a very strange way. After I had put out the candle, I tormented myself for a long time with the thought that I should never see La Colonna. As soon as I could rise from bed, I must flee Cotrone, and think myself fortunate in escaping alive; but to turn my back on the Lacinian promontory, leaving the Cape unvisited, the ruin of the temple unseen, seemed to me a miserable necessity which I should lament as long as I lived. I felt as one involved in a moral disaster; working in spite of reason, my brain regarded the matter from many points of view, and found no shadow of solace. The sense that so short a distance separated me from the place I desired to see added exasperation to my distress. Half-delirious, I at times seemed to be in a boat, tossing on wild waters, the Column visible afar, but only when I strained my eyes to discover it. In a description of the approach by land, I had read of a great precipice which had to be skirted, and this, too, haunted me with its terrors: I found myself toiling on a perilous road, which all at once crumbled into fearful depths just before me. A violent shivering fit roused me from this gloomy dreaming, and I soon after fell into a visionary state which, whilst it lasted, gave me such placid happiness as I had never known when in my perfect mind. Lying still and calm, and perfectly awake, I watched a succession of wonderful pictures. First of all I saw great vases, rich with ornament and figures; then sepulchral marbles, carved more exquisitely than the most beautiful I had ever known. The vision grew in extent, in multiplicity of detail; presently I was regarding scenes of ancient life—thronged streets, processions triumphal or religious, halls of feasting, fields of battle. What most impressed me at the time was the marvellously bright yet delicate colouring of everything I

La Colonna: Capo delle Colonne, a promontory on the Ionian Sea marking the beginning of the instep of the "boot" of Italy, inside which is the Gulf of Taranto. The ruin of an ancient Greek temple stands at its extremity.
Cotrone: now Crotone, a town at the northern base of La Colonna, once an important Greek colony and the seat of the school of the philosopher Pythagoras. It was occupied by the Romans in 277 B.C., and it was at Crotone that Hannibal embarked for his return to Africa in 203 B.C.
Column: natural feature after which the promontory of Colonne is named.

The Direct Experience

saw. I can give no idea in words of the pure radiance which shone from every object, which illumined every scene. More remarkable, when I thought of it next day, was the minute finish of these pictures, the definiteness of every point on which my eye fell. Things which I could not know, which my imagination, working in the service of the will, could never have bodied forth, were before me as in life itself. I consciously wondered at peculiarities of costume such as I have never read of; at features of architecture entirely new to me; at insignificant characteristics of that bygone world which by no possibility could have been gathered from books. I recall a succession of faces, the loveliest conceivable; and I remember, I feel to this moment, the pang of regret with which I lost sight of each when it faded into darkness.

As an example of the more elaborate visions that passed before me, I will mention the only one which I clearly recollect. It was a glimpse of history. When Hannibal, at the end of the second Punic War, was confined to the south of Italy, he made Croton his headquarters, and when, in reluctant obedience to Carthage, he withdrew from Roman soil, it was at Croton that he embarked. He then had with him a contingent of Italian mercenaries, and, unwilling that these soldiers should go over to the enemy, he bade them accompany him to Africa. The Italians refused. Thereupon Hannibal had them led down to the shore of the sea, where he slaughtered one and all. This event I beheld. I saw the strand by Croton; the promontory with its temple; not as I know the scene today, but as it must have looked to those eyes more than two thousand years ago. The soldiers of Hannibal doing massacre, the perishing mercenaries, supported my closest gaze, and left no curiosity unsatisfied. (Alas! could I but see it again, or remember clearly what was shown me!) And over all lay a glory of sunshine, an indescribable brilliancy which puts light and warmth into my mind whenever I try to recall it. The delight of these phantasms was well worth the ten days' illness which paid for them. After this night they never returned; I hoped for their renewal, but in vain. When I spoke of the experience to Dr. Sculco, he was much amused, and afterwards he often asked me whether I had had any more *visioni*. That gate of dreams was closed, but I shall always feel that, for an hour, it was granted me to see the vanished life so dear to my imagination. If the picture corresponded to nothing real, tell me who can, by what power I reconstructed, to the last perfection of intimacy, a world known to me only in ruined fragments.

Gissing in his fever sees in detail things that are not there; the neurotic often sees things as they really are with terrifying intensity, his illness at times dissolving the veil of insensitivity that most of us, in self-defense, keep between ourselves and the world. We have seen in "Old Houses" (p. 19) an example of the way Malte Laurids Brigge's neurosis intensifies his sensory awareness. (Brigge, you will recall, is a fictional character invented by Rainer Maria Rilke.) Again we are with him as an overwhelming combination of ordinary horrors builds into panic.

Rainer Maria Rilke

The Hospital

(1910)

The doctor did not understand me. Nothing. And certainly it was difficult to describe. They wanted to try electric treatment. Good. I received a slip of paper: I had to be at the Salpêtrière at one o'clock. I was there. I had to pass a long row of barracks and traverse a number of courtyards, where people in white bonnets stood here and there under the bare trees like convicts. Finally I entered a long, gloomy, corridor-like room, that had on one side four windows of dim, greenish glass, one separated from the other by a broad, black partition. In front of them a wooden bench ran along, past everything, and on this bench they who knew me sat and waited. Yes, they were all there. When I became accustomed to the twilight of the place, I noticed that among them, as they sat shoulder to shoulder in an endless row, there could also be other people, little people, artisans, char-women, truckmen. Down at the narrow end of this corridor, on special chairs, two stout women had spread themselves out and were conversing, concierges probably. I looked at the clock; it was five minutes to one. In five minutes, or say ten, my turn would come; so it was not so bad. The air was foul, heavy, impregnated with clothes and breaths. At a certain spot the strong, intensifying coolness of ether came through a crack in a door. I began to walk up and down. It crossed my mind that I had been directed here, among these people, to this overcrowded, general consultation. It was, so to speak, the first public confirmation of the fact that I belonged among the outcast; had the doctor known by my appearance? Yet I had paid my visit in a tolerably decent suit; I had sent in my card. Despite that he must have learned it somehow; perhaps I had betrayed myself. However, now that it was a fact I did not find it so bad after all; the people sat quietly and took no notice of me. Some were in pain and swung one leg a little, the better to endure it. Various men had laid their heads in the palms of their hands; others were sleeping deeply, with heavy, fatigue-crushed faces. A stout man with a red, swollen neck sat bending forward, staring at the floor, and from time to time spat with a smack at a spot he seemed to find suitable for the purpose. A child was sobbing in a corner; it had drawn its long thin legs close up on the bench, and now clasped and held them tightly to its body, as though it must bid them farewell. A small, pale woman on whose head a crape hat adorned with round, black flowers, sat awry, wore the grimace of a smile about her meager lips, but her sore eyes were constantly overflowing. Not far from her had been placed a girl with a

Salpetriere: an enormous public hospital in Paris.
char-women: cleaning women.
concierges: attendants, often female, at the doors of residence buildings in France. They handle mail, prevent strangers from entering, and sometimes serve as janitors.

round, smooth face and protruding eyes that were without expression; her mouth hung open, so that one saw her white, slimy gums with their old stunted teeth. And there were many bandages. Bandages that swathed a whole head layer upon layer, until only a single eye remained that no longer belonged to anyone. Bandages that hid, and bandages that revealed, what was beneath them. Bandages that had been undone, in which, as in a dirty bed, a hand now lay that was a hand no longer; and a bandaged leg that protruded from the row on the bench, as large as a whole man. I walked up and down, and endeavored to be calm. I occupied myself a good deal with the wall facing me. I noticed that it contained a number of single doors, and did not reach up to the ceiling, so that this corridor was not completely separated from the rooms that must adjoin it. I looked at the clock; I had been pacing up and down for an hour. A while later the doctors arrived. First a couple of young fellows who passed by with indifferent faces, and finally the one I had consulted, in light gloves, chapeau à huit reflets, impeccable overcoat. When he saw me he lifted his hat a little and smiled absent-mindedly. I now hoped to be called immediately, but another hour passed. I cannot remember how I spent it. It passed. An old man wearing a soiled apron, a sort of attendant, came and touched me on the shoulder. I entered one of the adjoining rooms. The doctor and the young fellows sat round a table and looked at me, someone gave me a chair. So far so good. And now I had to describe what it was that was the matter with me. As briefly as possible, s'il vous plaît. For much time these gentlemen had not. I felt very odd. The young fellows sat and looked at me with that superior, professional curiosity they had learned. The doctor I knew stroked his pointed black beard and smiled absently. I thought I should burst into tears, but I heard myself saying in French: "I have already had the honor, monsieur, of giving you all the details that I can give. If you consider it indispensable that these gentlemen should be initiated, you are certainly able, after our conversation, to do this in a few words, while I find it very difficult." The doctor rose, smiling politely, and going toward the window with his assistants said a few words, which he accompanied with a horizontal, wavering movement of his hands. Three minutes later one of the young men, short-sighted and jerky, came back to the table, and said, trying to look at me severely, "You sleep well, sir?" "No, badly." Whereupon he sprang back again to the group at the window. There they discussed a while longer, then the doctor turned to me and informed me that I would be summoned again. I reminded him that my appointment had been for one o'clock. He smiled and made a few swift, abrupt movements with his small white hands, which were meant to signify that he was uncommonly busy. So I returned to my hallway, where the air had become much more oppressive, and began again to pace up and down, although I felt mortally tired. Finally the moist, accumulated smell made me dizzy; I stopped at the entrance door and opened it a little. I saw that outside it was still afternoon, with some sun, and that

chapeau à huit reflets: shiny top hat.
s'il vous plaît: if you please.

did me ever so much good. But I had hardly stood a minute thus when I heard someone calling me. A female sitting at a table two or three steps away hissed something to me. Who had told me to open the door? I said I could not stand the atmosphere. Well, that was my own affair, but the door had to be kept shut. Was it not permissible, then, to open a window? No, that was forbidden. I decided to resume my walking up and down, for after all that was a kind of anodyne and it hurt nobody. But now this too displeased the woman sitting at the little table. Did I not have a seat? No, I hadn't. Walking about was not allowed; I would have to find a seat. There ought to be one. The woman was right. In fact, a place was promptly found next to the girl with the protruding eyes. There I now sat with the feeling that this state must certainly be the preparation for something dreadful. On my left, then, was this girl with the decaying gums; what was on my right I could not make out till after some time. It was a huge, immovable mass, having a face and a large, heavy, inert hand. The side of the face that I saw was empty, quite without features and without memories; and it was gruesome that the clothes were like those of a corpse dressed for the coffin. The narrow, black cravat had been buckled in the same loose, impersonal way around the collar, and the coat showed that it had been put on the will-less body by other hands. The hand had been placed on the trousers exactly where it lay, and even the hair looked as if it had been combed by those women who lay out the dead, and was stiffly arranged, like the hair of stuffed animals. I observed all these things with attention, and it occurred to me that this must be the place that had been destined for me; for I now believed I had at last arrived at that point of my life at which I would remain. Yes, fate goes wonderful ways.

Suddenly there rose quite nearby in quick succession the frightened, defensive cries of a child, followed by a low, hushed weeping. While I was straining to discover where this could have come from, a little, suppressed cry quavered away again, and I heard voices, questioning, a voice giving orders in a subdued tone, and then some sort of machine started up and hummed indifferently along. Now I recalled that half wall, and it was clear to me that all this came from the other side of the doors and that work was going on in there. Actually, the attendant with the soiled apron appeared from time to time and made a sign. I had given up thinking that he might mean me. Was it intended for me? No. Two men appeared with a wheel-chair; they lifted the mass beside me into it, and I now saw that it was an old paralytic who had another, smaller side to him, worn out by life, and an open, dim and melancholy eye. They wheeled him inside, and now there was lots of room beside me. And I sat and wondered what they were likely to do to the imbecile girl and whether she too would scream. The machines back there kept up such an agreeable mechanical whirring, there was nothing disturbing about it.

But suddenly everything was still, and in the stillness a superior, self-complacent voice, which I thought I knew, said: "Riez!" A pause. "Riez! Mais riez, riez!" I was already laughing. It was inexplicable that the man

Riez!: laugh!

on the other side of the partition didn't want to laugh. A machine rattled, but was immediately silent again, words were exchanged, then the same energetic voice rose again and ordered: "Dites-nous le mot: avant." And spelling it: "A-v-a-n-t." Silence. "On n'entend rien. Encore une fois..."

And then, as I listened to the hot, flaccid stuttering on the other side of the partition, then for the first time in many, many years it was there again. That which had struck into me my first, profound terror, when as a child I lay ill with fever: the Big Thing. Yes, that was what I had always called it, when they all stood around my bed and felt my pulse and asked me what had frightened me: the Big Thing. And when they got the doctor and he came and spoke to me, I begged him only to make the Big Thing go away, nothing else mattered. But he was like the rest. He could not take it away, though I was so small then and might so easily have been helped. And now it was there again. Later it had simply stayed away; it had not come back even on nights when I had fever; but now it was there, although I had no fever. Now it was there. Now it grew out of me like a tumor, like a second head, and was a part of me, though it could not belong to me at all, because it was so big. It was there like a huge, dead beast, that had once, when it was still alive, been my hand or my arm. And my blood flowed both through me and through it, as if through one and the same body. And my heart had to make a great effort to drive the blood into the Big Thing; there was hardly enough blood. And the blood entered the Big Thing unwillingly and came back sick and tainted. But the Big Thing swelled and grew over my face like a warm bluish boil and grew over my mouth, and already the shadow of its edge lay upon my remaining eye.

I cannot recall how I got out through the numerous courtyards. It was evening, and I lost my way in this strange neighborhood and went up boulevards with interminable walls in one direction and, when there was no end to them, returned in the opposite direction until I reached some square or other. Thence I began to walk along a street, and other streets came that I had never seen before, and still other streets. Electric cars would come racing up and past, too brilliantly lit and with harsh, beating clang of bells. But on their signboards stood names I did not know. I did not know in what city I was or whether I had a lodging somewhere here or what I must do in order not to have to go on walking.

DISCUSSION

1. Many have probably experienced Brigge's intensity of vision; few have conveyed it in words as well as Rilke does. Examine a section of fifteen or twenty lines anywhere in the passage. How does Rilke achieve the effect of intensity? What are the ingredients, and how are they combined?

Dites-nous le mot: avant: let's say the word "before."
On n'entend rien. Encore une fois...: I can't hear you. One more time...

2. The insensitive refuse to observe in self-defense; the morbid dwell on the unpleasant. How is Brigge's observation different from that of either the insensitive or the morbid?

3. Gissing is delighted by visions that include ruthless slaughter; Brigge is horrified by the sights in a hospital waiting room. Does this signify a profound difference of character in the two men, or is another factor involved? If the latter, what factor?

And now Malte Laurids Brigge recalls a childhood experience of a sort that is more common than we might suppose.

Rainer Maria Rilke

The Hand

(1910)

How small I must still have been I see from the fact that I was kneeling on the armchair in order to reach comfortably up to the table on which I was drawing. It was an evening, in winter, in our apartment in town, if I am not mistaken. The table stood in my room, between the windows, and there was no lamp in the room save that which shone on my papers and on Mademoiselle's book; for Mademoiselle sat next me, her chair pushed back a little, and was reading. She was far away when she read, and I don't know whether she was in her book; she could read for hours, she seldom turned the leaves, and I had the impression that the pages became steadily fuller under her eyes, as though she looked words into them, certain words that she needed and that were not there. So it seemed to me as I went on drawing. I was drawing slowly, without any very decided intention, and when I didn't know what to do next, I would survey the whole with head bent a little to the right; in that position it always came to me soonest what was lacking. They were officers on horseback, who were riding into battle, or they were in the midst of it, and that was far simpler, for in that case, almost all one needed to draw was the smoke that enveloped everything. Maman, it is true, always insists that they were islands I was painting; islands with large trees and a castle and a flight of steps and flowers along the edge that were supposed to be reflected in the water. But I think she is making that up, or it must have been later.

It is certain that on that particular evening I was drawing a knight, a solitary, easily recognizable knight, on a strikingly caparisoned horse. He became so gaily-colored that I had to change crayons frequently, but the red was most in demand, and for it I reached again and again. Now I needed it once more, when it rolled (I can see it yet) right across the

The Direct Experience

lighted sheet to the edge of the table and, before I could stop it, fell past me and disappeared. I needed it really urgently, and it was very annoying to clamber down after it. Awkward as I was, I had to make all sorts of preparations to get down; my legs seemed to me far too long, I could not pull them out from under me; the too-prolonged kneeling posture had numbed my limbs; I could not tell what belonged to me, and what to the chair. At last I did arrive down there, somewhat bewildered, and found myself on a fur rug that stretched from under the table as far as the wall. But here a fresh difficulty arose. My eyes, accustomed to the brightness above and all inspired with the colors on the white paper, were unable to distinguish anything at all beneath the table, where the blackness seemed to me so dense that I was afraid I should knock against it. I therefore relied on my sense of touch, and kneeling, supported on my left hand, I combed around with my other hand in the cool, long-haired rug, which felt quite friendly; only that no pencil was to be found. I imagined I must be losing a lot of time, and was about to call to Mademoiselle and ask her to hold the lamp for me, when I noticed that to my involuntarily strained eyes the darkness was gradually growing more penetrable. I could already distinguish the wall at the back, which ended in a light-colored molding; I oriented myself with regard to the legs of the table; above all I recognized my own outspread hand moving down there all alone, a little like an aquatic animal, examining the ground. I watched it, as I remember still, almost with curiosity; it seemed as if it knew things I had never taught it, groping down there so independently, with movements I had never noticed in it before. I followed it up as it pressed forward, I was interested in it, ready for all sorts of things. But how should I have been prepared to see suddenly come to meet it out of the wall another hand, a larger, extraordinarily thin hand, such as I had never seen before. It came groping in similar fashion from the other side, and the two outspread hands moved blindly toward one another. My curiosity was not yet used up but suddenly it came to an end, and there was only terror. I felt that one of the hands belonged to me, and that it was committing itself to something irreparable. With all the authority I had over it, I checked it and drew it back flat and slowly, without taking my eyes off the other, which went on groping. I realized that it would not leave off; I cannot tell how I got up again. I sat deep in the armchair, my teeth chattered, and I had so little blood in my face that it seemed to me there could be no more blue in my eyes. Mademoiselle—, I wanted to say and could not, but at that she took fright of her own accord, and, flinging her book away, knelt beside the chair and cried out my name; I believe she shook me. But I was perfectly conscious. I swallowed a couple of times; for now I wanted to tell about it.

But how? I made an indescribable effort to master myself, but it was not to be expressed so that anyone could understand. If there were words for this occurrence, I was too little to find them. And suddenly the fear seized me that nevertheless they might suddenly be there, beyond my years, these words, and it seemed to me more terrible than anything else that I should then have to say them. To live through once again the reality down there, differently, conjugated, from the beginning; to hear myself admitting it—for that I had no strength left.

It is of course imagination on my part to declare now that I already at that time felt that something had entered into my life, directly into mine, with which I alone should have to go about, always and always. I see myself lying in my little crib and not sleeping and somehow vaguely foreseeing that life would be like this: full of many special things that are meant for *one* person alone and that cannot be told. Certain it is that a sad and heavy pride gradually arose in me. I pictured to myself how one would go about, full of what is inside one, and silent. I felt an impetuous sympathy for grown-ups; I admired them, and proposed to tell them that I admired them. I proposed to tell it to Mademoiselle at the next opportunity.

DISCUSSION

1. What Brigge experienced, of course, was simply visual hallucination stimulated by retinal fatigue. As Chesterton said, the madman is the man who has lost everything except his reason. Relate the above two statements.
2. From the standpoint of writing technique, what is the function of the rather long beginning description of the circumstances of the experience—Mademoiselle reading, the "gaily colored" drawing, and so on?

Since opium-taking was common in Europe during one of its best literary periods, say 1750 to 1850, it is both puzzling and disappointing so few literary men left any more than hints about the effects of the drug. It is also unfortunate that the one who wrote most about the subject, Thomas De Quincey, was a writer of annoyingly elaborate and long-winded prose. In spite of the patience required to read it, however, his *Confessions of an English Opium-Eater* is a fascinating record and well worth the effort. The following excerpt has to do with the final stages of his experience.

Thomas De Quincey

The Pains of Opium

(1820)

The first notice I had of any important change going on in this part of my physical economy was from the re-awaking of a state of eye oftentimes incident to childhood. I know not whether my reader is aware that many children have a power of painting, as it were, upon the darkness all sorts of phantoms: in some that power is simply a mechanic affection of the eye; others have a voluntary or semi-voluntary power to dismiss or summon such phantoms; or, as a child once said to me, when I questioned him on this matter, "I can tell them to go, and they go; but sometimes they come when I don't tell them to come." He had by one-half as unlimited a command over apparitions as a Roman centurion over his soldiers. In the middle of 1817 this faculty became increasingly distressing to me: at night, when I lay awake in bed, vast processions moved along continually in mournful pomp; friezes of never-ending stories, that to my feelings were as sad and solemn as stories drawn from times before Oedipus or Priam, before Tyre, before Memphis. And, concurrently with this, a corresponding change took place in my dreams; a theatre seemed suddenly opened and lighted up within my brain, which presented nightly spectacles of more than earthly splendour. And the four following facts may be mentioned as noticeable at this time:—

1. That, as the creative state of the eye increased, a sympathy seemed to arise between the waking and the dreaming states of the brain in one point—that whatsoever I happened to call up and to trace by a voluntary act upon the darkness was very apt to transfer itself to my dreams; and at length I feared to exercise this faculty; for, as Midas turned all things to gold that yet baffled his hopes and defrauded his human desires, so whatsoever things capable of being visually represented I did but think of in the darkness immediately shaped themselves into phantoms for the eye; and, by a process apparently no less inevitable, when thus once traced in faint and visionary colours, like writings in sympathetic ink, they were drawn out by fierce chemistry of my dreams, into insufferable splendour that fretted my heart.

2. This and all other changes in my dreams were accompanied by deep-seated anxiety and funereal melancholy, such as are wholly incommunicable by words. I seemed every night to descend—not metaphorically, but literally to descend—into chasms and sunless abysses, depths below depths, from which it seemed hopeless that I could ever reascend. Nor did I, by waking, feel that I *had* re-ascended. Why should I dwell upon this? For indeed the state of gloom which attended these gorgeous spectacles, amounting at least to utter darkness, as of some suicidal despondency, cannot be approached by words.

3. The sense of space, and in the end the sense of time, were both powerfully affected. Buildings, landscapes, &c., were exhibited in proportions so vast as the bodily eye is not fitted to receive. Space swelled, and was amplified to an extent of unutterable and self-repeating infinity. This disturbed me very much less than the vast expansion of time. Sometimes I seemed to have lived for seventy or a hundred years in one night; nay, sometimes had feelings representative of a duration far beyond the limits of any human experience.

4. The minutest incidents of childhood, or forgotten scenes of later years, were often revived. I could not be said to recollect them; for, if

I had been told of them when waking, I should not have been able to acknowledge them as parts of my past experience. But, placed as they were before me in dreams like intuitions, and clothed in all their evanescent circumstances and accompanying feelings, I *recognised* them instantaneously. I was once told by a near relative of mine that, having in her childhood fallen into a river, and being on the very verge of death but for the assistance which reached her at the last critical moment, she saw in a moment her whole life, clothed in its forgotten incidents, arrayed before her as in a mirror, not successively, but simultaneously; and she had a faculty developed as suddenly for comprehending the whole and every part. This, from some opium experiences, I can believe; I have, indeed, seen the same thing asserted twice in modern books, and accompanied by a remark which probably is true—viz. that the dread book of account which the Scriptures speak of is, in fact, the mind itself of each individual. Of this, at least, I feel assured, that there is no such thing as ultimate *forgetting*; traces once impressed upon the memory are indestructible; a thousand accidents may and will interpose a veil between our present consciousness and the secret inscriptions on the mind. Accidents of the same sort will also rend away this veil. But alike, whether veiled or unveiled, the inscription remains for ever; just as the stars seem to withdraw before the common light of day, whereas, in fact, we all know that it is the light which is drawn over them as a veil, and that they are waiting to be revealed whenever the obscuring daylight itself shall have withdrawn.

Having noticed these four facts as memorably distinguishing my dreams from those of health, I shall now cite a few illustrative cases; and shall then cite such others as I remember, in any order that may give them most effect as pictures to the reader.

I had been in youth, and ever since, for occasional amusement, a great reader of Livy, whom I confess that I prefer, both for style and matter, to any other of the Roman historians; and I had often felt as solemn and appalling sounds, emphatically representative of Roman majesty, the two words so often occurring in Livy, *Consul Romanus;* especially when the consul is introduced in his military character. I mean to say that the words *king, sultan, regent,* &c., or any other titles of those who embody in their own persons the collective majesty of a great people, had less power over my reverential feelings. I had also, though no great reader of History, made myself critically familiar with one period of English history—viz. the period of the Parliamentary War—having been attracted by the moral grandeur of some who figured in that day, and by the interesting memoirs which survive those unquiet times. Both these parts of my lighter reading, having furnished me often with matter of reflection, now furnished me with matter for my dreams. Often I used to see, after painting upon the blank darkness a sort of rehearsal whilst waking, a crowd of ladies, and perhaps a festival and dances. And I heard it said, or I said to myself, "These are English ladies from the unhappy times of Charles I. These are the wives and daughters of those who met in peace, and sat at the same tables, and were allied by marriage or by blood; and yet, after a certain day in August, 1642, never smiled upon each other again, nor met but in the field of battle; and at Marston Moor, at Newbury, or at Naseby, cut asunder all ties of love by the cruel sabre, and washed away in blood the memory of ancient friendship." The ladies danced, and looked as lovely as at the court of George IV. Yet even in my dream I knew that they had been in the grave for nearly two centuries. This pageant would suddenly dissolve; and, at a clapping of hands, would be heard the heart-shaking sound of *Consul Romanus;* and immediately came "sweeping by," in gorgeous paludaments, Paullus or Marius, girt around by a company of centurions, with the crimson tunic hoisted on a spear, and followed by the *alalagmos* of the Roman legions.

Many years ago, when I was looking over Piranesi's "Antiquities of Rome," Coleridge, then standing by, described to me a set of plates from that artist, called his "Dreams," and which record the scenery of his own visions during the delirium of a fever. Some of these (I describe only from memory of Coleridge's account) represented vast Gothic halls; on the floor of which stood mighty engines and machinery, wheels, cables, catapults, &c., expressive of enormous power put forth, or resistance overcome. Creeping along the sides of the walls, you perceived a staircase; and upon this, groping his way upwards, was Piranesi himself. Follow the stairs a little farther, and you perceive them reaching an abrupt termination, without any balustrade, and allowing no step onwards to him who should reach the extremity, except into the depths below. Whatever is to become of poor Piranesi, at least you suppose that his labours must now in some way terminate. But raise your eyes, and behold a second flight of stairs still higher, on which again Piranesi is perceived, by this time standing on the very brink of the abyss. Once again elevate your eye, and a still more aerial flight of stairs is descried; and there, again, is the delirious Piranesi, busy on his aspiring labours: and so on, until the unfinished stairs and the hopeless Piranesi both are lost in the upper gloom of the hall. With the same power of endless growth and self-reproduction did my architecture proceed in dreams. In the early stage of the malady, the splendours of my dreams were indeed chiefly architectural; and I beheld such pomp of cities and palaces as never yet was beheld by the waking eye, unless in the clouds. . . .

To my architecture succeeded dreams of lakes and silvery expanses of water: these haunted me so much that I feared lest some dropsical state or tendency of the brain might thus be making itself (to use a metaphysical word) *objective,* and that the sentient organ might be projecting itself as its own object. For two months I suffered greatly in my head —a part of my bodily structure which had hitherto been so clear from all

a certain day in August, 1642: August 22, when Charles I raised his standard at Nottingham, escalating his conflict with Parliament from a political to a military one. Seven years later, Parliament declared itself the supreme power in the land, and Charles was beheaded.
George IV: king in De Quincey's own time.
alalagmos: war cries.
Piranesi: see Plate 16.

touch or taint of weakness (physically, I mean) that I used to say of it, as the last Lord Orford said of his stomach, that it seemed likely to survive the rest of my person. Till now I had never felt a headache even, or any the slightest pain, except rheumatic pains caused by my own folly.

The waters gradually changed their character—from translucent lakes, shining like mirrors, they became seas and oceans. And now came a tremendous change, which, unfolding itself slowly like a scroll, through many months, promised an abiding torment; and, in fact, it never left me, though recurring more or less intermittingly. Hitherto the human face had often mixed in my dreams, but not despotically, nor with any special power of tormenting. But now that affection which I have called the tyranny of the human face began to unfold itself. Perhaps some part of my London life (the searching for Ann amongst fluctuating crowds) might be answerable for this. Be that as it may, now it was that upon the rocking waters of the ocean the human face began to reveal itself; the sea appeared paved with innumerable faces, upturned to the heavens; faces, imploring, wrathful, despairing; faces that surged upwards by thousands, by myriads, by generations: infinite was my agitation; my mind tossed, as it seemed, upon the billowy ocean, and weltered upon the weltering waves....

. . . Under the connecting feeling of tropical heat and vertical sunlights, I brought together all creatures, birds, beasts, reptiles, all trees and plants, usages and appearances, that are found in all tropical regions, and assembled them together in China or Hindostan. From kindred feelings, I soon brought Egypt and her gods under the same law. I was stared at, hooted at, grinned at, chattered at, by monkeys, by paroquets, by cockatoos. I ran into pagodas, and was fixed for centuries at the summit, or in secret rooms; I was the idol; I was the priest; I was worshipped; I was sacrificed. I fled from the wrath of Brama through all the forests of Asia; Vishnu hated me; Seeva lay in wait for me. I came suddenly upon Isis and Osiris: I had done a deed, they said, which the ibis and the crocodile trembled at. Thousands of years I lived and was buried in stone coffins, with mummies and sphinxes, in narrow chambers at the heart of eternal pyramids. I was kissed, with cancerous kisses, by crocodiles, and was laid, confounded with all unutterable abortions, amongst reeds and Nilotic mud.

Some slight abstraction I thus attempt of my oriental dreams, which filled me always with such amazement at the monstrous scenery that horror seemed absorbed for a while in sheer astonishment. Sooner or later came a reflux of feeling that swallowed up the astonishment, and left me, not so much in terror, as in hatred and abomination of what I saw. Over every form, and threat, and punishment, and dim sightless incarceration, brooded a killing sense of eternity and infinity. Into these dreams only it was, with one or two slight exceptions, that any circumstances of physical horror entered. All before had been moral and spiritual terrors. But here the main agents were ugly birds, or snakes, or crocodiles, especially the last. The cursed crocodile became to me the object of more horror than all the rest. I was compelled to live with him; and (as was always the case in my dreams) for centuries. Sometimes I escaped, and found myself in Chinese houses. All the feet of the tables, sofas, &c., soon became instinct with life: the abominable head of the crocodile, and his leering eyes, looked out at me, multiplied into ten thousand repetitions; and I stood loathing and fascinated. So often did this hideous reptile haunt my dreams that many times the very same dream was broken up in the very same way: I heard gentle voices speaking to me (I hear everything when I am sleeping), and instantly I awoke; it was broad noon, and my children were standing, hand in hand, at my bedside, come to show me their coloured shoes, or new frocks, or to let me see them dressed for going out. No experience was so awful to me, and at the same time so pathetic, as this abrupt translation from the darkness of the infinite to the gaudy summer air of highest noon, and from the unutterable abortions of miscreated gigantic vermin to the sight of infancy and innocent *human* natures....

I thought that it was a Sunday morning in May; that it was Easter Sunday, and as yet very early in the morning. I was standing, as it seemed to me, at the door of my own cottage. Right before me lay the very scene which could really be commanded from that situation, but exalted, as was usual, and solemnised by the power of dreams. There were the same mountains, and the same lovely valley at their feet; but the mountains were raised to more than Alpine height, and there was interspace far larger between them of savannahs and forest lawns; the hedges were rich with white roses; and no living creature was to be seen, excepting that in the green churchyard there were cattle tranquilly reposing upon the verdant graves, and particularly round about the grave of a child whom I had once tenderly loved, just as I had really beheld them, a little before sunrise, in the same summer when that child died. I gazed upon the well-known scene, and I said to myself, "It yet wants much of sunrise; and it is Easter Sunday; and that is the day on which they celebrate the first-fruits of Resurrection. I will walk abroad; old griefs shall be forgotten to-day: for the air is cool and still, and the hills are high, and stretch away to heaven; and the churchyard is as verdant as the forest lawns, and the forest lawns are as quiet as the churchyard; and with the dew I can wash the fever from my forehead; and then I shall be unhappy no longer." I turned, as if to open my garden gate, and immediately I saw upon the left a scene far different; but which yet the power of dreams had reconciled into harmony. The scene was an oriental one; and there also it was Easter Sunday, and very early in the morning. And at a vast distance were visible, as a stain upon the horizon, the domes and cupolas of a great city—an image or faint abstraction, caught perhaps in childhood from some picture of Jerusalem. And not a bow-shot from me, upon a stone, shaded by Judean palms, there sat a woman; and I looked, and it was—Ann! She fixed her eyes upon me earnestly; and I said to her at length, "So, then, I have found you at last." I waited; but she answered me not a word. Her face was the same as when I saw it last; the same, and yet, again, how different! Seventeen years ago, when the lamp-light of mighty London fell upon her face, as for the last time

I kissed her lips (lips, Ann, that to me were not polluted!), her eyes were streaming with tears. The tears were now no longer seen. Sometimes she seemed altered; yet again sometimes *not* altered; and hardly older. Her looks were tranquil, but with unusual solemnity of expression, and I now gazed upon her with some awe. Suddenly her countenance grew dim; and, turning to the mountains, I perceived vapours rolling between us; in a moment all had vanished; thick darkness came on; and in the twinkling of an eye I was far away from mountains, and by lamp-light in London, walking again with Ann—just as we had walked, when both children, eighteen years before, along the endless terraces of Oxford Street.

Then suddenly would come a dream of far different character—a tumultuous dream—commencing with a music such as now I often heard in sleep—music of preparation and of awakening suspense. The undulations of fast-gathering tumults were like the opening of the Coronation Anthem; and, like *that*, gave the feeling of a multitudinous movement, of infinite cavalcades filing off, and the tread of innumerable armies. The morning was come of a mighty day—a day of crisis and of ultimate hope for human nature, then suffering mysterious eclipse, and labouring in some dread extremity. Somewhere, but I knew not where—somehow, but I knew now how—by some beings, but I knew not by whom—a battle, a strife, an agony, was travelling through all its stages—was evolving itself, like the catastrophe of some mighty drama, with which my sympathy was the more insupportable from deepening confusion as to its local scene, its cause, its nature, and its undecipherable issue. I (as is usual in dreams where, of necessity, we make ourselves central to every movement) had the power, and yet had not the power, to decide it. I had the power, if I could raise myself to will it; and yet again had not the power, for the weight of twenty Atlantics was upon me, or the oppression of inexpiable guilt. "Deeper than ever plummet sounded," I lay inactive. Then, like a chorus, the passion deepened. Some greater interest was at stake, some mightier cause, than ever yet the sword had pleaded, or trumpet had proclaimed. Then came sudden alarms; hurryings to and fro; trepidations of innumerable fugitives, I knew not whether from the good cause or the bad; darkness and lights; tempest and human faces; and at last, with the sense that all was lost, female forms, and the features that were worth all the world to me; and but a moment allowed—and clasped hands, with heart-breaking partings, and then— everlasting farewells! and, with a sigh such as the caves of hell sighed when the incestuous mother uttered the abhorred name of Death, the sound was reverberated—everlasting farewells! and again, and yet again reverberated—everlasting farewells!

And I awoke in struggles, and cried aloud, "I will sleep no more!"

Now, at last, I had become awestruck at the approach of sleep, under the condition of visions so afflicting, and so intensely life-like as those which persecuted my phantom-haunted brain. More and more also I felt violent palpitations in some internal region, such as are commonly, but erroneously, called palpitations of the heart—being, as I suppose, referable exclusively to derangements in the stomach. These were evidently increasing rapidly in frequency and in strength. Naturally therefore, on considering how important my life had become to others besides myself, I became alarmed; and I paused seasonably; but with a difficulty that is past all description. Either way it seemed as though death had, in military language, "thrown himself astride of my path." Nothing short of mortal anguish, in a physical sense, it seemed, to wean myself from opium; yet, on the other hand, death through overwhelming nervous terrors—death by brain-fever or by lunacy—seemed too certainly to besiege the alternative course. Fortunately I had still so much of firmness left as to face that choice, which, with most of instant suffering, showed in the far distance a possibility of final escape.

This possibility was realised: I *did* accomplish my escape. And the issue of that particular stage in my opium experiences (for such it was—simply a provisional stage, that paved the way subsequently for many milder stages, to which gradually my constitutional system accommodated itself) was, pretty nearly in the following words, communicated to my readers in the earliest edition of these Confessions:—

I triumphed. But infer not, reader, from this word *"triumphed,"* a condition of joy or exultation. Think of me as of one, even when four months had passed, still agitated, writhing, throbbing, palpitating, shattered; and much, perhaps, in the situation of him who has been racked, as I collect the torments of that state from the affecting account of them left by a most innocent sufferer in the time of James I. Meantime, I derived no benefit from any medicine whatever, except ammoniated tincture of valerian. The moral of the narrative is addressed to the opium-eater; and therefore, of necessity, limited in its application. If he is taught to fear and tremble, enough has been effected. But he may say that the issue of my case is at least a proof that opium, after an eighteen years' use, and an eight years' abuse, of its powers, may still be renounced; and that he may chance to bring to the task greater energy than I did, or that, with a stronger constitution, he may obtain the same results with less. This may be true; I would not presume to measure the efforts of other men by my own. Heartily I wish him more resolution; heartily I wish him an equal success. Nevertheless, I had motives external to myself which he may unfortunately want; and these supplied me with conscientious supports, such as merely selfish interests might fail in supplying to a mind debilitated by opium.

Lord Bacon conjectures that it may be as painful to be born as to die. That seems probable; and, during the whole period of diminishing the opium, I had the torments of a man passing out of one mode of existence into another, and liable to the mixed or the alternate pains of birth and death. The issue was not death, but a sort of physical regeneration; and I may add that ever since, at intervals, I have had a restoration of more than youthful spirits.

One memorial of my former condition nevertheless remains: my dreams are not calm; the dread swell and agitation of the storm have not wholly subsided; the legions that encamped in them are drawing off, but not departed; my sleep is still tumultuous; and, like the gates of Paradise to our first parents when looking back from afar, it is still (in the tremendous line of Milton)—

"With dreadful faces thronged and fiery arms."

DISCUSSION

1. Sometimes tediously elaborate, at other times De Quincey's language is remarkably powerful and effective. Take a passage such as the paragraph beginning, "Under the connecting feeling of tropical heat and vertical sunlights," and rephrase it in simpler, more direct language. What has been lost?
2. What governs the organization of this selection? Within this framework, do you find any sections organized in a different way? Which ones, and what is the type of organization?
3. De Quincey gives the specifics of his experience with opium. Using these as your basis, can you make two or three *general* statements about the effects of opium?
4. Through his opium experience, did De Quincey learn anything that might be significant? If so, what? Do you feel that his visions might tell us anything valid about the nature of the universe or of man? If so, try to formulate and express the ideas.

WRITING SUGGESTIONS

1. You, as a child, probably have had intense and memorable emotional experiences, perhaps in your first awareness of death, love, pain, loneliness, fear, joy, violence, poverty, discrimination, hypocrisy, courage, or strength. Write a careful account of such an experience, with particular attention to the circumstances that gave rise to it. Let the reader share the experience in detail.
2. Like Sherwood Anderson, you have probably changed your attitude toward someone as you grew up, perhaps a member of your family or someone else close to you. Can you recall one scene that seemed to mark the turning point? If so, write about it in three stages: (1) Explain the background; (2) Dramatize the scene; (3) Describe the change it made in you, and why.
3. Do you experience ambiguous or embarrassed feelings about certain situations you find yourself trapped in? For example, do you find formal social affairs silly and yet feel you are obliged to play the game? Do you do things that are expected of you even though they are not "you"? Are you polite to people you dislike? Do you avoid some people you do like because others make fun of them? Try to think of the situations that give rise to your most ambiguous or confused feelings. Explain some of them clearly, dramatizing examples. Then generalize if you can, trying to arrive at a valid conclusion that you will be able to act on in the future. But don't fake it. If you can't solve the problem, be honest and leave it hanging there, as Howells does in "Tribulations of a Cheerful Giver."

The Direct Experience

4. If you can recall clearly an unusual mental experience such as a hallucination, vision, illusion, or nightmare, write about it in enough detail that the reader will share your experience. Avoid general statement. Write as though you expected a movie to be made from your description.

5. Other people's dreams can be boring, but it is often because of the way they are told. Most people just outline the plot and fail to convey the emotional atmosphere of the dream. With that caution in mind, recount an impressive dream that you remember well. For an example of economical and effective dream description, take another look at Dag Hammarskjöld's "Three Dreams."

6. What were you most afraid of when you were a small child? Write a circumstantial account of the events or objects that gave rise to this fear and of how you felt. How did others regard your fear? Were they sympathetic or not? Try using Rilke's "The Hand" as a model.

Plate 15
Edvard Munch (1863–1944): *Puberty*

Every outward experience stimulates an inner experience, as we have seen in Hokusai's "The Great Wave off Kanagawa" (Plate 13) and Georges de la Tour's *Joseph the Carpenter* (Plate 14), as well as in the readings in Chapter 8. But often the inner experience can occur independently of the immediate outward experience and can have its origins inside the person. While Joseph's inner realization is triggered by what his eyes see, the emotions of the girl in Edvard Munch's *Puberty* arise from the biological changes within her, combined with her limited knowledge of their meaning.

1. What seems to be the dominant emotion felt by the girl? How has the artist made this clear?
2. What is the meaning of the girl's vaguely shaped, menacing shadow? What does it represent?
3. What does this painting have in common with *Joseph the Carpenter*?
4. Exactly what is the contrast in meaning with the "Venus" of Willendorf? With the *Venus de Milo*?
5. What relationship does it have with John Donne's "The Good-Morrow" (p. 229)? With Sherwood Anderson's "Discovery of a Father" (p. 231)?

PLATE 15 Edvard Munch (1863–1944), **Puberty.** *Nasjonalgalleriet, Oslo.*

Plate 16
Giovanni Battista Piranesi (1720–78): etching from
Imaginary Prisons

This etching is one of a series on the same theme called *Imaginary Prisons*. Edvard Munch in *Puberty* shows us a person having an inner experience in such a way that we can guess what the experience is; Piranesi here gives us an inner experience more directly, in the form of a vision. It is impossible for Munch to give us directly the feelings of a girl entering puberty, while Piranesi can give us some idea of the visions of a man dreaming or under the influence of drugs; often it is the subject itself that determines the approach. The etchings in this series of Piranesi's, by the way, are described in Thomas De Quincey's "The Pains of Opium" (p. 251).

1. The visions we experience in dreams are usually realistic but they combine things in an illogical way; in the case of visions experienced by a person under the influence of opium, the scale may become vast, and depth perception exaggerated. How are these two qualities developed in the picture?

2. Except for the *Imaginary Prisons,* most of Piranesi's etchings are literal representations of ancient Roman ruins; in fact, he made a career of depicting these. In what ways is Piranesi's absorption reflected in the "prison" etching? Can you describe a parallel experience where a dream reflected in a distorted way some activity you were absorbed in? If so, in what way did it appear distorted? Can you guess at any particular meaning communicated by the distortion that might have told you something about yourself or your experiences?

3. De Quincey describes strongly paranoid elements, such as "the tyranny of the human face" and the feeling of being pursued, in his opium dreams. Are any analogous feelings reflected in Piranesi's etching? If so, how are they expressed?

PLATE 16 Giovanni Battista Piranesi (1720–78), etching from **Carceri d'Invenzione.** From **The Prisons,** copyright 1973, *Dover Publications, Inc. New York.*

IV
Experiencing & Generalizing

We generalize about what we observe, but we also generalize on the basis of our inner feelings. To take an ordinary example, if we listen to a number of jazz records by groups with different styles and like most of them, we conclude that we like jazz. Though this is a purely subjective generalization about our own personal responses, it naturally leads us to believe that others would appreciate jazz too if they understood it, and we may start a campaign to persuade our friends to listen to jazz. We don't expect to convince them that jazz is good by lecturing about it; instead we lure them to a phonograph or a club and let the music itself do the persuading. The same principle applies to writing about what we feel: we do not expect our readers to be persuaded by generalizations, but rather we try to expose them to the experiences that gave rise to our feelings. We usually confined ourselves to a few generalizations, just enough to guide our readers in the direction we want them to go.

In this final part of *Experiences* we shall deal with writers who are trying to get us to see their personal points of view. Some will generalize almost entirely on the basis of their intimate experience; others will call on their objective observations as well, combining both experience and observation into a balanced whole.

10

Informal Generalizing

We now encounter three writers who offer their experiences, their feelings about them, and their conclusions. They display very different attitudes and use very different styles of writing. The first, Thoreau, gives us an intimate and personal view in a style that reflects conscientious and detailed description of both the things observed and his own feelings about them; the second, Stevenson, generalizes his observations more and presents his feelings in an open and sociable way, as though he expected them to be ours too; and the last, Heywood Broun, takes the reader even more for granted, assuming with his breezy, journalistic approach that the reader's experiences and conclusions must be the same as his.

Henry David Thoreau

A Moose Hunt

(1858)

Though I had not come a-hunting, and felt some compunctions about accompanying the hunters, I wished to see a moose near at hand, and was not sorry to learn how the Indian managed to kill one. I went as reporter or chaplain to the hunters,—and the chaplain has been known to carry a gun himself. After clearing a small space amid the dense spruce and fir trees, we covered the damp ground with a shingling of fir-twigs, and, while Joe was preparing his birch-horn and pitching his canoe,—for this had to be done whenever we stopped long enough to build a fire, and was

Experiencing and Generalizing

the principal labor which he took upon himself at such times,—we collected fuel for the night, large, wet, and rotting logs, which had lodged at the head of the island, for our hatchet was too small for effective chopping; but we did not kindle a fire, lest the moose should smell it.

At starlight we dropped down the stream, which was a dead-water for three miles, or as far as the Moosehorn; Joe telling us that we must be very silent, and he himself making no noise with his paddle, while he urged the canoe along with effective impulses. It was a still night, and suitable for this purpose,—for if there is wind, the moose will smell you,—and Joe was very confident that he should get some. The harvest moon had just risen, and its level rays began to light up the forest on our right, while we glided downward in the shade on the same side, against the little breeze that was stirring. The lofty, spiring tops of the spruce and fir were very black against the sky, and more distinct than by day, close bordering this broad avenue on each side; and the beauty of the scene, as the moon rose above the forest, it would not be easy to describe.

A bat flew over our heads, and we heard a few faint notes of birds from time to time, perhaps the myrtle-bird for one, or the sudden plunge of a musquash, or saw one crossing the stream before us, or heard the sound of a rill emptying in, swollen by the recent rain.

At length . . . Joe laid down his paddle, drew forth his birch-horn,—a straight one, about fifteen inches long and three or four wide at the mouth, tied round with strips of the same bark,—and standing up, imitated the call of the moose,—*ugh-ugh-ugh,* or *oo-oo-oo-oo,* and then a prolonged *oo-o-o-o-o-o-o-o,* and listened attentively for several minutes. We asked him what kind of noise he expected to hear. He said that if a moose heard it, he guessed we should find out; we should hear him coming half a mile off; he would come close up, perhaps into, the water, and my companion must wait till he got fair sight, and then aim just behind the shoulder.

The moose venture out to the river-side to feed and drink at night. Earlier in the season the hunters do not use a horn to call them out, but steal upon them as they are feeding along the sides of the stream, and often the first notice they have of one is the sound of the water dropping from its muzzle. An Indian whom I heard imitate the voice of the moose, and also that of the caribou and the deer, using a much longer horn than Joe's, told me that the first could be heard eight or ten miles, sometimes; it was a loud sort of bellowing sound, clearer and more sonorous than the lowing of cattle,—the caribou's a sort of snort,—and the small deer's like that of a lamb.

At length we turned up the Moosehorn, where the Indians at the carry had told us that they killed a moose the night before. This is a very meandering stream, only a rod or two in width, but comparatively deep, coming in on the right, fitly enough named Moosehorn, whether from its

Moosehorn, and so on: the area of Thoreau's travels is the wilderness of north central Maine, which remains much as it was in his time.
musquash: muskrat.

windings or its inhabitants. It was bordered here and there by narrow meadows between the stream and the endless forest, affording favorable places for the moose to feed, and to call them out on. We proceeded half a mile up this, as through a narrow, winding canal, where the tall, dark spruce and firs and arborvitae towered on both sides in the moonlight, forming a perpendicular forest-edge of great height, like the spires of a Venice in the forest. In two places stood a small stack of hay on the bank, ready for the lumberer's use in the winter, looking strange enough there. We thought of the day when this might be a brook winding through smooth-shaven meadows on some gentleman's grounds; and seen by moonlight then, excepting the forest that now hems it in, how little changed it would appear!

Again and again Joe called the moose, placing the canoe by some favorable point of meadow for them to come out on, but listened in vain to hear one come rushing through the woods, and concluded that they had been hunted too much thereabouts. We saw, many times, what to our imaginations looked like a gigantic moose, with his horns peering from out the forest edge; but we saw the forest only, and not its inhabitants, that night. So at last we turned about. There was now a litle fog on the water, though it was a fine, clear night above. There were very few sounds to break the stillness of the forest. Several times we heard the hooting of a great horned-owl, as at home, and told Joe that he would call out the moose for him, for he made a sound considerably like the horn,— but Joe answered, that the moose had heard that sound a thousand times, and knew better; and oftener still we were startled by the plunge of a musquash.

Once, when Joe had called again, and we were listening for moose, we heard, come faintly echoing, or creeping from far, through the moss-clad aisles, a dull, dry, rushing sound, with a solid core to it, yet as if half smothered under the grasp of the luxuriant and fungus-like forest, like the shutting of a door in some distant entry of the damp and shaggy wilderness. If we had not been there, no mortal had heard it. When we asked Joe in a whisper what it was, he answered, "Tree fall."

There is something singularly grand and impressive in the sound of a tree falling in a perfectly calm night like this, as if the agencies which overthrow it did not need to be excited, but worked with a subtle, deliberate, and conscious force, like a boa-constrictor, and more effectively then than even in a windy day. If there is any such difference, perhaps it is because trees with the dews of the night on them are heavier than by day .

Having reached the camp, about ten o'clock, we kindled our fire and went to bed. Each of us had a blanket, in which he lay on the fir-twigs, with his extremities toward the fire, but nothing over his head. It was worth the while to lie down in a country where you could afford such great fires; that was one whole side, and the bright side, of our world. We had first rolled up a large log some eighteen inches through and ten feet long, for a backlog, to last all night, and then piled on the trees to the height of three or four feet, no matter how green or damp. In fact, we burned as much wood that night as would, with economy and an air-tight stove, last a poor family in one of our cities all winter.

Experiencing and Generalizing

It was very agreeable, as well as independent, thus lying in the open air, and the fire kept our uncovered extremities warm enough. The Jesuit missionaries used to say, that, in their journeys with the Indians in Canada, they lay on a bed which had never been shaken up since the creation, unless by earthquakes. It is surprising with what impunity and comfort one who has always lain in a warm bed in a close apartment, and studiously avoided drafts of air, can lie down on the ground without a shelter, roll himself in a blanket, and sleep before a fire, in a frosty, autumn night just after a long rainstorm, and even come soon to enjoy and value the fresh air.

I lay awake awhile, watching the ascent of the sparks through the firs, and sometimes their descent in half-extinguished cinders on my blanket. They were as interesting as fireworks, going up in endless, successive crowds, each after an explosion, in an eager, serpentine course, some to five or six rods above the treetops before they went out. We do not suspect how much our chimneys have concealed; and now air-tight stoves have come to conceal all the rest. In the course of the night, I got up once or twice and put fresh logs on the fire, making my companions curl up their legs.

When we awoke in the morning (Saturday, September 17), there was considerable frost whitening the leaves. We heard the sound of the chickadee, and a few faintly lisping birds, and also of ducks in the water about the island. I took a botanical account of stock of our domains before the dew was off, and found that the ground hemlock, or American yew, was the prevailing under-shrub. We breakfasted on tea, hard bread, and ducks.

Before the fog had fairly cleared away we paddled down the stream again, and were soon past the mouth of the Moosehorn. These twenty miles of the Penobscot, between Moosehead and Chesuncook lakes, are comparatively smooth, and a great part dead-water; but from time to time it is shallow and rapid, with rocks or gravel beds, where you can wade across. There is no expanse of water, and no break in the forest, and the meadow is a mere edging here and there. There are no hills near the river nor within sight, except one or two distant mountains seen in a few places. The banks are from six to ten feet high, but once or twice rise gently to higher ground. In many places the forest on the bank was but a thin strip, letting the light through from some alder swamp or meadow behind.

Afer passing through some long rips, and by a large island, we reached an interesting part of the river called the Pine Stream Dead-Water, about six miles below Ragmuff, where the river expanded to thirty rods in width and had many islands in it, with elms and canoe-birches, now yellowing, along the shore, and we got our first sight of Ktaadn.

Here, about two o'clock, we turned up a small branch three or four rods wide, which comes in on the right from the south, called Pine Stream, to look for moose signs. We had gone but a few rods before we saw very recent signs along the water's edge, the mud lifted up by their feet being

Ktaadn: the highest mountain in Maine, 5268 feet.

quite fresh, and Joe declared that they had gone along there but a short time before. We soon reached a small meadow on the east side, at an angle in the stream, which was, for the most part, densely covered with alders. As we were advancing along the edge of this, rather more quietly than usual, perhaps, on account of the freshness of the signs,—the design being to camp up this stream, if it promised well,—I heard a slight crackling of twigs deep in the alders, and turned Joe's attention to it; whereupon he began to push the canoe back rapidly; and we had receded thus half a dozen rods, when we suddenly spied two moose standing just on the edge of the open part of the meadow which we had passed, not more than six or seven rods distant, looking round the alders at us.

They made me think of great frightened rabbits, with their long ears and half-inquisitive, half-frightened looks; the true denizens of the forest (I saw at once), filling a vacuum which now first I discovered had not been filled for me,—moose-men, wood-eaters, the word is said to mean,—clad in a sort of Vermont gray, or homespun. Our Nimrod, owing to the retrograde movement, was now farthest from the game; but being warned of its neighborhood, he hastily stood up, and, while we ducked, fired over our heads one barrel at the foremost, which alone he saw, though he did not know what kind of creature it was; whereupon this one dashed across the meadow and up a high bank on the northeast, so rapidly as to leave but an indistinct impression of its outlines on my mind.

At the same instant, the other, a young one, but as tall as a horse, leaped out into the stream, in full sight, and there stood cowering for a moment, or rather its disproportionate lowness behind gave it that appearance, and uttering two or three trumpeting squeaks. I have an indistinct recollection of seeing the old one pause an instant on the top of the bank in the woods, look toward its shivering young, and then dash away again. The second barrel was leveled at the calf, and when we expected to see it drop in the water, after a little hesitation, it, too, got out of the water, and dashed up the hill, though in a somewhat different direction.

All this was the work of a few seconds, and our hunter, having never seen a moose before, did not know but they were deer, for they stood partly in the water, nor whether he had fired at the same one twice or not. From the style in which they went off, and the fact that he was not used to standing up and firing from a canoe, I judged that we should not see anything more of them. The Indian said that they were a cow and her calf,—a yearling, or perhaps two years old, for they accompany their dams so long; but, for my part, I had not noticed much difference in their size. It was but two or three rods across the meadow to the foot of the bank, which, like all the world thereabouts, was densely wooded; but I was surprised to notice, that, as soon as the moose had passed behind the veil of the woods, there was no sound of footsteps to be heard from the soft, damp moss which carpets that forest, and long before we landed, perfect silence reigned. Joe said, "If you wound 'em moose, me sure get 'em."

We all landed at once. My companion reloaded; the Indian fastened his

Experiencing and Generalizing

birch, threw off his hat, adjusted his waistband, seized the hatchet, and set out. He told me afterward, casually, that before we landed he had seen a drop of blood on the bank, when it was two or three rods off. He proceeded rapidly up the bank and through the woods, with a peculiar, elastic, noiseless, and stealthy tread, looking to right and left on the ground, and stepping in the faint tracks of the wounded moose, now and then pointing in silence to a single drop of blood on the handsome, shining leaves of the *Clintonia borealis*, which, on every side, covered the ground, or to a dry fern-stem freshly broken, all the while chewing some leaf or else the spruce gum. I followed, watching his motions more than the trail of the moose. After following the trail about forty rods in a pretty direct course, stepping over fallen trees and winding between standing ones, he at length lost it, for there were many other moose tracks there, and, returning once more to the last blood-stain, traced it a little way and lost it again, and, too soon, I thought, for a good hunter, gave it up entirely. He traced a few steps, also, the tracks of the calf; but, seeing no blood, soon relinquished the search.

I observed, while he was tracking the moose, a certain reticence or moderation in him. He did not communicate several observations of interest which he made, as a white man would have done, though they may have leaked out afterward. At another time, when we heard a slight crackling of twigs and he landed to reconnoiter, he stepped lightly and gracefully, stealing through the bushes with the least possible noise, in a way in which no white man does,—as it were, finding a place for his foot each time.

About half an hour after seeing the moose, we pursued our voyage up Pine Stream, and soon, coming to a part which was very shoal and also rapid, we took out the baggage, and proceeded to carry it round, while Joe got up with the canoe alone. We were just completing our portage and I was absorbed in the plants, admiring the leaves of the *Aster macrophyllus*, ten inches wide, and plucking the seeds of the great round-leaved orchis, when Joe exclaimed from the stream that he had killed a moose. He had found the cow-moose lying dead, but quite warm, in the middle of the stream, which was so shallow that it rested on the bottom, with hardly a third of its body above water. It was about an hour after it was shot, and it was swollen with water. It had run about a hundred rods and sought the stream again, cutting off a slight bend. No doubt a better hunter would have tracked it to this spot at once.

I was surprised at its great size, horse-like, but Joe said it was not a large cow-moose. My companion went in search of the calf again. I took hold of the ears of the moose, while Joe pushed his canoe downstream toward a favorable shore, and so we made out, though with some difficulty, its long nose frequently sticking in the bottom, to drag it into still shallower water. It was a brownish black, or perhaps a dark iron-gray, on the back and sides, but lighter beneath and in front. I took the cord which served for the canoe's painter, and with Joe's assistance measured it carefully, the greatest distances first, making a knot each time. The painter being wanted, I reduced these measures that night with equal care to lengths and fractions of my umbrella, beginning with

Informal Generalizing

the smallest measures, and untying the knots as I proceeded; and when we arrived at Chesuncook the next day, finding a two-foot rule there, I reduced the last to feet and inches; and, moreover, I made myself a two-foot rule of a thin and narrow strip of black ash, which would fold up conveniently to six inches.

All this pains I took because I did not wish to be obliged to say merely that the moose was very large. Of the various dimensions which I obtained I will mention only two. The distance from the tips of the hoofs of the fore-feet, stretched out, to the top of the back between the shoulders, was seven feet and five inches. I can hardly believe my own measure, for this is about two feet greater than the height of a tall horse. (Indeed, I am now satisfied that this measurement was incorrect, but the other measures given here I can warrant to be correct, having proved them in a more recent visit to those woods.) The extreme length was eight feet and two inches. Another cow-moose, which I have since measured in those woods with a tape, was just six feet from the tip of the hoof to the shoulders, and eight feet long as she lay.

Here, just at the head of the murmuring rapids, Joe now proceeded to skin the moose with a pocket-knife, while I looked on; and a tragical business it was,—to see that still warm and palpitating body pierced with a knife, to see the warm milk stream from the rent udder, and the ghastly naked red carcass appearing from within its seemly robe, which was made to hide it. The ball had passed through the shoulder-blade diagonally and lodged under the skin on the opposite side, and was partially flattened. My companion keeps it to show to his grandchildren. He has the shanks of another moose which he has since shot, skinned and stuffed, ready to be made into boots by putting in a thick leather sole. Joe said, if a moose stood fronting you, you must not fire, but advance toward him, for he will turn slowly and give you a fair shot.

In the bed of this narrow, wild, and rocky stream, between two lofty walls of spruce and firs, a mere cleft in the forest which the stream had made, this work went on. At length Joe had stripped off the hide and dragged it trailing to the shore, declaring that it weighed a hundred pounds, though probably fifty would have been nearer the truth. He cut off a large mass of the meat to carry along, and another, together with the tongue and nose, he put with the hide on the shore to lie there all night, or till we returned. I was surprised that he thought of leaving this meat thus exposed by the side of the carcass, as the simplest course, not fearing that any creature would touch it; but nothing did. This could hardly have happened on the bank of one of our rivers in the eastern part of Massachusetts; but I suspect that fewer small wild animals are prowling there than with us. Twice, however, in this excursion, I had a glimpse of a species of large mouse.

This stream was so withdrawn, and the moose tracks were so fresh, that my companions, still bent on hunting, concluded to go farther up it and camp, and then hunt up or down at night. Half a mile above this, at a place where I saw the *Aster puniceus* and the beaked hazel, as we paddled along, Joe, hearing a slight rustling amid the alders, and seeing something black about two rods off, jumped up and whispered, "Bear!"

but before the hunter had discharged his piece, he corrected himself to "Beaver!"—"Hedgehog!" The bullet killed a large hedgehog more than two feet and eight inches long. The quills were rayed out and flattened on the hinder part of its back, even as if it had lain on that part, but were erect and long between this and the tail. Their points, closely examined, were seen to be finely bearded or barbed, and shaped like an awl, that is, a little concave, to give the barbs effect. After about a mile of still water, we prepared our camp on the right side, just at the foot of a considerable fall. Little chopping was done that night, for fear of scaring the moose. We had moose meat fried for supper. It tasted like tender beef, with perhaps more flavor,—sometimes like veal.

After supper, the moon having risen, we proceeded to hunt a mile up this stream, first "carrying" about the falls. We made a picturesque sight, wending single file along the shore, climbing over rocks and logs, —Joe, who brought up the rear, twirling his canoe in his hands as if it were a feather, in places where it was difficult to get along without a burden. We launched the canoe again from the ledge over which the stream fell, but after half a mile of still water, suitable for hunting, it became rapid again, and we were compelled to make our way along the shore, while Joe endeavored to get up in the birch alone, though it was still very difficult for him to pick his way amid the rocks in the night.

We on the shore found the worst of walking, a perfect chaos of fallen and drifted trees, and of bushes projecting far over the water, and now and then we made our way across the mouth of a small tributary on a kind of network of alders. So we went tumbling on in the dark, being on the shady side, effectually scaring all the moose and bears that might be thereabouts. At length we came to a standstill, and Joe went forward to reconnoiter; but he reported that it was still a continuous rapid as far as he went, for half a mile, with no prospect of improvement, as if it were coming down from a mountain. So we turned about, hunting back to the camp through the still water.

It was a splendid moonlight night, and I, getting sleepy as it grew late, —for I had nothing to do,—found it difficult to realize where I was. This stream was much more unfrequented than the main one, lumbering operations being no longer carried on in this quarter. It was only three or four rods wide, but the firs and spruce through which it trickled seemed yet taller by contrast. Being in this dreamy state, which the moonlight enhanced, I did not clearly discern the shore, but seemed, most of the time, to be floating through ornamental grounds,—for I associated the fir-tops with such scenes;—very high up some Broadway, and beneath or between their tops, I thought I saw an endless succession of porticoes and columns, cornices and façades, verandas and churches. I did not merely fancy this, but in my drowsy state such was the illusion. I fairly lost myself in sleep several times, still dreaming of that architecture and the nobility that dwelt behind and might issue from it; but all at once I would be aroused and brought back to a sense of my actual position by the sound of Joe's birch-horn in the midst of all this silence calling the moose, *ugh, ugh, oo,-oo-oo-oo-oo-oo*, and I prepared to hear a furious moose come rushing and crashing through the forest, and see him burst out on to the little strip of meadow by our side.

But, on more accounts than one, I had had enough of moose-hunting. I had not come to the woods for this purpose, nor had I foreseen it, though I had been willing to learn how the Indian maneuvered; but one moose killed was as good, if not as bad, as a dozen. That afternoon's tragedy, and my share in it, as it affected the innocence, destroyed the pleasure of my adventure. It is true, I came as near as possible to come to being a hunter and miss it, myself; and as it is, I think that I could spend a year in the woods, fishing and hunting just enough to sustain myself, with satisfaction. This would be next to living like a philosopher on the fruits of the earth which you had raised, which also attracts me.

But this hunting of the moose merely for the satisfaction of killing him,—not even for the sake of his hide,—without making any extraordinary exertion or running any risk yourself, is too much like going out by night to some wood-side pasture and shooting your neighbor's horses. These are God's own horses, poor, timid creatures, that will run fast enough as soon as they smell you, though they *are* nine feet high. Joe told us of some hunters who a year or two before had shot down several oxen by night, somewhere in the Maine woods, mistaking them for moose. And so might any of the hunters; and what is the difference in the sport, but the name? In the former case, having killed one of God's and *your own* oxen, you strip off its hide,—because that is the common trophy, and, moreover, you have heard that it may be sold for moccasins,—cut a steak from its haunches, and leave the huge carcass to smell to heaven for you. It is no better, at least, than to assist at a slaughterhouse.

This afternoon's experience suggested to me how base or coarse are the motives which commonly carry men into the wilderness. The explorers and lumberers generally are all hirelings, paid so much a day for their labor, and as such they have no more love for wild nature than wood-sawyers have for forests. Other white men and Indians who come here are for the most part hunters, whose object is to slay as many moose and other wild animals as possible. But, pray, could not one spend some weeks or years in the solitude of this vast wilderness with other employments than these—employments perfectly sweet and innocent and ennobling? For one that comes with a pencil to sketch or sing, a thousand come with an axe or rifle. What a coarse and imperfect use Indians and hunters make of Nature! No wonder that their race is so soon exterminated. I already, and for weeks afterward, felt my nature the coarser for this part of my wood-land experience, and was reminded that our life should be lived as tenderly and daintily as one would pluck a flower.

With these thoughts, when we reached our camping-ground, I decided to leave my companions to continue moose-hunting down the stream, while I prepared the camp, though they requested me not to chop much nor make a large fire, for fear I should scare their game. In the midst of the damp fir-wood, high on the mossy bank, about nine o'clock of this bright moonlight night, I kindled a fire, when they were gone, and sitting on the fir-twigs, within sound of the falls, examined by its light the botanical specimens which I had collected that afternoon, and wrote down some of the reflections which I have here expanded; or I walked along the shore and gazed up the stream, where the whole space above the falls was filled with mellow light. As I sat before the fire on my fir-twig seat, without walls above or around me, I remembered how far on every hand that wilderness stretched, before you came to cleared or cultivated fields, and wondered if any bear or moose was watching the light of my fire; for Nature looked sternly upon me on account of the murder of the moose.

Strange that so few ever came to the woods to see how the pine lives and grows and spires, lifting its evergreen arms to the light,—to see its perfect success; but most are content to behold it in the shape of many broad boards brought to market, and deem *that* its true success! But the pine is no more lumber than man is, and to be made into boards and houses is no more its true and highest use than the truest use of man is to be cut down and made into manure. There is a higher law affecting our relation to pines as well as to men.

A pine cut down, a dead pine, is no more a pine than a dead human carcass is a man. Can he who has discovered only some of the values of whalebone and whale oil be said to have discovered the true use of the whale? Can he who slays the elephant for his ivory be said to have "seen the elephant"? These are petty and accidental uses; just as if a stronger race were to kill us in order to make buttons and flageolets of our bones; for everything may serve a lower as well as a higher use. Every creature is better alive than dead, men and moose and pine-trees, and he who understands it aright will rather preserve its life than destroy it.

Is it the lumberman, then, who is the friend and lover of the pine, stands nearest to it, and understands its nature best? Is it the tanner who has barked it, or he who has boxed it for turpentine, whom posterity will fable to have been changed into a pine at last? No! no! it is the poet; he it is who makes the truest use of the pine,—who does not fondle it with an axe, nor tickle it with a saw, nor stroke it with a plane,—who knows whether its heart is false without cutting into it,—who has not bought the stumpage of the township on which it stands. All the pines shudder and heave a sigh when *that* man steps on the forest floor. No, it is the poet, who loves them as his own shadow in the air, and lets them stand.

I have been into the lumber-yard, and the carpenter's shop, and the tannery, and the lampblack factory, and the turpentine clearing; but when at length I saw the tops of the pines waving and reflecting the light at a distance high over all the rest of the forest, I realized that the former were not the highest uses of the pine. It is not their bones or hide or tallow that I love most. It is the living spirit of the tree, not its spirit of turpentine, with which I sympathize, and which heals my cuts. It is as immortal as I am, and perchance will go to as high a heaven, there to tower above me still.

DISCUSSION

1. Thoreau evokes vividly the feeling of being on a river and in camp at night. Other than vision, which sense does he use most to get this effect? What circumstances cause him to use this sense a great deal?
2. Thoreau combines sensory data, matter-of-fact statement, and opinion in such a way that there are no abrupt transitions from one to another. What proportions of each does he seem to use? Which does he use most effectively? What are some examples?
3. At first Thoreau's generalizations in the last section seem to wander away from the subject of hunting. Is this inconsistency a real one or merely apparent? Can you make adequate connections between these generalizations and the experience he describes? If so, then what is really the subject of the piece?
4. Thoreau illustrates for several paragraphs and then generalizes for several paragraphs. Is the generalization necessary or has he already made his point by describing the experience? If you feel that the generalizations have added something essential, try to define accurately what it is.

Robert Louis Stevenson

Walking Tours

(1876)

It must not be imagined that a walking tour, as some would have us fancy, is merely a better or worse way of seeing the country. There are many ways of seeing landscape quite as good; and none more vivid, in spite of canting dilettantes, than from a railway train. But landscape on a walking tour is quite accessory. He who is indeed of the brotherhood does not voyage in quest of the picturesque, but of certain jolly humours —of the hope and spirit with which the march begins at morning, and the peace and spiritual repletion of the evening's rest. He cannot tell whether he puts his knapsack on, or takes it off, with more delight. The excitement of the departure puts him in a key for that of the arrival. Whatever he does is not only a reward in itself, but will be further rewarded in the sequel; and so pleasure leads on to pleasure in an endless chain. It is this that so few can understand; they will either be always lounging or always at five miles an hour; they do not play off the one against the other, prepare all day for the evening, and all evening for the next day. And, above all, it is here that your overwalker fails of comprehension. His heart rises against those who drink their curaçoa in liqueur glasses, when he himself can swill it in a brown John. He will not believe

humours: moods.
brown John: earthenware jug.

that the flavour is more delicate in the smaller dose. He will not believe that to walk this unconscionable distance is merely to stupefy and brutalise himself, and come to his inn, at night, with a sort of frost on his five wits, and a starless night of darkness in his spirit. Not for him the mild luminous evening of the temperate walker! He has nothing left of man but a physical need for bedtime and a double nightcap; and even his pipe, if he be a smoker, will be savourless and disenchanted. It is the fate of such an one to take twice as much trouble as is needed to obtain happiness, and miss the happiness in the end; he is the man of the proverb, in short, who goes further and fares worse.

Now, to be properly enjoyed, a walking tour should be gone upon alone. If you go in a company, or even in pairs, it is no longer a walking tour in anything but name; it is something else and more in the nature of a picnic. A walking tour should be gone upon alone, because freedom is of the essence; because you should be able to stop and go on, and follow this way or that, as the freak takes you; and because you must have your own pace, and neither trot alongside a champion walker, nor mince in time with a girl. And then you must be open to all impressions and let your thoughts take colour from what you see. You should be as a pipe for any wind to play upon. "I cannot see the wit," says Hazlitt, "of walking and talking at the same time. When I am in the country I wish to vegetate like the country,"—which is the gist of all that can be said upon the matter. There should be no cackle of voices at your elbow, to jar on the meditative silence of the morning. And so long as a man is reasoning he cannot surrender himself to that fine intoxication that comes of much motion in the open air, that begins in a sort of dazzle and sluggishness of the brain, and ends in a peace that passes comprehension.

During the first day or so of any tour there are moments of bitterness, when the traveller feels more than coldly towards his knapsack, when he is half in a mind to throw it bodily over the hedge and, like Christian on a similar occasion, "give three leaps and go on singing." And yet it soon acquires a property of easiness. It becomes magnetic; the spirit of the journey enters into it. And no sooner have you passed the straps over your shoulders than the lees of sleep are cleared from you, you pull yourself together with a shake, and fall at once into your stride. And surely, of all possible moods, this, in which a man takes the road, is the best. Of course, if he *will* keep thinking of his anxieties. if he *will* open the merchant Abudah's chest and walk arm-in-arm with the hag—why, wherever he is, and whether he walk fast or slow, the chances are that he will not be happy. And so much the more shame to himself! There are perhaps thirty men setting forth at that same hour, and I would lay a large wager there is not another dull face among the thirty. It would be a fine thing to follow, in a coat of darkness, one after another of these wayfarers, some summer morning, for the first few miles upon the road. This one, who walks fast, with a keen look in his eyes, is all concentrated in his own mind; he is up at his loom, weaving and weaving, to set the

freak: notion, whim.
Christian: hero of John Bunyan's *Pilgrim's Progress*.

landscape to words. This one peers about, as he goes, among the grasses; he waits by the canal to watch the dragonflies; he leans on the gate of the pasture, and cannot look enough upon the complacent kine. And here comes another, talking, laughing, and gesticulating to himself. His face changes from time to time, as indignation flashes from his eyes or anger clouds his forehead. He is composing articles, delivering orations, and conducting the most impassioned interviews by the way. A little farther on, and it is as like as not he will begin to sing. And well for him, supposing him to be no great master in that art, if he stumble across no stolid peasant at a corner; for on such an occasion, I scarcely know which is the more troubled, or whether it is worse to suffer the confusion of your troubadour, or the unfeigned alarm of your clown. A sedentary population, accustomed, besides, to the strange mechanical bearing of the common tramp, can in no wise explain to itself the gaiety of these passers-by. I knew one man who was arrested as a runaway lunatic, because although a full-grown person with a red beard, he skipped as he went like a child. And you would be astonished if I were to tell you all the grave and learned heads who have confessed to me that, when on walking tours, they sang—and sang very ill—and had a pair of red ears when, as described above, the inauspicious peasant plumped into their arms from round a corner. And here, lest you should think I am exaggerating, is Hazlitt's own confession, from his essay *On Going a Journey*, which is so good that there should be a tax levied on all who have not read it:—

"Give me the clear blue sky over my head," says he, "and the green turf beneath my feet, a winding road before me, and a three hours' march to dinner—and then to thinking! It is hard if I cannot start some game on these lone heaths. I laugh, I run, I leap, I sing for joy."

Bravo! After that adventure of my friend with the policeman, you would not have cared, would you, to publish that in the first person? But we have no bravery nowadays, and, even in books, must all pretend to be as dull and foolish as our neighbors. It was not so with Hazlitt. And notice how learned he is (as, indeed, throughout the essay) in the theory of walking tours. He is none of your athletic men in purple stockings, who walk their fifty miles a day: three hours' march is his ideal. And then he must have a winding road, the epicure!

Yet there is one thing I object to in these words of his, one thing in the great master's practice that seems to me not wholly wise. I do not approve of that leaping and running. Both of these hurry the respiration; they both shake up the brain out of its glorious open-air confusion; and they both break the pace. Uneven walking is not so agreeable to the body, and it distracts and irritates the mind. Whereas, when once you have fallen into an equable stride, it requires no conscious thought from you to keep it up, and yet it prevents you from thinking earnestly of anything else. Like knitting, like the work of a copying clerk, it gradually neutralises and sets to sleep the serious activity of the mind. We can think of this or that, lightly and laughingly, as a child thinks, or as we think

clown: country person, bumpkin.

in a morning doze; we can make puns or puzzle out acrostics, and trifle in a thousand ways with words and rhymes; but when it comes to honest work, when we come to gather ourselves together for an effort, we may sound the trumpet as loud and long as we please; the great barons of the mind will not rally to the standard, but sit, each one, at home, warming his hands over his own fire and brooding on his own private thought!

In the course of a day's walk, you see, there is much variance in the mood. From the exhilaration of the start to the happy phlegm of the arrival, the change is certainly great. As the day goes on, the traveller moves from the one extreme towards the other. He becomes more and more incorporated with the material landscape, and the open-air drunkenness grows upon him with great strides, until he posts along the road, and sees everything about him, as in a cheerful dream. The first is certainly brighter, but the second stage is the more peaceful. A man does not make so many articles towards the end, nor does he laugh aloud; but the purely animal pleasures, the sense of physical well-being, the delight of every inhalation, of every time the muscles tighten down the thigh, console him for the absence of the others, and bring him to his destination still content.

Nor must I forget to say a word on bivouacs. You come to a milestone on a hill, or some place where deep ways meet under trees; and off goes the knapsack, and down you sit to smoke a pipe in the shade. You sink into yourself, and the birds come round and look at you; and your smoke dissipates upon the afternoon under the blue dome of heaven; and the sun lies warm upon your feet, and the cool air visits your neck and turns aside your open shirt. If you are not happy, you must have an evil conscience. You may dally as long as you like by the roadside. It is almost as if the millennium were arrived, when we shall throw our clocks and watches over the housetop, and remember time and seasons no more. Nor to keep hours for a lifetime is, I was going to say, to live for ever. You have no idea, unless you have tried it, how endlessly long is a summer's day, that you measure out only by hunger, and bring to an end only when you are drowsy. I know a village where there are hardly any clocks, where no one knows more of the days of the week than by a sort of instinct for the fête on Sundays, and where only one person can tell you the day of the month, and she is generally wrong; and if people were aware how slow Time journeyed in that village, and what armfuls of spare hours he gives, over and above the bargain, to its wise inhabitants, I believe there would be a stampede out of London, Liverpool, Paris, and a variety of large towns, where the clocks lose their heads, and shake the hours out each one faster than the other, as though they were all in a wager. And all these foolish pilgrims would each bring his own misery along with him, in a watch-pocket! It is to be noticed, there were no clocks and watches in the much-vaunted days before the flood. It follows, of course, there were no appointments, and punctuality was not yet thought upon. "Though ye take from a covetous man all his treasure," says Milton, "he has yet one jewel left; ye cannot deprive him of his covet-

phlegm: calm, indifference.

ousness." And so I would say of a modern man of business, you may do what you will for him, put him in Eden, give him the elixir of life—he has still a flaw at heart, he still has his business habits. Now, there is no time when business habits are more mitigated than on a walking tour. And so during these halts, as I say, you will feel almost free.

But it is at night, and after dinner, that the best hour comes. There are no such pipes to be smoked as those that follow a good day's march; the flavour of the tobacco is a thing to be remembered, it is so dry and aromatic, so full and so fine. If you wind up the evening with grog, you will own there was never such grog; at every sip a jocund tranquillity spreads about your limbs, and sits easily in your heart. If you read a book—and you will never do so save by fits and starts—you find the language strangely racy and harmonious; words take a new meaning; single sentences possess the ear for half-an-hour together; and the writer endears himself to you, at every page, by the nicest coincidence of sentiment. It seems as if it were a book you had written yourself in a dream. To all we have read on such occasions, we look back with special favour. "It was on the 10th of April, 1789," says Hazlitt, with amorous precision, "that I sat down to a volume of the new *Héloïse*, at the Inn at Llangollen, over a bottle of sherry and a cold chicken." I should wish to quote more, for though we are mighty fine fellows nowadays, we cannot write like Hazlitt. And, talking of that, a volume of Hazlitt's essays would be a capital pocket-book on such a journey; so would a volume of Heine's songs; and for *Tristram Shandy* I can pledge a fair experience.

If the evening be fine and warm, there is nothing better in life than to lounge before the inn door in the sunset, or lean over the parapet of the bridge, to watch the weeds and the quick fishes. It is then, if ever, that you taste Joviality to the full significance of that audacious word. Your muscles are so agreeably slack, you feel so clean and so strong and so idle, that whether you move or sit still, whatever you do is done with pride and a kindly sort of pleasure. You fall in talk with any one, wise or foolish, drunk or sober. And it seems as if a hot walk purged you, more than of anything else, of all narrowness and pride, and left curiosity to play its part freely, as in a child or a man of science. You lay aside all your own hobbies, to watch provincial humours develop themselves before you, now as a laughable farce, and now grave and beautiful like an old tale.

Or perhaps you are left to your own company for the night, and surly weather imprisons you by the fire. You may remember how Burns, numbering past pleasures, dwells upon the hours when he has been "happy thinking." It is a phrase that may well perplex a poor modern, girt about on every side by clocks and chimes, and haunted, even at night, by flaming dial-plates. For we are all so busy, and have so many far-off projects to realise, and castles in the fire to turn into solid habitable mansions

grog: liquor.
Joviality: from Jove (or Zeus) chief god of the Greeks. Originally the word meant "god-like feelings."
dial-plates: clock faces.

on a gravel soil, that we can find no time for pleasure trips into the Land of Thought and among the Hills of Vanity. Changed times, indeed, when we must sit all night, beside the fire, with folded hands; and a changed world for most of us, when we find we can pass the hours without discontent, and be happy thinking. We are in such haste to be doing, to be writing, to be gathering gear, to make our voice audible a moment in the derisive silence of eternity, that we forget that one thing, of which these are but the parts—namely, to live. We fall in love, we drink hard, we run to and fro upon the earth like frightened sheep. And now you are to ask yourself if, when all is done, you would not have been better to sit by the fire at home and be happy thinking. To sit still and contemplate,—to remember the faces of women without desire, to be pleased by the great deeds of men without envy, to be everything and everywhere in sympathy, and yet content to remain where and what you are—is not this to know both wisdom and virtue, and to dwell with happiness? After all, it is not they who carry flags, but they who look upon it from a private chamber, who have the fun of the procession. And once you are at that, you are in the very humour of all social heresy. It is no time for shuffling, or for big, empty words. If you ask yourself what you mean by fame, riches, or learning, the answer is far to seek; and you go back into that kingdom of light imaginations, which seem so vain in the eyes of Philistines perspiring after wealth, and so momentous to those who are stricken with the disproportions of the world, and, in the face of the gigantic stars, cannot stop to split differences between two degrees of the infinitesimally small, such as a tobacco-pipe or the Roman Empire, a million of money or a fiddlestick's end.

You lean from the window, your last pipe reeking whitely into the darkness, your body full of delicious pains, your mind enthroned in the seventh circle of content; when suddenly the mood changes, the weathercock goes about, and you ask yourself one question more: whether, for the interval, you have been the wisest philosopher or the most egregious of donkeys? Human experience is not yet able to reply; but at least you have had a fine moment, and looked down upon all the kingdoms of the earth. And whether it was wise or foolish, to-morrow's travel will carry you, body and mind, into some different parish of the infinite.

DISCUSSION

1. Comparing "A Moose Hunt" and "Walking Tours" you will find that there is a difference in the level of generalization at which most of the evidence is presented. Try to define what that difference is.
2. There is also a difference in the order in which evidence and generalization are presented. We have already examined the order of Thoreau's piece; what is the order Stevenson uses?
3. Thoreau uses "I" throughout; Stevenson uses "you," "we," and "he" more often than "I." Try reading a typical paragraph from each, substituting the other's pronouns. What is the effect? What reason does each writer have for his choice of pronouns?

4. Try to disregard your feelings about each author's opinion. Which do you find to be the more persuasive writer? Why?

Heywood Broun

Holding a Baby

(1921)

When Adam delved and Eve span, the fiction that man is incapable of housework was first established. It would be interesting to figure out just how many foot-pounds of energy men have saved themselves, since the creation of the world, by keeping up the pretense that a special knack is required for washing dishes and for dusting, and that the knack is wholly feminine. The pretense of incapacity is impudent in its audacity, and yet it works.

Men build bridges and throw railroads across deserts, and yet they contend successfully that the job of sewing on a button is beyond them. Accordingly, they don't have to sew buttons.

It might be said, of course, that the safety of suspension bridges is so much more important than that of suspenders that the division of labor is only fair, but there are many of us who have never thrown a railroad in our lives, and yet swagger in all the glory of masculine achievement without undertaking any of the drudgery of odd jobs.

Probably men alone could never have maintained the fallacy of masculine incapacity without the aid of women. As soon as that rather limited sphere, once known as woman's place, was established, women began to glorify and exaggerate its importance, by the pretense that it was all so special and difficult that no other sex could possibly begin to accomplish the tasks entailed. To this declaration men gave immediate and eager assent and they have kept it up. The most casual examination will reveal the fact that all the jokes about the horrible results of masculine cooking and sewing are written by men. It is all part of a great scheme of sex propaganda.

Naturally there are other factors. Biology has been unscrupulous enough to discriminate markedly against women, and men have seized upon this advantage to press the belief that, since the bearing of children is exclusively the province of women, it must be that all the caring for them belongs properly to the same sex. Yet how ridiculous this is.

Most things which have to be done for children are of the simplest sort. They should tax the intelligence of no one. Men profess a total lack of ability to wash baby's face simply because they believe there's no great fun in the business, at either end of the sponge. Protectively, man must go the whole distance and pretend that there is not one single thing which he can do for baby. He must even maintain that he doesn't know how to hold one. From this pretense has grown the shockingly transparent fallacy that holding a baby correctly is one of the fine arts; or, perhaps even more fearsome than that, a wonderful intuition, which has come down after centuries of effort to women only.

"The thing that surprised Richard most," says a recent woman novelist, "was the ease and the efficiency with which Eleanor handled Annabel. . . . She seemed to know by instinct, things that Richard could not understand and that he could not understand how she came by. If she reached out her hands to take Annabel, her fingers seemed, of themselves, to curve into the places where they would fit the spineless bundle and give it support."

At this point, interruption is inevitable. Places indeed! There are one hundred and fifty-two distinctly different ways of holding a baby—and all are right! At least all will do. There is no need of seeking out special places for the hands. A baby is so soft that anybody with a firm grip can make places for an effective hold wherever he chooses. But to return to our quotation: "If Richard tried to take up the bundle, his fingers fell away like the legs of the brittle crab and the bundle collapsed, incalculable and helpless. 'How do you do it?' he would say. And he would right Annabel and try to still her protests. And Eleanor would only smile gently and send him on some masculine errand, while she soothed Annabel's feelings in the proper way."

You may depend upon it that Richard also smiled as soon as he was safely out of the house and embarked upon some masculine errand, such as playing eighteen holes of golf. Probably, by the time he reached the tenth green, he was too intent upon his game to remember how guile had won him freedom. Otherwise, he would have laughed again, when he holed a twenty-foot putt over a rolling green and recollected that he had escaped an afternoon of carrying Annabel because he was too awkward. I once knew the wife of the greatest billiard player in the world, and she informed me with much pride that her husband was incapable of carrying the baby. "He doesn't seem to have the proper touch," she explained.

As a matter of fact, even if men in general were as awkward as they pretend to be at home, there would still be small reason for their shirking the task of carrying a baby. Except that right side up is best, there is not much to learn. As I ventured to suggest before, almost any firm grip will do. Of course the child may cry, but that is simply because he has become over-particular through too much coddling. Nature herself is cavalier. Young rabbits don't even whimper when picked up by the ears, and kittens are quite contented to be lifted by the scruff of the neck.

This same Nature has been used as the principal argument for woman's exclusive ability to take care of the young. It is pretty generally held that all a woman needs to do to know all about children is to have some. This wisdom is attributed to instinct. Again and again we have been told by rapturous grandmothers that: "It isn't something which can be read in a book or taught in a school. Nature is the great teacher." This simply isn't true. There are many mothers in America who have learned far more from the manuals of Dr. Holt than instinct ever taught them—and

Dr. Holt is a man. I have seen mothers give beer and spaghetti and Neapolitan ice-cream to children in arms, and, if they got that from instinct, the only conclusion possible is that instinct did not know what it was talking about. Instinct is not what it used to be.

I have no feeling of being a traitor to my sex, when I say that I believe in at least a rough equality of parenthood. In shirking all the business of caring for children we have escaped much hard labor. It has been convenient. Perhaps it has been too convenient. If we have avoided arduous tasks, we have also missed much fun of a very special kind. Like children in a toy shop, we have chosen to live with the most amusing of talking-and-walking dolls, without ever attempting to tear down the sign which says, "Do not touch." In fact we have helped to set it in place. That is a pity.

Children mean nothing at long range. For our own sake we ought to throw off the pretense of incapacity and ask that we be given a half share in them. I hope that this can be done without its being necessary for us to share the responsibility of dishes also. I don't think there are any concealed joys in washing dishes. Washing children is quite a different matter. After you have washed somebody else's face you feel that you know him better. This may be the reason why so many trained nurses marry their patients—but that is another story. A dish is an unresponsive thing. It gives back nothing. A child's face offers competitive possibilities. It is interesting to see just how high a polish can be achieved without making it cry.

There is also a distinct sense of elation in doing trifling practical things for children. They are so small and so helpless that they contribute vastly to a comforting glow in the ego of the grown-up. When you have completed the rather difficult task of preparing a child for bed and actually getting him there, you have a sense of importance almost divine in its extent. This is to feel at one with Fate, to be the master of another's destiny, of his waking and his sleeping and his going out into the world. It is a brand-new world for the child. He is a veritable Adam and you loom up in his life as more than mortal. Golf is well enough for a Sunday sport, but it is a trifling thing beside the privilege of taking a small son to the zoo and letting him see his first lion, his first tiger and, best of all, his first elephant. Probably he will think that they are part of your own handiwork turned out for his pleasure.

To a child, at least, even the meanest of us may seem glamourous with magic and wisdom. It seems a pity not to take the fullest advantage of this chance before the opportunity is lost. There must come a day when even the most nimble-witted father has to reply, "I don't know." On that day the child comes out of Eden and you are only a man again. Cortes on his lonely peak in Darien was a pigmy discoverer beside the child eating his first spoonful of ice-cream. There is the immediate frightened and angry rebellion against the coldness of it, and then the amazing sensation as the strange substance melts into magic of pleasant sweetness. The child will go on to high adventure, but I doubt whether the world holds for any one more soul-stirring surprise than the first adventure with ice-cream. No, there is nothing dull in feeding a child.

There is less to be said for dressing a child, from the point of view of recreation. This seems to us laborious and rather tiresome, both for father and child. Still I knew one man who managed to make an adventure of it. He boasted that he had broken all the records of the world for changing all or any part of a child's clothing. He was a skilled automobile mechanic, much in demand in races, where tires are whisked on and off. He brought his technic into the home. I saw several of his demonstrations. He was a silent man who habitually carried a mouthful of safety pins. Once the required youngster had been pointed out, he wasted no time in preliminary wheedlings but tossed her on the floor without more ado. Even before her head had bumped, he would be hard at work. With him the thrill lay in the inspiration of the competitive spirit. He endeavored always to have his task completed before the child could begin to cry. He never lost. Often the child cried afterward, but by that time my friend felt that his part of the job was completed—and would turn the youngster over to her mother.

DISCUSSION

1. Heywood Broun is even more impersonal in his language than Stevenson, using expressions such as "It might be said," and "It would be interesting." Are his ideas and feelings actually more impersonal than Stevenson's? Does he support them in such a way that we find it difficult to disagree? If so, why? Point out examples of his opinions and the facts or experiences that support them.
2. What parts of "Holding a Baby" seem to be derived from the author's personal experience and what parts from his observation of others? Can you always tell? What is the evidence?
3. Heywood Broun was a popular writer. Can you suggest reasons for his popularity?
4. Thoreau has never been a popular writer, though he is more widely read today than he was in his own time. If he had used a style like Broun's, do you think he would have been more successful? Why, or why not? How would you describe Broun's style?

WRITING SUGGESTIONS

1. Have you ever found yourself, like Thoreau, a good deal at odds with a majority attitude? If so, give a careful and concrete account of the circumstances that aroused your feeling of rebellion. If you still believe you were right, say so in measured terms, giving your reasons clearly.
2. Is there an activity, or nonactivity, that you enjoy as much as Stevenson enjoys walking-tours? If so, try to convince the reader that he would enjoy it as much as you do. Use Stevenson's method of depicting scenes and describing pleasurable sensations rather than making assertions. Make the reader feel strongly the pleasures you have experienced.

3. What are your opinions regarding the roles of the sexes? We have all been exposed to too many emotional generalizations on this subject; do not bore your reader with such stuff. Be specific instead, writing in terms of your own experience and observation. What sort of relationship do you find just and rewarding, with what kinds of equalities and what kinds of allowances for difference? Make no generalizations without relevant and concrete examples.

Plate 17
Gnosis (c. 300 B.C.): *Stag Hunt*

In this and the following picture two artists are, by their manner of presenting their subjects, offering us an informal but definite opinion of the values involved. There are many ways in which a stag hunt could be depicted; in Thoreau's "A Moose Hunt" we have a hint as to how a person unsympathetic with hunting might show the killing of an animal. Here, clearly, hunting is shown as a hazardous and noble sport.

1. What qualities in the mosaic make it clear that the artist regards hunting favorably? Or, to put the question in another way, what details would you change if you wanted the picture to convey a distaste for the sport?
2. For centuries hunting was the sport most favored by chieftains, warriors, and kings. Does the picture suggest reasons for this preference?
3. In ancient Greek times when this mosaic was laid, it is unlikely that anyone opposed hunting. Yet in modern times Thoreau is not alone in disliking it; many writers and others have expressed distaste. Can you suggest any reasons for this change in attitude, aside from the personalities of the writers?
4. In your imagination, try substituting female figures for the male ones shown in the mosaic. Is the result absurd or is it just as natural as the original? What social or personal attitudes lie behind this emotional effect?

PLATE 17 Gnosis, **Stag Hunt**, c. 300 B.C. *Pebble mosaic at Pella. Rev. Raymond Schader, S.J.*

Plate 18
Mary Cassatt (1845–1926): *The Bath*

Mary Cassatt is best known for her paintings of mothers and children, and no artist has more strongly represented the pleasures of motherhood. Though she might not have agreed with Heywood Broun ("Holding a Baby," p. 283) that fathers are just as capable of handling babies as mothers, the values she communicates are similar to those in "Holding a Baby": nothing, she seems to believe, is more rewarding than caring for a child.

1. Look at the painting with the idea of expressing another informal generalization, such as that small children are a nuisance. What details of the painting would you have to change to make it express this idea?

2. Test Heywood Broun's generalization by substituting a father for the mother in the picture. What is the result in terms of emotional tone? Does the picture then become comical or absurd, or does it retain the same tenderness and dignity? What basic personal or social attitudes determine this emotional effect? Are they valid and natural, or superficial?

3. Aside from expressing an informal generalization, what does this painting have in common with *The Stag Hunt*? With the "Venus" of Willendorf or the *Venus de Milo*?

PLATE 18   Mary Cassatt (1845–1926), **The Bath.** *Courtesy of the Art Institute of Chicago.*

11

Expressing a View of Life

We can infer a general view of life from the evidence in almost any of the previous selections in this book. From Benjamin Franklin's "Whirlwind," for example, we see that his mind is an open, free-ranging and curious one; we can guess that nature and its investigation are important to him and that his view of life is both scientific and optimistic. Leigh Hunt in "The Inside of an Omnibus" makes it clear that nothing is of more interest to him than his fellow human beings, and we can infer that his view of life is social and humanistic. But our previous writers have not been concerned to tell us what their philosophies of life are, how they believe life should be lived, or even what they consider the highest values. The writers in this chapter do tell us these things. They see people, and even whole societies, living in ways that do not lead to happiness and they offer suggestions as to how we might live better.

Robert Louis Stevenson

An Apology for Idlers

(1876)

"BOSWELL: We grow weary when idle.

"JOHNSON: That is, sir, because others being busy, we want company; but if we were idle, there would be no growing weary; we should all entertain one another."

Just now, when every one is bound, under pain of a decree in absence convicting them of *lèse*-respectability, to enter on some lucrative profession, and labour therein with something not far short of enthusiasm, a cry from the opposite party who are content when they have enough, and like to look on and enjoy in the meanwhile, savours a little of bravado and gasconade. And yet this should not be. Idleness so called, which does not consist in doing nothing, but in doing a great deal not recognised in the dogmatic formularies of the ruling class, has as good a right to state its position as industry itself. It is admitted that the presence of people who refuse to enter in the great handicap race for sixpenny pieces, is at once an insult and a disenchantment for those who do. A fine fellow (as we see so many) takes his determination, votes for the sixpences, and in the emphatic Americanism, "goes for" them. And while such an one is ploughing distressfully up the road, it is not hard to understand his resentment, when he perceives cool persons in the meadows by the wayside, lying with a handkerchief over their ears and a glass at their elbow. Alexander is touched in a very delicate place by the disregard of Diogenes. Where was the glory of having taken Rome for these tumultuous barbarians, who poured into the Senate house, and found the Fathers sitting silent and unmoved by their success? It is a sore thing to have laboured along and scaled the arduous hilltops, and when all is done, find humanity indifferent to your achievement. Hence physicians condemn the unphysical; financiers have only a superficial toleration for those who know little of stocks; literary persons despise the unlettered; and people of all pursuits combine to disparage those who have none.

But though this is one difficulty of the subject, it is not the greatest. You could not be put in prison for speaking against industry, but you can be sent to Coventry for speaking like a fool. The greatest difficulty with most subjects is to do them well; therefore, please to remember this is an apology. It is certain that much may be judiciously argued in favour of diligence; only there is something to be said against it, and that is what, on the present occasion, I have to say. To state one argument is not necessarily to be deaf to all others, and that a man has written a book of travels in Montenegro, is no reason why he should never have been to Richmond.

It is surely beyond a doubt that people should be a good deal idle in youth. For though here and there a Lord Macaulay may escape from

lèse-respectability: injured respectability. The "lèse" is borrowed from "lèse majesté," injured majesty.
gasconade: boasting.
Alexander . . . Diogenes: according to legend, when Alexander, who had conquered the world, sought out Diogenes the philosopher and asked what he could do for him, Diogenes replied that he might move over a little and stop blocking the sun.
sent to Coventry: excluded from society. During the Great Rebellion in England, Royalist prisoners were sent to Coventry.
Richmond: a suburb of London.
Lord Macaulay: a British historian whom Stevenson judges to have escaped stuffiness, despite his education.

Expressing a View of Life

school honours with all his wits about him, most boys pay so dear for their medals that they never afterwards have a shot in their locker, and begin the world bankrupt. And the same holds true during all the time a lad is educating himself, or suffering others to educate him. It must have been a very foolish old gentleman who addressed Johnson at Oxford in these words: "Young man, ply your book diligently now, and acquire a stock of knowledge; for when years come upon you, you will find that poring upon books will be but an irksome task." The old gentleman seems to have been unaware that many other things besides reading grow irksome, and not a few become impossible, by the time a man has to use spectacles and cannot walk without a stick. Books are good enough in their own way, but they are a mighty bloodless substitute for life. It seems a pity to sit, like the Lady of Shalott, peering into a mirror, with your back turned on all the bustle and glamour of reality. And if a man reads very hard, as the old anecdote reminds us, he will have little time for thought.

If you look back on your own education, I am sure it will not be the full, vivid, instructive hours of truantry that you regret; you would rather cancel some lack-lustre periods between sleep and waking in the class. For my own part, I have attended a good many lectures in my time. I still remember that the spinning of a top is a case of Kinetic Stability. I still remember that Emphyteusis is not a disease, nor Stillicide a crime. But though I would not willingly part with such scraps of science, I do not set the same store by them as by certain other odds and ends that I came by in the open street while I was playing truant. This is not the moment to dilate on that mighty place of education, which was the favourite school of Dickens and of Balzac, and turns out yearly many inglorious masters in the Science of the Aspects of Life. Suffice it to say this: if a lad does not learn in the streets, it is because he has no faculty of learning. Nor is the truant always in the streets, for if he prefers, he may go out by the gardened suburbs into the country. He may pitch on some tuft of lilacs over a burn, and smoke innumerable pipes to the tune of the water on the stones. A bird will sing in the thicket. And there he may fall into a vein of kindly thought, and see things in a new perspective. Why, if this be not education, what is? We may conceive Mr. Worldly Wiseman accosting such an one, and the conversation that should thereupon ensue:—

"How now, young fellow, what dost thou here?"

"Truly, sir, I take mine ease."

"Is not this the hour of the class? and should'st thou not be plying thy Book with diligence, to the end thou mayest obtain knowledge?"

"Nay, but thus also I follow after Learning, by your leave."

Johnson: Samuel Johnson. See Plate 4 and "Letter to Lord Chesterfield," p. 334.
Lady of Shalott: in Tennyson's poem of the same name, a lady who was not permitted to look at the world directly, but only through her mirror.
Emphyteusis: a contract by which a man had a right to land as long as he kept it under cultivation.
Stillicide: a continual succession of drops, as dripping rainwater from eaves.
burn: brook.

"Learning, quotha! After what fashion, I pray thee? Is it mathematics?"
"No, to be sure."
"Is it metaphysics?"
"Nor that."
"Is it some language?"
"Nay, it is no language."
"Is it a trade?"
"Nor a trade neither."
"Why, then, what is't?"
"Indeed, sir, as a time may soon come for me to go upon Pilgrimage, I am desirous to note what is commonly done by persons in my case, and where are the ugliest Sloughs and Thickets on the Road; as also, what manner of Staff is of the best service. Moreover, I lie here, by this water, to learn by root-of-heart a lesson which my master teaches me to call Peace, or Contentment."

Hereupon Mr. Worldly Wiseman was much commoved with passion, and shaking his cane with a very threatful countenance, broke forth upon this wise: "Learning, quotha!" said he; "I would have all such rogues scourged by the Hangman!"

And so he would go his way, ruffing out his cravat with a crackle of starch, like a turkey when it spread its feathers.

Now this, of Mr. Wiseman's, is the common opinion. A fact is not called a fact, but a piece of gossip, if it does not fall into one of your scholastic categories. An inquiry must be in some acknowledged direction, with a name to go by; or else you are not inquiring at all, only lounging; and the workhouse is too good for you. It is supposed that all knowledge is at the bottom of a well, or the far end of a telescope. Sainte-Beuve, as he grew older, came to regard all experience as a single great book, in which to study for a few years ere we go hence; and it seemed all one to him whether you should read in Chapter xx., which is the differential calculus, or in Chapter xxxix., which is hearing the band play in the gardens. As a matter of fact, an intelligent person, looking out of his eyes and hearkening in his ears, with a smile on his face all the time, will get more true education than many another in a life of heroic vigils. There is certainly some chill and arid knowledge to be found upon the summits of formal and laborious science; but it is all round about you, and for the trouble of looking, that you will acquire the warm and palpitating facts of life. While others are filling their memory with a lumber of words, one-half of which they will forget before the week be out, your truant may learn some really useful art: to play the fiddle, to know a good cigar, or to speak with ease and opportunity to all varieties of men. Many who have "plied their book diligently," and know all about some one branch or another of accepted lore, come out of the study with an ancient and owl-like demeanour, and prove dry, stockish and dyspeptic in all the better and brighter parts of life. Many make a large fortune, who remain under-bred and pathetically stupid to the last. And meanwhile there goes the idler, who began life along with them—by your leave, a different pic-

Sainte-Beuve: French essayist and critic (1804–69).

ture. He has had time to take care of his health and his spirits; he has been a great deal in the open air, which is the most salutary of all things for both body and mind; and if he has never read the great Book in very recondite places, he has dipped into it and skimmed it over to excellent purpose. Might not the student afford some Hebrew roots, and the business man some of his half-crowns, for a share of the idler's knowledge of life at large, and Art of Living? Nay, and the idler has another and more important quality than these. I mean his wisdom. He who has much looked on at the childish satisfaction of other people in their hobbies, will regard his own with only a very ironical indulgence. He will not be heard among the dogmatists. He will have a great and cool allowance for all sorts of people and opinions. If he finds no out-of-the-way truths, he will identify himself with no very burning falsehood. His way takes him along a byroad, not much frequented, but very even and pleasant, which is called Commonplace Lane, and leads to the Belvedere of Commonsense. Thence he shall command an agreeable, if no very noble prospect; and while others behold the East and West, the Devil and the Sunrise, he will be contentedly aware of a sort of morning hour upon all sublunary things, with an army of shadows running speedily and in many different directions into the great daylight of Eternity. The shadows and the generations, the shrill doctors and the plangent wars, go by into ultimate silence and emptiness; but underneath all this, a man may see, out of the Belvedere windows, much green and peaceful landscape; many fire-lit parlours; good people laughing, drinking, and making love as they did before the Flood or the French Revolution; and the old shepherd telling his tale under the hawthorn.

Extreme *busyness*, whether at school or college, kirk or market, is a symptom of deficient vitality; and a faculty for idleness implies a catholic appetite and a strong sense of personal identity. There is a sort of dead-alive, hackneyed people about, who are scarcely conscious of living except in the exercise of some conventional occupation. Bring these fellows into the country or set them aboard ship, and you will see how they pine for their desk or their study. They have no curiosity; they cannot give themselves over to random provocations; they do not take pleasure in the exercise of their faculties for its own sake; and unless Necessity lays about them with a stick, they will even stand still. It is no good speaking to such folk: they *cannot* be idle, their nature is not generous enough; and they pass those hours in a sort of coma, which are not dedicated to furious moiling in the gold-mill. When they do not require to go to the office, when they are not hungry and have no mind to drink, the whole breathing world is a blank to them. If they have to wait an hour or so for a train, they fall into a stupid trance with their eyes open. To see them, you would suppose there was nothing to look at and no one to speak with; you would imagine they were paralysed or alienated; and yet very possibly they are hard workers in their own way, and have good eyesight

Belvedere: a building with a good view.
sublunary: under the moon.
kirk: church.

for a flaw in a deed or a turn of the market. They have been to school and college, but all the time they had their eye on the medal; they have gone about in the world and mixed with clever people, but all the time they were thinking of their own affairs. As if a man's soul were not too small to begin with, they have dwarfed and narrowed theirs by a life of all work and no play; until here they are at forty, with a listless attention, a mind vacant of all material of amusement, and not one thought to rub against another, while they wait for the train. Before he was breeched, he might have clambered on the boxes; when he was twenty, he would have stared at the girls; but now the pipe is smoked out, the snuff-box empty, and my gentleman sits bolt upright upon a bench, with lamentable eyes. This does not appeal to me as being Success in Life.

But it is not only the person himself who suffers from his busy habits, but his wife and children, his friends and relations, and down to the very people he sits with in a railway-carriage or an omnibus. Perpetual devotion to what a man calls his business, is only to be sustained by perpetual neglect of many other things. And it is not by any means certain that a man's business is the most important thing he has to do. To an impartial estimate it will seem clear that many of the wisest, most virtuous, and most beneficent parts that are to be played upon the Theatre of Life are filled by gratuitous performers, and pass, among the world at large, as phases of idleness. For in that Theatre, not only the walking gentlemen, singing chambermaids, and diligent fiddlers in the orchestra, but those who look on and clap their hands from the benches, do really play a part and fulfil important offices towards the general result. You are no doubt very dependent on the care of your lawyer and stockbroker, of the guards and signalmen who convey you rapidly from place to place, and the policemen who walk the streets for your protection; but is there not a thought of gratitude in your heart for certain other benefactors who set you smiling when they fall in your way, or season your dinner with good company? Colonel Newcome helped to lose his friend's money; Fred Bayham had an ugly trick of borrowing shirts; and yet they were better people to fall among than Mr. Barnes. And though Falstaff was neither sober nor very honest, I think I could name one or two long-faced Barabbases whom the world could better have done without. Hazlitt mentions that he was more sensible of obligation to Northcote, who had never done him anything he could call a service, than to his whole circle of ostentatious friends; for he thought a good companion emphatically the greatest benefactor. I know there are people in the world who cannot feel grateful unless the favour has been done them at the cost of pain and difficulty. But this is a churlish disposition. A man may send you six sheets of letter-paper covered with the most entertaining gossip, or you

breeched: put in trousers.
Success in Life: a humorous reference to a passage from Walter Pater appearing on p. 301, it was published just a few years before "An Apology for Idlers."
Colonel Newcome, and so on: characters in William Makepeace Thackeray's novel, *The Newcomes.*
Barabbases: Pontius Pilate offered to free either Barabbas the robber or Jesus; the crowd preferred he free Barabbas.

may pass half-an-hour pleasantly, perhaps profitably, over an article of his; do you think the service would be greater, if he had made the manuscript in his heart's blood, like a compact with the devil? Do you really fancy you should be more beholden to your correspondent, if he had been damning you all the while for your importunity? Pleasures are more beneficial than duties because, like the quality of mercy, they are not strained, and they are twice blest. There must always be two to a kiss, and there may be a score in a jest; but wherever there is an element of sacrifice, the favour is conferred with pain, and, among generous people, received with confusion. There is no duty we so much underrate as the duty of being happy. By being happy, we sow anonymous benefits upon the world, which remain unknown even to ourselves, or when they are disclosed, surprise nobody so much as the benefactor. The other day, a ragged, barefoot boy ran down the street after a marble, with so jolly an air that he set every one he passed into a good humour; one of these persons, who had been delivered from more than usually black thoughts, stopped the little fellow and gave him some money with this remark: "You see what sometimes comes of looking pleased." If he had looked pleased before, he had now to look both pleased and mystified. For my part, I justify this encouragement of smiling rather than tearful children; I do not wish to pay for tears anywhere but upon the stage; but I am prepared to deal largely in the opposite commodity. A happy man or woman is a better thing to find than a five-pound note. He or she is a radiating focus of goodwill; and their entrance into a room is as though another candle had been lighted. We need not care whether they could prove the forty-seventh proposition; they do a better thing than that, they practically demonstrate the great Theorem of the Liveableness of Life. Consequently, if a person cannot be happy without remaining idle, idle he should remain. It is a revolutionary precept; but thanks to hunger and the workhouse, one not easily to be abused; and within practical limits, it is one of the most incontestable truths in the whole Body of Morality. Look at one of your industrious fellows for a moment, I beseech you. He sows hurry and reaps indigestion; he puts a vast deal of activity out to interest, and receives a large measure of nervous derangement in return. Either he absents himself entirely from all fellowship, and lives a recluse in a garret, with carpet slippers and a leaden inkpot; or he comes among people swiftly and bitterly, in a contraction of his whole nervous system, to discharge some temper before he returns to work. I do not care how much or how well he works, this fellow is an evil feature in other people's lives. They would be happier if he were dead. They could easier do without his services in the Circumlocution Office than they can tolerate his fractious spirits. He poisons life at the well-head. It is better to be beggared out of hand by a scapegrace nephew, than daily hag-ridden by a peevish uncle.

And what, in God's name, is all this pother about? For what cause do they embitter their own and other people's lives? That a man should publish three or thirty articles a year, that he should finish or not finish his great allegorical picture, are questions of little interest to the world. The ranks of life are full; and although a thousand fall, there are always

Experiencing and Generalizing

some to go into the breach. When they told Joan of Arc she should be at home minding women's work, she answered there were plenty to spin and wash. And so, even with your own rare gifts! When nature is "so careless of the single life," why should we coddle ourselves into the fancy that our own is of exceptional importance? Suppose Shakespeare had been knocked on the head some dark night in Sir Thomas Lucy's preserves, the world would have wagged on better or worse, the pitcher gone to the well, the scythe to the corn, and the student to his book; and no one been any the wiser of the loss. There are not many works extant, if you look the alternative all over, which are worth the price of a pound of tobacco to a man of limited means. This is a sobering reflection for the proudest of our earthly vanities. Even a tobacconist may, upon consideration, find no great cause for personal vainglory in the phrase, for although tobacco is an admirable sedative, the qualities necessary for retailing it are neither rare nor precious in themselves. Alas and alas! you may take it how you will, but the services of no single individual are indispensable. Atlas was just a gentleman with a protracted nightmare! And yet you see merchants who go and labour themselves into a great fortune and thence into the bankruptcy court; scribblers who keep scribbling at little articles until their temper is a cross to all who come about them, as though Pharaoh should set the Israelites to make a pin instead of a pyramid: and fine young men who work themselves into a decline, and are driven off in a hearse with white plumes upon it. Would you not suppose these persons had been whispered, by the Master of the Ceremonies, the promise of some momentous destiny? and that this lukewarm bullet on which they play their farces was the bull's-eye and centre-point of all the universe? And yet it is not so. The ends for which they give away their priceless youth, for all they know, may be chimerical or hurtful; the glory and riches they expect may never come, or may find them indifferent; and they and the world they inhabit are so inconsiderable that the mind freezes at the thought.

DISCUSSION

1. Robert Louis Stevenson lived to be only forty-four and yet his writings fill quite a large bookshelf. How do you reconcile this fact with the philosophy expressed in "An Apology for Idlers"?
2. Most people, when they present a view of life, argue in terms of a "false dilemma"; that is, they state matters as though there were only two extreme choices with nothing in between. Does Stevenson give us such a false dilemma here? Can you suggest alternatives he does not seem to take into account?
3. The usual question of Mr. Worldly Wiseman when confronted with the philosophy of idleness is, "Who's going to get the world's work done if everybody's idle?" Can you suggest one or more answers Stevenson might be able to give him?

Walter Pater suggests a way of life in terms more general than Stevenson's.

Walter Pater

Success in Life

(1868)

The service of philosophy, of speculative culture, towards the human spirit is to rouse, to startle it into sharp and eager observation. Every moment some form grows perfect in hand or face; some tone on the hills or the sea is choicer than the rest; some mood of passion or insight or intellectual excitement is irresistibly real and attractive for us—for that moment only. Not the fruit of experience, but experience itself, is the end. A counted number of pulses only is given to us of a variegated, dramatic life. How may we see in them all that is to be seen in them by the finest senses? How shall we pass most swiftly from point to point, and be present always at the focus where the greatest number of vital forces unite in their purest energy?

To burn always with this hard, gem-like flame, to maintain this ecstasy, is success in life. In a sense it might even be said that our failure is to form habits; for, after all, habit is relative to a stereotyped world, and meantime it is only the roughness of the eye that makes any two persons, things, situations, seem alike. While all melts under our feet, we may well catch at any exquisite passion, or any contribution to knowledge that seems by a lifted horizon to set the spirit free for a moment, or any stirring of the senses, strange dyes, strange colours, and curious odours, or work of the artist's hands, or the face of one's friend. Not to discriminate every moment some passionate attitude in those about us, and in the brilliancy of their gifts some tragic dividing of forces on their ways, is, on this short day of frost and sun, to sleep before evening. With this sense of the splendour of our experience and of its effort to see and touch, we shall hardly have time to make theories about the things we see and touch. What we have to do is to be for ever curiously testing new opinions and courting new impressions, never acquiescing in a facile orthodoxy of Comte, or of Hegel, or of our own. Philosophical theories or ideas, as points of view, instruments of criticism, may help us to gather up what might otherwise pass unregarded by us. "Philosophy is the microscope of thought." The theory or idea or system which requires of us the sacrifice of any part of this experience, in consideration of some interest into which we cannot enter, or some abstract theory we have not identified with ourselves, or what is only conventional, has no real claim upon us.

One of the most beautiful passages in the writings of Rousseau is that in the sixth book of the *Confessions*, where he describes the awakening in him of the literary sense. An undefinable taint of death had always clung about him, and now in early manhood he believed himself smitten by mortal disease. He asked himself how he might make as much as possible of the interval that remained; and he was not biassed by anything in his previous life when he decided that it must be by intellectual excitement, which he found just then in the clear, fresh writings of Voltaire. Well! we are all *condamnés,* as Victor Hugo says: we are all under sentence of death, but with a sort of indefinite reprieve—*les hommes sont tous condamnés à mort avec des sursis indéfinis*: we have an interval, and then our place knows us no more. Some spend this interval in listlessness, some in high passions, the wisest, at least among "the children of this world," in art and song. For our one chance lies in expanding that interval, in getting as many pulsations as possible into the given time. Great passions may give us this quickened sense of life, ecstasy and sorrow of love, the various forms of enthusiastic activity, disinterested or otherwise, which come naturally to many of us. Only be sure it is passion—that it does yield you this fruit of a quickened, multiplied consciousness. Of this wisdom, the poetic passion, the desire of beauty, the love of art for art's sake, has most; for art comes to you professing frankly to give nothing but the highest quality to your moments as they pass, and simply for those moments' sake.

DISCUSSION

1. What is the difference between Pater's point of view and Stevenson's—that is, exactly at what point would they disagree if they were to debate? Is their difference an essential one or not?
2. On what points would Pater and Stevenson agree?
3. Do you find Pater or Stevenson more persuasive? Aside from your natural inclination to agree with the ideas of one or the other, why?
4. Whenever anyone claims to possess the one key to successful living, it is well to pause and think whether there are alternatives. First, formulate Pater's idea briefly and clearly, but without oversimplifying. Then see if you can formulate in similar terms a different and equally attractive philosophy.
5. Try a simple but revealing philosophical exercise. First, state what you want most in life. Then get someone to ask you, "What do you want that *for?*" Answer, and then repeat the process until you arrive at something basic, about which your answer is, "I want that for its own sake, because it is good in itself." Swimming, for example, is basic; marriage is not. One does not swim *for* anything, but because swimming is pleasurable, that is a good in itself. But no one marries just in order to marry; he expects the process to lead to benefits beyond standing in church in an uncomfortable costume. Beware of simple, vague answers like "happiness"; if *all* you wanted was to be happy, you would have had your brain disconnected.

Pater believes that art is the concentrated essence of life. John Ruskin might have agreed, but first, he says, certain things are essential. His angry appeal, addressed to representatives of industrial England a century ago, might well be aimed at us today.

John Ruskin

The Essential Things

(1871)

There are three material things, not only useful but essential to life. No one "knows how to live" till he has got them.

These are Pure Air, Water, and Earth.

There are three immaterial things, not only useful, but essential to life. No one knows how to live till he has got them also.

These are Admiration, Hope, and Love.

Admiration—the power of discerning and taking delight in what is beautiful in visible Form and lovely in human Character, and, necessarily, striving to produce what is beautiful in form and to become what is lovely in character.

Hope—the recognition, by true foresight, of better things to be reached hereafter, whether by ourselves or others; necessarily issuing in the straightforward and undisappointable effort to advance, according to our proper power, the gaining of them.

Love—both of family and neighbour, faithful and satisfied.

These are the six chiefly useful things to be got by Political Economy, when it *has* become a science. I will briefly tell you what modern Political Economy—the great *savoir mourir*—is doing with them.

The first three, I said, are Pure Air, Water, and Earth.

Heaven gives you the main elements of these. You can destroy them at your pleasure, or increase, almost without limit, the available quantities of them.

You can vitiate the air by your manner of life and of death, to any extent. You might easily vitiate it so as to bring such a pestilence on the globe as would end all of you. You, or your fellows, German and French, are at present vitiating it to the best of your power in every direction—chiefly at this moment with corpses, and animal and vegetable ruin in war, changing men, horses, and garden-stuff into noxious gas. But everywhere, and all day long, you are vitiating it with foul chemical exhalations; and the horrible nests, which you call towns, are little more than laboratories for the distillation into heaven of venomous smokes and smells, mixed with effluvia from decaying animal matter and infectious miasmata from purulent disease.

On the other hand, your power of purifying the air, by dealing properly and swiftly with all substances in corruption, by absolutely forbidding noxious manufactures, and by planting in all soils the trees which cleanse and invigorate earth and atmosphere, is literally infinite. You might make every breath of air you draw, food.

Secondly, your power over the rain and river-waters of the earth is

---

savoir mourir: this is a play on *savoir faire*, "knowing how to do," substituting *mourir*, "to die." Ruskin is saying that political economy is the science of death.
miasmata: noxious gases.

infinite. You can bring rain where you will, by planting wisely and tending carefully; drought where you will, by ravage of woods and neglect of the soil. You might have the rivers of England as pure as the crystal of the rock; beautiful in falls, in lakes, in living pools; so full of fish that you might take them out with your hands instead of nets. Or you may do always as you have done now—turn every river of England into a common sewer, so that you cannot so much as baptize an English baby but with filth, unless you hold its face out in the rain; and even *that* falls dirty.

Then for the third, earth, meant to be nourishing for you and blossoming. You have learned about it that there is no such thing as a flower; and as far as your scientific hands and scientific brains, inventive of explosive and deathful instead of blossoming and life-giving dust, can contrive, you have turned the Mother Earth, Demeter, into the Avenger Earth, Tisiphone—with the voice of your brother's blood crying out of it in one wild harmony round all its murderous sphere.

That is what you have done for the Three Material Useful Things.

Then for the Three Immaterial Useful Things. For Admiration, you have learned contempt and conceit. There is no lovely thing ever yet done by man that you care for, or can understand; but you are persuaded you are able to do much finer things yourselves. You gather and exhibit together, as if equally instructive, what is infinitely bad with what is infinitely good. You do not know which is which; you instinctively prefer the Bad, and do more of it. You instinctively hate the Good, and destroy it.

Then, secondly, for Hope. You have not so much spirit of it in you as to begin any plan which will not pay for ten years; nor so much intelligence of it in you (either politicians or workmen) as to be able to form one clear idea of what you would like your country to become.

Then, thirdly, for Love. You were ordered by the Founder of your religion to love your neighbour as yourselves. You have founded an entire science of Political Economy on what you have stated to be the constant instinct of man—the desire to defraud his neighbour. And you have driven your women mad, so that they ask no more for Love nor for fellowship with you, but stand against you, and ask for "justice."

Are there any of you who are tired of all this? Any of you Landlords or Tenants? Employers or Workmen? Are there any landlords, any masters, who would like better to be served by men than by iron devils? Any tenants, any workmen, who can be true to their leaders and to each other? who can vow to work and to live faithfully, for the sake of the joy of their homes?

Will any such give the tenth of what they have, and of what they earn, not to emigrate with, but to stay in England with, and do what is in their hands and hearts to make her a happy England?

I am not rich (as people now estimate riches), and great part of what

Demeter: Greek goddess of fertlity and growth, especially with reference to crops.
Tisiphone: one of the three Furies of Greek mythology, the one who punishes the guilty in the underworld who have escaped punishment during their lives.

I have is already engaged in maintaining art-workmen, or for other objects more or less of public utility. The tenth of whatever is left to me, estimated as accurately as I can (you shall see the accounts), I will make over to you in perpetuity, with the best security that English law can give, on Christmas Day of this year, with engagement to add the tithe of whatever I earn afterwards. Who else will help, with little or much? the object of such fund being to begin, and gradually—no matter how slowly—to increase the buying and securing of land in England, which shall not be built upon, but cultivated by Englishmen with their own hands and such help of force as they can find in wind and wave. I do not care with how many or how few this thing is begun, nor on what inconsiderable scale—if it be but in two or three poor men's gardens. So much, at least, I can buy, myself, and give them. If no help come, I have done and said what I could, and there will be an end. If any help come to me, it is to be on the following conditions:—

We will try to make some small piece of English ground beautiful, peaceful, and fruitful. We will have no steam-engines upon it, and no railroads; we will have no untended or unthought-of creatures on it; none wretched but the sick; none idle but the dead. We will have no liberty upon it, but instant obedience to known law and appointed persons; no equality upon it, but recognition of every betterness that we can find, and reprobation of every worseness. When we want to go anywhere, we will go there quietly and safely, not at forty miles an hour in the risk of our lives; when we want to carry anything anywhere, we will carry it either on the backs of beasts, or on our own, or in carts or boats. We will have plenty of flowers and vegetables in our gardens, plenty of corn and grass in our fields,—and few bricks. We will have some music and poetry; the children shall learn to dance to it and sing it; perhaps some of the old people, in time, may also. We will have some art, moreover; we will at least try if, like the Greeks, we can't make some pots. The Greeks used to paint pictures of gods on their pots. We, probably, cannot do as much; but we may put some pictures of insects on them, and reptiles—butterflies and frogs, if nothing better. There was an excellent old potter in France who used to put frogs and vipers into his dishes, to the admiration of mankind; we can surely put something nicer than that. Little by little, some higher art and imagination may manifest themselves among us, and feeble rays of science may dawn for us:—botany, though too dull to dispute the existence of flowers; and history, though too simple to question the nativity of men; nay, even perhaps an uncalculating and uncovetous wisdom, as of rude Magi, presenting, at such nativity, gifts of gold and frankincense.

DISCUSSION

1. Ruskin speaks in pretty general terms. What is the purpose of his appeal? Would this purpose be better served if he gave more concrete evidence than he does? Why, or why not?

tithe: tenth.

Experiencing and Generalizing

2. What evidence of his own sincerity does he offer? Was his appeal successful? How do you know?

Sometimes poetry can express a view more pungently than prose, and more economically. Here Tu Fu conveys not only the oppressiveness of continuing war, but a tragic view of life itself.

Tu Fu

Chariots Go Forth to War

(760)

Chariots rumble and roll; horses whinney and neigh;
Men are marching with bows and arrows at their hips.
Their parents and wives hurry to bid farewell,
Raising clouds of dust over Hsien-yang Bridge.
They pull at the soldiers' clothes, stamp their feet and cry out.
The sound of their crying soars to the clouds.

Some passers-by speak to the soldiers;
They shake their heads dumbly and say:
"Since the age of fifteen we have defended the northern rivers.
Till we are forty we shall serve on the western front.
We leave our homes as youths and return as gray-haired men.
Along the frontiers there flows the sea of our blood.
The King hungers for territory—therefore we fight.

"Have you not heard, sir,
How through two hundred countries east of the Tai-yeng Mountains
Through thousands of villages and tens of thousands of hamlets
Thorns and nettles run wild?
Sturdy peasant women swing the hoes and drive the plow,
But neither in the east nor west is anything raised or sown.
The soldiers of Sh'and will fight to the end,
But they cannot be slain like dogs or like hens.

"Oh, sir, it is kind of you to ask me,
But how dare we express our resentment?
Winter has come and the year is passing away;
The war on the western passes is still going on.
The magistrates are pressing us to pay our taxes,
But where shall we get the money?
If only I had known the fate in store for boys,

I would have had my children all girls,
For girls may be married to the neighbors,
But boys are born only to be cut down and buried beneath the grass.

"Do you not see, sir,
The long dead ancient bones near the Blue Sea bleached by the sun?
And now the lament of those who have just died
Mingles with the voices of those who died long ago,
And darkness falls, and the rain, and the ghostly whimpering of voices."

DISCUSSION

1. "Between 751 and 763 China lost most of its fighting manpower." What does the poem communicate that this factual statement does not?
2. Point out two or three lines that seem to work well in the poem, but that would not function well in prose.
3. For its effect, poetry depends on creating images in the mind. What are some images here that help the poet to express the immense tragedy of war? How do they create their effect?

A view of life both broad and deep can be expressed in a few words.

Ryokan

The Thief and the Moon

(1830)

The thief
 Left it behind—
  The moon at the window.

DISCUSSION

1. What scene and situation are implied by the poem?
2. Why doesn't the poet tell us what was stolen?
3. What is the philosophy of life expressed? Have any other writers in this book expressed a similar view? If so, which ones, where, and how?
4. Make a simple one-sentence statement of this philosophy. How does it differ in effect from the poem? Which do you find more convincing? Why?

Experiencing and Generalizing

WRITING SUGGESTIONS

1. What is "success in life"?

2. What do you believe is the best way to live, day by day, hour by hour? Describe as attractively as you can the best way to make the most of a day: not a holiday or an exceptional day, but the best kind of typical day in a life as you would like to live it. Be practical. This is not to be a dream, but a way of life that can be achieved in the world as it is.

3. What is your present belief about the nature of the universe we live in? Describe it as clearly as you can and with some attention to detail. Or, if you feel no need for a belief about the ultimate nature of the universe, describe the degree of belief that you find necessary in order to live. Just how much do you need to know or believe in order to make your own decisions with some assurance they are the right ones?

4. Do you feel a sweeping pessimism about mankind, or an equally sweeping optimism? Or is your feeling a more subtle and mixed one? Try to express your feeling about the human world as a whole in terms of images—of what you see and hear, smell and touch, when you let your imagination wander about all the parts of the earth. This time do not confine yourself to firsthand experience, but give us your imaginary experience, a vast and sweeping view of what the world means to you.

Plate 19
Mathias Grünewald (1480–1530): *Crucifixion*

Every age expresses its views of life in the language of its beliefs. In Christian Europe for several hundred years the artist's ideas were communicated through religious paintings, often of the Crucifixion. Comparing this painting with the following one, we see how divergent these views could be.

1. What aspects of the death of Jesus does Grünewald emphasize? Apart from specifically Christian belief, what generalizations can you make about the way he sees life? What details communicate this view?

2. Among the authors you have read in this book, do any express views that are in any way comparable to Grünewald's? If so, which authors? In what way are their attitudes like his? In what ways do they differ?

3. What emotions does Grünewald seem to want to arouse in the observer of his painting? What thoughts, as opposed to emotions, does the painting suggest? With or without particular reference to Christian belief, can you make a general philosophical statement that you feel Grünewald might subscribe to?

PLATE 19   Mathias Grünewald (1480?–1530?), **Crucifixion.** *Colmar/ d'Unterlinden Museum, from Giraudon.*

PLATE 20   Alessandro Allori (1535–1607), **The Trinity.** *Santissima Annunziata, Chapel of the Academy of Artists, Florence, from Scala New York/Florence.*

Plate 20
Alessandro Allori (1535–1607): *Trinity*

Again, as in Grunewald's *Crucifixion*, a view of life is communicated through the medium of a conventional religious subject. While the subject is nearly the same, the artist's attitude toward it is conspicuously different.

1. What might be some of Grunewald's objections to this painting? What might be some of Allori's objections to Grunewald's *Crucifixion*? What would their reasons be in each case?
2. What differences are there in the backgrounds of each picture? How do these differences reflect the artist's attitude toward the scene?
3. What are the important values expressed in Allori's fresco? What takes up most of the surface area, and what does the style of its arrangement tell us?
4. What element is conspicuous in Grunewald's painting and nearly invisible in Allori's? What does this tell us about what the artist regards as important?
5. Using *Trinity* as your only evidence, what would you say was Allori's philosophy of life? What particulars lead you to this conclusion?

Plate 21
Winslow Homer (1836–1910): "Old Friends"

In this and the following picture, views of life are expressed by showing human figures in a natural environment. The two artists not only employ widely differing techniques, but also reflect widely differing cultures and ways of seeing their subjects. Winslow Homer's background was that of America about a century ago, when many who were still living had experienced the wilderness.

1. What is the relationship between the old man and the tree? Exactly how has the artist communicated this relationship?
2. What general view of life is expressed by the painting? How do you know this?
3. An artist can tell us as much by what he leaves out of a picture as by what he includes. This picture is a simple one, including just enough to tell the story. What are some details a lesser artist might have been tempted to put in "because they were there"? Why is the picture more effective without them?
4. Do you feel that "Old Friends" is a first-rate painting or not? Do you feel that the same view of life could have been expressed in a more significant way? If so, in what way?
5. The picture is done in watercolor, using rapid, simple strokes of the brush. Do you think it would have been more effective if it had been done in oils, with greater attention to detail? Why, or why not?

PLATE 21 Winslow Homer (1836–1910), **Old Friends.** *Worcester Art Museum, Worcester, Mass.*

PLATE 22   Ma Lin, **Listening to the Wind in the Pines,** 1246. *Collection of the National Palace Museum, Taipei, Taiwan, Republic of China.*

Plate 22
Ma Lin (1246): *Listening to the Wind in the Pines*

As the courts of China became more and more refined and luxurious, writers and artists dwelt on the theme of man and nature and on the necessity of remaining in close touch with the natural world. Many Chinese paintings show artists and scholars walking among trees, contemplating mountains, or sitting beside streams. This painting, however, adds another dimension to these activities.

1. What specific evidences can you find that tell us something about this scholar's attitude toward nature? For example, what is the object lying near his right foot?
2. Is the scholar listening to the wind in the pines? What evidence is there that he is or is not? (The boy in the lower left corner is his servant.)
3. For what real purpose is the scholar sitting out among the trees? What generalization can you make about his relationship with nature?
4. The artist, of course, is making fun of the scholar and other people like him, much in the same tolerant spirit we find in Erasmus ("Fools Art Happy," p. 335). What do you think might be the artist's own attitude toward nature—"the wind in the pines"? What evidence can you point out to support this idea?
5. Recalling William McFee's "The Pattern-Makers" (p. 115), which of these two artists, Homer or Ma Lin, do you feel represents more clearly McFee's value of careful craftsmanship? What are your reasons in support of this judgment?
6. How do you think Ma Lin might have regarded the scene depicted by Winslow Homer in "Old Friends"? Aside from differences in technique, how might he arrange the scene differently?

12

Giving Advice

Nothing is more freely given or more reluctantly received than advice. Perhaps giving advice directly is the least effective of all literary devices; nevertheless, some kinds of advice are more welcome than others, as we shall see.

There are probably few kinds of advice less needed than advice from a confirmed bachelor to a bride, and, after reading Jonathan Swift's try at it, we might conclude that there were good reasons for his being a bachelor.

Jonathan Swift

To a Young Lady on Her Marriage

(1727)

MADAME,—The Hurry and Impertinence of receiving and paying Visits on account of your Marriage being now over, you are beginning to enter into a Course of life, where you will want much advice to divert you from falling into many Errors, Fopperies, and Follies to which your Sex is subject. I have always born an entire friendship to your father and mother; and the person they have chosen for your Husband, hath been for some years past my particular Favourite; I have long wished you might come together, because I hoped, that from the goodness of your Disposition,

Foppery: foolishness, especially with regard to fancy clothing and elegant manners.

317

and by following the Counsel of wise Friends, you might in time make yourself worthy of him. Your Parents were so far in the right, that they did not produce you into the World, whereby you avoided many wrong steps which others have taken, and have fewer ill Impressions to be removed. But they failed, as it is generally the case, in too much neglecting to cultivate your Mind; without which it is impossible to acquire or preserve the Friendship and Esteem of a wise man, who soon grows weary of acting the Lover and treating his wife like a mistress, but wants a reasonable Companion, and a true Friend, through every stage of his life. It must be therefore your Business to qualify yourself for those offices; wherein I will not fail to be your Director, as long as I shall think you deserve it, by letting you know how you are to act, and what you ought to avoid.

And beware of despising or neglecting Instructions, whereon will depend not only your making a good Figure in the World, but your own real Happiness, as well as that of the person who ought to be the dearest to you.

I must therefore desire you, in the first place, to be very slow in changing the *modest behaviour of a Virgin*. It is usual in young Wives, before they have been many weeks married, to assume a bold forward Look and manner of talking, as if they intended to signify in all companies, that they were no longer Girls, and consequently that their whole Demeanor, before they got a Husband, was all but a Countenance and Constraint upon their Nature; whereas, I suppose, if the Votes of wise men were gathered, a very great Majority would be in favour of those Ladies, who, after they were entered into that state, rather chose to double their portion of Modesty and Reservedness.

I must likewise warn you strictly against the least degree of *Fondness* to your Husband before any Witness whatsoever, even before your nearest Relations, or the very Maids of your chamber. This Proceeding is so exceeding odious and disgustful to all who have either good Breeding or good Sense, that they assign two very unamiable reasons for it; the one is gross Hypocrisy, and the other has too bad a name to mention. . . . Conceal your Esteem and Love in your own breast, and reserve your kind looks and language for private Hours, which are so many in the four and twenty, that they will afford Time to employ a passion as exalted as any that was ever described in a *French* Romance.

Upon this head, I should likewise advise you to differ in practice from those Ladies who affect abundance of *Uneasiness* while their Husbands are abroad; start with every knock at the door, and ring the bell incessantly for the servants to let in their master; will not eat a bit at dinner or supper, if the Husband happens to stay out; and receive him at his return with such a medley of Chiding and Kindness, and catechising him where he has been, that a Shrew from *Billingsgate* would be a more easy and eligible companion.

produce you into the World: introduce into society, as with a "coming out" party.
Countenance: false face.
Billingsgate: fish market, where fishwives screamed and swore at each other.

Of the same leaven are those Wives, who, when their Husbands are gone a Journey, must have a Letter every post, upon pain of Fits and Hystericks; and a Day must be fixed for their return home, without the least Allowance for business, or sickness, or accidents, or weather; upon which, I can only say, that in my observation, those Ladies who are apt to make the greatest Clutter on such occasions, would liberally have paid a messenger for bringing them news, that their Husbands had broke their necks on the road.

You will perhaps be offended, when I advise you to abate a little of that violent Passion for *fine Clothes*, so predominant in your Sex. It is a little hard, that ours, for whose Sake you wear them, are not admitted to be of your council. I may venture to assure you, that we will make an abatement at any time of four pounds a yard in a Brocade, if the Ladies will but allow a suitable addition of care in the *Cleanliness* and Sweetness of their Persons. For the satyrical part of Mankind will needs believe, that it is not impossible to be very fine and very filthy; and that the Capacities of a lady are sometimes apt to fall short in cultivating Cleanliness and Finery together. . . .

I am wholly at a loss how to advise you in the choice of *Company*, which, however, is a point of as great importance as any in your life. If your general Acquaintance be among Ladies who are your equals or superiors, provided they have nothing of what is commonly call'd an ill Reputation, you think you are safe; and this in the Style of the world will pass for good Company. Whereas I am afraid it will be hard for you to pick out one Female Acquaintance in this town, from whom you will not be in manifest danger of contracting some Foppery, Affectation, Vanity, Folly, or Vice. Your only safe way of conversing with them, is by a firm resolution to proceed in your Practice and Behaviour directly contrary to whatever they shall say or do. And this I take to be a good general rule, with very few exceptions. For instance, in the doctrines they usually deliver to young married Women in managing their Husbands; their several Accounts of their own Conduct in that particular, to recommend it to your imitation; the Reflections they make upon others of their sex for acting differently; their Directions how to come off with Victory upon any Dispute or Quarrel you may have with your husband; the Arts by which you may discover and practise upon his weak side; when to work by Flattery and Insinuation, when to melt him with Tears, and when to engage with a high Hand. In these, and a thousand other cases, it will be prudent to retain as many of their lectures in your memory as you can, and then determine to act in full Opposition to them all.

I hope your Husband will interpose his Authority to limit you in the trade of *Visiting:* half a dozen Fools are in all conscience as many as you should require; and it will be sufficient for you to see them twice a year. For I think, the Fashion does not exact, that Visits would be paid to Friends.

I advise, that your Company at home should consist of Men, rather than Women. To say the truth, I never yet knew a tolerable Woman to be fond of her own Sex. I confess, when both are mixed and well chosen, and put their best Qualities forward, there may be an Intercourse of civility and good-will; which, with the addition of some degree of Sense, can make conversation or any amusement agreeable. But a knot of Ladies, got together by themselves, is a very school of Impertinence and Detraction, and it is well if those be the worst.

Let your Men-Acquaintance be of your Husband's choice, and not recommended to you by any she-companions; because they will certainly fix a Coxcomb upon you, and it will cost you some time and pains, before you can arrive at the knowledge of distinguishing such a one from a Man of Sense.

Never take a *favourite Waiting-Maid* into your cabinet-council, to entertain you with Histories of those ladies, whom she hath formerly served, of their Diversions and their Dresses; to insinuate how great a Fortune you brought, and how little you are allowed to squander; to appeal to her from your husband, and to be determined by her judgment, because you are sure it will be always for you; to receive and discard Servants by her approbation, or dislike; to engage you, by her Insinuations, into Misunderstandings with your best Friends; to represent all things in false colours, and to be the common Emissary of Scandal.

But the grand Affair of your Life will be to gain and preserve the Friendship and Esteem of your *Husband*. You are married to a man of good Education and Learning, of an excellent understanding, and an exact Taste. It is true, and it is happy for you, that these qualities in him are adorned with great Modesty, a most amiable Sweetness of Temper, and an unusual disposition to Sobriety and Virtue. But neither good-nature nor virtue will suffer him to *esteem* you against his Judgment; and although he is not capable of using you ill, yet you will in time grow a thing indifferent and perhaps contemptible; unless you can supply the loss of Youth and Beauty with more durable qualities. You have but a very few Years to be young and handsome in the eyes of the World; and as few Months to be so in the eyes of a Husband, who is not a Fool; for I hope you do not still dream of Charms and Raptures, which Marriage ever did, and will, put a sudden end to. Besides, yours was a match of Prudence and common good-liking, without any mixture of that ridiculous Passion, which has no Being but in Play-books and Romances. . . .

As little Respect as I have for the generality of your Sex, it hath sometimes moved me with Pity, to see the Lady of the house forced to withdraw immediately after dinner, and this in Families where there is not much drinking; as if it were an established maxim, that Women are uncapable of all Conversation. In a room where both sexes meet, if the Men are discoursing upon any general subject, the Ladies never think it their business to partake in what passes, but in a separate club entertain each other with the Price and Choice of Lace, and Silk, and what Dresses they liked or disapproved at the Church or the Play-house. And when you are among yourselves, how naturally, after the first compliments, do you apply your hands to each others Lappets and Ruffles and Mantua's, as if the whole Business of your lives, and the publick Concern of the World,

Coxcomb: conceited fool.

depended upon the Cut or Colour of your dresses. As Divines say, that some people take more pains to be damned, than it would cost them to be saved; so your Sex employs more Thought, Memory, and Application to be fools, than would serve to make them wise and useful. When I reflect on this, I cannot conceive you to be human Creatures, but a sort of Species hardly a degree above a Monkey; who has more diverting Tricks than any of you, is an animal less mischievous and expensive, might in time be a tolerable critick in Velvet and Brocade, and, for ought I know, would equally become them.

I would have you look upon Finery as a necessary Folly, as all great Ladies did, whom I have ever known. I do not desire you to be out of the Fashion, but to be the last and least in it. I expect that your Dress shall be one degree lower than your fortune can afford; and in your own heart I would wish you to be an utter Contemner of all Distinctions which a finer Petticoat can give you; because it will neither make you richer, handsomer, younger, better-natured, more virtuous, or wise, than if it hung upon a Peg.

If you are in company with men of learning, though they happen to discourse of Arts and Sciences out of your compass, yet you will gather more Advantage by listening to them, than from all the Nonsense and Frippery of your own Sex; but if they be Men of Breeding as well as Learning, they will seldom engage in any conversation where you ought not to be a Hearer, and in time have your part. If they talk of the Manners and Customs of the several Kingdoms of *Europe*, of Travels into remoter Nations, of the State of their own Country, or of the great men and actions of *Greece* and *Rome*; if they give their judgment upon *English* and *French* Writers, either in Verse or Prose, or of the nature and limits of Virtue and Vice, it is a shame for an *English* Lady not to relish such discourses, not to improve by them, and endeavour, by reading and information, to have her Share in those entertainments, rather than turn aside, as is the usual custom, and consult with the Woman, who sits next her, about a new cargo of Fans.

It is a little hard, that not one Gentleman's Daughter in a thousand should be brought to read or understand her own natural Tongue, or be judge of the easiest Books that are written in it, as any one may find, who can have the Patience to hear them, when they are disposed to mangle a Play or a Novel, where the least Word out of the common road is sure to disconcert them. It is no wonder, when they are not so much as taught to spell in their childhood, nor can ever attain to it in their whole lives. I advise you therefore to read aloud, more or less, every day to your Husband, if he will permit you, or to any other Friend (but not a female one), who is able to set you right; and as for spelling, you may compass it in time, by making collections from the books you read.

I know very well, that those who are commonly called Learned Women, have lost all manner of credit by their impertinent Talkativeness and Conceit of themselves: but there is an easy Remedy for this, if you once consider, that after all the pains you may be at, you never can arrive in point of learning to the perfection of a School-boy. The Reading I would advise you to, is only for improvement of your own good Sense, which will never fail of being mended by Discretion. It is a wrong method, and ill Choice of Books, that makes those learned ladies just so much worse for what they have read. And therefore it shall be my Care to direct you better, a Task for which I take myself to be not ill qualified; because I have spent more time, and have had more opportunities than many others, to observe and discover from what Sources the various Follies of Women are derived....

There is never wanting in this Town a Tribe of bold, swaggering, rattling Ladies, whose Talents pass among Coxcombs for Wit and Humour; their Excellency lies in rude choquing Expressions, and what they call *running a Man down*. If a Gentleman in their company happens to have any Blemish in his birth or person, if any Misfortune hath befallen his Family or himself for which he is ashamed, they will be sure to give him broad Hints of it without any provocation. I would recommend you to the acquaintance of a common Prostitute, rather than to that of such Termagants as these. I have often thought that no man is obliged to suppose such Creatures to be Women; but to treat them like insolent Rascals disguised in female habits, who ought to be stript and kickt down stairs....

I desire you will keep this Letter in your cabinet, and often examine impartially your whole Conduct by it. And so God bless you and make you a fair Example to your Sex, and a perpetual Comfort to your Husband, and your Parents. I am with great Truth and Affection

MADAM
Your most faithful Friend, and humble Servant.

If Jonathan Swift seems to be the model for Theophrastus' tactless man, Lord Chesterfield doesn't seem to be much better. He appears to have a genius for saying the things no son wants to hear from his father. The following letter is not the only example of his talent for alienating people: he also provoked Samuel Johnson's letter, offered in Chapter 13, which became one of the world's most famous put-downs. Compounding the sins of this letter to his son, he quotes Pope incorrectly.

Philip Stanhope, Lord Chesterfield

Letter to His Son

(1746)

Bath, October 4, O.S. 1746

Dear Boy,

Though I employ so much of my time in writing to you, I confess I have often my doubts whether it is to any purpose. I know how unwel-

Termagants: nagging women.

come advice generally is; I know that those who want it most, like it and follow it least; and I know, too, that the advice of parents, more particularly, is ascribed to the moroseness, the imperiousness, or the garrulity of old age. But then, on the other hand, I flatter myself, that as your own reason, though too young as yet to suggest much to you of itself, is however, strong enough to enable you, both to judge of, and receive plain truths: I flatter myself (I say) that your own reason, young as it is, must tell you, that I can have no interest but yours in the advice I give you; and that consequently you will at least weigh and consider it well: in which case, some of it will, I hope, have its effect. Do not think that I mean to dictate as a parent; I only mean to advise as a friend, and an indulgent one too: and do not apprehend that I mean to check your pleasures; of which, on the contrary, I only desire to be the guide, not the censor. Let my experience supply your want of it, and clear your way, in the progress of your youth, of those thorns and briars which scratched and disfigured me in the course of mine. I do not, therefore, so much as hint to you, how absolutely dependent you are upon me; that you neither have, nor can have a shilling in the world but from me; and that, as I have no womanish weakness for your person, your merit must, and will, be the only measure of my kindness. I say, I do not hint these things to you, because I am convinced that you will act right, upon more noble and generous principles: I mean, for the sake of doing right, and out of affection and gratitude to me.

I have so often recommended to you attention and application to whatever you learn, that I do not mention them now as duties; but I point them out to you as conducive, nay, absolutely necessary to your pleasures; for can there be a greater pleasure than to be universally allowed to excel those of one's own age and manner of life? And, consequently, can there be anything more mortifying than to be excelled by them? In this latter case, your shame and regret must be greater than anybody's, because everybody knows the uncommon care which has been taken of your education, and the opportunities you have had of knowing more than others of your age. I do not confine the application which I recommend, singly to the view and emulation of excelling others (though that is a very sensible pleasure and a very warrantable pride); but I mean likewise to excel in the thing itself; for, in my mind, one may as well not know a thing at all, as know it but imperfectly. To know a little of anything, gives neither satisfaction nor credit; but often brings disgrace or ridicule.

Mr. Pope says, very truly,

> A little knowledge is a dangerous thing;
> Drink deep, or taste not the Castalian spring.

And what is called a *smattering* of everything, infallibly constitutes a coxcomb. I have often, of late, reflected what an unhappy man I must now have been, if I had not acquired in my youth some fund and taste of learning. What could I have done with myself, at this age, without them?

A little knowledge: Pope's lines are, "A little learning is a dangerous thing;/ Drink deep, or taste not the Pierian Spring," from his "Essay on Criticism."

I must, as many ignorant people do, have destroyed my health and faculties by sotting away the evenings; or, by wasting them frivolously in the tattle of women's company, must have exposed myself to the ridicule and contempt of those very women; or, lastly, I must have hanged myself, as a man once did, for weariness of putting on and pulling off his shoes and stockings every day. My books, and only my books, are now left me; and I daily find what Cicero says of learning, to be true: *Hæc studia* (says he) *adolescentium alunt, senectutem oblectant, secundas res ornant, adversis perfugium ac solatium præbent, delectant domi, non impediunt foris, pernoctant nobiscum, peregrinantur, rusticantur.*

I do not mean, by this, to exclude conversation out of the pleasures of an advanced age; on the contrary, it is a very great and a very rational pleasure, at all ages; but the conversation of the ignorant is no conversation, and gives even them no pleasure: they tire of their own sterility, and have not matter enough to furnish them with words to keep up a conversation.

Let me, therefore, most earnestly recommend to you to hoard up, while you can, a great stock of knowledge; for though, during the dissipation of your youth, you may not have occasion to spend much of it, yet, you may depend upon it, that a time will come when you will want it to maintain you. Public granaries are filled in plentiful years; not that it is known that the next, or the second, or third year will prove a scarce one; but because it is known, that, sooner or later, such a year will come, in which the grain will be wanted.

I will say no more to you upon this subject; you have Mr. Harte with you to enforce it; you have Reason to assent to the truth of it; so that, in short, "you have Moses and the Prophets; if you will not believe them, neither will you believe, though one rose from the dead." Do not imagine that the knowledge which I so much recommend to you, is confined to books, pleasing, useful, and necessary as that knowledge is: but I comprehend in it the great knowledge of the world, still more necessary than that of books. In truth, they assist one another reciprocally; and no man will have either perfectly, who has not both. The knowledge of the world is only to be acquired in the world, and not in a closet. Books alone will never teach it you; but they will suggest many things to your observation, which might otherwise escape you; and your own observations upon mankind, when compared with those which you will find in books, will help you to fix the true point.

To know mankind well, requires full as much attention and application as to know books, and, it may be, more sagacity and discernment. I am at this time, acquainted with many elderly people, who have all passed their whole lives in the great world, but with such levity and inattention, that

---

sotting: excessive drinking.
Hæc . . . rusticantur: "These studies nourish youth, please old age, adorn good fortune, offer a refuge and solace in adversity; they delight at home and do no harm in public places; they share the night with us, travel abroad with us, dwell in the country with us."
Mr. Harte: his private tutor.

they know no more of it now, than they did at fifteen. Do not flatter yourself, therefore, with the thought that you can acquire this knowledge in the frivolous chit-chat of idle companies; no, you must go much deeper than that. You must look into people, as well as at them. Almost all people are born with all the passions, to a certain degree; but almost every man has a prevailing one, to which the others are subordinate. Search every one for that ruling passion; pry into the recesses of his heart, and observe the different workings of the same passion in different people. And, when you have found out the prevailing passion of any man, remember never to trust him where that passion is concerned. Work upon him by it, if you please; but be upon your guard yourself against it, whatever professions he may make you.

I would desire you to read this letter twice over, but that I much doubt whether you will read once to the end of it. I will trouble you no longer now; but we will have more upon this subject hereafter. Adieu.

I have this moment received your letter from Schaffhausen: in the date of it you forgot the month.

Knowing Mark Twain, we would expect a different sort of advice from him, and we are not disappointed. He offers an amiable antidote for those who have had too large a dose of Chesterfield and Swift.

Mark Twain

Advice to Youth

(1882)

Being told I would be expected to talk here, I inquired what sort of a talk I ought to make. They said it should be something suitable to youth—something didactic, instructive, or something in the nature of good advice. Very well. I have a few things in my mind which I have often longed to say for the instruction of the young; for it is in one's tender early years that such things will best take root and be most enduring and most valuable. First, then, I will say to you, my young friends—and I say it beseechingly, urgingly——

Always obey your parents, when they are present. This is the best policy in the long run, because if you don't they will make you. Most parents think they know better than you do, and you can generally make more by humoring that superstition than you can by acting on your own better judgment.

Be respectful to your superiors, if you have any, also to strangers, and sometimes to others. If a person offend you, and you are in doubt as to whether it was intentional or not, do not resort to extreme measures; simply watch your chance and hit him with a brick. That will be sufficient. If you shall find that he had not intended any offense, come out frankly and confess yourself in the wrong when you struck him; acknowledge it like a man and say you didn't mean to. Yes, always avoid violence; in this age of charity and kindliness, the time has gone by for such things. Leave dynamite to the low and unrefined.

Go to bed early, get up early—this is wise. Some authorities say get up with the sun; some others say get up with one thing, some with another. But a lark is really the best thing to get up with. It gives you a splendid reputation with everybody to know that you get up with the lark; and if you get the right kind of a lark, and work at him right, you can easily train him to get up at half past nine, every time—it is no trick at all.

Now as to the matter of lying. You want to be very careful about lying; otherwise you are nearly sure to get caught. Once caught, you can never again be, in the eyes of the good and the pure, what you were before. Many a young person has injured himself permanently through a single clumsy and ill-finished lie, the result of carelessness born of incomplete training. Some authorities hold that the young ought not to lie at all. That, of course, is putting it rather stronger than necessary; still, while I cannot go quite so far as that, I do maintain, and I believe I am right, that the young ought to be temperate in the use of this great art until practice and experience shall give them that confidence, elegance, and precision which alone can make the accomplishment graceful and profitable. Patience, diligence, painstaking attention to detail—these are the requirements; these, in time, will make the student perfect; upon these, and upon these only, may he rely as the sure foundation for future eminence. Think what tedious years of study, thought, practice, experience, went to the equipment of that peerless old master who was able to impose upon the whole world the lofty and sounding maxim that "truth is mighty and will prevail"—the most majestic compound fracture of fact which any of woman born has yet achieved. For the history of our race, and each individual's experience, are sown thick with evidence that a truth is not hard to kill and that a lie told well is immortal. There in Boston is a monument of the man who discovered anesthesia; many people are aware, in these latter days, that that man didn't discover it at all, but stole the discovery from another man. Is this truth mighty, and will it prevail? Ah no, my hearers, the monument is made of hardy material, but the lie it tells will outlast it a million years. An awkward, feeble, leaky lie is a thing which you ought to make it your unceasing study to avoid; such a lie as that has no more real permanence than an average truth. Why, you might as well tell the truth at once and be done with it. A feeble, stupid, preposterous lie will not live two years—except it be a slander upon somebody. It is indestructible, then, of course, but that is no merit of yours. A final word: begin your practice of this gracious and beautiful art early—begin now. If I had begun earlier, I could have learned how.

Never handle firearms carelessly. The sorrow and suffering that have been caused through the innocent but heedless handling of firearms by the young! Only four days ago, right in the next farmhouse to the one where I am spending the summer, a grandmother, old and gray and sweet, one of the loveliest spirits in the land, was sitting at her work, when her young grandson crept in and got down an old, battered, rusty gun which had not been touched for many years and was supposed not to be loaded, and pointed it at her, laughing and threatening to shoot. In her fright she ran screaming and pleading toward the door on the other side of the room; but as she passed him he placed the gun almost against her very breast and pulled the trigger! He had supposed it was not loaded. And he was right—it wasn't. So there wasn't any harm done. It is the only case of that kind I ever heard of. Therefore, just the same, don't you meddle with old unloaded firearms; they are the most deadly and unerring things that have ever been created by man. You don't have to take any pains at all with them; you don't have to have a rest, you don't have to have any sights on the gun, you don't have to take aim, even. No, you just pick out a relative and bang away, and you are sure to get him. A youth who can't hit a cathedral at thirty yards with a Gatling gun in three-quarters of an hour, can take up an old empty musket and bag his grandmother every time, at a hundred. Think what Waterloo would have been if one of the armies had been boys armed with old muskets supposed not to be loaded, and the other army had been composed of their female relations. The very thought of it makes one shudder.

There are many sorts of books; but good ones are the sort for the young to read. Remember that. They are a great, an inestimable, an unspeakable means of improvement. Therefore be careful in your selection, my young friends; be very careful; confine yourselves exclusively to Robertson's Sermons, Baxter's *Saint's Rest*, *The Innocents Abroad*, and works of that kind.

But I have said enough. I hope you will treasure up the instructions which I have given you, and make them a guide to your feet and a light to your understanding. Build your character thoughtfully and painstaking upon these precepts, and by and by, when you have got it built, you will be surprised and gratified to see how nicely and sharply it resembles everybody else's.

One of the most famous books of advice is Niccolò Machiavelli's *Prince*. ("Prince" is used to mean any sort of ruler.) It is suspected that many politicians have applied its advice and would not want to admit that they did so. Indeed, *The Prince* has long functioned as the practical politician's handbook. Here is a chapter.

Niccolò Machiavelli

In What Way Princes Must Keep Faith

(1513)

How laudable it is for a prince to keep good faith and live with integrity, and not with astuteness, every one knows. Still the experience of our times shows those princes to have done great things who have had little regard for good faith, and have been able by astuteness to confuse men's brains, and who have ultimately overcome those who have made loyalty their foundation.

You must know, then, that there are two methods of fighting, the one by law, the other by force: the first method is that of men, the second of beasts; but as the first method is often insufficient, one must have recourse to the second. It is therefore necessary for a prince to know well how to use both the beast and the man. This was covertly taught to rulers by ancient writers, who relate how Achilles and many others of those ancient princes were given to Chiron the centaur to be brought up and educated under his discipline. The parable of this semi-animal, semi-human teacher is meant to indicate that a prince must know how to use both natures, and that the one without the other is not durable.

A prince being thus obliged to know well how to act as a beast must imitate the fox and the lion, for the lion cannot protect himself from traps, and the fox cannot defend himself from wolves. One must therefore be a fox to recognise traps, and a lion to frighten wolves. Those that wish to be only lions do not understand this. Therefore, a prudent ruler ought not to keep faith when by so doing it would be against his interest, and when the reasons which made him bind himself no longer exist. If men were all good, this precept would not be a good one; but as they are bad, and would not observe their faith with you, so you are not bound to keep faith with them. Nor have legitimate grounds ever failed a prince who wished to show colourable excuse for the non-fulfillment of his promise. Of this one could furnish an infinite number of modern examples, and show how many times peace has been broken, and how many promises rendered worthless, by the faithlessness of princes, and those that have been best able to imitate the fox have succeeded best. But it is necessary to be able to disguise this character well, and to be a great feigner and dissembler; and men are so simple and so ready to obey present necessities, that one who deceives will always find those who allow themselves to be deceived.

I will only mention one modern instance. Alexander VI did nothing else but deceive men, he thought of nothing else, and found the occasion for it; no man was ever more able to give assurances, or affirmed things with stronger oaths, and no man observed them less; however, he always succeeded in his deceptions, as he well knew this aspect of things.

centaur: a mythical creature, half man, half horse.
feigner: pretender.
Alexander VI: a member of the Borgia family who was Pope from 1492 to 1503.

It is not, therefore, necessary for a prince to have all the above-named qualities, but it is very necessary to seem to have them. I would even be bold to say that to possess them and always to observe them is dangerous, but to appear to possess them is useful. Thus it is well to seem merciful, faithful, humane, sincere, religious, and also to be so; but you must have the mind so disposed that when it is needful to be otherwise you may be able to change to the opposite qualities. And it must be understood that a prince, and especially a new prince, cannot observe all those things which are considered good in men, being often obliged, in order to maintain the state, to act against faith, against charity, against humanity, and against religion. And, therefore, he must have a mind disposed to adapt itself according to the wind, and as the variations of fortune dictate, and, as I said before, not deviate from what is good, if possible, but be able to do evil if constrained.

A prince must take great care that nothing goes out of his mouth which is not full of the above-named five qualities, and, to see and hear him, he should seem to be all mercy, faith, integrity, humanity, and religion. And nothing is more necessary than to seem to have this last quality, for men in general judge more by the eyes than by the hands, for every one can see, but very few have to feel. Everybody sees what you appear to be, few feel what you are, and those few will not dare to oppose themselves to the many, who have the majesty of the state to defend them; and in the actions of men, and especially of princes, from which there is no appeal, the end justifies the means. Let a prince therefore aim at conquering and maintaining the state, and the means will always be judged honourable and praised by every one, for the vulgar is always taken by appearances and the issue of the event; and the world consists only of the vulgar, and the few who are not vulgar are isolated when the many have a rallying point in the prince. A certain prince of the present time, whom it is well not to name, never does anything but preach peace and good faith, but he is really a great enemy to both, and either of them, had he observed them, would have lost him state or reputation on many occasions.

DISCUSSION

1. Whether Swift is being serious or facetious in "To a Young Lady on Her Marriage" is not easy to determine, since he is known both for his satire and his deeply critical attitude toward women. What internal evidence can you find on either side? What is your conclusion?
2. There is no doubt about Lord Chesterfield's intentions; he is entirely serious. Do you find most of his advice basically good, or bad? What is the philosophical basis, or attitude toward life, that lies behind it? What statements support this conclusion?
3. What is implied by the last sentence, the "punch line," of "Advice to Youth"?

vulgar: the common people.

Experiencing and Generalizing

4. In "Advice to Youth," a certain slyness is concealed in the paragraph about firearms. What advice is Mark Twain really giving here? How can you tell?
5. Is "Advice to Youth" ironic or not? (See "A Note on Irony," p. 107).
6. Do any of Mark Twain's recommendations have anything in common with Machiavelli's? Which ones? In what way are they similar?
7. *The Prince* has generally been taken seriously. However, Machiavelli wrote it after a new administration (so to speak) had fired him and thrown him out of the country. Can you make a case, from the chapter given here, that it is not advice on how princes should behave but satire on how they do behave?
8. Assuming that Machiavelli's advice is offered in all seriousness, it clearly recommends opportunism rather than idealism for the ruler. It suggests that what is desirable is getting and keeping power, deceiving the people, and creating a good "image" to conceal that one is not really good. What do you feel are the moral implications of writing such a book? Do you think a good man would have refrained from writing it? Why, or why not?
9. What are the philosophical implications of *The Prince*, as nearly as you can judge from this single chapter? That is, what does it imply about the nature of the universe Machiavelli believes in and his belief about the nature of mankind?

WRITING SUGGESTIONS

1. Both Swift's letter to the bride and Chesterfield's to his son seem to invite *parody*—burlesque imitation exaggerating the comic qualities that are already there. Write a letter to a modern bride advising her how to make her husband happy or write a letter from a modern father to his son, repeating all the unwelcome clichés that fathers tend to use in giving sons advice.
2. A variation of the above suggestion is to reverse the situation. Write a letter to a newly wed husband on how to be good to his wife or a letter from a son giving his father the benefit of his worldy wisdom.
3. By pretending to give advice, it is possible to make fun of someone. Tom Brown, a wit of about Swift's time, wrote a letter that purported to be from an experienced wine seller to a young man entering the trade, in which he advised him on how to water his wine, how to sell his worst wine at high prices, and so on. Try writing a letter of advice to a novice in one of the following trades.

    A secondhand car dealer
    A plumber
    A beggar (see "Tribulations of a Cheerful Giver" in Chapter 9 for hints)
    A pickpocket
    A politician (see "In What Way Princes Must Keep Faith" in this chapter)
    A writer of popular novels
    A portrait photographer
    An airline hostess
    A rooming-house landlady (see "Hall-Bedrooms" in Chapter 1)

A fortuneteller
An antique dealer

4. Write a chapter from your own book, *How to Be a Successful Politician.* The chapter might be about

What to Say in Speeches
How to Appear on Television
What to Do When the Scandal Breaks
How to Deal with Honest Opponents
Who You Can Afford to Ignore
Who You Cannot Afford to Ignore
How to Create an Image
Friends and How to Reward Them
How to Deal with Reporters

13

Satire and Fable

Satire is ridicule in literary form. The "character" we encountered in Chapter 6 is a form of satire; there are elements of satire in Mark Twain's "House Beautiful" and "Advice to Youth," Jonathan Swift's "City Shower," and Robert Lynd's "Conversation," among others. There are a number of ways a writer can ridicule his subject: he can exaggerate or distort, he can understate, he can parody, he can use allegory (that is, represent abstract ideas as persons as Erasmus does in "Fools Are Happy"), or he can employ the commonest and most effective device, irony. Often, of course, the devices are combined. The writer's purpose may range all the way from simple entertainment to social reform.

Siegfried Sassoon

Base Details

(1918)

If I were fierce, and bald, and short of breath,
  I'd live with scarlet Majors at the Base,
And speed glum heroes up the line to death.
  You'd see me with my puffy petulant face,
Guzzling and gulping in the best hotel,
  Reading the Roll of Honour. 'Poor young chap,'

I'd say—'I used to know his father well;
   Yes, we've lost heavily in this last scrap.'
And when the war is done and youth stone dead,
I'd toddle safely home and die—in bed.

Arthur Hugh Clough

The Latest Decalogue

(1862)

Thou shalt have one God only; who
Would be at the expense of two?
No graven images may be
Worshipped, except the currency:
Swear not at all; for, for thy curse
Thine enemy is none the worse:
At church on Sunday to attend
Will serve to keep the world thy friend:
Honour thy parents; that is, all
From whom advancement may befall;
Thou shalt not kill; but need'st not strive
Officiously to keep alive:
Do not adultery commit;
Advantage rarely comes of it:
Thou shalt not steal; an empty feat,
When it's so lucrative to cheat:
Bear not false witness; let the lie
Have time on its own wings to fly:
Thou shalt not covet, but tradition
Approves all forms of competition.

DISCUSSION

1. What techniques of satire do these two poems have in common?
2. If the purpose of both poets is reform, which poem do you think might be the more effective? Why?
3. Which of the two poems has an important poetic element that is lacking in the other? Does this lack have any connection with its effectiveness?
4. "Chariots Go Forth to War" (p. 306) and "Base Details" are both anti-war poems. The first does not use satire, while the second is entirely satiric. Which do you find communicates the stronger feeling against war? By what means?

5. The title "Base Details" is a double pun. What three meanings does it suggest?

Satire can be conveyed through an ironic tone. In the following letter to Lord Chesterfield, who offered help only when no longer needed, Samuel Johnson simply states the facts and his own feelings without much exaggeration. But the respectful and formal tone in which he writes is opposed to the feelings he expresses, and therein lies his irony.

Samuel Johnson

Letter to Lord Chesterfield

February 7, 1755

My Lord,

I have been lately informed, by the proprietor of the World, that two papers, in which my Dictionary is recommended to the public, were written by your Lordship. To be so distinguished is an honour which, being very little accustomed to favours from the great, I know not well how to receive, or in what terms to acknowledge.

When, upon some slight encouragement, I first visited your Lordship, I was overpowered, like the rest of mankind, by the enchantment of your address, and could not forebear to wish that I might boast myself *Le vainqueur du vainqueur de la terre*—that I might obtain that regard for which I saw the world contending; but I found my attendance so little encouraged, that neither pride nor modesty would suffer me to continue it. When I had once addressed your Lordship in public, I had exhausted all the art of pleasing which a retired and uncourtly scholar can possess. I had done all that I could; and no man is well pleased to have his all neglected, be it ever so little.

Seven years, my Lord, have now passed, since I waited in your outward rooms, or was repulsed from your door; during which time I have been pushing on my work through difficulties, of which it is useless to complain, and have brought it, at last, to the verge of publication, without one act of assistance, one word of encouragement, or one smile of favour. Such treatment I did not expect, for I never had a Patron before.

The shepherd in Virgil grew at last acquainted with Love, and found him a native of the rocks.

Is not a Patron, my Lord, one who looks with unconcern on a man struggling for life in the water, and, when he has reached ground, en-

World: a London newspaper.
Le vainqueur . . . : "The conqueror of the conqueror of the world."
Patron: a wealthy person who supports someone engaged in the arts.

cumbers him with help? The notice which you have been pleased to take of my labours, had it been early, had been kind; but it has been delayed till I am indifferent, and cannot enjoy it; till I am solitary, and cannot impart it; till I am known, and do not want it. I hope it is no very cynical asperity, not to confess obligations where no benefit has been received, or to be unwilling that the public should consider me as owing that to a Patron which Providence has enabled me to do for myself.

Having carried on my work thus far with so little obligation to any favourer of learning, I shall not be disappointed though I should conclude it, if less be possible, with less; for I have long wakened from that dream of hope, in which I once boasted myself with so much exultation,

My Lord,
Your Lordship's most humble
Most obedient servant,
Sam. Johnson

DISCUSSION

1. Although most of the letter is straightforward, there are a few phrases that might be called ironic. What are these phrases? Why would they be called ironic?
2. Since Dr. Johnson is obviously angry, why doesn't he express his feelings more openly to Lord Chesterfield and just "tell him off"? (There are at least two or three good reasons why such an approach would be less effective than the one Johnson chose.)

The next two satirists are in sharp contrast to each other. Both use irony, but whereas Jonathan Swift employs it with savagery to force his readers to face an equally savage social injustice, Erasmus uses it to entertain us by pointing out the kinds of human weakness that are never likely to change. In the book from which the following passage was taken, *In Praise of Folly*, it is Folly herself who speaks, in the form of a goddess of foolishness defending her own worshippers.

Erasmus of Rotterdam

Fools Are Happy

(1510)

... By the gods above, is there anything that is better off than that class of men whom we generally call morons, fools, halfwits, and zanies —the most beautiful names I know of! You see, I am telling you what at first blush may seem silly and absurd but is true many times over. For first of all, these folk are free from all fear of death—and this fear, by Jove, is no piddling evil! They are free from tortures of conscience. They are not frightened by tales of ghosts, or scared to death by specters and goblins. They are not tormented by dread of impending evils, and they are not blown up with hope of future good. In short, they are not vexed by the thousand cares to which this life is subject. They do not feel shame or fear, they are not ambitious, they do not envy, they do not love. And finally, if they should approach even more closely to the irrationality of dumb animals they would not sin, according to the writers of theology. I wish you would think over for me, you wise fool, how by night and by day your soul is torn by so many carking cares; I wish you would gather into one heap all the discommodities of your life: then you will begin to understand from how many evils I have delivered my fools. Remember also that they are continually merry, they play, sing, and laugh; and what is more, they bring to others, wherever they may come, pleasure, jesting, sport, and laughter, as if they were created, by a merciful dispensation of the gods, for this one purpose—to drive away the sadness of human life.

Thus it comes about that, in a world where men are differently affected toward each other, all are at one in their attitude toward these innocents; all seek them out, give them food, keep them warm, embrace them, and give them aid, if occasion rises; and all grant them leave to say and to do what they wish, with impunity. So true it is that no one wishes to hurt them that even wild beasts, by a certain natural sense of their innocence, will refrain from doing them harm. They are indeed held sacred by the gods, especially by me; and not impiously do all men pay such honor to them. Thus kings find such consummate pleasure in my naturals that they cannot eat, or go on a progress, or even pass an hour, without them. The fact is that in some degree they prefer these simpletons to their crabbed wise men, whom yet they support for dignity's sake. That kings have this preference ought not, I suggest, seem remarkable or difficult of explanation: the wise men make a habit of bringing before them only serious matters, and, confident in their learning, will not fear at times "to grate their tender ears with rasping truths"; but fools furnish the one kind of thing that rulers are glad to get from any quarter and in any shape—jests, japes, laughter, pastime.

Notice also this estimable gift of fools, that they alone are frank and ingenuous. What is more praiseworthy than truth? Granted that the proverb of Alcibiades in Plato attributes truth to drunkards and children, yet all its merit is peculiarly mine, even as Euripides witnesses; his famous saying has come down to us: "A fool speaks foolish things." Whatever a fool has in his heart, that he sets also in his face and utters in his speech. But your wise man has two tongues, as this same Euripides mentions, one used for speaking truth, the other for speaking what he judges most opportune at the moment. Black is turned into white by these men of wisdom; they blow hot and cold with the same breath,

progress: a royal journey with an elaborate retinue.

and hidden in the breast they have something quite different from what they frame in speech. With all their felicity, indeed, the princes of earth seem to me most unfortunate in this respect, that they have no one to tell them the truth, but are compelled to have toadies instead of friends. But, some one will say, the ears of princes have an antipathy to truth, and for this reason the princes shun wise counsellors, fearing that possibly one more free than the others will stand forth and dare to speak things true rather than pleasant. Yes, by and large, veracity is disliked by kings. And yet a remarkable thing happens in the experience of my fools: from them not only true things, but even sharp reproaches, will be listened to; so that a statement which, if it came from a wise man's mouth, might be a capital offense, coming from a fool gives rise to incredible delight. Veracity, you know, has a certain authentic power of giving pleasure, if nothing offensive goes with it: but this the gods have granted only to fools. And for more or less the same reasons women are wont to take vast delight in men of this class, women being by nature more inclined to pleasure and toys. And however they may carry on with fools, even if it begins to wax a little too serious, they pass it off as a joke or a game—for the sex is ingenious, especially in veiling its own lapses.

Let me return to the topic of the happiness of fools. After a life lived out in much jollity, with no fear of death, or sense of it, they go straight to the Elysian Fields, there to entertain the pious and idle shades with their jests. Let us go about, then, and compare the lot of the wise man with that of the fool. Fancy some pattern of wisdom to put up against him, a man who wore out his whole boyhood and youth in pursuing the learned disciplines. He wasted the pleasantest time of life in unintermitted watchings, cares, and studies; and through the remaining part of it he never tasted so much as a tittle of pleasure; always frugal, impecunious, sad, austere; unfair and strict toward himself, morose and unamiable to others; afflicted by pallor, leanness, invalidism, sore eyes, premature age and white hair; dying before his appointed day. By the way, what difference does it make when a man of that sort dies? He has never lived. There you have a clear picture of the wise man.

But here those Stoic frogs begin to croak at me again. Nothing, they say, is sadder than madness; flagrant folly is either very near madness, or, what is more likely, it is the same thing. For what is madness but a wandering of the wits? (But they themselves wander the whole way.) Come now, with the Muses prospering us, we shall also tear this syllogism wide open. Subtly argued, indeed; but just as, in Plato, Socrates teaches us to make two Venuses by splitting the usual one, and two Cupids by cutting Cupid apart, so in this case it would behoove our dialecticians to distinguish madness from madness—at least if they wish

---

Stoic frogs: Stoicism was a school of philosophy founded by Zeno (fourth century B.C.). Stoics emphasized individual free will and responsibility, with virtuous action the absolute value by which to live. They believed that happiness could not be obtained except as an occasional and accidental byproduct of virtue.
Muses: goddesses of the arts.

to be thought sane themselves. For certainly all madness is not calamitous. Otherwise Horace would not have said, "Does a dear madness play upon me?" Nor would Plato have placed that friendly fury of poets, prophets, and lovers among the chief blessings of life. Nor would the Sibyl have spoken of the "insane labor" of Aeneas. The fact is that "madness" is a genus comprising two species: one the revenging Furies send secretly from hell whenever, with their snaky locks unbound, they put into the hearts of mortal men lust for war, or insatiable thirst for wealth, shameful and illicit love, parricide, incest, sacrilege, or any other bane of the sort; or when they hound the guilty and stricken soul with fiends or with torch-bearing goblins. The other kind is far different from this. It comes, you see, from me; and of all things is most to be desired. It is present whenever an amiable dotage of the mind at once frees the spirit from carking cares and anoints it with a complex delight. And such a dotage of the mind Cicero, writing to Atticus, wished for as a special bounty of the gods, for thereby he could lose his sense of the great evils of the time. Nor was that Greek in Horace far afield, whose madness took the form of sitting alone in the theater all day long, laughing, applauding, cheering, because he thought fine tragedies were being acted before him (though nothing at all was on the stage); yet he conducted himself acceptably in other relations of life—"pleasant with his friends, kind to his wife, and so indulgent to his servants that they might open a bottle of his wine without his going into a rage." When the care of his family and medical treatment had driven away these fits, and he was fully restored to himself, he protested to his friends. "By Pollux, you have killed me, not saved me," he said, "taking away my enjoyments this way and destroying by force the very pleasant illusion of my mind." And rightly; for they were themselves doting and had more need for hellebore, when they looked upon such a lucky and pleasant delusion as a disease to be driven out by potions.

To be sure, I have not yet decided whether every deviation of the senses or the faculties ought to be called by the name of madness. To a man with weak eyes a mule may seem to be an ass; another man may admire some vulgar song as the finest poetry; neither will forthwith be considered mad. But a man who is deceived not only in his senses but also in the judgment of his mind, and this beyond what is ordinary, and upon all occasions, is bound to be considered as close to madness; if, for example, he thinks he is listening to a fine orchestra whenever he hears an ass braying; or if some beggar, born to low station, believes himself to be Croesus, King of the Lydians. And yet this kind of madness, assum-

the Sibyl: sibyls were women with powers of prophecy who lived alone in caves or beside sacred springs. Aeneas, a refugee from the defeat of Troy, consulted the sibyl at Cumae, who helped him with his "insane labor" of founding Rome. (Virgil's *Aeneid*, Book VI)
Furies: in Greek mythology, three female deities of unpleasant aspect, who hunted down and punished the guilty.
hellebore: a medicinal herb supposed to cure insanity.
Croesus: lived in the sixth century B.C. and noted for his enormous wealth.

ing, as is usually the case, that it tends to give pleasure, can bring a delight above the common both to those who are seized by it and to those who look on but are not mad in the same way. This variety of madness is much more widespread than people generally realize. Thus one madman laughs at another, turn about, and they minister to each other's mutual pleasure. You will often see it happen that the madder man laughs more uproariously at the one who is not so mad.

The fact is that the more ways a man is deluded, the happier he is, if Folly is any judge. Only let him remain in that kind of madness which is peculiarly my own, and which is so widespread that I do not know whether out of the whole world of mortals it is possible to find one who is wise at all times of day, and who is not subject to some extravagance. It may be only that a man seeing a pumpkin believes it is a woman, and others give him the epithet of "mad," simply because so few people share his belief. But when another man swears roundly that his wife (whom he holds in common with many others) is a Penelope, only more virtuous, and thus flatters himself in the key of C-major, happily deluded; nobody calls him mad, because they see that this happens to other husbands here and there.

To this order belong the fellows who renounce everything else in favor of hunting wild game, and protest they feel an ineffable pleasure in their souls whenever they hear the raucous blast of the horns and the yelping of the hounds. Even the dung of the dogs, I am sure, smells like cinnamon to them. And what is so sweet as a beast being butchered? Cutting up bulls and oxen is properly given over to the humble plebeian, but it is a crime for game to be slaughtered except by a gentleman! There, with his head bared, on bended knees, with a knife designed just for this (for it is sacrilege to use any other), with certain ceremonial gestures he cuts just the proper members in the approved order. The company stands in silence, wondering as at some great novelty, although it has seen the same spectacle a thousand times. And if some bit of the animal is handed one of them to taste, he thinks he has gone up a step or so in the ranks of nobility. And thus with their butchering and eating of beasts they accomplish nothing at all unless it be to degenerate into beasts themselves, though they think, all the while, they are living the life of a king.

Very like to these is the class of men who suffer from an incurable itch to be abuilding. They transform round structures into square ones, and presently square ones into round ones. Nor is there any limit, any moderation, in this until by dint of having built themselves into utter poverty, they have nowhere to live and nothing to eat. What then? No matter, they have passed a number of years in complete happiness.

Next to these, it seems to me, come those who keep on trying, by new and secret skills, to transmute the forms of things, and who ransack earth and sea for a certain fifth essence. A honeyed hope cajoles them,

Penelope: Odysseus' wife, who waited faithfully for him during the twenty years of his absence.
fifth essence: the alchemists used to search for a fifth element (in addition to earth, air, fire, and water) that would enable them to make base metals into gold.

so that they begrudge no pains or costs, but with marvellous ingenuity contrive that by which they may deceive themselves; and they go on in this pleasant imposture till, having gone through their possessions, there is not enough left to build a new furnace. Even then they do not leave off dreaming their pleasant dreams, but with all their strength they urge others to seek the same happiness. And when at last they are robbed of all hope, there remains this sentiment as a great solace, "In great things 'tis enough to have tried." Then they complain that life is too brief and does not suffice for the magnitude of their project.

As for gamblers, I have some doubt whether they should be admitted to our college. And yet it is a foolish and wholly ridiculous sight to see some of these addicts; as soon as they hear the rattle of the dice, their hearts leap and begin to beat faster. When, drawn further and further by hope of winning, they have made a wreck of all their resources, splitting the ship on Dice-Box Rock (which is even more deadly than the promontory Malea), and have just come through with their shirts, they choose to defraud anyone else but the winner, for fear they will get the reputation of not being men of their word. And what about those old gamesters, half-blind, who have to wear spectacles to play at all? At the last, when a justly earned gout has tied their joints in knots, they hire an assistant to put the dice into the box for them. A sweet business, indeed, were it not that the game usually passes over into an angry quarrel, so that it appertains to the Furies, not to me.

Here is a sort of men who beyond any doubt bear my trademark wholly —the ones who find joy in either hearing or telling monstrous lies and strange wonders. They never get enough of such stories, so long as prodigies are recounted, involving banshees, goblins, devils, or the like. The farther these are from the truth, the more they tickle the ears of our friends with pleasing sensations. These wonders serve very well to lighten tedious hours, but they also provide a way to make money, particularly for priests and pardoners.

And next to these come the folk who have arrived at the foolish but gratifying belief that if they gaze on a picture of Polyphemus-Christopher they will not die that day, or that whoever salutes in certain prescribed words an image of Barbara will come through a battle unharmed, or that by making application to Erasmus on certain days, using a certain kind of candles and certain prayers, one will shortly become rich. Indeed, they have discovered another Hercules, and even another Hippolytus, in George; whose horse, piously decked out with trappings and bosses, they all but worship, often commending themselves to him by some little gift; while to swear by St. George's brass helmet is an oath

---

Malea: Cape Malea, a promontory at the southern tip of Greece, long a hazard to sailors.
pardoners: people through whom one could pay money to the Church and thus be pardoned for a sin. The pardon was called an indulgence.
Polyphemus-Christopher, and so on: the names in this paragraph are those of Christian saints and their pagan counterparts to whom people offered prayers for help.

for a king. Then what shall I say of the people who so happily fool themselves with forged pardons for sins, measuring out time to be spent in purgatory as if with an hour-glass, and figuring its centuries, years, months, days, and hours as if from a mathematical table, beyond possibility of error? Or I might speak of those who will promise themselves any and every thing, relying upon certain charms or prayers devised by some pious impostor either for his soul's sake or for money, to bring them wealth, reputation, pleasure, plenty, good health, long life, and a green old age, and at last a seat next to Christ's in heaven—but they do not wish to get it too soon. That is to say, when the pleasures of this life have finally failed them, willy-nilly, though they struggled tooth and nail to hold on to them, then it is time for the bliss of heaven to arrive.

I fancy that I see some merchant or soldier or judge laying down one small coin from his extensive booty and expecting that the whole cesspool of his life will be at once purified. He conceives that just so many perjuries, so many lustful acts, so many debauches, so many fights, murders, frauds, lies, and so many breaches of faith, are bought off as by contract; and so bought off that with a clean slate he may start from scratch upon a new round of sins. And who are more foolish, yet who more happy, than those who promise themselves something more than the highest felicity if they daily recite those seven verses of the *Psalms?* The seven, I mean, which some devil, a playful one, but blabbing rather than crafty, is believed to have pointed out to St. Bernard after he had been duped by the saint's trick. Things like that are so foolish, you know, that I am almost ashamed of them myself; yet they stand approved not only by the common people but even by teachers of religion. And is it not almost as bad when the several countries each lay claim to a particular saint of their own, and then assign particular powers respectively to the various saints and observe for each one his own peculiar rites of worship? One saint assists in time of toothache, another in propitious to women in travail, another recovers stolen goods, a fourth stands by with help in a shipwreck, and still another keeps the sheep in good repair; and so of the rest, though it would take too long to specify all of them. Some of them are good for a number of purposes, particularly the Virgin Mother, to whom the common people tend to attribute more than to the Son.

Yet what do men ask of these saints except things that pertain to folly? Think a bit: among all those consecrated gifts which you see covering the walls of some churches, and even hung on the ceiling, do you ever find one given in gratitude for an escape from folly, or because the giver has been made any whit wiser? One person has come safe to land. A second survived being run through in a duel. One no less fortunately than bravely got away from a battlefield, leaving the rest to fight. Another was brought near to the gallows, but by favor of some saint who is friendly to thieves he has decided that he should go on relieving those who are burdened with too much wealth. Another escaped in a jail-break. Another came through a fever, in spite of his doctor. The poisoned drink of another, by loosening his bowels, served to cure him instead of kill him, not at all to the joy of his wife, who lost both her labor and her expenses. Another's cart was turned over, but he drove both horses home safely. Another was dug out of the debris of a fallen house. Another, caught in the act by a husband, made good his escape. No one gives thanks for a recovery from being a fool. So sweet it is not to be wise that mortal men will pray to be delivered from anything sooner than from Folly.

DISCUSSION

1. Since Folly is doing the talking, we would expect all her statements to be foolish and to be opposed to our own beliefs and those of the author. Is this the case or do some of her statements make sense? If so, which ones?
2. In this passage, there is an orderly progression from one kind of fool to another. How are the kinds of fools described in the last pages different from those in the first? What is the reason for this shift—that is, how does it function as satire? What is the effect on the reader?
3. Are all kinds of fools really happy or is there a double irony in parts of this passage in which the unhappy are described as happy? If so, what are some examples?

"A Modest Proposal" is Jonathan Swift's reaction to England's treatment of the Irish. In effect he is saying, "Since it is obvious from your actions that you do not regard the Irish as human, here is a nonhuman solution to the Irish problem." His weapon is irony.

Jonathan Swift

A Modest Proposal

(1729)

It is a melancholy object to those who walk through this great town, or travel in the country, when they see the streets, the roads, and cabin doors crowded with beggars of the female sex, followed by three, four, or six children, all in rags, and importuning every passenger for an alms. These mothers, instead of being able to work for their honest livelihood, are forced to employ all their time in strolling to beg sustenance for their helpless infants; who, as they grow up, either turn thieves, for want of work, or leave their dear native country to fight for the pretender in Spain, or sell themselves to the Barbadoes.

this great town: Dublin.
Barbadoes: island in the West Indies where men could sell themselves as slaves.

I think it is agreed by all parties, that this prodigious number of children in the arms, or on the backs, or at the heels of their mothers, and frequently of their fathers, is, in the present deplorable state of the kingdom, a very great additional grievance; and therefore whoever could find out a fair, cheap, and easy method of making these children sound useful members of the commonwealth, would deserve so well of the public, as to have his statue set up for a preserver of the nation.

But my intention is very far from being confined to provide only for the children of professed beggars: it is of a much greater extent, and shall take in the whole number of infants at a certain age, who are born of parents in effect as little able to support them, as those who demand our charity in the streets.

As to my own part, having turned by thoughts for many years upon this important subject, and maturely weighed the several schemes of our projectors, I have always found them grossly mistaken in their computation. It is true, a child just dropped from its dam may be supported by her milk for a solar year, with little other nourishment: at most not above the value of two shillings, which the mother may certainly get, or the value in scraps, by her lawful occupation of begging; and it is exactly at one year old that I propose to provide for them in such a manner, as, instead of being a charge upon their parents, or the parish, or wanting food and raiment for the rest of their lives, they shall, on the contrary, contribute to the feeding, and partly to the clothing of many thousands.

There is likewise another great advantage in my scheme, that it will prevent those voluntary abortions, and that horrid practice of women murdering their bastard children, alas too frequent among us! sacrificing the poor innocent babes, I doubt more to avoid the expense than the shame, which would move tears and pity in the most savage and inhuman breast.

The number of souls in this kingdom being usually reckoned one million and a half, of these I calculate there may be about two hundred thousand couple whose wives are breeders; from which number I subtract thirty thousand couple, who are able to maintain their own children (although I apprehend there cannot be so many, under the present distresses of the kingdom); but this being granted, there will remain a hundred and seventy thousand breeders. I again subtract fifty thousand, for those women who miscarry, or whose children die by accident or disease within the year. There only remain a hundred and twenty thousand children of poor parents annually born. The question therefore is, How this number sh ll be reared and provided for? which, as I have already said, under the present situation of affairs, is utterly impossible by all the methods hitherto proposed. For we can neither employ them in handicraft or agriculture; we neither build houses (I mean in the country), nor cultivate land; they can very seldom pick up a livelihood by stealing, till they arrive at six years old, except where they are of towardly parts; although I confess they learn the rudiments much earlier; during which time they can however be properly looked upon only as probationers; as I have been informed by a principal gentleman in the county of Cavan, who protested to me, that he never knew above one or two instances under the age of six, even in a part of the kingdom so renowned for the quickest proficiency in that art.

I am assured by our merchants, that a boy or a girl before twelve years old is no saleable commodity; and even when they come to this age they will not yield above three pounds, or three pounds and half-a-crown at most, on the exchange; which cannot turn to account either to the parents or kingdom, the charge of nutriment and rags having been at least four times that value.

I shall now therefore humbly propose my own thoughts, which I hope will not be liable to the least objection.

I have been assured by a very knowing American of my acquaintance in London, that a young healthy child, well nursed, is at a year old a most delicious, nourishing, and wholesome food, whether stewed, roasted, baked, or boiled; and I make no doubt that it will equally serve in a fricassee or a ragout.

I do therefore humbly offer it to public consideration, that of the hundred and twenty thousand children already computed, twenty thousand may be reserved for breed, whereof only one-fourth part to be males; which is more than we allow to sheep, black-cattle, or swine; and my reason is, that these children are seldom the fruits of marriage, a circumstance not much regarded by our savages, therefore one male will be sufficient to serve four females. That the remaining hundred thousand may, at a year old, be offered in sale to the persons of quality and fortune through the kingdom; always advising the mother to let them suck plentifully in the last month, so as to render them plump and fat for a good table. A child will make two dishes at an entertainment for friends; and when the family dines alone, the fore or hind quarter will make a reasonable dish, and seasoned with a little pepper or salt, will be very good boiled on the fourth day, especially in winter.

I have reckoned, upon a medium, that a child just born will weigh twelve pounds, and in a solar year, if tolerably nursed, will increase to twenty-eight pounds.

I grant this food will be somewhat dear, and therefore very proper for landlords, who, as they have already devoured most of the parents, seem to have the best title to the children.

Infants' flesh will be in season throughout the year, but more plentifully in March, and a little before and after: for we are told by a grave author, an eminent French physician, that fish being a prolific diet, there are more children born in Roman catholic countries about nine months after Lent, than at any other season; therefore, reckoning a year after Lent, the markets will be more glutted than usual, because the number of popish infants is at least three to one in this kingdom; and therefore it will have one other collateral advantage, by lessening the number of papists among us.

I have already computed the charge of nursing a beggar's child (in which list I reckon all cottagers, labourers, and four-fifths of the farmers) to be about two shillings per annum, rags included; and I believe no gentleman would repine to give ten shillings for the carcass of a good fat child, which, as I have said, will make four dishes of excellent nutritive meat, when he has only some particular friend or his own family to dine with him. Thus the squire will learn to be a good landlord, and grow popular among his tenants; the mother will have eight shillings neat profit, and be fit for work till she produces another child.

Those who are more thrifty (as I must confess the times require) may flay the carcass; the skin of which, artificially dressed, will make admirable gloves for ladies, and summer-boots for fine gentlemen.

As to our city of Dublin, shambles may be appointed for this purpose in the most convenient parts of it, and butchers we may be assured will not be wanting; although I rather recommend buying the children alive, than dressing them hot from the knife, as we do roasting pigs.

A very worthy person, a true lover of his country, and whose virtues I highly esteem, was lately pleased, in discoursing on this matter, to offer a refinement upon my scheme. He said, that many gentlemen of this kingdom, having of late destroyed their deer, he conceived that the want of venison might be well supplied by the bodies of young lads and maidens, not exceeding fourteen years of age, nor under twelve; so great a number of both sexes in every county being now ready to starve for want of work and service; and these to be disposed of by their parents if alive, or otherwise by their nearest relations. But with due deference to so excellent a friend, and so deserving a patriot, I cannot be altogether in his sentiments; for as to the males, my American acquaintance assured me, from frequent experience, that their flesh was generally tough and lean, like that of our schoolboys, by continual exercise, and their taste disagreeable; and to fatten them would not answer the charge. Then as to the females, it would, I think, with humble submission, be a loss to the public, because they soon would become breeders themselves: and besides, it is not improbable that some scrupulous people might be apt to censure such a practice, (although indeed very unjustly) as a little bordering upon cruelty; which, I confess, has always been with me the strongest objection against any project, how well soever intended.

But in order to justify my friend, he confessed that this expedient was put into his head by the famous Psalmanazar, a native of the island Formosa, who came from thence to London above twenty years ago; and in conversation told my friend, that in his country, when any young person happened to be put to death, the executioner sold the carcass to persons of quality as a prime dainty; and that in his time the body of a plump girl of fifteen, who was crucified for an attempt to poison the emperor, was sold to his imperial majesty's prime-minister of state, and other great mandarins of the court, in joints from the gibbet at four hundred crowns. Neither indeed can I deny, that if the same use were made of several plump young girls in this town, who without one single groat to their fortunes, cannot stir abroad without a chair, and appear at a playhouse and assemblies in foreign fineries which they never will pay for, the kingdom would not be the worse.

Some persons of a desponding spirit are in great concern about that

flay: skin.
groat: fourpence.

vast number of poor people who are aged, diseased, or maimed; and I have been desired to employ my thoughts, what course may be taken to ease the nation of so grievous an incumbrance. But I am not in the least pain upon that matter, because it is very well known, that they are every day dying, and rotting, by cold and famine, and filth and vermin, as fast as can be reasonably expected. And as to the young labourers, they are now in almost as hopeful a condition: they cannot get work, and consequently pine away for want of nourishment, to a degree, that if at any time they are accidentally hired to common labour, they have not strength to perform it; and thus the country and themselves are happily delivered from the evils to come.

I have too long digressed, and therefore shall return to my subject. I think the advantages by the proposal which I have made, are obvious and many, as well as of the highest importance.

For first, as I have already observed, it would greatly lessen the number of papists, with whom we are yearly over-run, being the principal breeders of the nation, as well as our most dangerous enemies; and who stay at home on purpose to deliver the kingdom to the pretender, hoping to take their advantage by the absence of so many good protestants, who have chosen rather to leave their country, than stay at home and pay tithes against their conscience to an episcopal curate.

Secondly, The poorer tenants will have something valuable of their own, which by law may be made liable to distress, and help to pay their landlord's rent; their corn and cattle being already seized, and money a thing unknown.

Thirdly, Whereas the maintenance of a hundred thousand children, from two years old and upward, cannot be computed at less than ten shillings a piece per annum, the nation's stock will be thereby increased fifty thousand pounds per annum, beside the profit of a new dish introduced to the tables of all gentlemen of fortune in the kingdom, who have any refinement in taste. And the money will circulate among ourselves, the goods being entirely of our own growth and manufacture.

Fourthly, The constant breeders, beside the gain of eight shillings sterling per annum by the sale of their children, will be rid of the charge of maintaining them after the first year.

Fifthly, This food would likewise bring great custom to taverns; where the vintners will certainly be so prudent as to procure the best receipts for dressing it to perfection, and consequently, have their houses frequented by all the fine gentlemen, who justly value themselves upon their knowledge in good eating: and a skilful cook, who understands how to oblige his guests, will contrive to make it as expensive as they please.

Sixthly, This would be a great inducement to marriage, which all wise nations have either encouraged by rewards, or enforced by laws and penalties. It would increase the care and tenderness of mothers toward their children, when they were sure of a settlement for life to the poor babes, provided in some sort by the public, to their annual profit or expense. We should see an honest emulation among the married women which of them could bring the fattest child to the market. Men would become as fond of their wives during the time of their pregnancy, as they are now of the mares in foal, their cows in calf, their sows when they are ready to farrow; nor offer to beat or kick them (as is too frequent a practice) for fear of a miscarriage.

Many other advantages might be enumerated. For instance, the addition of some thousand carcasses in our exportation of barreled beef; the propagation of swine's flesh, and improvement in the art of making good bacon, so much wanted among us by the great destruction of pigs, too frequent at our table; which are no way comparable in taste or magnificence to a well grown, fat, yearling child, which roasted whole will make a considerable figure at a lord mayor's feast, or any other public entertainment. But this, and many others, I omit, being studious of brevity.

Supposing that one thousand families in this city would be constant customers for infants' flesh, beside others who might have it at merrymeetings, particularly at weddings and christenings, I compute that Dublin would take off annually about twenty thousand carcasses; and the rest of the kingdom (where probably they will be sold somewhat cheaper) the remaining eighty thousand.

I can think of no one objection, that will possibly be raised against this proposal, unless it should be urged, that the number of people will be thereby much lessened in the kingdom. This I freely own, and it was indeed one principal design in offering it to the world. I desire the reader will observe, that I calculate my remedy for this one individual kingdom of Ireland, and for no other that ever was, is, or I think ever can be upon earth. Therefore let no man talk to me of other expedients: of taxing our absentees at five shillings a pound: of using neither clothes, nor household-furniture, except what is our own growth and manufacture: of utterly rejecting the materials and instruments that promote foreign luxury: of curing the expensiveness of pride, vanity, idleness, and gaming in our women: of introducing a vein of parsimony, prudence and temperance; of learning to love our country, in the want of which we differ even from LALANDERS, and the inhabitants of TOPINAMBOO: of quitting our animosities and factions, nor acting any longer like the Jews, who were murdering one another at the very moment their city was taken: of being a little cautious not to sell our country and conscience for nothing: of teaching landlords to have at least one degree of mercy toward their tenants: lastly, of putting a spirit of honesty, industry, and skill into our shopkeepers; who, if a resolution could now be taken to buy only our negative goods, would immediately unite to cheat and exact upon us in the price, the measure, and the goodness, nor could ever yet be brought to make one fair proposal of just dealing, though often and earnestly invited to it.

Therefore I repeat, let no man talk to me of these and the like expedients, till he has at least some glimpse of hope, that there will ever be some hearty and sincere attempt to put them in practice.

But, as to myself, having been wearied out for many years with offering

Topinamboo: a place name invented by Swift as the nation of the Tupi Indians (who are real) in South America.

vain, idle, visionary thoughts, and at length utterly despairing of success, I fortunately fell upon this proposal; which, as it is wholly new, so it has something solid and real, of no expence and little trouble, full in our own power, and whereby we can incur no danger in disobliging ENGLAND. For this kind of commodity will not bear exportation, the flesh being of too tender a consistence to admit a long continuance in salt, although perhaps I could name a country, which would be glad to eat up our whole nation without it.

After all, I am not so violently bent upon my own opinion as to reject any offer proposed by wise men, which shall be found equally innocent, cheap, easy, and effectual. But before something of that kind shall be advanced in contradiction to my scheme, and offering a better, I desire the author or authors will be pleased maturely to consider two points. First, as things now stand, how they will be able to find food and raiment for a hundred thousand useless mouths and backs. And secondly, there being a round million of creatures in human figure throughout this kingdom, whose whole subsistence put into a common stock would leave them in debt two millions of pounds sterling, adding those who are beggars by profession, to the bulk of farmers, cottagers, and labourers, with the wives and children, who are beggars in effect; I desire those politicians who dislike my overture, and may perhaps be so bold as to attempt an answer, that they will first ask the parents of these mortals, whether they would not at this day think it a great happiness to have been sold for food at a year old, in the manner I prescribe, and thereby have avoided such a perpetual scene of misfortunes, as they have since gone through, by the oppression of landlords, the impossibility of paying rent without money or trade, the want of common sustenance, with neither house nor clothes to cover them from the inclemencies of the weather, and the most inevitable prospect of entailing the like, or greater miseries, upon their breed for ever.

I profess, in the sincerity of my heart, that I have not the least personal interest in endeavouring to promote this necessary work, having no other motive than the public good of my country, by advancing our trade, providing for infants, relieving the poor, and giving some pleasure to the rich. I have no children by which I can propose to get a single penny; the youngest being nine years old, and my wife past child-bearing.

DISCUSSION

1. Swift's real feeling is indignation at the way the Irish are treated. What attitude does he assume, in contrast, for the purpose of his satire? Point out statements that make this clear.
2. What assumption does Swift seem to make about his readers? What is his actual assumption about them? How do you know?
3. Reinforcing the main satire are a number of jibes at particular groups or types of people. What are some of these? Who are they aimed at?
4. As a brief exercise to help you see how the satirist begins, try thinking

of some contemporary injustice that makes you angry and then think of a radical solution such as Swift's that would solve the problem by carrying the injustice to its logical extreme, rendering the outrage more outrageous. But keep in mind that your solution ought to be funny, not merely outrageous. Swift does not suggest genocide, which is not funny, but cannibalism, which in this context, is.

A fable is a simple story that illustrates a truth, sometimes using animal characters and sometimes people. There is usually an element of satire in the fable.

Robert Louis Stevenson

The Penitent

(1888)

A man met a lad weeping. "What do you weep for?" he asked.
"I am weeping for my sins," said the lad.
"You must have little to do," said the man.
The next day they met again. Once more the lad was weeping. "Why do you weep now?" asked the man.
"I am weeping because I have nothing to eat," said the lad.
"I thought it would come to that," said the man.

James Thurber

Four Fables for Our Time

(1940)

The Moth and the Star

A young and impressionable moth once set his heart on a certain star. He told his mother about this and she counselled him to set his heart on a bridge lamp instead. "Stars aren't the thing to hang around," she said; "lamps are the thing to hang around." "You get somewhere that way," said the moth's father. "You don't get anywhere chasing stars." But the moth would not heed the words of either parent. Every evening at dusk when the star came out he would start flying toward it and every morning at dawn he would crawl back home worn out with his vain endeavor. One day his father said to him, "You haven't burned a wing in months, boy, and it looks to me as if you were never going to. All your brothers have been badly burned flying around street lamps and all your sisters have been terribly singed flying around house lamps. Come on, now, get out of here and get yourself scorched! A big strapping moth like you without a mark on him!"

The moth left his father's house, but he would not fly around street lamps and he would not fly around house lamps. He went right on trying to reach the star, which was four and one-third light years, or twenty-five trillion miles, away. The moth thought it was just caught in the top branches of an elm. He never did reach the star, but he went right on trying, night after night, and when he was a very, very old moth he began to think that he really had reached the star and he went around saying so. This gave him a deep and lasting pleasure, and he lived to a great old age. His parents and his brothers and his sisters had all been burned to death when they were quite young.

MORAL: Who flies afar from the sphere of our sorrow is here today and here tomorrow.

The Courtship of Arthur and Al

Once upon a time there was a young beaver named Al and an older beaver named Arthur. They were both in love with a pretty little female. She looked with disfavor upon the young beaver's suit because he was a harum-scarum and a ne'er-do-well. He had never done a single gnaw of work in his life, for he preferred to eat and sleep and to swim lazily in the streams and to play Now-I'll-Chase-You with the girls. The older beaver had never done anything but work from the time he got his first teeth. He had never played anything with anybody.

When the young beaver asked the female to marry him, she said she wouldn't think of it unless he amounted to something. She reminded him that Arthur had built thirty-two dams and was working on three others, whereas he, Al, had never even made a bread-board or a pin tray in his life. Al was very sorry, but he said he would never go to work just because a woman wanted him to. Thereupon she offered to be a sister to him, but he pointed out that he already had seventeen sisters. So he went back to eating and sleeping and swimming in the streams and playing Spider-in-the-Parlor with the girls. The female married Arthur one day at the lunch hour—he could never get away from work for more than one hour at a time. They had seven children and Arthur worked so hard supporting them he wore his teeth down to the gum line. His health broke in two before long and he died without ever having had a vacation in his life. The young beaver continued to eat and sleep and swim in the streams and play Unbutton-Your-Shoe with the girls. He never Got Anywhere, but he had a long life and a Wonderful Time.

MORAL: It is better to have loafed and lost than never to have loafed at all.

The Rabbits Who Caused All the Trouble

Within the memory of the youngest child there was a family of rabbits who lived near a pack of wolves. The wolves announced that they did not like the way the rabbits were living. (The wolves were crazy about the way they themselves were living, because it was the only way to live.) One night several wolves were killed in an earthquake and this was blamed on the rabbits, for it is well known that rabbits pound on the ground with their hind legs and cause earthquakes. On another night one of the wolves was killed by a bolt of lightning and this was also blamed on the rabbits, for it is well known that lettuce-eaters cause lightning. The wolves threatened to civilize the rabbits if they didn't behave, and the rabbits decided to run away to a desert island. But the other animals, who lived at a great distance, shamed them, saying, "You must stay where you are and be brave. This is no world for escapists. If the wolves attack you, we will come to your aid, in all probability." So the rabbits continued to live near the wolves and one day there was a terrible flood which drowned a great many wolves. This was blamed on the rabbits, for it is well known that carrot-nibblers with long ears cause floods. The wolves descended on the rabbits, for their own good, and imprisoned them in a dark cave, for their own protection.

When nothing was heard about the rabbits for some weeks, the other animals demanded to know what had happened to them. The wolves replied that the rabbits had been eaten and since they had been eaten the affair was a purely internal matter. But the other animals warned that they might possibly unite against the wolves unless some reason was given for the destruction of the rabbits. So the wolves gave them one. "They were trying to escape," said the wolves, "and, as you know, this is no world for escapists."

MORAL: Run, don't walk, to the nearest desert island.

The Unicorn in the Garden

Once upon a sunny morning a man who sat in a breakfast nook looked up from his scrambled eggs to see a white unicorn with a gold horn quietly cropping the roses in the garden. The man went up to the bedroom where his wife was still asleep and woke her. "There's a unicorn in the garden," he said. "Eating roses." She opened one unfriendly eye and looked at him. "The unicorn is a mythical beast," she said, and turned her back on him. The man walked slowly downstairs and out into the garden. The unicorn was still there; he was now browsing among the tulips. "Here, unicorn," said the man, and he pulled up a lily and gave it to him. The unicorn ate it gravely. With a high heart, because there was a unicorn in his garden, the man went upstairs and roused his wife again. "The unicorn," he said, "ate a lily." His wife sat up in bed and looked at him, coldly. "You are a booby," she said, "and I am going to have you put in the booby-hatch." The man, who had never liked the words, "booby" and "booby-hatch," and who liked them even less on a shining morning when there was a unicorn in the garden, thought for a moment. "We'll see about that," he said. He walked over to the door. "He has a golden horn in the middle of his forehead," he told her. Then he went back to the garden to watch the unicorn; but the unicorn had gone away. The man sat down among the roses and went to sleep.

As soon as the husband had gone out of the house, the wife got up and dressed as fast as she could. She was very excited and there was a gloat in her eye. She telephoned the police and she telephoned a psychiatrist; she told them to hurry to her house and bring a strait-jacket. When the police and the psychiatrist arrived they sat down in chairs and looked at her, with great interest. "My husband," she said, "saw a unicorn this morning." The police looked at the psychiatrist and the psychiatrist looked at the police. "He told me it ate a lily," she said. The psychiatrist looked at the police and the police looked at the psychiatrist. "He told me it had a golden horn in the middle of its forehead," she said. At a solemn signal from the psychiatrist, the police leaped from their chairs and seized the wife. They had a hard time subduing her, for she put up a terrific struggle, but they finally subdued her. Just as they got her into the strait-jacket, the husband came back into the house.

"Did you tell your wife you saw a unicorn?" asked the police. "Of course not," said the husband. "The unicorn is a mythical beast." "That's all I wanted to know," said the psychiatrist. "Take her away. I'm sorry, sir, but your wife is as crazy as a jay bird." So they took her away, cursing and screaming, and shut her up in an institution. The husband lived happily ever after.

MORAL: Don't count your boobies until they are hatched.

Ethiopian Folk Tale

Justice

A woman one day went out to look for her goats that had wandered away from the herd. She walked back and forth over the fields for a long time without finding them. She came at last to a place by the side of the road where a deaf man sat before a fire brewing himself a cup of coffee. Not realizing he was deaf, the woman asked:

"Have you seen my herd of goats come this way?"

The deaf man thought she was asking for the water hole, so he pointed vaguely toward the river.

The woman thanked him and went to the river. And there, by coincidence, she found the goats. But a young kid had fallen among the rocks and broken its foot.

She picked it up to carry it home. As she passed the place where the deaf man sat drinking his coffee, she stopped to thank him for his help. And in gratitude she offered him the kid.

But the deaf man didn't understand a word she was saying. When she held the kid toward him he thought she was accusing him of the animal's misfortune, and he became very angry.

"I had nothing to do with it!" he shouted.

"But you pointed the way," the woman said.

"It happens all the time with goats!" the man shouted.

"I found them right where you said they would be," the woman replied.

"Go away and leave me alone, I never saw him before in my life!" the man shouted.

People who came along the road stopped to hear the argument.

The woman explained to them:

"I was looking for the goats and he pointed toward the river. Now I wish to give him this kid."

"Do not insult me in this way!" the man shouted loudly. "I am not a leg breaker!" And in his anger he struck the woman with his hand.

"Ah! did you see? He struck me with his hand!" the woman said to the people. "I will take him before the judge!"

So the woman with the kid in her arms, the deaf man, and the spectators went to the house of the judge. The judge came out before his house to listen to their complaint. First, the woman talked, then the man talked, then people in the crowd talked. The judge sat nodding his head. But that meant very little, for the judge, like the man before him, was very deaf. Moreover, he was also very nearsighted.

At last, he put up his hand and the talking stopped. He gave them his judgment.

"Such family rows are a disgrace to the Emperor and an affront to the Church," he said solemnly. He turned to the man.

"From this time forward, stop mistreating your wife," he said.

He turned to the woman with the young goat in her arms.

"As for you, do not be so lazy. Hereafter do not be late with your husband's meals."

He looked at the baby goat tenderly.

"And as for the beautiful infant, may she have a long life and grow to be a joy to you both!"

The crowd broke up and the people went their various ways.

"Ah, how good it is!" they said to each other. "How did we ever get along before justice was given us?"

DISCUSSION

1. The six preceding fables all have at least two elements in common. Can you identify these similarities?
2. What belief is Stevenson making fun of in "The Penitent"? What do you infer is his own belief concerning this matter?
3. The "morals" at the end of "The Moth and the Star" and "The Rabbits Who Caused All the Trouble" do not fully sum up the meaning of the fables. If you were afraid the reader might miss the point, what "moral" would you attach to each of these two fables?

Experiencing and Generalizing

4. What kind of advice is Thurber offering, by implication, in all four of his fables? Can you make a general statement that would make a "moral" for all four?
5. What group's attitude is being satirized in "Justice"? What is the attitude?

Like "The Unicorn in the Garden" and "Justice," our last fable uses people rather than animals as characters; unlike these fables, it has no obvious "moral." It is the unlikely sequence of events and their illustrative quality that make "Lie Thee Down, Oddity" a fable rather than a short story, but its purpose is to communicate a total approach to life rather than a comment on one aspect of it. It may seem to you a strange and even incomprehensible fable, for the point of view it represents is opposed to most common opinion.

T. F. Powys

Lie Thee Down, Oddity

(1934)

Though the sun shone with summer heat, the damp August warmth, giving the rather faded countryside a new glow in her cheeks—for there had been a good all-night's rain—yet Mr. Cronch wore his black felt hat, of the cut that used to be worn by evangelical clergymen in the last century.

The Honourable George Bullman, who employed Mr. Cronch as head-gardener, had spoken to him some years before about this hat of his, which was the only thing about Mr. Cronch that gave a hint of peculiarities. 'Your Methodist hat will be the ruin of you one day, Cronch,' Mr. Bullman had observed, while discussing with his gardener about the making of a new lawn.

Mr. Cronch was mowing the lawn; he had bid the under-gardener work elsewhere. To please and humour Cronch, Mr. Bullman used no motor mowing-machine. Cronch did not like them. But the under-gardener had hardly looked at the old-fashioned mower before he complained that such labour was beyond his power. To push all day such an awkward instrument 'that might,' the young man said, 'have been used by Adam,' was out of the question for anyone who understood the arts and fancies of oil-driven machinery.

Mr. Cronch did the work himself. 'One has, you know, to pay for one's oddities,' he told his wife, Jane.

At Green Gate House the grounds were always in the best order; there was never a weed in the kitchen-garden or a plantain on the lawn, but at

plantain: here, a kind of weed.

one place, bordering the lawn, there were railings, and over these railings there was the heath.

A different world, that looked with contempt upon the soft pelt of a smooth lawn, which was indeed like the skin of a tamed beast that did nothing else but lie and bask in the sun while its sleek hide was being curry-combed by Mr. Cronch. The heath was a different matter from the garden. All was nature there, and she is a wild, fierce, untutored mother. Flowers and weeds, unnoticed, lived there, fighting the battle of their lives, careless of man, but living as they were commanded to live at the first moving of the waters. The raven and the falcon nested in the tall trees beyond a desolate swamp, and only a solitary heath-cutter might sometimes be seen with his load, taking a long track towards the waste land. Who, indeed, would view such barrenness when there was the Honourable George Bullman's garden to admire?

Mr. Bullman could afford a good gardener. The head-gardener's cottage, where Mr. Cronch and his wife lived, had every comfort of a modern well-built house. No servant of Mr. Bullman had anything to complain of. No one would leave such service, could they avoid doing so.

Over the heath, even the winds blew differently from the gentle garden ones. Out there the blasts could roar and bellow, wrench the boughs from the trees, and rush along madly, but in the summer-time garden all winds were soft.

Mr. Cronch stopped. He took the box from the mower and tipped the cut grass into the wheelbarrow. The wheelbarrow was full of sweet-smelling grass. Mr. Cronch then whistled softly, and Robert, the under-gardener, left his weeding and trundled the barrow to the cucumber-frames. He returned with the empty barrow at a slow, even pace—the gait of a well-paid gardener, as learned from Mr. Cronch.

Mr. Cronch began to mow again. He came near to the railings beyond which was the heath. Then he stopped. He took off his hat and looked into it. He looked at the lawn. Nowhere in the world, out of England, could any lawn have been smoother or more green. There was not the smallest clover leaf there that was not consecrated to the fine taste of a proper gentleman and ready to be pressed by the elegant foot of a real lady. The smooth banks, the beds of flowers nearby, might have been a modern picture in colours; they were so unlike nature. There was nothing rude or untidy there, and every cabbage in the kitchen-garden wore a coronet.

Mr. Cronch had not changed, as the garden was changed when it became the heath. He was the same Mr. Cronch who had, at one o'clock, cut the finest cucumber in the garden for Mr. Bullman's lunch. He waited for another moment or two and then softly put on his hat. After doing so, he spoke aloud, 'Lie thee down, Oddity!' said Mr. Cronch.

Then Mr. Cronch shook his head, as much as to say that if the Oddity would not lie down, it was no fault of his. For such a being it was impossible to control. Had the Oddity lain down, then Mr. Cronch would have gone on with his work, as a wise man should who earns four pounds a week, with a good house and garden, and with leave to sell whatever he likes from his master's.

But Mr. Cronch did not start work again. It was no good; whatever happened to him the Oddity must be obeyed. The Oddity knew best. Mr. Cronch left the machine where it was, near to the railings. He walked, with the same slow gardener's walk—that showed, as much as any walk could, a hatred of all untidiness and disorder—and came to the potting-shed. There he put on his coat.

The hour was three in the afternoon. Mr. Cronch learned that from his watch. Then he listened. What he expected, happened; the church clock that was just across the way struck three.

Mr. Cronch's watch was always right.

It was no use mentioning that to the Oddity. He would not lie down the more because Mr. Cronch's gold watch—a gift of Mr. Bullman's—went with the Church time.

Mr. Cronch shut the potting-shed door and went home. He remarked, when he saw his wife, as though he said nothing of particular interest, that he had given up work at Green Gate House. He told her to begin to pack, for they were leaving the gardener's cottage as soon as possible.

Jane thought him mad, and when the under-gardener, Robert, heard of it, he blamed the mowing-machine. 'To have to push anything like that would drive any man away,' he said to Mr. Bullman.

The Honourable George Bullman was anxious that Mr. Cronch should still remain in the gardener's cottage. He would give him a pension, he said, for he did not want to lose so good a neighbour, whose advice he valued so highly. Mr. Bullman, of course, blamed the hat for the trouble.

Jane wished to stay, but as the Oddity would not lie down, Mr. Cronch said they must go.

About two miles away from Green Gate House, upon the heath, there was a wretched cottage that had once been inhabited by a rabbit-catcher. Mr. Cronch chose this hut as a residence. About an acre of land went with it. Mr. Cronch repaired the cottage with his own hands, and put up new railings round the garden. In order to do this neatly, he spent most of the money he had saved in service. Then he began to reclaim the garden, that was fallen out of cultivation and was become heath again.

The wild spirit of the waste land struggled against him. But here the poverty of the soil met its match. Nature is no respecter of persons; she gives alike to the good and to the evil. The potato-blight will ruin a good man's crop as well as a naughty one's. The heath was not a curry-combed creature, tamed with milk and wine. It was a savage animal, now friendly and kind, now cruel and vindictive, then mild. One day smiling like a pretty maid, and the next biting at you with ugly-shaped teeth.

There was no pleasant shelter there, no glass-houses, no high walls, no trimmed box-hedges. The winds of heaven had free passage, a snake could roam at large and find only its natural enemies to attack it. The wild birds had rest. Mr. Cronch bowed his head and laboured. It needed a better man than nature to cast him down. With the Oddity asleep, he could go on with his work. There was no need for him to rest, he was an obedient servant. He required no telling what to do in the way of work; even the Honourable George Bullman had put himself under Mr. Cronch's

Satire and Fable

guidance. While he had hands and tools he could compel the most sour-tempered soil to serve his needs. His broad shoulders were ever bent over the ground as he turned the earthen clod.

It was not long before Mr. Cronch compelled the heath to pay him tribute, and soon a pleasant cottage and a large well-cultivated garden arose in the wilderness. There were many who respected Mr. Cronch for leaving so much good at Mr. Bullman's to do battle with nature upon the heath, but others said he only left his master out of pride. Mr. Cronch smiled when he heard that. 'Here was a fine matter, indeed,' he thought, 'that a mortal man should have pride—a nice folly to call a leaf proud that is driven willy-nilly before a November gale. A fine pride that leaf must have when, at the last, it is buried in a dung-hill!'

But if Mr. Cronch was proud, as some thought, it was only because he had the knowledge that, within him, something slept. . . .

Mr. Cronch was resting contentedly one Sunday, reading a country paper. Even that morning he had been busy in his garden, and was glad now to rest while Jane prepared the dinner.

Mr. Cronch sat there, a simple respectable working-class man—in years too—wearing spectacles, and reading his paper.

He found something to read that interested him, for he read the same paragraph three times.

This was a police case. An old woman, who was employed on Saturdays by the Stonebridge town clerk to scrub his floors, had found upon the dining-room floor a blank cheque. This cheque she had filled in herself, and because she was a simple woman, without pride, she had written the town clerk's name instead of her own.

For thirty years Mrs. Tibby had kept herself and her husband, John—who spent all his time in leaning over the town bridge to watch the water flow under—and now his one wish was to go to London to see the king. His wife wished to give him this treat; "E do need a holiday,' she said.

When a charwoman picks up money she has a right to it. Mrs. Tibby thought the cheque money. Money, after a card-party, which there had been at the clerk's, is often left on the floor for the sweeper—that is the custom of the country.

Mrs. Tibby was not greedy: she only wrote 'four pounds' upon the cheque. She supposed that sum to be enough to take her husband to see the king. If the clerk were annoyed, she knew she could work the money out in scrubbing the floors.

When she was taken up, she could get no bail, so she went to prison.

Mr. Cronch carefully folded the paper.

The month was November. Over the heath, dark sweeping clouds, like great besoms, were driving. The two ravens, who nested in the high fir tree, enjoyed the wind. The mist from the sea brought memories to their minds; they remembered stories told of men hanged in chains on Blacknoll Mound, whose bones could be pecked clean. The ravens flew off and looked for a lamb to kill.

besoms: brooms.

Mr. Cronch laid the paper on the table, beside a smoking dish of fried beef and onions—there were other vegetables to come—and a rice pudding.

Mr. Cronch rose slowly and sniffed.

But the Oddity would not lie down. So Mr. Cronch told his wife he was going out. The distance to Stonebridge was twelve miles. Mr. Cronch put on his overcoat; he went to a drawer and took out twenty-five pounds. He put on his large black hat, opened the cottage-door and went out—the rain greeted him with a lively shower of water-drops. Jane let him go. She supposed him to be in one of his mad fits, that the Giant Despair in the Pilgrim's Progress used to have.

Mr. Cronch walked along, with his usual slow steady step—the gait of a careful gardener. When he reached Stonebridge he was not admitted into the jail, and so he took a lodging for the night.

In the morning he visited Mrs. Tibby. 'I wish to be your bail,' he said, cheerfully.

Mrs. Tibby was in a maze. She did not know what she had done wrong. She was happy where she was, she was allowed to gossip with the prison charwoman, who was an old friend of hers. She begged Mr. Cronch, if he wished to be good to her, to allow her to stay with her friend, and to take her husband to London to see the king. Mrs. Tibby liked the prison, 'Everyone is so kind,' she said, 'and when I complained to the doctor about my headaches, he ordered me gin. I have never been so happy before.'

Mr. Cronch found Mr. Tibby smoking his pipe and leaning over the town bridge. He told him he was going to take him to see the king, and Mr. Tibby agreed to go, but first he knocked his pipe out on the stone coping of the bridge.

When they reached London, the king was out of town. He was soon to return, and Mr. Tibby spent the time happily, smoking his pipe and leaning over Waterloo Bridge, although the fog was so dense he could not see the river. When the king came, Mr. Cronch took Mr. Tibby into the crowd to see the king go by. Mr. Tibby sang 'God Save the King,' and shouted 'Hurrah!' The king bowed.

'Now I shall die happy,' said Mr. Tibby, 'but how shall I get home?'

Mr. Cronch paid his fare to Stonebridge, and saw him off at the station.

The weather had improved; a brisk wind from the south-west had driven off the fog. Mr. Cronch, to please himself, walked into the city. He had fifteen pounds in his pocket, and he looked into the shop-windows. He still wore his large black hat, and the beggars avoided him. They thought him a Jewish money-lender, or else a Baptist minister. Beggars are shrewd judges of character. They have to decide quickly. Their income depends upon it. To beg from the wrong man means loss of time—perhaps prison.

Mr. Cronch went down a narrow street where some offices were. One of these was the office of a money-lender. A gentleman, who looked worn out by sickness and trouble, came out of that door. A woman, his wife, who carried a baby in her arms, waited for him in the street. The gentleman shook his head. Evidently the security that he had to offer was not good enough.

Then there arose a little conversation between them.

'I could go to mother's,' the woman said.

'If I had money, I could go with you,' the man observed, 'the change would do me good, and I might get work in Bristol.'

'Baby will be easier to manage in a few months,' the woman said. 'Mother will not mind taking us, but you will have to stay here.'

'I can't let you go,' said the man.

He made a curious sound in his throat.

Mr. Cronch stood near on the pavement. Who would have noticed Mr. Cronch? The couple paid no heed to him. But presently they turned to where he stood, for Mr. Cronch spoke.

'Lie thee down, Oddity!' he said, aloud.

The gentleman smiled, he could do nothing else. The baby held out her arms to Mr. Cronch; she wanted his hat. Mr. Cronch took two five pound notes from his wallet and gave them to the woman. Then he walked away.

For his own pleasure, he walked out of the city into the poor parts of the town. He walked along slowly and looked at the vegetables in the greengrocers' shops. He wondered that people could buy such old stuff. If he offered anything like that at the Weyminster market, he would never find a purchaser. He remembered the lordly freedom of the wild heath. There, nature might be cruel, but life and death joined hands in the dance. The sun could shine, and when darkness came it was the darkness of God. The town was different.

Mr. Cronch went down a dingy court. Clothes were hung from house to house, and barefooted children played in the gutter. The air was heavy with human odours and factory stench. Then Mr. Cronch came upon something worse than misery.

A man sat leaning against a wall, with half his face eaten away. His eyes were gone; he cried out to everyone whose footstep he heard, to lead him to the river. When Mr. Cronch came by, he cried out the more. Mr. Cronch stopped.

'Lie thee down, Oddity!' he said, angrily.

'Lead me to the river,' the man begged.

'Come,' said Mr. Cronch, and led the man to the river. A policeman who knew the man's wish, followed them. At the brink of the river, the man said, 'I am afraid; only give me one little push, and I shall die.'

'Certainly,' said Mr. Cronch, and pushed him into the river. The man sank like a stone.

The police officer came up to demand Mr. Cronch's name and address; he had made a note of what had happened.

'You will appear at court, charged with murder,' he said. 'But now you may go!'

Mr. Cronch walked out of the great city. He had enough money to take him home by train, but he liked walking. As he went along he decided to plant a part of his garden with spinach. He had seen a good deal of this green stuff in the London shops, and he thought he could sell it at home.

Experiencing and Generalizing

He walked ten miles out of town, and then took a lodging for the night. Since the Oddity had risen last, Mr. Cronch had behaved just as a sober gardener would when out for a holiday. When he came to an allotment, he would look into it to see what was grown. He found the ground good. But he believed that more glass might be used, and the city dung, he thought, too heating for the soil. He was especially interested in the window-flowers that he saw, but wondered that no hyacinths were seen, the bulbs having been all planted too late to bloom at that season.

Starting his walk again the next morning, Mr. Cronch came upon a large crowd watching a high factory chimney. This immense chimney, as high as the clouds and weighing many thousands of tons, was being brought down. The workmen were busy at its base, and the crowd watched from a safe distance.

All was ready for the fall; the masons and engineers left the chimney. But one of the men remained to give the final stroke that would cause the huge structure to sway and fall. This mason completed his task, and began to walk to safety.

When he was a few yards off the chimney, he trod upon a wet plank, hidden in the mud, and fell heavily. The spectators expected him to jump up and run off. But he did not do so.

An official held his watch in his hand, 'One, two, three,' he counted. When he reached sixty seconds the chimney would fall.

Its direction was known. It would fall directly upon the man. He tried to rise, but his leg was broken. He tried to crawl, but the pain prevented him. He raised himself up, and looked at the huge mass above him; he knew what was coming. None of the onlookers moved. It was too late to save the man; to go to him would mean certain death.

The chimney began to totter, to rock.

Then Mr. Cronch said softly, 'Lie thee down, Oddity!' but the Oddity would not listen to him. Mr. Cronch spoke in so low a tone that perhaps the Oddity never even heard what he said.

Mr. Cronch walked, with his slow gardener's step, to the man.

'What are you afraid of?' he asked him.

'Of the chimney,' cried the man, 'it's falling.'

'What if it does fall,' observed Mr. Cronch, looking up as though he thought the huge mass above him was a small pear-tree.

'It's coming,' cried the man.

Mr. Cronch took off his hat. The man smiled.

DISCUSSION

1. On five occasions the Oddity refuses to lie down, and Mr. Cronch acts. What do all five actions have in common?
2. The conventional person would judge some of Mr. Cronch's actions right and others wrong. But if Mr. Cronch is to follow a principle consistently, all his actions are right. What is the principle?

allotment: garden plot.

Satire and Fable

3. What is the significance of Mr. Cronch's old black hat? At what times does he take it off or raise it?
4. Mr. Cronch's attitude toward life is expressed at one point in his own words. What is his attitude?
5. What is the Oddity?

WRITING SUGGESTIONS

1. Using personification, as Erasmus does, or simple ironic argument, write a strong defense of some human weakness such as laziness, greed, vanity, gullibility, envy, jealousy, habitual lying, or ignorance. Make it appear practical and virtuous.
2. Injustice and violence are as common in the world today as they were in Swift's century. Try a satire like "A Modest Proposal" on a contemporary subject. Offer, with every appearance of sincerity, a logical but humanly unacceptable case for any evil that would make a good target, such as war, poverty, political dishonesty, exploitation of labor, traffic slaughter, or destruction of the environment. Be as concrete as possible in giving the details of your solution and keep a straight face while you argue that it is practical.
3. It has been said that television has saved many marriages by preventing the partners from becoming acquainted. This might suggest a satire on the benefits of television.
4. Few things are funnier than seeing someone imitating a public figure—the boy who lets a cigarette dangle from his lips like Bogart and gets smoke in his eyes, the girl who borrows everything from her hairdo to her tone of voice from a rock singer. A good subject for satire might be a party in which several people are ineptly trying to imitate somebody else.
5. Try a parody of some writer, novelist, poet, or journalist, who has a unique and recognizable style. (See "A Note on Parody" at the end of this chapter.) Apply the writer's style in an exaggerated form to an unsuitable subject. For example, "Dear Abby" might offer advice to a mass-murderer, the elaborate style of Henry James might be used to describe the emotional relationships of your pet dog, the rolling rhythms of Walt Whitman could be applied to a cat fight, or one of television's laconic detectives might investigate the activities of a small boy skipping a day of school. Pay close attention to the style you are imitating; the parody won't be successful unless the reader recognizes the original.
6. Deceptively simple, the fable is one of the hardest literary forms to use successfully. But it's worth a try. Take another look at what Thurber does in his animal fables and in his human fable, "The Unicorn in the Garden." Begin with a humorous and ironic statement such as the "moral" at the end of each of these fables; then work backward and see if you can illustrate that statement by a simple tale with a surprise twist at the end. For a beginning, you might try casting Goldsmith's "On the Use of Language" into fable form, using perhaps mice or squirrels as characters. Other themes that could be treated this way are found in Llewellyn Powys' "House of Correction," George Orwell's "Marrakech," Samuel Butler's "Darwin among the Machines," Soame Jenyn's "The Country Visit," Robert Louis Stevenson's "An Apology

Experiencing and Generalizing

for Idlers," John Ruskin's "The Essential Things," Niccolò Machiavelli's "In What Way Princes Must Keep Faith," and perhaps other pieces in this book.

7. Many people have a block against writing verse. While it is true that really good poetry is mastered by only a few people, writing amusing satiric verse is easy. Begin by imitating "Base Details." Write a first line starting, "If I were an English teacher," "If I were a little brother," or something of the sort, and just go on from there, giving your sense of irony free rein.

A NOTE ON PARODY

A parody is a comical imitation of another writer's style, usually applied to an unsuitable subject. In "A City Shower," for example, Jonathan Swift applies the grand and formal style of Virgil to an everyday subject that is comical in itself. In order for parody to be effective, the original writer must have a distinctive style that is easily recognizable, and of course the reader of the parody must have some acquaintance with the original. Parody may serve as criticism of the original, but does not necessarily do so: excellent writers such as Shakespeare and Walt Whitman can be parodied without damage because of their highly recognizable styles. Probably the best known recent parodists are James Thurber and S. J. Perelman, to whose works the student is directed.

Rupert Brooke

Heaven

(1911)

Fish (fly-replete, in depth of June,
Dawdling away their wat'ry noon)
Ponder deep wisdom, dark or clear,
Each secret fishy hope or fear.
Fish say, they have their Stream and Pond;
But is there anything Beyond?
This life cannot be All, they swear,
For how unpleasant, if it were!
One may not doubt that, somehow, Good
Shall come of Water and of Mud;
And, sure, the reverent eye must see
A Purpose in Liquidity.
We darkly know, by Faith we cry,
The future is not Wholly Dry.
Mud unto mud!—Death eddies near—
Not here the appointed End, not here!
But somewhere, beyond Space and Time.

Is wetter water, slimier slime!
And there (they trust) there swimmeth One
Who swam ere rivers were begun,
Immense, of fishy form and mind,
Squamous, omnipotent, and kind;
And under that Almighty Fin,
The littlest fish may enter in.
Oh! never fly conceals a hook,
Fish say, in the Eternal Brook,
But more than mundane weeds are there,
And mud, celestially fair;
Fat caterpillars drift around,
And Paradisal grubs are found;
Unfading moths, immortal flies,
And the worm that never dies.
And in that Heaven of all their wish,
There shall be no more land, say fish.

Plate 23
George Grosz (1893–1959): "Couple"

Most of us see more examples of satirical art than of any other kind, for of course that is what newspaper and magazine cartoons are. Generally these cartoons are based on fads or happenings of the moment and are out of date in a few months or a few years; but occasionally an excellent cartoonist like Herblock or George Price will, like Jonathan Swift in "A Modest Proposal" (p. 342), produce a work broad enough in its scope to become a classic. The key is "universality," the quality of applying not only to a particular occasion, but to all men in all times. "A Modest Proposal" is a comment not just on England's treatment of the Irish in the eighteenth century, but of man's inhumanity to man at all periods and in all nations. George Grosz' "Couple" has this quality: while the costumes are dated, the pinched, self-satisfied faces are common to selfish and class-conscious people of all times and places.

1. Most people base their concept of their own virtue on what they don't do rather than on what they do. What are some things you might guess this couple are proud of not doing? What evidence in the picture supports this conjecture?
2. Snobbishness and narrowness are based on fear. What things might Grosz' couple be afraid of? Would this fear be justified or not? What evidence, in the picture and from your own experience, are you using as the basis of your guesses?
3. What readings in this book have something in common with "Couple"?
4. Recall Mark Twain's "House Beautiful" (p. 13). Does his presentation of the "principal citizen's" home have anything in common with Grosz' presentation of this couple? If so, what?

PLATE 23 George Grosz (1893–1959), **Couple.** *Collection of the Whitney Museum of American Art, New York.*

Plate 24
Richard Stankiewicz (1922–   ): *Secretary*

George Grosz' "Couple" is not funny; there is no incongruity in it, only exaggeration of selected features. But *Secretary* makes us laugh first, before we receive the more serious message.

1. "Incongruity" means a combination of things that don't belong together, and it is the chief ingredient of humor. What are the things in *Secretary* that don't belong together?
2. Aside from fun, what might be the artist's purpose in putting them together in this way?
3. A statement cannot, of course, communicate the total meaning of a work of art any more than the word "chocolate" will melt on your tongue. All the same, it might be a good exercise to attempt a carefully qualified statement of what you think the artist intended *Secretary* to communicate. Try to include the element of humor in your statement, for it is an essential part of the sculpture.
4. The artist could have carved his sculpture out of a block of wood or stone, but instead he assembled it out of junk. Other than making the job easier for himself, might he have had a meaningful reason for using junk?
5. Do you find any common idea in *Secretary* and Samuel Butler's "Darwin among the Machines" (p. 140)? Can you state this idea clearly?

PLATE 24 Richard Stankiewicz (1922–   ), **Secretary.** *Courtesy Mrs. Martin L. Cannon, Charlotte, N.C., from Sandak.*

Index of Authors and Titles

Advice to Youth   325
Anderson, Sherwood
   Discovery of a Father   231
Apology for Idlers, An   293
Arab Feasting   58
Ascham, Roger
   On Quick and Slow Wits of Pupils   135
   The Wind   9
Auda   30
Autumn Night in the Hills, An   72

Bacon, Francis
   Idols of the Mind   144
Base Details   332
Beer and My Cat   91
Blyth, R. H.
   What Is Zen?   178
Brooke, Rupert
   Heaven   362
   The Great Lover   3
Broun, Heywood
   Holding a Baby   283
Butler, Samuel
   Beer and My Cat   91
   Darwin among the Machines   140
   The Finger-Nail and the Note   90
   The Hunter   132

Chariots Go Forth to War   306
Chesterton, G. K.
   Madness   137
Clough, Arthur Hugh
   The Latest Decalogue   333
Conversation   66
Country Visit, The   205

Darwin among the Machines   140
Description of a City Shower   56
De Quincey, Thomas
   The Pains of Opium   251
Discovery of a Father   231
Donne, John
   Song   134
   The Good-Morrow   229
Dying   139

Eiseley, Loren
   The Judgment of the Birds   88
Erasmus of Rotterdam
   Fools Are Happy   335
Essential Things, The   303
Ethiopian Folk Tale
   Justice   352
Evelyn, John
   A Slave Galley   54
Evolution of the Horse, The   176

Fight, A   52

Finger-Nail and the Note, The   90
Flatterer, The   131
Fools Are Happy   335
Four Fables for Our Time   349
Franklin, Benjamin
   The Whirlwind   10

Garland, Hamlin
   The Grasshopper and the Ant   207
Gaskell, Elizabeth Cleghorn
   Small Economies   92
Getting Up on Cold Mornings   203
Gissing, George
   Visions in a Fever   243
Goldsmith, Oliver
   On the Use of Language   94
Good-Morrow, The   229
Governor of Los Teques, The   164
Grasshopper and the Ant, The   207
Great Lover, The   3

Hall-Bedrooms   16
Hammerskjöld, Dag
   Three Dreams   230
Hand, The   249
Hawthorne, Nathaniel
   Shanties at Walden Pond   12
   The Old Apple Dealer   32
Heaven   362
Hoggart, Richard
   A Working Class Mother   28
   Old Men in Libraries   70
Holding a Baby   283
Hospital, The   245
House Beautiful, The   13
House of Correction, A   104
Howells, William Dean
   Tribulations of a Cheerful Giver   235
Hunt, Leigh
   Getting Up on Cold Mornings   203
   The Inside of an Omnibus   62
Hunter, The   132

Idols of the Mind   144
Inside of an Omnibus, The   62
In What Way Princes Must Keep Faith   328

James, Henry
   Miss Birdseye   27
Jenyns, Soame
   The Country Visit   205
Johnson, Samuel
   Letter to Lord Chesterfield   334
Judgment of the Birds, The   88
Justice, an Ethiopian folk tale   352

Index of Authors and Titles

LaFarge, Oliver
   Old Man Facing Death   35
Languid Lady, The   133
Latest Decalogue, The   333
Lawrence, T. E.
   Arab Feasting   58
   Auda   30
Lee, Laurie
   London Road   213
Letter to His Son   322
Letter to Lord Chesterfield   334
Lie Thee Down, Oddity   354
Line, The   113
Livingstone, David
   Mauled by a Lion   201
London Road   213
Lynd, Robert
   Conversation   66

Machiavelli, Niccolò
   In What Way Princes Must
      Keep Faith   328
Madness   137
Marrakech   98
Mauled by a Lion   201
McFee, William
   The Pattern-Makers   115
Melville, Herman
   The Line   113
Miss Birdseye   27
Modest Proposal, A   342
Moose Hunt, A   267

Old Apple Dealer, The   32
Old Houses   19
Old Man Facing Death   35
Old Men in Libraries   70
On Quick and Slow Wits
   of Pupils   135
On the Use of Language   94
Orwell, George
   Marrakech   98

Pains of Opium, The   251
Pater, Walter
   Success in Life   301
Pattern-Makers, The   115
Peloponnesian War: Final Defeat of
   the Athenian Forces, The   167
Penitent, The   349
Powys, Llewellyn
   A House of Correction   104
   Hall-Bedrooms   16
Powys, T.F.
   Lie Thee Down, Oddity   354

Red   40
Reid, Leslie
   The Evolution of the Horse   176

Rilke, Rainer Maria
   Old Houses   19
   The Hand   249
   The Hospital   245
Ruskin, John
   The Essential Things   303
Ryokan
   The Thief and the Moon   307

Sassoon, Siegfried
   Base Details   332
Shanties at Walden Pond   12
Slave Galley, A   54
Small Economies   92
Social Instinct among Animals,
   The   87
Song   134
Stanhope, Philip, Lord Chesterfield
   Letter to His Son   322
Stevenson, Robert Louis
   An Apology for Idlers   293
   The Penitent   349
   Walking Tours   277
Stifter, Adalbert
   The Thunderstorm   7
Storm, A   5
Success in Life   301
Swift, Jonathan
   A Modest Proposal   342
   Description of a City Shower   56
   To a Young Lady on Her
      Marriage   317
Synge, J.M.
   An Autumn Night in the Hills   72

Tactless Man, The   131
Taylor, Jeremy
   Dying   139
Theocritus
   A Fight   52
Theophrastus
   The Flatterer   131
   The Tactless Man   131
Thief and the Moon, The   307
Thoreau, Henry David
   A Moose Hunt   267
Three Dreams   230
Thucydides
   The Peloponnesian War: Final
      Defeat of the Athenian
      Forces   167
Thunderstorm, The   7
Thurber, James
   Four Fables for Our Time   349
To a Young Lady on Her
   Marriage   317
Tribulations of a Cheerful Giver   235
Tucci, Niccolo
   Red   40

Tu Fu
    Chariots Go Forth to War   306
Twain, Mark
    Advice to Youth   325
    A Storm   5
    The House Beautiful   13

Visions in a Fever   243

Walking Tours   277
What Is Zen?   178

Whirlwind, The   10
White, Gilbert
    The Social Instinct among Animals   87
Wind, The   9
Working Class Mother, A   28

Ybarra, T.R.
    The Governor of Los Teques   164
Young, Edward
    The Languid Lady   133

Index of Plates and Artists

Allori, Allessandro
    The Trinity   312
Audubon, John James
    "Snowy Egret"   128
Bath, The   290
Bellows, George Wesley
    Stag at Sharkey's   83
Benton, Thomas Hart
    Persephone   198
Cassatt, Mary
    The Bath   290
Ch'i, Mu
    Six Persimmons   23
"Couple"   364
Crucifixion   309
de La Tour, Georges
    Joseph the Carpenter   226
Dr. Johnson   50
Dürer, Albrecht
    "The Vision of St. John"   195
Erasmus   48
Feast of St. Nicholas, The   81
Gauguin, Paul
    The Spirit of the Dead Watching   162
Gnosis
    Stag Hunt   288
Great Wave off Kanagawa, The   224
Grosz, George
    Couple   364
Grünewald, Mathias
    Crucifixion   309
Hokusai
    The Great Wave off Kanagawa   224
Holbein, Hans
    Erasmus   48
Homer, Winslow

"Old Friends"   313
"Palm Tree, Nassau"   26
Imaginary Prisons, etching from   263
Joseph the Carpenter   226
Lin, Ma
    Listening to the Wind in the Pines   316
Listening to the Wind in the Pines   316
Maxime Dethomas   110
Munch, Edward
    Puberty   261
Old Friends   313
"Palm Tree, Nassau"   26
Persephone   198
Piranesi, Giovanni Battista
    Etching from *Imaginary Prisons*   263
Puberty   261
Reynolds, Sir Joshua
    Dr. Johnson   50
Secretary   366
Six Persimmons   23
Snowy Egret   128
Spirit of the Dead Watching, The   162
Stag at Sharkey's   83
Stag Hunt   288
Stankiewicz, Richard
    Secretary   366
Steen, Jan
    The Feast of St. Nicholas   81
Toulouse-Lautrec, Henri de
    Maxime Dethomas   110
Trinity, The   312
Venus de Milo   160
"Venus" of Willendorf   160
Vision of St. John, The   195